WOLF of the DEEP

WOLF of the DEEP

RAPHAEL SEMMES

AND THE NOTORIOUS CONFEDERATE RAIDER

CSS ALABAMA

Stephen Fox

ALFRED A. KNOPF

New York

2007

THIS IS A BORZOI BOOK
PUBLISHED BY ALFRED A. KNOPF

Copyright © 2007 by Stephen Fox

Library of Congress Cataloging-in-Publication Data
Fox, Stephen R.
Wolf of the deep : Raphael Semmes and the notorious Confederate raider
CSS Alabama / by Stephen Fox.—1st ed.
p.   cm.
Includes bibliographical references and index.
ISBN 978-1-4000-4429-0
1. Semmes, Raphael, 1809–1877.   2. Alabama (Screw sloop).   3. Admirals—
Confederate States of America—Biography.   4. Ship captains—Confederate States
of America—Biography.   5. Confederate States of America. Navy—Biography.
6. United States—History—Civil War, 1861–1865—Naval operations, Confederate.
I. Title.
E467.1.S47F68   2007
973.7'5092—DC22
[B]
2007014668
Manufactured in the United States of America
First Edition

Frontispiece: Raphael Semmes, courtesy of the Naval Historical Foundation

For Robin Straus

Semmes has been a wolf of the deep
For many a day to harmless sheep;
Ships he scuttled and robbed and burned,
Watches pilfered and pockets turned.

—GEORGE H. BOKER, PHILADELPHIA, 1864

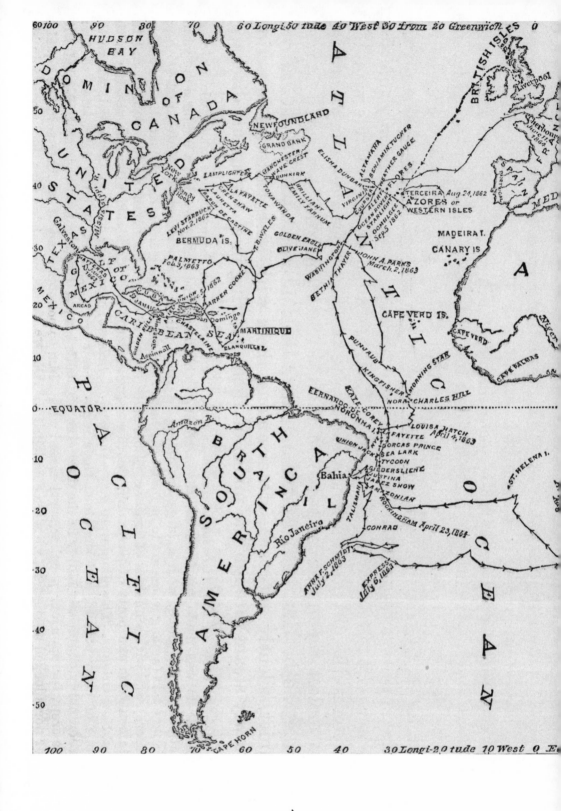

CHART OF THE CRUISE OF THE "ALABAMA."

NOTE: of the 66 captures, given on this chart, 52 were burned; 10 were released on bond, namely, the *Emily Farnum*, *Tonawanda*, *Baron de Castine*, *Union*, *Ariel*, *Washington*, *Bethia Thayer*, *Punjaub*, *Morning Star*, and *Justina*; of the 4 not accounted for above, the *Hatteras* was sunk in action; the *Conrad* was named the *Tuscaloosa*, and became a cruiser, or "tender to the *Alabama*"; the *Sea Bride* was sold; the *Martha Wenzell*, captured in neutral waters, was released.

The cruise of the *Alabama*, from Liverpool to the Azores and the Newfoundland Banks, down to the Gulf of Mexico, into the Caribbean and south to Brazil, across the South Atlantic to the Cape of Good Hope, to Singapore and back, again to Brazil, then to Cherbourg: 22 months, 75,000 miles, and 65 captures. One of the 66 captures named in the illustration has been excluded, as it was caught and released in neutral waters. (*Battles and Leaders of the Civil War*, 1887)

Contents

WOLF of the DEEP

Escape and Debut

July 1862. Captain Raphael Semmes of the Confederate Navy was biding his time in Nassau, the Bahamas, waiting for a ship to take him
back to England. He had arrived from London a few weeks earlier, on
his way home (or so he thought) after a daringly fruitful cruise on the
CSS *Sumter.* That six-month voyage, ranging from New Orleans into
the Caribbean and then across the ocean to Gibraltar, had made
Semmes the first Confederate naval hero. In the Bahamas he hoped to
find a fast blockade-runner that would take him to a friendly secessionist port in the South for a new role in the war—and then eventually
home to see his wife, Anne Elizabeth, and their six children for the first
time since March 1861.

Instead he was handed orders in Nassau to return at once to
England and take command of a new ship. As a sailor and veteran naval
officer, he was naturally intrigued by his new command; this mysterious gunboat was supposed to be bigger, faster, more heavily armed,
and more seaworthy than the leaky little *Sumter.* Semmes guessed and
hoped that he might soon control an instrument of real historical
potential. But as a man, husband, and father he had to confront
another extended, indefinite separation from home and family. "You

cannot conceive, my dear wife," he wrote Anne from Nassau, "how my heart yearns towards you and our dear children. It is now some sixteen months since I saw your dear faces, and this time seems to me an age; doubly an age, as measured by my absence from you, and by the many and stirring events which have passed."

The war, well into its second year, was writhing through transformations that nobody had expected. The initial success of Confederate forces in 1861 had raised Southern hopes for a quick and easy conclusion. In the winter and spring of 1862, however, those expectations were turned upside down by a series of Union victories. McClellan's army won at Williamsburg and the siege of Yorktown, and approached within six miles of Richmond. Out west, Grant and Buell also made grinding progress. Forts Henry and Donelson were taken, along with the major Confederate cities of Nashville and Memphis. In late April, in the biggest Union triumph yet, New Orleans fell with hardly a battle, delivering the Confederacy's most important port to the enemy. "It now requires no very far-reaching prophet," announced Horace Greeley in his *New York Tribune*, "to predict the end of the struggle."

The meaning of the war remained a matter of noisy dispute. Southerners believed they were fighting for independence from a bullying tyrant, in the same tradition as their ancestors from 1776. Northerners believed they were putting down a treasonous rebellion, launched in open defiance of the United States Constitution. Neither side chose to discuss slavery much. "My paramount object in this struggle," Lincoln explained to Greeley that summer, "is to save the Union, and is not either to save or to destroy slavery." That moral dimension of the conflict was, as yet, absent.

The tumbling chaos of events kept redefining the war into unanticipated hopes and durations. All the players felt swept along by forces beyond anyone's control or vision toward an ever-receding conclusion. Raphael Semmes's two oldest sons, Spencer and Oliver, were fighting somewhere in the Confederate Army. They were perhaps still alive; for a year Semmes had heard nothing about them. "But whatever may betide them or me, my dear wife," he wrote Anne, "you must keep ever present to your mind, that we are engaged in a holy cause, fighting for all that is dear to man." The daily barrage of war news proclaimed battles lost and won, hope and despair, deaths dealt and borne. The recent downturn in Confederate fortunes hardly mattered to Semmes. "Every day of the war serves but to strengthen my conviction," he assured Anne. "The war may last years—we may be prostrated, exhausted, but never conquered." (And in case Anne was faltering in his absence: "And the glorious women of the South are as hopeful and enthusiastic as the men.")

Finally, after four weeks of waiting, Semmes took passage on a steamship to Liverpool. Arriving on August 5, he was told to embark, yet again, for a secret rendezvous, somewhere at sea, with his new command. Just before leaving England, he wrote a discreet letter to his older daughter, Electra, veiling his words in case the enemy intercepted it. "I am sorry, my darling daughter, that I cannot inform you of my movements. I have something in hand," he allowed, "of which you will probably hear in due time, but for the present you must curb your curiosity."

The new ship emerged from a delicate, shadowy fandango among Confederate agents, Union spies, waterfront characters, and assorted diplomats, politicians, lawyers, and shipbuilders. The central figures were two resourceful, adroit Americans in Liverpool, each devoted to his cause and intent on deceiving and frustrating the other. James D. Bulloch of Georgia pursued the Confederate Navy's interests in Britain. A former lieutenant in the United States Navy, he was living in New York when the war came, working for a steamship line that ran vessels down to New Orleans. "My personal interests were wholly, and my personal friendships were chiefly, in the North," he later wrote, but his deeper ancestral sympathies and convictions took him south. He was sent to England to acquire ships and naval supplies for the Confederacy. Thirty-nine years old in 1862, still a sailor at heart, he longed to leave his landlocked duties and—striking more directly—take command of a fine warship at sea. (Many years later, his nephew Theodore Roosevelt fondly compared Uncle Jimmy to a chivalrous gentleman in a Thackeray novel—"the nearest approach to Col. Newcome of any man I ever met in actual life," said TR, "that most beautiful of all characters in fiction.")

Bulloch's nemesis, Thomas H. Dudley of New Jersey, was the U.S. consul in Liverpool. Of Quaker heritage, ardently antislavery and pro-Union, he felt surrounded by enemies in Liverpool, the center of Con-

James D. Bulloch of Georgia, godfather to the *Alabama*. (*Battles and
Leaders of the Civil War*, 1887)

federate activities in England. Stalking through the dark labyrinths
of docks and dripping fogs along the river Mersey, Dudley—quite
reasonably—suspected foul plots and conspirators against the Union.
Provided with a small budget of $2,000 a year for espionage, to pene-
trate these mysteries he paid detectives, spies, stray sailors and shipyard
workers, self-proclaimed insiders found in dives and bars: "not as a
general thing very esteemable men," he admitted to his boss, Secretary
of State William H. Seward, "but [they] are the only persons we can
get to engage in this business, which I am sure you will agree with me
is not a very pleasant one." It was murky, uncertain, exasperating work;
Dudley could never compel anyone's testimony, and the best-informed
men were also the least willing to provide evidence. Nonetheless he
dispatched a stream of alarmed, mostly accurate reports on local Confederate movements to Seward and to Charles Francis Adams, the U.S.
minister in London.

In the summer of 1861, Bulloch crossed the Mersey to Birkenhead
and toured the impressive Laird shipyard—one of the most respected

shipbuilding firms in Britain, technically innovative, with deep experience at turning out warships for Her Majesty's Navy. John Laird had recently retired and left the business to his three sons. Bulloch quickly came to terms with them for a fast wooden-hulled gunboat, 220 feet long, powered by both sail and steam. He signed the contract in his own name alone, without reference to the Confederacy. "They did not know for what purpose the ship was intended when they agreed to build her," Bulloch later insisted. "They, on their part, asked no questions." They hardly needed to: Bulloch's Southern accent and his well-known local affiliations made his purpose obvious, and the details of the contract explicitly defined a ship intended for war. It was so self-evident that the matter needed no discussion, indeed demanded a careful, evasive silence. British law forbade the building of such a ship for such a combatant during a war in which the government was officially neutral. But the Lairds, like many Liverpudlians, sympathized with the Southern side in the American war.

As the 290th vessel built by the Laird family, the ship was initially just called the *290*. Bulloch hoped for swift completion by the spring of 1862. But the wooden construction went slowly, stuttering during Bulloch's occasional absences from Liverpool, and delayed by the builder's insistence on the finest materials and highest standards. "The foreman who had charge of building her says that no boat was ever built stronger or better than her," Thomas Dudley reported to Seward in May. "There is no doubt but what she is intended for the Rebels." After the launch on May 15, the ship's steam engine and machinery were installed quickly amid conditions of accelerating urgency. A trial run on the Mersey proved satisfactory. Dudley's spies reported alarming news: the *290* was designed not as a blockade-runner, for sneaking cargoes in and out of Confederate ports, but as a well-armed commerce raider, able to stay at sea indefinitely, picking off defenseless Union merchant ships. The Lairds floated a report that she was actually contracted for the government of Spain. Dudley checked with the Spanish legation in London and found—not to his surprise—the report was false.

Adams and Dudley began desperate attempts to stop the ship through diplomatic channels. All the British authorities, from local customs officials in Liverpool all the way up to the foreign secretary, Lord John Russell, in London, already knew on some commonsense level that the *290* was a Confederate warship and therefore an outlaw. But for their own unstated, mostly political reasons they demanded unreasonably meticulous legal proof backed by sworn affidavits. So Dudley assembled nine signed affidavits from himself, his main detective, a Laird shipwright, a sailor signed up for the ship who had been told her purpose, and others. The Union men hired their own lawyer and obtained a favorable opinion from a substantial legal authority, Robert Collier, a queen's counsel and judge advocate of the Admiralty. The legal process shifted against the *290*. "I think we shall stop her," Dudley hoped on July 22; "that the case is so bald they will not dare to let her go."

Meantime Bulloch was working briskly to prepare the ship for sea and battle. In secret he bought an old sailing bark, the *Agrippina*, in London, and very discreetly, without being detected, had her loaded with 350 tons of coal—and cannon, guns, ammunition, and other warlike supplies that the *290* could not legally take from Britain. In Liverpool, his agents scrounged the waterfront for sailors to hazard a secret voyage. The men were told "they were going to have some fun," maybe to Nassau, maybe through the Union blockade into a Confederate port. Matthew Butcher, the first officer of a Cunard Line transatlantic steamship, was hired to take the *290* somewhere out to sea. (Captain Semmes still had not arrived in Liverpool.) Everything was ready to go.

The entire tightening drama was proceeding down conventional and deliberate legal, diplomatic, and naval lines toward a rational denouement. Then it turned on two bizarre, inexplicable twists. On Saturday, July 26, Bulloch heard from what he later described as "a private but most reliable source" that the *290* had better leave Liverpool within forty-eight hours. (The source's identity has puzzled many speculating historians ever since but still remains unknown.) At about that same moment, Sir John Harding went insane. As the queen's advocate, he was supposed to convey Dudley's legal documents to the attorney general and solicitor general. But instead, Harding, his mind blinking out, took the documents to an asylum and refused to surrender them. This further delay in the legal proceedings against the *290* proved decisive.

Bulloch assigned his clerk, Clarence Yonge of the Confederate Navy, to join the new ship as its paymaster. When first at sea, Bulloch instructed, "you are strictly enjoined not to mention that you are in any way connected with the C.S. Navy, but you will simply act as the purser of a private ship." Mingle with the British warrant and petty officers, Bulloch urged Yonge, and attempt to convert them to the cause. "Show interest in their comfort and welfare, and endeavor to excite their interest in the approaching cruise of the ship. Talk to them of the Southern States, and how they are fighting against great odds for only what every Englishman enjoys—liberty." Don't be too obvious or persistent, Bulloch cautioned, but aim to spread the message from the officers down to the British sailors on the berth deck. "Seamen are very impressionable, and can be easily influenced by a little tact and management."

On Tuesday, the twenty-ninth, Bulloch cued his actors with a sly piece of staged diversionary theater. He assembled a disguising party of ladies and gentlemen, including two of the Laird brothers and two of their daughters, and took the *290* down the Mersey and into the Irish Sea on what was supposed to be just another trial run. It was intended to look like a festive day's outing on the new ship, of no real significance. At a safe distance from Dudley and his agents, a tugboat took the ladies and gentlemen back to Liverpool. The *290* kept going.

A Union warship was lurking to the south, in St. George's Channel between England and Ireland, keeping watch for the Confederate vessel. So Captain Butcher, as instructed by Bulloch, took his ship in the opposite direction, through the North Channel between Scotland and northern Ireland, and then out into the Atlantic Ocean. An order from London to stop the ship, delayed long enough by Harding's helpful mental breakdown, came by telegraph—just six hours too late.

Captain Semmes arrived in Liverpool from Nassau a few days later. Already notorious, and so hoping to muffle his presence, he rested for a while at Bulloch's home in the nearby village of Waterloo. Then both men quietly embarked on the steamer *Bahama* for an announced but false destination. Three ships—the *Agrippina* from London and the *290* and *Bahama* from the Mersey—converged on the secret rendezvous, the island of Terceira in the Azores, nine hundred miles west of Portugal.

Two days after leaving the northwest coast of Ireland, the *290* sailed into strong gales with hard squalls and heavy seas, testing the new ship and her untried crew. The vessel rolled deliriously and shipped dense sluices of water, roaring over the bulwarks and gushing out the scuppers. At two o'clock in the morning, the portside swinging boom was washed away. Later that morning another fresh breeze blew in, forcing the sailors aloft to take in all sails, and causing more damage. But overall, Captain Butcher recalled, even in these storms his charge "proved herself an excellent sea boat and very comfortable."

The speedy *290* reached Terceira on August 10 and waited. The lumbering, heavily loaded *Agrippina* finally arrived eight days later, to the exhaling relief of the Confederates on their unarmed new cruiser. The crews started the toiling dogwork of transferring coal, cannon, gun carriages, rifles and small arms, shells and ammunition, gunpowder, clothing, and stores. The officers kept a sharp, fretful watch for curious Union warships; nobody on the other side knew about the secret rendezvous, but an enemy captain could always get lucky. On August 20 the *Bahama* appeared, bringing more cannon and their carriages, as well as Bulloch, Semmes, and a small group of his young officers from the *Sumter*.

Intensely curious about his new ship, Semmes finally got a first glimpse of her. She looked especially sleek and sharp lying next to the dumpy *Agrippina*. He was at once and permanently smitten. "She was, indeed, a beautiful thing to look upon," he exulted. "Her model was of the most perfect symmetry, and she sat upon the water with the lightness and grace of a swan." Designed for speed, for pursuit and flight, she was long and narrow, the black hull of English oak sitting low in the water. A flaring clipper bow, an extended bowsprit, and a fiddlehead cutwater dominated the forequarters. Three masts of the best yellow pine were raked backward, imparting a look of nimble swiftness even when the ship lay at anchor. The stumpy black smokestack protruded above the bridge, just forward of the middle mast. Two lifeboats, also painted black, hung aft on each side, and a fifth boat dangled across the trim elliptical stern. Once the supplies were properly stowed, the coal dust and rubbish cleaned up, and the decks scraped down with holystones, "she became sweet and clean," Semmes noted, "and when her awnings were snugly spread, her yards squared, and her rigging hauled taut, she looked like a bride, with the orange-wreath about her brows, ready to be led to the altar." As the avid groom, Semmes relished the prospect of taking possession.

The *Alabama* at sea. (*Frank Leslie's Illustrated Newspaper*, March 14, 1863)

The captain's most essential task was to recruit an adequate crew from the dubious collection of sailors at hand—who had not signed on for anything like the extended cruise that now opened before them, and as British citizens felt no loyalty to the Confederate cause. Semmes hoped for a full complement of 105 hands to man his guns and sails in a crisis. Like an evangelist seeking converts, he had to stand forth and address the men—first on the *Bahama*, then on the *290*—and preach his case. Without enough men, the cruise was already over, and the lovely new ship was vulnerable to any passing enemy.

The sailors, given their first extended chance to examine the famous Captain Semmes, and accustomed to judging men by their physical force and presence, could not have been impressed. About to turn fifty-three, he looked older, perhaps too old for the job he was undertaking. He was a small man, below the average height for his time, and very slim, weighing no more than 130 pounds. The thick woolen coat of his uniform made him seem more substantial and less bony than he really was. The face looked weather-beaten and sallow. The generous ears, slightly protruding, were partly camouflaged by flaps of iron-gray hair. The forehead was broad, the nose and chin assertive. Two aspects most defined him. The gray eyes were hard, glittering, determined, as though he had spent a lifetime being underestimated and grimly having to compensate for what people saw. And a peculiar mustache soared out and above his lips like the wings of a gull in flight, extending laterally for inches away from his face, thin and waxed to its extended points. Hardly any of his Civil War contemporaries wore such a mustache. It demanded constant, attentive care and grooming—especially on the windblown seas. Vaguely French, preening, and madcap, it suggested another dimension to Semmes's otherwise disciplined, contained nature.

Standing on the bridge of the *Bahama*, he addressed her men gathered below him. "Now, my lads," he said, as a crewman remembered it, "there is the ship" (pointing to the 290). "She is as fine a vessel as ever floated. There is a chance which seldom offers itself to a British seaman, that is, to make a little money. I am not going to put you alongside of a frigate at first, but after I have got you drilled a little, I will give you a nice fight." Of all the ships of the Union Navy, he feared only six. "We are going to burn, sink, and destroy the commerce of the United States. Your prize money will be divided proportionably according to each man's rank, something similar to the English Navy." The captain was dangling the lures of easy fortune, adventure, and the sporting, double-edged excitement of deadly combat at sea. But only about half the men on the *Bahama* were persuaded to join the cruise. "The others hung back, perhaps for better terms," Semmes confided to his shipboard journal. "There are, perhaps, some sea lawyers among them influencing their determination."

A few days later he tried again, this time on the 290 amid a panoply of patriotic display designed to arouse a sailor's generally latent sense of any higher purpose. Calling all hands aft to the quarterdeck, backed by his own zealous officers in their uniforms, he read aloud his commission and sailing orders from the Confederate government in Richmond. Then he officially named the cruiser the CSS *Alabama*. While the ship's band played "Dixie," the informal anthem of the infant nation, the British flag was lowered. The Confederate Stars and Bars and the pennant of the new cruiser were raised to the topmasts and set snapping in the breeze. The *Bahama* boomed a gun in salute.

Mounting the carriage of a broadside cannon, swinging into the fervor of the moment, Semmes "said he was deranged in his mind," as the boatswain's mate, Henry Redden, recalled it a few weeks later, "to see his country going to ruin, and had to steal out of Liverpool like a thief. That instead of them watching him, he was now going after them. He wanted all of us to join him—that he was going to sink, burn, and destroy all his enemy's property, and that any that went with him was entitled to two-twentieths prize money. It did not matter whether the prize was sunk, or burned, or sold, the prize money was to be paid." Sharpening his earlier argument, he said he actually feared only four or five of the enemy's warships, not six of them. Again he offered the thrill and challenge of fighting, "but any of you that thinks he cannot stand to his gun, I don't want" (thereby implicating anybody who turned him down as a coward).

In conclusion—this no doubt clinched his case—he reluctantly gave in and agreed to double the usual wages, as proposed by the resisting men, and to pay them in gold. Semmes offered four pounds, ten shillings a month to the seamen, five or six pounds to the petty officers, and seven pounds to the hard-duty firemen, who sweated and shoveled coal into furnaces down in the hot, smoky bowels of the ship. To pay these high wages, he said, he had a war chest of £20,000 on board. The men were also promised ample food, grog (rum and water) twice a day, the occasional delights of liberty on shore, and, at least in their own imaginations, the happy prospect of freelance pillaging on condemned ships before they were sunk. With these practical inducements, surely more compelling than the alien patriotic flourishes, Semmes brought his crew up to eighty men: fewer than he hoped for, but enough to start cruising. "The modern sailor has greatly changed in character," he grumbled in his journal that night, "as he now stickles for pay like a sharper, and seems to have lost his former love of adventure and of recklessness."

At midnight the *Bahama* left for Liverpool, taking Bulloch and the men whom Semmes could not persuade. It was a beautiful clear night at sea, the stars multiplied and brilliant in the infinite black inverted bowl overhead. A blazing comet lit up the sky to the northwest. Bulloch watched the bright lanterns of the *Alabama* recede and felt like a man leaving home behind. He had hoped to command the cruiser himself, had seen to her construction and escape with that understanding, and then felt crushed when he was directed to hand her over to Semmes. Like the noble Colonel Newcome, he subdued his own private regrets for the larger cause. "Banishing every sentiment but hope," as he reported his departure to his superiors in Richmond, "I predicted a glorious cruise for the dashing little craft and her gallant commander."

On the *Alabama*, Captain Semmes turned toward a northeast heading. He ordered the fore and main trysails set and told the chief engineer to let the boiler fires go down. After evening hours of drudging paperwork to sign up his crew, he collapsed into bed, physically and emotionally exhausted at the end of that long, anxious, momentous day: August 24, 1862. A moderate gale blew in, making the ship roll and tumble uncomfortably through the night. The gagging stench of roiling bilge water wafted up from the hold. The captain, prone to seasickness, slept uneasily.

The *Alabama* went hunting for prey. Semmes knew that plump commercial fleets of Yankee whaling ships—slow, unarmed, wooden, and easy to burn—would cluster around the Azores until about the first of October. Until then he could just linger in the vicinity ("It was the most obvious thing in the world," he reflected) and wait at the top of the predator chain. The local ocean currents at certain times of year collected enticing clumps of small marine organisms and fishes, which drew the whales, which drew the whalers, which drew the *Alabama*.

For eleven days she sailed in a clockwise direction around the Azores and then struck off toward the northwest. During this time the lookouts sighted six ships, but they all proved to be out of reach or not Yankees. Just as well for the Confederates; the captain needed this respite to get his ship and guns in order. The seams of the upper deck, caulked during the cold of a northern English winter, were leaking badly under the relentless sun of the mid-Atlantic summer. Against a background of the steady, obnoxious clanking of the pump, sailors knelt down and recaulked the deck. Others stowed the ammunition magazine and secured loose objects below. The cannon, especially the most valuable pivot guns fore and aft, remained in disarray and could not yet be fired. "We are still quite defenseless," Semmes worried in his journal. With the ship so undermanned, he had to assign six of his junior officers to one of the gun crews. By September 3 they could finally practice shooting their guns—but only the pivot cannon. The broadside guns were still not ready.

Two days later, they happened on an American whaler, the *Ocmulgee*, out of Martha's Vineyard in Massachusetts. (A perfectly arrayed political symbolism: the Confederate cruiser meeting a ship from the hated state that had launched and led the abolitionist movement.) Deploying a traditional disguising tactic of naval combat, Semmes ran up his British flag; the *Ocmulgee*, reassured, hoisted the Stars and Stripes of the United States. The whaler was lying at rest next to a huge dead sperm whale, harvesting the blubber. As the *Alabama* drew near, Semmes revealed himself by striking the British colors and raising the Confederate flag. He fired a warning shot, not aimed to harm but firmly asserting his purpose. The skipper of the *Ocmulgee*—expecting a friendly encounter at sea, and having heard nothing about the escape or whereabouts of the *Alabama*—looked puzzled, then blankly astonished as he suddenly understood his implacable predicament.

Semmes sent a lieutenant to board the whaler. The lieutenant politely told the skipper, sir, that he was sorry to inform him that they were now a prize to the Confederate cruiser *Alabama*. It was quite gentlemanly and businesslike; no lives were in danger. The thirty-seven men of the *Ocmulgee* came aboard the *Alabama*. The skipper and first mate were allowed to bring a trunk of clothes apiece, the rest of the men just a bag of clothing each. A scavenging squad from the cruiser went through the whaler and brought back some rigging (which they needed) and barrels of salt beef and pork and other small stores. Next day they shot two dogs, the last living creatures aboard the *Ocmulgee*, and set her on fire. On the *Alabama*, the Yankees were lightly sheltered under a blanketing sail on the exposed deck, with the officers clamped in irons. After two days and nights on deck, six miles off the island of Flores, they were released and sent ashore in their own whaleboats. An officer of the *Alabama* estimated the value of this first prize at $50,000.

The blazing debut started two weeks of easy pickings, pulling in a merchant schooner from Boston and eight more New England whalers. On September 9 Semmes relished the delicious pleasure of burning three Yankee ships in a single day. But after the tenth prize, on September 18, the lookouts strained and squinted yet saw nothing for ten long, slow days. "We seem to be in a desert part of the ocean," Semmes fretted. With the approaching end of whaling season near the Azores, he hauled away, far to the northwest, toward the Grand Banks of Newfoundland, the crowded crossroads of traffic in the North

Atlantic. There he waited to ambush laden Yankee grain ships bringing the fall wheat harvests to Europe. They obligingly appeared. Again the captain had chosen an obvious, packed seasonal hunting ground.

During the two months that started with the capture of the *Ocmulgee*, the *Alabama* burned twenty prizes, an average of one every three days. She also captured three more U.S. ships that could not be burned because of neutral cargoes or too many passengers; Semmes released them on bonds to be redeemed by the Confederacy after the end of the war. Union property and sailing schedules remained the only victims. The cruiser had, as yet, caused no human casualties. By the rough estimates of her officers, the twenty burned ships and their cargoes were together worth $1,184,311—more than four times the cost of building and equipping the cruiser herself. James Bulloch's secret investment with the Lairds was already amply repaid.

The most significant warship of the Civil War, and ultimately the most effective commerce raider in the entire history of naval warfare, was loose on the vast, concealing ocean. Where would she turn up next? How could she ever be stopped? "A splendid vessel," reported Theodore Julius, master of the captured *Tonawanda*, after being held prisoner for four days, "and the fastest under canvas I ever had my foot on board of, and I have no doubt she is the same under steam, as she has very powerful machinery. . . . I do not think there is a ship in our navy that can catch her." In London, Charles Francis Adams urged the Union warships *Kearsarge* and *Tuscarora*, patrolling nearby, to move into position to protect Yankee ships returning from India. But he was not hopeful. "I fear that neither of them separately," he wrote to Washington, "nor indeed both together, are any match for the shrewdness and enterprise of Captain Semmes, who has a vessel very capable of escaping from every risk of encounter. The exploits of this vessel by no means give rise to a feeling of entire satisfaction on this side of the water."

Adams recognized the doubled threat that was looming somewhere out there. Semmes and the ship, groom and bride, were well matched: both of rare and ruthless attributes, and thus worthy of each other. Together they sailed away into history. Far at sea, months removed from any two-way contact with his naval superiors, Semmes had to set his own course. That isolated circumstance gave him nearly absolute freedom to roam and hunt as he chose. Under his firm command, the ship faithfully expressed the captain—his skinny ferocity, risks and hunches, fears and courage, skill and will. The ship became the captain became the ship.

Men from the bonfired prizes of the Confederate cruiser gradually found their ways home. In the manner of Theodore Julius, they told excited stories to the newspapers, stoking the newborn legend of Semmes and the *Alabama*. The Yankee skipper of the captured *Baron de Castine*, released and relieved, arrived in Boston on November 2. Several officers of the *Alabama*, he said, had told him they were next bound for New York—and they were planning to shell the city. "Can one vessel do as she pleases on the high seas," demanded the *New York Herald*, the largest newspaper in the United States, "and we, with all our resources of ships, guns, men and money, be unable to prevent it? The people ask the question, How long is this to last?"

ONE

The Captain and the Ship

Like most of the military heroes of the Civil War, Raphael Semmes burst into that sudden historical spotlight after an earlier career of no particular distinction. During thirty-five years in the Navy of the United States, he had often clashed with his superiors and railed at the clogged pipelines of promotion. He seemed distracted by intellectual and literary interests, or his second career as a lawyer, or the needs and pulls of his large family. Naval colleagues such as David Dixon Porter, more single-minded than Semmes, doubted his seriousness. "While in the United States Navy, Semmes had little reputation as an officer," Porter recalled after the war.

> He was indolent and fond of his comfort, so that altogether his associates in the Navy gave him credit for very little energy. What was, then, the astonishment of his old companions to find that Semmes was pursuing a course that required the greatest skill and vigor; for there never was a naval commander who in so short a time committed such depredations on an enemy's commerce, or who so successfully eluded the vessels sent in pursuit of him.

Porter's later praise and criticism of Semmes were both filtered through the distorting passions of the opposite sides they had taken in the war. Porter was himself one of the many frustrated Union pursuers of the Confederate commander, and that public failure no doubt sharpened the edges of his dismissal of the prewar Semmes. Yet his final judgment of a former colleague who was so often underestimated seems balanced and well deserved. "The inertness he had displayed while in the United States Navy had disappeared," Porter wrote of the captain who bestrode the deck of the *Alabama*. "He had become a new man."

At the core of this transformation was Semmes's internal sense of himself as a Southerner—evolving over many years, prodded along by events, and not finally firmed until after the start of the war. His Roman Catholic ancestors had for five generations lived in the border state of Maryland, a terrain contentiously split between its free-labor northern counties and slaveowning southern regions. In Charles County, twenty-five miles south of Washington, the Semmeses of the seventeenth and eighteenth centuries grew tobacco and owned slaves. At times they attained wealth and prominence as members of the local Catholic gentry.

Raphael was born on September 27, 1809, at Effton Hills, Charles County, on the family's tobacco farm. His only brother, Samuel, was born two years later. Their mother, Catherine Middleton Semmes, died when the boys were young. Their father, Richard Thompson Semmes, then married again and moved the family into town, to the Georgetown district of Washington, where his brothers Alexander and Raphael were thriving in business. But Richard also died young, only thirty-nine years old, leaving no money and two sons who were just fourteen and twelve. The orphans, Raphael and Samuel, were very close, often sleeping in each other's arms.

Instead of being separated, they were delivered to the joint care of the families of Uncle Raphael and a third uncle, Benedict Joseph Semmes, a physician, farmer, and politician out in Piscataway, Prince George's County. Even before this formal arrangement, though, young Raphael had already learned important lessons from all his uncles. In the fluid country households of the time, children moved around and spent occasional seasons with their favorite relations. Raphael later remembered being "reared on the banks of the Potomac," acquiring the swimming skills that, in future naval combats and disasters, would save his life more than once. Another relative, Joseph Semmes, ran the City Tavern near the corners of High and Bridge streets in Georgetown. More than just a drinking joint, it functioned as a major business, transportation, and cultural center— and doubtless a fertile source of practical education for the curious young boy.

Uncle Benedict, an eminent graduate of the Baltimore Medical College with a statewide practice, taught his nephew the private joys and haven of serious reading. "The habit of study is in itself a great comfort," Raphael later instructed one of his own children. "I formed this habit myself in early life, under the wise counsels of your Uncle Ben, and it has been a great resource to me ever since." Though he may have spent a few years at a military academy in St. Mary's County, and once even offhandedly referred to "the shreds and patches of our college learning," he was essentially self-educated: a lifelong, intent autodidact, never more at home than when lost in a book.

His uncles Alexander and Raphael inspired a naval career by giving the boy a taste for salt water and distant ports. Alexander owned a fleet of merchant ships sailing out of Georgetown, down the Potomac and on to the sea. Uncle Raphael's merchant shipping interests often took him across the Atlantic, then home with expansive stories to tell. Hanging around the ships and sailors, perhaps even venturing a quick coastal voyage, young Raphael decided to try life on the ocean. His main home, Uncle Raphael's crowded house in Georgetown, included five other children, with more to come. It seemed time to venture out on his own. In April 1826, with the necessary political help of his well-connected Uncle Ben, he was appointed a midshipman in the U.S. Navy. The boy, not yet seventeen years old, was now a man.

Years before the founding of the Naval Academy at Annapolis in 1845, Semmes was entering a kind of apprenticeship for future naval officers. On a man-of-war, the midshipmen stood between the officers and the sailors, taking orders from above and delivering them below. A tutor gave lessons in the arcane shipboard skills of navigation, astronomy, and artillery. The middies ate together, in messes of eight to twelve men, and slept together in the steerage. As a tight cluster of young men, they inevitably arranged themselves into a pecking order. Within this group, status depended on muscle and assertion. Raphael Semmes, small and bookish, lacked the usual credentials. It could not have been an easy initiation.

In confined circumstances at sea, with hundreds of rough men crowded into tight spaces for months at a time, often through severe and dangerous weather, survival depended on ruthless order and discipline. Every man and object claimed an assigned place. A typical Navy sailing ship of this period had four decks and three masts. (Steam power still lay in the future.) On the top deck, aft of the mainmast at the center of the vessel, the coveted quarterdeck was just for officers; midshipmen could not even set foot on its starboard side. Everyone, the captain included, had to touch his hat or cap upon entering the quarterdeck to acknowledge its significance. Toward the stern, aft of the mizzenmast, lay the raised poop deck. Ringed by bulwarks that held the sailors' hammocks during the day, it also formed the roof of the captain's cabin.

The ship's clock hung over the door of this cabin. In an era when American life on shore was still gearing up to the industrial cadence of clock time, everyday shipboard routine moved to the precise, relentless ticking of that timepiece. The twenty-four hours were sliced into five watches of four hours each and two more—the dog watches—of two hours. Within each watch, the ship's bell was struck once after thirty minutes, twice after sixty, and so on. The constant question was not What time is it? but How many bells is it? At eight bells the watch changed and men shifted in synchronized patterns among their prescribed spots (below, above, and aloft), in the clockworked rhythms of working, sleeping, and eating.

The food and water were generally terrible. Water stored in large wooden casks smelled and tasted rank; it improved slightly when iron tanks replaced the casks. The daily staples of salt beef and rice were so blandly indigestible that they made occasional dishes of salt pork and bean soup seem like treats. The hard bread, veined by worms, was often rebaked until crisp; if this didn't improve the flavor, at least it killed the worms. The characteristic overpowering ship odor belowdecks—of cooking, rotting food, cockroaches and vermin, and human waste, all mingling in a bracing stew of bilgewater—did not improve appetites. A prolonged storm meant battened hatches and heavy, stifling air below, with all hands yearning for their first relieving gulps of the sweet oceanic atmosphere up on deck.

Yet Semmes, young and small as he was, found a place in these ships that felt comfortable and kept pulling him back. The basic social unit of shipboard life was the mess. For the middies, that meant about eight men in a small, low-ceilinged room, ten feet by ten feet, somewhere between decks. Each guy had a chest for his clothes. In the center of the room was a table for eating; off to one side, a small pantry for crockery and supplies. A lattice grating overhead let in some light and air, but the room was dark and poorly ventilated. The men were allowed only two candles a day and no open flames at night. They slept on the gun or berth decks, hanging their hammocks from hooks in the overhead beams. Like the members of an infantry unit, or harassed pledges of a college fraternity, the messmates drew together in their shared hardships and common needs—and for lighter moments too. As young men away from home for the first time, exulting in their relative freedom, they all cracked jokes and pulled pranks, and kept each other loose. Semmes even developed a betting habit that frequently cost him his month's pay.

For Semmes, the ship functioned like a college. He excelled at the educational aspects, broadly defined. Aside from the formal shipboard instruction, he seized the many chances for self-instruction. As his later ship journals and published writings make obvious, he was fascinated by oceans and exotic ports of call. Almost anything might catch his attention: tide rips, the Gulf Stream, whales and fishes, a lunar rainbow, the alternation of land and sea breezes in tropical countries, an odd cloud of golden dust far at sea, coral reefs and the tiny creatures that built them, the landscape of the Venezuelan coast, the winds and currents at Gibraltar, the fierce storms of the North Atlantic. The Navy took him around the world, and he noticed details everywhere he went. He admired the great harbor at Rio de Janeiro. He traveled in Europe, standing on the shore of Lake Geneva and watching a storm in the Alps.

After six years, including a stint at the school in the Norfolk Navy Yard in Virginia, he ripped through the required examination and advanced to the rank of passed midshipman. Semmes thereby became eligible for promotion and collided with the aspect of naval life he came most to detest. Preparing for war, the Navy trained far too many men for the available postings in peace. When promotions did arrive, they were doled out by seniority and favoritism, not merit. For Semmes and most other officers, that meant long, slow years of waiting, with extended leaves on shore at reduced pay. He was not promoted to lieutenant until 1837. To occupy his time ashore and bring in some needed extra money, he read law with his brother, Samuel. In 1834 he was admitted to the Maryland bar. A lawyer's work suited his studious habits and command of written language, and it remained an intermittent occupation for the rest of his life.

In the Navy, though, it helped set his reputation as, literally, a "sea lawyer," a malcontent overly inclined to question and quibble. "As a controversialist," a Southern colleague later recalled, "he was unequalled in the Navy." Whenever he disagreed with a decision, or felt slighted, he could not resist speaking out: candid behavior appropriate for a private citizen but, in a military structure based on rank and deference, a pattern not endearing to his superiors or liable to advance his career. At times the issues were external, with Semmes merely responding to public reports that he thought unfair. In 1833, after a military magazine criticized his revered mathematics teacher at Norfolk, Semmes sent a sharp rebuttal to the publication. This began a lifelong pattern of firing off polemics to the editors of newspapers and magazines.

Three years later, after a steamship under his command ran aground and sank on the Withlacoochee River in Florida, the *Pensacola Gazette* reported that the accident had harmed a related military operation against the Seminole Indians. Semmes submitted an extended counterargument, bristling with italics, which the *Gazette* printed. "The public will see the undue importance which has been attached to the loss of this vessel," he asserted. "If there is blame to be attached to myself or my officers, this will be a proper subject for a *Court of Inquiry*, and not for newspaper discussions."

In 1843 Semmes clashed with his boss at the Pensacola Navy Yard, Commodore Alexander Dallas, over the appointment of a chief clerk at the yard. Instead of giving the job to the man Semmes favored, Dallas named the son of a friend. Semmes then recklessly sidestepped Dallas and sent a complaint up to the Navy Department in Washington, accusing the commodore of signing a false muster for the new clerk, who furthermore—Semmes charged—was neglecting his duties.

When Dallas heard about it, he roared at Semmes and suspended him from duty for six weeks. Semmes at once wrote another broadside and tried to deliver it to Dallas. The enraged commodore menacingly stalked toward him, sending Semmes at a brisk run back to his quarters. A later court-martial cleared Dallas of any misconduct. The Navy brass surely took note of the bumptious behavior of their troublesome Lieutenant Semmes.

A career in the U.S. Navy, defending his country's flag all around the world, reinforced for Semmes a sense of national identity over any sectional loyalty. His marriage to a woman from the North both reflected and extended the same tendency. In 1834, during one of his prolonged shore leaves, Semmes for obscure reasons ventured out to Cincinnati, Ohio, across the Ohio River from Kentucky. It was then a young, booming town of about 28,000 people, not long matured from the frontier. Boarding at the home of Oliver and Electra Spencer, the naval officer noticed their teenaged daughter, Anne Elizabeth. She was easy to notice. An acquaintance at the time described her as "a stately, handsome girl with regular chiseled features, brilliant brunette complexion and hazel eyes." An early photograph adds details: dark, shiny hair parted in the middle and gathered at the nape of her neck, a tiny waist, and a steady, composed gaze at the camera.

Her father came from an old New England Yankee family. Oliver Spencer was born in New Jersey, then as a boy moved to the Ohio frontier with his family. In 1792, at the age of ten, he was kidnapped by Indians. For seven months he lived and moved with them, in reasonable contentment, until a British agent bought him back. (Later Spencer wrote a short book about his captivity, a deadpan narrative bearing no anger, and his Indian guardian paid him an annual friendly visit.) Settled in Cincinnati, he at first enjoyed a successful career in banking and river commerce. By 1815 he was president of the Miami Exporting Company. But its bank failed five years later, swallowing the savings of many customers. An angry mob marched on the bank and almost sacked it. In the messy aftermath, Spencer managed to keep his family's fine house on Sixth Street, between Broadway and Sycamore, but he had lost a fortune and his good name.

Oliver Spencer emerged from this disaster with a call to preach. At a time of burning Protestant zeal and sharply felt differences among warring denominations, he moved easily from one sect to another, like a man leaping among bobbing ice floes in a swift river. Cincinnati was founded by Presbyterians; in 1812 he pledged one hundred dollars toward the construction of a new Presbyterian church. At the same time, he opened his home to the newly arrived Quakers for their first meetings in town. After his bank went under, he declared himself a Methodist minister, the Reverend Spencer, and president of the Miami District Bible Society linked with the Methodist Episcopal church. His wife, Electra, presided over the associated Female Branch Bible Society. The Reverend Spencer never claimed a church of his own, but he did apparently preach here and there. The family scraped by in reduced circumstances—in part by taking in boarders such as Raphael Semmes.

Breaking into this Northern, antislavery, militantly Protestant household, at some point Semmes asked for Anne's hand in marriage. He was ten years older than she, embarked on a naval career that would mean frequent moves and long absences from home, and—worst of all—a devout Roman Catholic from the slave state of Maryland. Oliver and Electra Spencer must have been aghast at the notion of their beautiful only daughter marrying a dreaded papist. Indeed, it is a certain measure of the youthful passion between Raphael and Anne, and their mutual persistence and strength of character, that the union took place. In May 1837, three months after his promotion to lieutenant (perhaps a parental requirement for the marriage), they were married in Cincinnati, twenty-seven and seventeen years old. They skirted the family religious quarrel by holding separate Episcopal and Catholic ceremonies. Their first child, arriving ten months later, was named Samuel Spencer, after Raphael's brother and Anne's father.

Within the family he was called Spencer, a gentle but telling self-assertion on Anne's part. She converted to Roman Catholicism and attended mass faithfully, but the elaborate ritual annoyed her, after the plain Protestant worship of her youth, and her devoutness never matched her husband's. Their children were all baptized as Catholics, but Raphael did not insist on their confirmation in the faith. Later two of them became Episcopalians. Anne and Raphael also disagreed about finances. After growing up in genteel poverty, and hearing sad stories about her family's former wealth, Anne worried about money. Her husband preferred to think about other matters. "Money has no charms for me," he once told her, doubtless to her knowing exasperation. Anne always remained her own person, forthright and independent.

In 1841 Semmes contrived his own self-assertion by moving his family down to Alabama. Within the sectional politics of the period, it seems a balancing act, conscious or otherwise: given a Northern wife, his family would henceforth live in the Deep South. At the time he was assigned to the Pensacola Navy Yard, making surveys of the coasts of Florida and the Gulf of Mexico. He bought farmland in Baldwin County, Alabama, on the west bank of the Perdido River, near the gulf and with convenient access to Pensacola. Other Navy colleagues purchased farms nearby, forming "a very pleasant colony of nautical farmers." The family, by then including another son, Oliver, gradually put down Alabama roots in a house that Semmes called Prospect Hill. Two more children, daughters Electra (1843) and Katherine (1844), were born there. It meant a stable mooring for a migratory naval family—but not an immediate shift of state allegiances for the lieutenant. As late as 1848, he still privately referred to "my fellow citizens of Maryland."

Semmes's service in the Mexican War, however, again confirmed his national loyalties. For fifteen months, from September 1846 through November 1847, he acted almost continuously in various war capacities in the Eastern theater; his later claim to have "served during the whole of the Mexican War, either afloat, or on shore," was no exaggeration. First assigned to the Home Squadron, which patrolled around the Gulf of Mexico, he itched for a more active role in charge of a ship. He got his chance when he was given command of the *Somers*, a small, speedy, well-armed brig with a checkered history.

On blockade duty off Vera Cruz, in December 1846, he was caught fatally unprepared by a sudden squall blowing in from the north. The *Somers* was lightly ballasted and running under full sail after a suspected enemy. Semmes ordered the helmsman to bring her around to face into the wind; too late; in thirty seconds the ship was blown onto her beam ends, the masts and sails spanking flat on the sea. Semmes, thrown overboard, was pulled up onto the side of the capsized hull. Water flooded into every scuttle and hatchway, and in just ten minutes she sank. Again in the water, having shed all his clothes except his shirt and drawers, Semmes swam toward a stray piece of grating and held on. Crewmen who had managed to launch a single lifeboat in the swirling final moments rescued Semmes, by then exhausted and help-less, and thirty-eight others. But thirty-seven men, nearly half the crew, were drowned. Semmes had lost his second ship and suffered his first fatalities. He requested an investigation, which cleared him of any misconduct.

Within days of the loss of the *Somers*, Commodore David Conner of the Home Squadron assigned Semmes to his flagship, the *Raritan*, as first lieutenant. That conspicuous expression of confidence made Semmes the second in command on the commodore's own vessel. The winter of 1847 passed in blockade duty, dull but effective. In February the pace and tension started humming as an army of ten thousand men under General Winfield Scott prepared to invade Vera Cruz. Ships and supplies arrived every day. "Our hitherto quiet head-quarters," Semmes later wrote, "in which we had stagnated all winter, became daily more animated."

On March 9 the troops were landed in the largest amphibious operation to that point in American military history. The *Raritan* and other ships exchanged cannon lobs with Mexican batteries on shore; for the first time Semmes watched the deadly spectacle, and felt the awful thrills, of being under serious fire. Scott asked that some of the Navy ordnance be brought ashore to help the siege. On March 24, a moonless night, Semmes accompanied this landing force. They camped out and boomed away for three days. Semmes commanded one of the thirty-two-pound cannon, advised in its placement by Cap-tain Robert E. Lee. The Mexican forces surrendered Vera Cruz on March 27.

After two more weeks of fighting at Tuspan, a town northwest of Vera Cruz, Semmes was sent inland, bearing a special message, to catch up with Scott's army as it headed toward Mexico City. In effect he had left the Navy and joined the Army, leading an escort of twenty soldiers that followed the route of Cortéz up the Valley of Mexico. He spent the next six months making himself useful and traversing the country, inevitably studying its history, customs, and landscapes along the way. In one of the last battles outside Mexico City, he and Lieu-tenant Ulysses S. Grant both mounted howitzers on the roof of a church. The American forces finally broke through the walls of the city in September.

The easy American triumph in the war, propelled by superior guns and machinery, added over a million square miles to the national domain and set the patriotic eagle screaming. For Semmes, it brought commendations from his superiors and a resolution from the Maryland General Assembly in praise of his "distinguished gallantry." His most cherished reward, though, was the publication and success of his first book. For years he had harbored literary ambitions—as an outlet for his essential bookishness, and as a gesture, presumably goaded by Anne, toward extra family income. In 1846 he wrote a 239-page manuscript describing the recent cruise of the Navy warship *Porpoise* through the Caribbean to Santo Domingo after the latest round of political unrest there. Semmes served as first lieutenant on the mission, with David Dixon Porter among his shipmates. But that intended book did not find a publisher.

The Mexican War and his varied roles in the conflict presented the aspiring author the richer material he needed. *Service Afloat and Ashore During the Mexican War*, an impressive tome of 480 pages, was issued in the summer of 1851 by William H. Moore and Company of Cincinnati. His wife's hometown ties may have assisted the publishing process; brother Henry was then in his fourth term as mayor, and brother Oliver was a prominent attorney. Semmes borrowed part of his title from *Afloat and Ashore; or, The Adventures of Miles Wallingford*, a recent seafaring novel by James Fenimore Cooper. He dedicated the book to his Uncle Benedict Semmes, his foster father and intellectual mentor, "as a tribute to his many virtues, public and private; and as a slight return for the many kindnesses received at his hands." (Uncle Raphael Semmes, his other foster father, had died a few years earlier.)

As a writer, Semmes could never contain his omnivorous curiosity. The book offered more pages on Mexican history, society, mores, lands, and climates than on the war itself. But the digressions were interesting and usually relevant, placing the conflict in a layered context that expanded its meanings. Semmes's accounts of his own participation in the war were crisp and exciting without being too self-serving. For the most part, he stepped offstage and let the more significant players command the spotlight. The author remained nearby, watching, recording, and reflecting. "There never yet was a campaign without a blunder," he declared, so his book would avoid "the puerilities and puffings that have been bestowed upon the Mexican War." He regretted the siege of Vera Cruz, his own bloody initiation, because the imprecise cannon fire had caused so many civilian casualties. He heard women screaming during the shelling—a sound he could not shake. Semmes's worst villains were the American political figures who, for selfish reasons of fame and career, had fomented the war and then exploited its success. "Politicians, with a few honorable exceptions, have descended to the position of mere office-seekers," he regretted. Political life, once the domain of statesmen, had become merely "the petty theater of events, on which the fleeting generations of politicians play hide-and-go-seek, and then pass away and are forgotten."

Yet Semmes was a patriot, a military man, who saw the Mexican War as part of white America's inexorable, beneficial march across the continent. By spreading into Texas, New Mexico, and California, his countrymen were replacing "an inferior people," he insisted, and bringing new energy, courage, arts, letters—also, by the way, at great political and commercial advantage to themselves. "Time, with his scythe and hour-glass, had brought another and a newer race, to sweep away the moldered and moldering institutions of a worn-out people, and replace them with a fresher and more vigorous civilization. The descendant of the Dane and the Saxon, with 'progress' inscribed on his helmet, had come to supplant the never-changing Visigoth."

Most Americans agreed. The book quickly sold out its first edition and went into a second printing. Praise came from all around the country. "One of the most interesting of all the publications to which the late war with Mexico gave rise," said the voice of the South, *De Bow's Review* of New Orleans. "The battles are minutely described with military skill." "The most unprejudiced and truly historical record of those events that has yet been given to the public," concluded the most influential women's magazine, *Godey's Lady's Book* of Philadelphia. "A graphic and lively style." "A work of standard merit, and does honor to the growing literature of the West," announced the major literary monthly, *Harper's Magazine* of New York. "We congratulate the noble-spirited author on the signal success of his work, and hope that we shall again hear of his name in the field of literature, as well as in the service of his country." The war, the book, and its smiling reviews all seemed to confirm a triumphantly united nation.

· · ·

Coming into middle age, Semmes had split his life into four major aspects, interrelated but also independent—and sometimes mutually contradictory. He was a husband and father, a reader and writer, a lawyer, and a naval officer. Each of the four roles by itself might have exhausted his time and energy. He worked hard, persistently, at all four. They called on different skills and personality traits; at any particular moment, a deep immersion in one inevitably meant slighting the others. This daily juggling act, being always pressed for time, exacted a psychic toll. Semmes spent his days, in general, quite tightly wound, tense, striving, seldom at rest or content. Sometimes he smiled, but he hardly ever laughed. Observers often thought him aloof and unfriendly.

The most severe cost of these separate roles has long remained a guarded family secret. At the end of his Mexican War service, in November 1847, he was granted permission to return home to Prospect Hill in Alabama. Anne gave birth to her fifth child in December. The awkward fact was that Semmes could not have been the father. Between February and May of that year, seven to ten months before the birth, he was intensely involved in preparations for the landing and siege at Vera Cruz, and in related actions on shore for many weeks afterward. He was a thousand miles across the gulf from Prospect Hill, with no chance whatever of making a quick trip home and back.

Anne named the baby Anna Spencer Semmes, a version of her own name. At an early point Anna was dispatched to a Roman Catholic convent school outside Philadelphia—a long way from Prospect Hill—while the four older children remained at home. The Academy of the Sacred Heart, Eden Hall, was also known as the Eden Hall Institution for Young Ladies. Located in Holmesburg, at the northeastern edge of the city, the boarding school of about fifty students was run by French-speaking nuns from the Sacred Heart order. Board and tuition cost $180 a year, with extra fees for books, stationery, music, drawing, and languages other than French—a large imposition on Semmes's modest Navy salary. (During the Civil War, with her husband away at sea for years, Anne would bring her child back into the family home.) As an adult Anna claimed a birth date of May 27, 1846. It was unusual for a woman of that time to pretend to be *older* than her actual age— but she could thereby avoid the potential embarrassment of the true date.

No letters between Raphael and Anne survive from this period of the late 1840s; that is perhaps no accident. How they dealt with this family crisis, what they said to each other, and the identity of the real father cannot be known. For Semmes, a devout nineteenth-century Roman Catholic, divorce could not be considered. They might have separated, but they didn't. Perhaps in some ways, up to a limited point, he understood. At the time of the child's conception, the war had apparently kept him away for eight or nine months already, since a brief visit in early July 1846. Anne was at home alone with four children, ages nine and under. She was still just twenty-seven years old, still a beautiful young woman in her sexual prime. Any helpful male acquaintance might have wished to keep her company. Semmes perhaps felt guilty over his long naval absences, the simple companionship and comforts he could not provide. The Roman Catholic mind-set, unlike its demanding Protestant counterpart, expects that human beings, being so human, will sin—and therefore arranges a formal, elaborate mediating structure of confession and eventual expiation and forgiveness. Semmes apparently forgave her. The marriage survived. Later on, with Anna removed from the family circle, they could almost pretend she had not happened.

It seems that Semmes did thereafter try harder to stay nearby. In mid-January 1848, just a month after Anna's birth, he asked for command of the storeship *Electra*, based in Pensacola, "to be near my family," as he put it. He left a month later for a ninety-day cruise around the gulf in the *Electra*. "I feel sad at the prospect of so long a separation from my family," he wrote in his shipboard journal on March 4, the tenth birthday of his oldest child. "Those who see only the bright side of our profession have no idea of the almost life-long privations we suffer." At various ports of call, he hoped for reassuring letters from Anne—but none came. He must inevitably have started to worry about what she might be doing, again, in his absence. "Every day I am becoming more and more sick of the sea," he wrote on April 1, "and its privations—one of the chief of which is the hard fate of banishment from one's family." A week later, "No letters yet from home! and I am forty six days absent." Finally, after another week, some letters reached him. He got back to Prospect Hill for three days in May ("<u>At Home!</u>"), then for good in early July. He found the welcome news of his appointment to a shore job at the Pensacola yard. Within two weeks Anne was pregnant again, with a boy they would name Raphael. The namesake son sealed and symbolized their reconciliation.

The few surviving letters from Semmes to Anne, from a later period, show no overt emotional residue of her extramarital affair and child. Their agreed-upon explanation, that the child was his, required a rigid façade to outsiders and even to themselves. On a deeper level, though, unexpressed and perhaps even unconscious, the shock and pain must have always stayed with them. Anna Spencer, even far away in Philadelphia, of course reminded Semmes of his wife's betrayal—and reminded Anne of the child she had borne but could not raise. When he later, in 1862, wrote a fond letter to his wife, mentioning their five children by name, one by one, but making no reference to Anna, it amounted to an oblique yet pointed rebuke, again, for her wayward behavior back in 1847. Their deepest feelings about their gravest crisis probably had to remain walled off, unspoken and unacknowledged.

One other document, ambiguous and tantalizing, is pertinent here. An old Semmes family Bible was passed down through various descendants and is now in the custody of Thomas Middleton Semmes of Gladstone, Oregon. In some blank pages at the start of the New Testament, Raphael Semmes recorded the birth and death dates of his Semmes grandfather, father, and mother. He then wrote the dates of his own birth and marriage to Anne, and the birthdates of their first four children from 1838 to 1844. Semmes did not record Anna's birth in 1847 in this sequence. Later, at the bottom of the page, someone else added the birth of Raphael Jr., in 1849.

Two more full pages of handwritten family genealogy follow, with the marriages and children of Samuel Spencer Semmes and Electra Semmes Colston. On the last blank page, in an otherwise empty space, somebody at some point added a final entry: the birth of Anna, described as the daughter of Raphael and Anne Semmes, on May 27, 1846.

In the fall of 1849, Semmes moved his family into town, near Mobile. Prospect Hill now seemed too isolated. With five kids in need of schooling, he made the move "for the convenience of educating my children," he explained. He spent the next few years writing his Mexico book and acting as a judge and attorney for courts-martial in Pensacola. His naval life at sea was suspended, and he could focus on his three other callings of family, writing, and law. As any writer comes to know too acutely, intellectual life and family life pull in opposite directions. A writer needs solitude, quiet, and long blocks of private time—not the usual conditions in a home with young children. When the work is going well, the writer looks down at the papers on the desk, locks into them, and becomes engrossed. Hours flit by like minutes. The writer then looks up, notices the time of day, and with muttering regrets has to stop because the family is waiting.

At most levels, Semmes was most truly himself alone in his study, reading and writing. It was his own private, stable universe, consistent from childhood on—and wonderfully portable, available anywhere on land or sea. Books could, at least for a while, even relieve the tedium of an extended naval cruise. "I read, and read," he noted on the *Electra*, "and get tired of reading—then walk until I tire myself, and then in my desperation, go to reading again." Over his lifetime of reading, he took up some fiction (Washington Irving and the sea novelist Frederick Marryat), but generally preferred history (Thomas Macaulay), sociology (Alexis de Tocqueville), ocean lore (Matthew Maury), and poetry. He admired the works of Walter Scott, as many Southerners of the time did—but Semmes favored the Scotsman's poetry over his fiction.

In his Mexico book and later published writings, Semmes followed the nineteenth-century practice of sprinkling his prose with snatches of unidentified poetry. Of some three dozen such quotations, all but a few came from British authors: Scott, Macaulay, Oliver Goldsmith, the poet James Montgomery. That preference is not surprising; with American literature far from matured, Semmes's intellectual generation had grown up mainly on the mother country's writers. But his runaway favorite source for poetry quotations, with fourteen hits, seems out of character: George Gordon, Lord Byron, the Romantic poet, political liberal, and notorious sexual outlaw. The choice might be taken as a literary counterpart to Semmes's loopy French mustache: a revealingly odd touch that doesn't seem to fit him. Perhaps Semmes simply admired Byron's work but not the man. And perhaps—this is only speculation—he had come to understand that sexual behavior could not be contained within facile categories of proper and improper.

Semmes had a classic writer's personality, quiet and solitary. He was more inclined to listen than talk, to watch than do. In any social group, he was the silent one off to the side, keeping to himself, wishing he could go read. Like many shy people, he longed for the effortless social ease and skills he could never attain. His description of a rollicking naval colleague, John Newland Maffitt, at a congenial hotel in Nassau included hints of jealousy peeping between the lines: "He knew everybody, and everybody knew him, and he passed in and out of all the rooms. . . . He was equally at home, with men or women, it being all the same to him, whether he was wanted to play a game of billiards, take a hand at whist, or join in a duet with a young lady—except that he had the good taste always to prefer the lady. Social, gay, and convivial, he was much courted and flattered." Semmes could admire such a performance and covet it for himself—even while knowing it was impossibly beyond him. He was forever small and skinny, not handsome, socially uneasy, with "a voice like a woman's." His charm, subtler than conventional physical gifts, relied on spirit and intellect.

At sea, as well, Semmes was socially and intellectually out of place. Those studious tendencies puzzled his shipmates. "He had no particular taste for his profession, but had a fondness for literature and was a good talker and writer," according to David Dixon Porter. "Although his courage was undoubted, his tastes were rather those of the scholar than of the dashing naval officer." Few of his naval colleagues shared his passions for books and writing. Of necessity he kept to himself aboard ship, staring out to sea and contentedly lost in his own rich but private world. "He had the rare un-American quality of an economy, a parsimony, of speech," recalled Robert Rogers, one of his officers on the *Somers*. "Indeed, he was a silent man. I have seen him, almost daily, standing aft, clinging to a back-stay, looking in a fixed direction . . . as if in reflection or introspection. He would remain for hours in that Carthusian closure of the lips."

People who met him after he became famous during the Civil War were typically surprised—and often disappointed. "Nothing particularly striking in his appearance," noted a friendly observer, "except his eye, which is very fine and piercing." He did not look or carry himself like a naval hero. He ventured no swagger; he buckled no swashes. "For he was a man of very fine and sensitive feelings," wrote his English friend William S. Lindsay. "He was one of the quietest and most unassuming men I ever met. He was nothing of the buccaneer either in his mind or manners—made no boast of his exploits—on the contrary never spoke of them when he could normally avoid doing so." Lindsay, also surprised at first, eventually penetrated the introverted American's social barricades and recognized, underneath, "my warm hearted, gentle friend."

As the nation tore itself apart during the 1850s, Semmes spent most of the decade in professional frustration. Despite his distinguished war record, he was still just a lieutenant, confined to shore duties and leaves. That extended time at home did help restore his marriage. But his legal work bored him, and he missed the snap and tang of the ocean. The call of the sea again trumped the rest of his life. He kept asking for cruises but was denied. No doubt his reputation as a troublous sea lawyer helped block his way; but the larger impediment was the Navy's senseless seniority-based promotion system. "We of the naval service are dead—dead of old age and decrepitude," he warned in the Mexico book. It was slow death by seniority, "that preposterous cry which insists that a man's years, and not his brains, should be the test of promotion and employment. A more perfect system could not have been invented, by our worst enemies, if their object had been to destroy us. It dampens hope, it stifles talent, it cripples energy."

Such stinging public criticism presumably did not help his chances with the Navy brass. Semmes watched his naval contemporaries—men he had started with as midshipmen, messed and grown up with—pass him in the lists and take command of frigates. He remained on shore, furious. "Ambitious as I am to fill the higher posts in my profession, to which I have already devoted the best energies of my life," he wrote to a senator from Florida, "I would rather be 'retired' tomorrow than continue to wear away my life, with the blank and hopeless prospect at present before me." He thought about getting out and attempting other kinds of work. In the spring of 1852 he rented some field slaves and tried lumbering the fine stands of live oak and yellow pine in Washington County, north of Mobile. But the project was made difficult by illness and muddy roads, and the heavy physical labor did not suit him.

Back to naval life and waiting. After eighteen years as a lieutenant, he was at last promoted to commander late in 1855. A commander in sea service made $2,500 a year; in shore duty, $2,100, and just $1,800 on leave. The attractions of the ocean included extra pay. Semmes wrote to the secretary of the Navy in October 1855, asking for a command at sea. "I have not been afloat, since the spring of 1849," he pointed out. "In the mean time, almost all the newly promoted commanders, who rank me, have made one or more cruises." Four months later he tried again, noting that two new sloops of war were being fitted out, and requesting "the first vacant command afloat." Semmes was soon tossed a short-term bone: the mail steamer *Illinois*. It turned out to be his final command on a ship of the U.S. Navy.

Having returned to Mobile, late in 1856 he was offered yet another shore posting, as inspector of lighthouses for the local district. He wrote a letter of acceptance with this added condition: "I respectfully request, however, that the Department will continue to regard me as an applicant for sea-service, and that it will not pass me by." On reflection, though, he crossed that sentence out before sending the letter. It epitomized his ambivalence. For himself he craved the command of a ship at sea; but the rest of his life, his other passions and responsibilities, pulled him back to shore. At the age of forty-seven, nearly too old for the rigors of the ocean, he was giving up on his lifelong ambition.

Two years later he was promoted to a desk job in Washington, as secretary of the lighthouse board in the Treasury Department. By the spring of 1859, he had settled into the position—"a perfectly independent one, and of no little importance," he wrote to his son Spencer, then studying law in New Orleans. He functioned as his own boss, like the commander of a ship at sea, and supervised a million-dollar budget and lighthouses along three thousand miles of American coastline. But he still could not command his wife. Anne, independent as ever, visited her relatives in Cincinnati, then came to spend the summer with her husband before deciding about moving herself and the younger children. "It will depend," Semmes told Spencer, "upon how your mother likes Washington, whether [we will] make a temporary location here or not." She liked the city well enough, and the family was reunited.

Living in the national capital, Semmes could observe at close proximity the thrashings and flailings of the politicians who were driving the country toward catastrophe. Ever since the Mexican War, hatred of such officeholders had always tinged his patriotism. "I love my country as a sort of <u>identity</u>," he reflected then, "while I despise its hordes of demagogues who yearly struggle for office, and without other thoughts than how they may best provide for themselves." In general, he agreed with other white Southerners in their political quarrels with the North over tariffs and slavery. He also accepted the common Southern notion that North and South comprised two diverging, incompatible cultures: Puritan, industrial, and Saxon against Cavalier, agrarian, and Norman. But to Semmes these differences did not require secession and war.

As the national crisis tightened, he remained detached and moderate, and skeptical of mere politicians. In the summer of 1860, after the approaching presidential campaign had splintered into four parties and candidates, he made a lighthouse tour of the Great Lakes. He sent a cheerful, chatty report to Anne, marveling at "the great extent and rapid growth of this country," and saying nothing whatever about political conditions or the looming crisis. On election day he voted for Stephen Douglas, the relative centrist in the presidential field.

His detachment meant that Semmes would be swept along by events, making decisions by responding to the latest news. Though naturally sympathetic to the South, he temporized over leaving a secure government position for an uncertain future. Lincoln's election set the secessionists of the Lower South on fire. On December 11 Semmes contacted a political acquaintance and fellow moderate, Alexander Stephens of Georgia. "The great government," he wrote Stephens, "under which we have lived so long, and prospered so greatly, is probably destroyed." How could the Union now be preserved? Failing that, how could the South unite in a Confederacy? "My judgment, my inclinations, and my affections all incline me to link my fate with the first movement of the South, if I can be cordially received and appointed a place in the movement." His decision, that is, depended on getting a job; and if his own state—Maryland, not Alabama—did not secede, could he obtain such an appointment? Meantime he remained at his lighthouse duties, "but listening with an aching ear, and a beating heart for the first sounds of the great disruption which is at hand."

Nine days later, South Carolina bolted, followed quickly by six other Lower South states. Semmes stayed on in Washington, working for the federal government and waiting. "I think States enough have gone out to determine me as to the course I shall pursue," he guessed in late January. Alabama had seceded, tempting him to switch his state allegiance; "I am in some sort claimed as a citizen of Alabama, having resided in that state several years," so perhaps that would bring him a post in the Navy of the new Confederacy. But he still did not expect a war, writing on February 6 to another Southern politician: "I do not think you will have any war." At last, on February 14, the decision was made for him. A telegram from the provisional government in Montgomery, Alabama, summoned him to naval duty. A day later he resigned his commission in the U.S. Navy, and a day after that he left for Montgomery.

In his temporizing he was also trying to straddle the divisions within his own family. His beloved only brother, Samuel, had for decades lived in the free-labor region of northwestern Maryland. As the country fell apart, he assumed a leading role among the Unionists in his town of Cumberland. A cousin, Alexander Semmes, later became a flag officer in the Union Navy. Within his own household, Anne lined up with her relatives in Cincinnati and chose the Union while the children all fervently cheered for the Confederacy. The two oldest boys, Spencer and Oliver, at once joined the Southern army; in fact, Oliver, a cadet at West Point, resigned *his* United States commission four weeks before his father did. "Kiss your dear Mother for me," Semmes wrote his daughter Electra in March, "and tell her she hardly deserves to hear that her Ollie has been made a captain, so much has she lamented over what she terms my false movement."

That fond, bantering tone could not conceal the lacerating wounds of this family quarrel. The war had begun. No one could say when it would end. Semmes hoped Anne would take the children back to Alabama for the duration. "If you can get safely down to Mobile, I think you would be better satisfied," he urged her. "You would there be out of the tainted atmosphere of Abolitionism, and would not be compelled to witness the sad spectacle of your own brothers enlisting in this Northern crusade against your husband's section, and the birth place of your children." As for Samuel, "I am disappointed and mortified at the course of my own brother, for whom there is less excuse than for yours. It is in times like these that men are tried, and we shall hereafter know who are our friends. . . . Even our own blood relatives fall away from us." Anne, again, went her own way. She took Electra, Kate, and young Raphael to stay with Samuel for a while in Cumberland, then settled herself and her brood with her own Unionist kinfolk in Cincinnati.

For Semmes, events had transformed Hamlet into Hotspur. The sharp early battles of the war, played against the defections of his wife and brother and the secessionist loyalties of his children, turned him into a roaring Confederate patriot. His long period of moderate equivocation suddenly accelerated into bellicose zeal; the internal pressures that he had contained now exploded. In May he wrote to Electra:

> The fierce and savage war which is being waged against us, by the fanatic and the half civilized hordes of the North, strikes a serious and an alarming blow at the principle of self-government—not only in these states, but throughout the world. Our revolution is far more important, viewed in this light, than was the first revolution of the colonies against the mother country. The rude, rough, unbridled, and corrupt North threatens us with nothing less than utter <u>subjugation</u>, and yet strange to say, the <u>entire</u> <u>North</u> seems to approve of this design. I have almost lost my faith in mankind.

Semmes had, indeed, become a new man.

He urged the newborn Confederate Navy to deploy "a small organized system of private armed ships, known as privateers." From his saltwater vantage point, he saw the North as a commercial power dependent on seagoing enterprise. Its ability to harm the South "will consist chiefly in ships and shipping," Semmes argued. "It is at ships and shipping, therefore, that you must strike." Privateers were a traditional weapon of a weaker nation against a stronger; the United States had used them effectively in two wars against Great Britain, the dominant naval force in the world, and had made heroes of dashing privateer captains like John Paul Jones. But they veered close to piracy as freelancers operating outside normal naval chains of command, seizing spoils and selling prizes for money. "There is a growing disposition among civilized nations," Semmes himself had written in his Mexico book, "to put an end to this disreputable mode of warfare, under any circumstances. It had its origin in remote and comparatively barbarous ages, and has for its object rather the plunder of the bandit, than honorable warfare. . . . They are little better than licensed pirates." The

Semmes in a Richmond photographer's studio, at
some point during the war. (Cook Collection,
Valentine Richmond History Center)

major European powers had outlawed the practice in 1856. But now
the Confederacy was arrayed against a much stronger enemy, and
Semmes—with more ethical flexibility than he might have cared to
admit—aimed to revive this "disreputable mode of warfare."

The Confederacy desperately needed a legitimate naval force to
attack Northern seaborne commerce, protect its ports, and counter
the Union blockade of the entire Southern coastline. Though many
U.S. Navy officers headed home to the South after secession, the new
nation could claim no great seafaring tradition like the North's; most
of its existing vessels were designed for river and coastal traffic, not the
deep ocean, and the South generally lacked the shipyards and iron
foundries to build oceangoing steamships. Stephen Mallory of Florida,
secretary of the Navy, dispatched James Bulloch to England to acquire
the ships of war that the Confederacy could not construct for itself.

Mallory "was like a chieftain without a clan, or an artizan without the tools of his art," Bulloch noted. "The task before him was to create."

In New Orleans, Semmes creatively took command of the *Sumter,* a small, three-masted propeller steamship of only five hundred tons, formerly employed in the easy two-day run between Havana and New Orleans. For two months Semmes oversaw her refitting as a warship. Cabins and public rooms gave way to water tanks and more space for coal. To protect the five guns and the upper parts of the engine, a light flush deck was added on top. The extra ten feet looked in odd proportion to the masts and funnel. The wooden hull seemed fragile; "I could have kicked her bows in, she was so unseaworthy," one of her officers said later. Her first trial run yielded a top speed of just under ten knots, disappointing Semmes. But she was buoyant and dry, with fine sailing qualities: the first oceangoing ship of the Confederate Navy.

The *Brooklyn* and other Union warships were blockading the mouth of the Mississippi. On the morning of June 30, the *Sumter* crossed the bar and ran. The *Brooklyn,* four miles away, gave chase. She was four times larger than the *Sumter,* with five times the firepower and a reputation for speed. Both ships put out all their sails. The *Sumter* was strangely out of trim, heavy at the bow, plunging deeply and keeping her forecastle doused in spray. Semmes ordered a field howitzer and 1,500 gallons of water thrown overboard. His little ship put on more steam pressure, from the previous limit of eighteen pounds up to twenty-seven, risking the boilers. The *Brooklyn* started to fall back on the leeward side, toward which the breeze was blowing. The *Sumter* was now eating the wind of her pursuer, running interference as they bowled along. Semmes kept his ship in that tactical advantage. After four hours the race was over. He convened his officers in the wardroom for a celebratory glass of wine. Five years after Semmes had given up his last hopes for an oceangoing command, he was at sea once again. "Night beautiful and starlight," he exulted in his journal, "with a light in the north throwing a pencil of rays to the northeast as if lighting our way."

Just three days later, off the western tip of Cuba, Semmes caught his first Yankee. The *Golden Rocket* of Bangor, Maine, was sailing in ballast, with no cargo. Semmes took her crew aboard, plus some provisions and other supplies. It was ten o'clock on a very black night. The prize was made of old, seasoned lumber, with pine decks and pitch-

and-oakum caulking, and some paints and oils stowed in the forecastle. The boarding officer lit her afire in three places at once. The flames jumped up and engulfed the ship, sucking air into the burning holds and cabins, the indrafts roaring like so many furnaces. The sails were hanging loose aloft. The fires ran up the shrouds and rigging; flaming spars and sails broke apart and silted down into the ocean. Each mast fell in turn, crashing heavily like an old oak tree in a forest. All that fire in the midst of all that water, looking and sounding so out of place, was beautiful and terrible: Semmes's first bonfire at sea.

Over the next month, Semmes captured nine more ships—all of Union registry, but carrying cargoes owned by people from other countries, and thus protected from Confederate flames. Instead the nine were sent or towed into a putatively friendly port, in the hope of selling them or using the ships as Confederate vessels. But it didn't work, for legal or diplomatic or other reasons. Semmes could never risk the blockade by attempting to bring his prizes into Confederate ports. Lacking other options, he decided to focus on Union ships bearing Union cargoes that he could burn at sea.

The limitations of the *Sumter* were already becoming apparent. When she was under sail alone, the propeller could not be lifted out of the water; this created drag and slowed the vessel. Under steam, she could carry only enough coal for eight days of continuous power. Semmes wanted to head for the teeming crossroads of South Atlantic ship traffic, off the northeast coast of Brazil, and squat there for a while, waiting for prey. But in that exposed, distant spot, he needed the insurance of emergency steaming—which his coal supply would not allow. Instead he had to stay near shore, hopping around the Caribbean, with regular stops for coaling.

The *Sumter* seemed more formidable back home, in various Union ports and the Navy Department in Washington. As the ship's captures piled up, the alarmed news reports created their own kind of bonfire. Rumors flew around that one prize had yielded $5,000 in cash, and another $13,000. (The actual total for the first ten ships taken was $200.) Gideon Welles, Lincoln's secretary of the Navy, ordered fleets of ships in pursuit. David Dixon Porter, cruising in the Caribbean on the *Powhatan*, sent his boss some captured letters of Semmes's. "He is in a position now where he can't escape, if properly looked after," Porter announced. "He is out of coal and out of credit." A few days later, off Cuba, Porter was sure: "The *Sumter*, sir, will not likely leave the Caribbean sea." But he suggested sending eight more ships in pursuit. A month later, off Brazil, "I have chased her from point to point, and have gained on her at every place." Not that he had the slightest notion of the cruiser's whereabouts: "I can form no idea where the *Sumter* is at this time, but I think she is off Cape St. Roque." The problem, Porter concluded, was that his own ship was too big; "With a smaller vessel I would have caught the *Sumter* ten days ago." But he hoped the government would persist, "even if it has to send all the navy afloat after the *Sumter*, and go to the expense of building a hundred new vessels for this purpose." (Perhaps Porter now sensed he was dealing with a different Raphael Semmes than the unimpressive man he had known in the old Navy.)

Meantime, after his initial flurry, Semmes went two months without any captures. He burned one ship, the *Joseph Park* of Massachusetts, trolled through another month, then burned the *Daniel Trowbridge* of Connecticut. After ten prizes in the first month, he took just two in the next three. On November 9, needing a break from all that fruitless cruising, the *Sumter* anchored at the town of St. Pierre on Martinique, among the Windward Islands off the coast of Venezuela. Semmes needed coal, as usual, and water. He ventured ashore, spoke to the governor, attended mass, went shopping. The visit stretched on into two pleasant weeks. The crew, given its first liberty since departing New Orleans, descended on the bars and brothels to indulge in traditional rounds of drunken misbehavior.

The Union Navy's *Iroquois*, 1,500 tons and six guns, was then chasing the *Sumter* around the Caribbean. Her captain, James S. Palmer, had been told to "use every endeavor, notwithstanding the time it may take, to hunt her down, as her capture is of great moment to our commercial interests." At St. Thomas, Palmer learned his quarry was at St. Pierre. The *Iroquois* arrived there on November 14. She was a true warship, much stauncher and a couple of knots faster than the converted Havana boat. Within the harbor, hostilities were forbidden; but at 1:30 in the morning, the Union ship steamed toward the Confederate cruiser. Semmes, awakened, called all hands to quarters, ready for action. The *Iroquois* sheered off, turned, did it again, and yet again, once approaching within a ship's length. "Great excitement pervades the entire city," Semmes recorded in his journal. "The market square, the quays, and the windows of the houses are thronged by an eager and curious multitude, expecting every moment to see a combat."

The *Iroquois* steamed out of the harbor to wait outside the three-mile limit. "I have at last got hold of the *Sumter*," Palmer wrote home. "This ship ought to knock her to pieces in ten minutes." The harbor was fifteen miles long, with passages at the northern and southern ends. Semmes wanted to leave on the first dark night, but his chief engineer was repairing the pumps, taking longer than expected. He finished work on November 22, but that night was brightly starlit, without a cloud anywhere. Next day brought welcome rain and darkened skies, then problematic clearing before sundown. Semmes couldn't wait any longer.

He had learned that another Yankee ship in the harbor was going to signal the *Iroquois*: two blue lights if the *Sumter* went south, red lights if she went north. Semmes headed south, saw the blue lights, kept going for a few hundred yards, and halted. The *Iroquois* could be seen charging for the southern exit. The harbor was deep in close to the land, and a blocky rock formation rose high near the water's edge. Snuggling up to this cover, blending into the land and its shadow, Semmes came about and ran for the north point. The engine had to be stopped, briefly, because the bearings became too hot. "This was truly an anxious moment for me," Semmes noted. A friendly rain squall blew in, hiding the telltale plumes of black smoke pouring from the *Sumter*'s funnel. After a taut, watchful half hour, the lights of the town winked out behind them, and they knew they had escaped again.

During the long fallow periods between captures by the *Sumter*, little news of her whereabouts reached the newspapers back home. That only stoked the growing legend of "Semmes the pirate." In the absence of any real news, rumors could spawn and prosper. The *Sumter* was wrecked off Trinidad. No, but she was captured near Barbados. No, but Semmes had left the ship and was on his way to England. Aboard the steamship *Edinburgh*, during her passage from New York to England in October, an impostor claimed to be Raphael Semmes. American passengers with divided loyalties, North and South, had been picking at each other. A pretty young widow from Baltimore even came to dinner one night wrapped in a Confederate flag. In the uproar that followed, a man who had previously identified himself as a Briton named Burnside, but who seemed like a Southerner, now confessed that he was instead the famous Semmes. He had been introduced to William Seward in Washington, he said, and had also visited the Army of the Potomac. He was drunk, but several Confederate ladies agreed that, yes, they had been told in New York that Semmes was on board. After a prolonged row, the ship's captain was summoned to restore peace, and "Semmes" retired to bed.

The real Semmes was in fact heading toward Europe. His heart-thumping flight from the *Iroquois*, given any number of the slightest twists of contingency, could have tumbled into a disaster. He and his men were tired of lean pickings, weeks and weeks of no captures, not even any Union sails in sight. Many of the enemy's ships, well aware of him by now, were hiding in port or avoiding the Caribbean. "It is of no use to chase sails any more in these waters," Semmes decided; "the Yankees have nearly all disappeared, and even those who do show themselves are small lumbermen from Maine, or provision and live-stock dealers from Connecticut and Massachusetts." He took two final Caribbean prizes, burning one of them, and then plotted a course to the northeast.

Crossing the fierce North Atlantic Ocean under the darkening skies of December, the *Sumter* struggled through overwhelming waves and weather for which she was not designed. About a third of the way across, on December 6, she sailed into three days of gales and squalling rains. The ship began to leak copiously, mainly through the propeller sleeve, forcing the pumps to jog away through half a night. They did have the brief pleasure of burning a whaler, the *Eben Dodge* from New Bedford, Massachusetts, but that added twenty-two more prisoners to the twenty-one already on board, everyone crowded into grim conditions below.

December 11: "As ugly looking a morning as one could well conceive," Semmes noted, brought "thick, dark, gloomy weather, with the wind blowing fresh from the east and threatening a gale." It proved worse than a mere gale. A cyclone blew in that night, with pounding, irregular seas, high winds and hard rain, and flashes of incandescent lightning against the turbulent night sky. Just after midnight, a quartermaster knocked on the captain's door to report that a porthole on the starboard bow was stove in. Semmes sent his first lieutenant to plug the leak. Nobody slept that night.

The *Sumter* was crippled from that point on. She had to be

pumped out twice every four hours, and still the gun deck was ankle-deep in water. Running short of coal, the ship had to proceed under sail alone. Semmes considered a stop at the Azores for rest and supplies, but the danger of winter storms there changed his mind. He aimed for Gibraltar instead. Christmas Day brought inevitable thoughts of home, family, friends, and church. "Alas!" Semmes journalized. "How great the contrast between these things and our present condition." After a brief stay at the neutral port of Cádiz, Spain, for only the most essential hull repairs, he took two final prizes—bringing the *Sumter*'s total bag to eighteen captures, seven of them burned. On January 18, 1862, she limped into the harbor at Gibraltar. And there she stopped.

The *Sumter* was too damaged to be repaired. A local correspondent for *The Times* of London went to see the storied ship. "I could scarcely believe that so poor a vessel could have escaped so many dangers," he reported. "She is crank and leaky." (Captain Semmes, he added, was "a reserved, determined-looking man, whose left hand knows not what his right hand doeth.") The captain asked his men to survey the ship. They found some of the wooden planking and beams

The worn-out *Sumter* entering the harbor at Gibraltar.
(*Frank Leslie's Illustrated Newspaper*, November 8, 1862)

rotten. On the hull, planks above the copper sheathing were worm-eaten. The condenser and boilers needed to be lifted out for repairs that could only be done in a fully equipped machine shop—which Gibraltar did not have. The boilers were lightly patched and dangerous. In a test, at only twelve pounds of pressure a patch sprung two heavy leaks, which doused a fire in the boiler.

The *Sumter* was done, but Semmes was not. "The crippled condition of my ship," he wrote to Confederate agents in London, "and the want of funds have deprived me of the power of scouring the Mediterranean, the whole of which sea I could have swept without molestation in from fifteen to twenty days." Semmes paid off his crew and laid up the *Sumter*. He spent a few restful weeks in England in May, waiting to hear about his next assignment. When nothing appeared, he started for home and got as far as Nassau. There he was summoned back to England to take command of a new ship.

The *Alabama* was designed mainly by Henry Laird, the most technically inclined of the three brothers who had inherited the family shipyard from their father, John Laird. "There is not a shipbuilding firm in the country enjoying a higher reputation than his," declared a British engineering magazine when John retired, "either for excellence of materials or faithfulness of workmanship." Since 1831 the Lairds had built almost three hundred vessels of all kinds, including about forty for the Royal Navy. In 1857 they opened their imposing "New Yard" just south of Woodside, across the river Mersey from Liverpool. It was a busy place, noisy and smoky, extending for 650 feet along the river, with several ships rising at once and its Birkenhead Ironworks hammering out steam engines and boilers. Henry Laird had spent nearly three years apprenticing at the state-of-the-art shipyard of the French steamship line Messageries Imperiales, in La Ciotat, east of Marseilles. At a time when French shipbuilding led the world in scientific precision and progress, Laird learned the latest techniques at La Ciotat for improving hull design, to make a ship faster and more fuel-efficient. He was only twenty-three when he applied these lessons to the *Alabama*, his early masterpiece.

The Lairds had pioneered iron shipbuilding in Britain. But James Bulloch, the Confederate agent in Liverpool who contracted for the

Alabama, wanted a wooden hull of strong English oak. Bulloch knew the cruiser would spend most of her career at sea, with uncertain port facilities available. To repair an iron hull required special tools, materials, and craftsmen, found only in the most advanced dockyards. Almost any port in the world, though, would have lumber and ship carpenters. In addition, the *Alabama* would probably have to sail for indefinitely long stretches without having her bottom scoured. A copper-sheathed wooden hull resisted thick fouling by marine plants and organisms better than an iron hull did. Again the need for speed: a clean hull slipped more easily through the water. At the Laird shipyard in 1861–62, a wooden hull cost more and took longer to build than did an iron ship, but for the Confederate cruiser, the advantages of wood were compelling.

Henry Laird thus crafted the vessel for speed, deception, and extended cruising periods at sea. For a warship of the time, she was rakishly narrow, more like a yacht, at 220 feet long and 32 feet wide. That length-to-beam ratio of about seven to one made her less roomy, but faster. The clipper bow was cut sharply, flowing back into graceful lines. The hull, masts, lifeboats, and other fittings were painted black to blend into the ocean. For the same reason, the hull rode low in the water—dangerously so at times, especially when she was fully coaled.

The steam engine, of three hundred horsepower, was built on the compact and durable "oscillating" arrangement of shafts and gearing, the most advanced marine engine design of the day. (In the engineering lexicon of the nineteenth century, "engine" meant "cylinder," leading to some confusion among later historians. Though the ship was often said to have two engines, it was actually a single engine of two cylinders, each fifty-six inches in diameter with a twenty-seven-inch stroke.) The *Alabama* had room for 350 tons of coal, enough for eighteen days of continuous steaming. Her two-bladed propeller could be steam-lifted out of the water and into its own well in just fifteen minutes. A condenser attached to the engine turned enough salt water into fresh water for all hands. The *Sumter*'s endemic limitations of coal, water, and a dragging propeller were all addressed.

The three masts of yellow pine—foremast, mainmast, and mizzenmast, going from bow to stern—looked especially long and high in proportion to the low-riding hull. The bowsprit extended forward, connected by ropes to the foremast, above the modest figurehead of a red shield adorned with a gilt anchor. The sails and rigging were generally arranged in the style of a sailing East Indiaman. The *Alabama* usually sailed configured in a "barkentine" rig, with long lower masts and therefore an enormous spread of canvas, which let her lie close to the wind. At sea, from a distance, vessels might be identified by their rigs; after adjustments to the spars and sails on the mizzenmast, the *Alabama* could be disguised as a "ship-rigged" vessel. When running to windward, fighting the prevailing breeze, with her square sails furled she became a swift three-masted schooner, still faster than practically any ship she cared to chase or escape.

Captain Semmes and his men worked and lived on two decks. At the stern of the exposed upper deck, near the flag locker and arms chest, was the horse block, a raised platform that gave the officers clear sight lines for surveying the whole ship. Moving forward from there, the ship's wheel and compass binnacles were just ahead of the mizzenmast. The wheel was inscribed *"Aide-toi et Dieu t'aidera,"* Help Yourself and God Will Help You—a general motto of the Confederacy. Next came shot racks, the aft pivot gun, the skylight over the engine room, scuttles for loading coal, the ventilator to the aft stokehole (where the overheated firemen fed coal to the boilers), and the mainmast. Six other coal scuttles surrounded the funnel, squat and black, and the steam pipe for venting off excess steam. Just forward of the funnel, the bridge ran across the ship. Water closets here reigned on both sides of the deck. Last came the forward pivot gun, the ventilator for the other stokehole, the chain pipes and anchor chains, the capstan for raising the anchor, the foremast, sail room, and—hanging out over the bow—the bowsprit.

Of the guns that defined the *Alabama* as a warship, the most formidable was the rifled Blakely forward pivot gun; it fired one-hundred-pound shells, seven inches in diameter, though in use it tended to overheat too quickly. The aft pivot gun, unrifled, threw sixty-eight-pound shells that were eight inches in diameter. Both these guns, mounted on slides on the fore-to-aft midline of the deck, could be turned and aimed through wide arcs. Six other cannon on wheeled carriages peeked out gun ports cut through the bulwarks on the sides of the deck. Each weighed over two tons and fired thirty-two-pound shells, but could not be aimed from left to right. The pivot guns got the most action for enforcing Semmes's authority.

Living quarters were on the lower deck. By the mizzenmast, a ladderway descended to the captain's small, plainly furnished stateroom at the stern. Twelve feet long and twenty feet across at the widest point, it had slightly convex side walls tapering with the mold of the hull into a point at the back. A horsehair sofa ran around the edge of the cabin, ringed by Semmes's ever-growing collection of chronometers from captured ships. A profusion of maps, also lifted from prizes, overflowed the room, stowed behind the chronometers, against the bulkheads and crossbeams, and scattered on the sofa, table, chairs, and floor. A shelf held the captain's law books and a few other volumes. The small sideboard stood near the steward's pantry. At times the cabin included a canary and potted geraniums at a porthole. It was in many ways a typical dark, wood-toned Victorian room, ugly and cluttered, comfortable and functional.

Semmes ate, usually by himself, and worked at a long, U-shaped table across the middle of his quarters. On the walls hung a colored engraving of the *Alabama* and photographs of Jefferson Davis, Robert E. Lee, and a few others. To one side, a door opened into the captain's tiny sleeping room, barely large enough for a narrow bunk with drawers beneath and a strongbox, chair, and washstand. On the opposite side, another door led to a similar room for the captain's hardtoiling clerk. In everyday operations, the reclusive captain spent more time with his clerk than with anybody else on board.

Moving forward on the lower deck, next came the gun room (placed where the captain could supervise its use), followed by a small dining saloon, galley, and cabins for the main officers. After them were cabins for midshipmen to starboard and for engineers to port. As on any oceangoing vessel, the living quarters defined a man's shipboard status, gradually diminishing in both size and privacy as the room assignments descended the ranks.

The engine room and boilers dominated the middle of the ship, surrounded and protected by coal holds. From there to the bow, the sailors and firemen ate and slept in one big room, fifty-two feet long, reached from a ladderway by the capstan. A galley dispensed food to rows of tables ranged to port and starboard; under the seats were lockers for the sailors' bags and their hammocks, which only came out for sleeping. Beneath the lower deck were storage compartments for food, water, ammunition, liquor, sails, and other supplies. The magazines holding shells and powder were lined with three layers of oak and two layers of lead, in the hope of insulating them from moisture or a stray, disastrous spark.

At sea, capturing merchant vessels and lighting bonfires, the *Alabama* was remarkably self-contained and self-sufficient. Her speed under sail alone ranged from ten to thirteen knots, ample for catching most whalers and cargo ships. With steam power added, she could reach fifteen knots—but she seldom needed that boost. Semmes could save his coal for the vital condensing of water. Captured ships replenished the *Alabama*'s staple food stores, often with occasional extra treats such as cigars, meat on the hoof, and fresh fruits and vegetables. From their own separate supplies, the ship's boatswain, gunner, sailmaker, and carpenter could manage most routine repairs on board. As one of the officers later remarked, "It is rarely that a ship has such a complete dock-yard within herself."

Henry Laird designed the *Alabama* for certain predatory functions: to chase, kill, hide, and run, and in the process to stay at sea for months at a time. Her looks were an incidental by-product of those ruthless purposes. As it happened, though, she was by any standard quite pretty. Under full sail, with her ugly funnel pulled down for disguise, she looked like one of the legendary American clipper ships. Lean and graceful, skipping lightly over the waves, she could have been a crack racer in the China trade, rounding the Horn with a cargo of tea for the people of Boston. "I think," recalled her first lieutenant, yielding to a fond bias, "she was the most beautiful ship that ever touched the sea."

TWO

"A Pirate on the High Seas"

Semmes and the *Alabama* made their historical reputations during the first five months of the cruise. It happened so quickly, so many Union ships destroyed in so many different spots from the Azores to the Gulf of Mexico, that the captain and the ship became instant legends. To the Confederacy, Captain Semmes seemed like a heroic Stonewall Jackson of the sea, launching swift strikes now here, now there, and then disappearing again. To the Union, the *Alabama*—elusive, omnipresent, and deadly—seemed at times to vault beyond everyday realities and drift into mythology, like the storied Flying Dutchman of the oceans: a phantom ship from nowhere that could abruptly show up anywhere, bringing bad luck and a fiery trail of quite real bonfires.

After his blazing but brief rehearsal on the overachieving little *Sumter*, Captain Semmes at once established a workable routine for his longer run on the *Alabama*. Whenever the ship was cruising at sea, a lookout— a sailor with especially sharp eyesight—was always kept aloft, high in the foremast or mainmast. He continuously scanned the vast, circular horizon that surrounded the ship, looking for any sign of another vessel. Sometimes it was a smudge of black coal smoke, indicating a steamship. More typically it was a sail—or what looked like a sail. It might turn out to be a low-lying cloud, an iceberg, a flare of spindrift, or some unaccountable mystery of the deep. When the lookout thought he was sure, or sure enough, he shouted, "Sail ho!"

The cry, always welcome, and particularly after a dreary dry period of no prizes, sparked a series of actions below. If the captain was down in his cabin, he was called to the upper deck at any time of day or moonlit night. He and his top officers trained their telescopes on the sail. Semmes had to make a fast, perilous decision whether to chase or not. It depended on their best guess as to the identity of the distant ship; it also hinged on their current course and that of the target, on the wind direction, the weather, and the prevailing turbulence of the sea, even on the time of day. By instinct, Semmes and his men wanted to chase. They craved action and the task for which they were spending long months at sea. But if the sail was in fact a bristly Union warship with more men and firepower than the *Alabama*, the decision to pursue could prove irrevocable and suicidal.

Usually Semmes decided to go. All hands were called to their stations, eyes snapping, everybody keyed up to the bracing challenge of dangerous fun. Sailors danced up the rigging, waiting for orders to unfurl more sail. Down in the boiler room, the chief engineer stood ready to throw more coal on his banked fires in case the captain needed the extra speed of steam power. The chase was on. As the *Alabama* closed the distance between herself and the retreating sail, the identity of the intended quarry became clearer. American ships had a characteristic design, a peculiar cut of the canvas and taper of the spars, and their sails tended to be fuller and whiter than those of other nations. Closer, closer; the swift Confederate cruiser was typically a few knots faster than any fleeing vessel. Semmes could now, through his telescope, see the national flag flying at the stern, perhaps even make out the ship's name and home port painted over the transom. To avoid early detection, the *Alabama* chased under the disguise of a British or Union flag.

Pulled up within hailing distance, Semmes signaled the other ship to come about and wait to be boarded. If the other captain, on his unarmed ship, did not comply, Semmes fired a blank but noisy shot from his forward pivot gun. If that did not work, he aimed a live shell just off the bow of the quarry. Finally, if necessary, he threw a shell between the masts of the resisting ship, just a little above the upper deck. The men on the other ship could see, feel, and hear the shot skimming over their heads; it made them ponder what such a shell might do if aimed a bit lower. At that point they almost always decided to comply.

With the prey under his control, Semmes ordered his camouflaging flag pulled down and the Confederate colors run up. Launching one of his lifeboats, he dispatched a boarding party of an officer and a half dozen sailors, all armed with pistols and cutlasses and looking menacingly piratical. The intruders came aboard the captured ship, which was evidently of Union registry and ownership. They told her captain that they were now all in possession of the CSS *Alabama* of the Confederate Navy, and would he please with his ship's papers accompany them back to the off-lying cruiser? They also asked, right away, for any late newspapers from shore; Semmes and his men liked to read about themselves, about any Union ships sent to catch them, and the war news in general. Once on the *Alabama*, the captured captain— presumably worried yet curious, but with an overwhelming sense that matters were careening out of his control—descended the aft ladderway by the mizzenmast and was ushered into the captain's stateroom.

Semmes sat there behind his long table. It stretched across the room from port to starboard, forming a defined boundary between the contending sides. If the chase had been short, and the quarry quick to cave in, Semmes was gracious and good-humored, even sympathetic. On the other hand, any prolonged resistance or lack of cooperation could send him into a dark storm cloud of ill humor, curt and profanely impatient. Semmes asked the captain for the legal papers that identified the owners of the ship and cargo. If the papers hinted at any attempt to deceive, to disguise the owners as not Yankees, Semmes pounced without mercy. In his own special courtroom, he served as judge, jury, and prosecuting attorney. Sometimes he decided that the ship or cargo did indeed belong to neutral owners. More typically, with his authority so tilted Southward, he found in his own favor and condemned the ship and cargo as a prize to the Confederacy.

When the captured captain emerged from his hearing, the look on his face predicted what would happen next. The men waiting on the upper deck knew at once. In most cases the captain was rowed back to his ship with instructions for a hasty departure. With just a bag or trunk of clothing allowed to each man, he and his crew were brought back to the *Alabama* and confined, either out on deck or somewhere below. (The captured men were soon sent ashore or transferred to a passing vessel.) A few trusted men from the Confederate cruiser delved into the condemned ship, looking for food, money, and naval stores and—for Semmes's private collection—the charts, nautical instruments, and ship's chronometer. All the captured chronometers were hung on Semmes's wall like scalps, as both trophies of the hunt and valuable booty for later sale.

After a short interval, a couple of hours or a couple of days (depending on what else Semmes was planning), a firing squad made a final visit to the doomed vessel. They went through the cabins and forecastle, breaking up the pine bunks and straw mattresses, making piles of kindling. They poured an accelerant around—lard, butter, liquor, or lubricating oil—and opened the portholes and hatches for ventilation. After starting fires in several places at once, they headed briskly for the boat back to the *Alabama*. A New England whaler, if caught on the way home well filled with barrels of pungent whale oil, exploded into an especially dense, smoky bonfire. These spectacles, though repeated so often, never bored the men on the *Alabama*. If the burning ship was especially fine, sparkling new or unusually plush, they might even feel a sailorlike twinge of regret over destroying a comely, kindred sea spirit. But they all still looked forward to the next prize.

The trail of fiery captures began before Semmes really knew his own ship. Any captain of a brand-new vessel must pass through an acquainting period—complicated in this case by already being at sea, at war, and at risk. A wooden sailing ship like the *Alabama* gradually took on a distinct personality approaching that of a living, sentient creature. The particular arrangement of masts, sails, and ropes, the vibrations from the rudder that the man at the wheel could feel in his hands, the hum and pitch of the wind as it blew through the rigging, the cut of the jib and the curve of the hull were all unique to this singular cruiser. Taken together, exposed over time to variable seas and weathers, they came to define the *Alabama*. For a barnacled old sailor as experienced and observant as Raphael Semmes, she was both comfortably familiar and completely unknown.

Three weeks into the cruise, on September 13, 1862, the *Alabama* was about five hundred miles west-northwest of the Azores. In sparkling, tranquil weather, Semmes took the sixth prize for his new command, a small whaler out of New Bedford, Massachusetts, and burned her at nightfall. With no other actions pending, he retired early, at nine o'clock, and fell sound asleep. At 11:30 a quartermaster came down from the upper deck, gently shook the captain's cot, and announced a large ship passing to windward on the opposite tack from the *Alabama*'s. Semmes threw on his clothes and went up on deck. Under bright moonlight, he could see enough of the other vessel to order a chase—the first real test of his new ship's speed and sailing qualities.

At that hour of night, with only a minimum crew standing watch, it took precious time to make adjustments. Semmes wore his ship onto the needed tack, bringing her head away from the wind until it was blowing from behind him, then turning the bow toward the wind on the other side. By then the quarry—the whaler *Benjamin Tucker* from New Bedford—was about two and a half miles away, partly to windward, on the side from which the wind was blowing. Semmes hauled in his topsails (the squared-off banks of canvas at the midpoints of the masts) and put out his enormous trysails, the assertive triangular sails hanging diagonally from the foremast and mainmast. The *Alabama* was now positioned at her optimal point of sailing, as Semmes had learned, either toward or across from the wind. The men on the *Tucker*, taking note, ran out their royals and flying jib, reaching for more speed. The moonlit sport of hound-and-hare was under way: one ship running for a prize, the other running for her life.

Semmes moved to windward of the quarry, cutting the *Tucker* out of the breeze. He also headreached the enemy skipper, obliging him to tack toward the *Alabama*, slicing the distance between them. After a couple of hours, when they were still a mile apart, Semmes fired his usual introductory blank cartridge. The crack of the cannon split open the still night air. The *Tucker* paid no attention and kept fleeing. Watching through special night glasses, Semmes saw her try to regain the tactical advantage. The whaler moved off the wind, slackened her ropes, and started to put out the booms for her studding sails.

Semmes jumped on this lull and bore down on the *Tucker*. At half a mile he fired a second shot. The captain of the whaler gave up, brought his ship into the wind and started taking in sail. This chase and capture enabled Semmes to know the *Alabama* better. Under sudden, unexpected pressure, both man and ship had performed superbly. With daylight approaching, Semmes handed off his command and went back to bed. The *Tucker*, eight months out from home, was carrying 340 barrels of whale oil. After the *Alabama* took on her crew of thirty, along with forty boxes of soap and three thousand pounds of tobacco, she provided a dramatic fire. (The tobacco, stockpiled for a whaling voyage intended to last years, was especially welcome on a cruiser originally supplied from Britain, where the war was causing a shortage of American tobacco.)

Four days later, after two more prizes, the weather turned stormy under a darker sky, with a fresh, building wind from the west and southwest. Shortly before noon, yet another New Bedford whaler, the *Elisha Dunbar*, hove into sight of the lookout. Semmes again wore about and started to chase. Another test for the *Alabama*: Already proven fast in smooth water, could she also run in half a gale? Many fast ships could not handle such extreme conditions. With the wind pushing from astern, Semmes kept his topgallant sails billowed and stretched at the tops of his three masts. The yellow-pine masts, flexible and resilient, bent and buckled, edging close to their breaking points, but were not quite there. The captain of the *Dunbar* put out all his sails and whipped his vessel up to ten knots, a giddy pace for a whaler. The *Alabama* kept gaining under sail alone, sometimes hitting a top speed of thirteen knots.

For three hours the chase continued through mounting waves under ugly skies. Semmes, holding on, could feel his vessel coming alive as she bucked and bounced. "My gallant little ship was entirely at home in the roughest weather," he later noted. "She seemed, like a trained racer, to enjoy the sport, and though she would tremble, now and then, as she leaped from sea to sea, it was the tremor of excitement, not of weakness." In a futile attempt at deception, the *Dunbar* was showing no flag. The weather was getting worse; Semmes was running short of patience (with which he was never oversupplied). He fired his starboard bow gun, just a blank cartridge, and ran up the Confederate flag. Captain David Gifford of the *Dunbar* at once raised his U.S. flag in a gesture of defeat. He pulled in his sails and gave up.

At that moment, Gifford might actually have saved his ship by waiting a bit longer. On the heaving ocean it would have been impossible to aim and fire a gun effectively. The sea was so rough that Semmes hesitated to send any boats to the whaler. With the gale strengthening, Gifford might have stood by until nightfall and then escaped into the stormy darkness. Instead Semmes positioned his ship to windward of the *Dunbar* and launched his two staunchest boats, which then could row toward the whaler with the wind pushing them along. These boarding parties managed to reach the prize. Collecting only her chronometer, sextant, flag, and crew, they started rowing back through the storm. Semmes meantime had brought the *Alabama* around to the lee side of the whaler, so the boats once more had the wind helping them. Everybody got safely on board. Captain Semmes had outmaneuvered another Yankee skipper.

Just before leaving the *Dunbar,* afraid to try to return, they set her on fire. Weather had trumped the law: because the screeching storm was threatening to swamp his boats, Semmes had decided to skip the usual legal proceeding in his cabin. The unsanctioned bonfire in the late afternoon burned like an outlaw, wild and ferocious. Overhead, the black clouds delivered thunder and lightning. All around the cruiser and dying whaler, the clumpy seas rose and fell. The helpless *Dunbar* flailed and pitched, rolled and dipped, in constant eccentric motion. The wind caught a burning sail and flew it away. The wooden masts and spars burned and dropped. The naked hull filled with water—the fire nearly out—and sank. The *Alabama* had notched her tenth prize in two weeks.

Afterward, Semmes headed west and north, moving from his first hunting grounds near the Azores to the heavily trafficked shipping lanes off the crowded Grand Banks of Newfoundland. For two weeks they made no captures, the longest dead period so far. Gun crews were put to practicing with cannon and small arms. Carpenters built chests for the weapons, and engineers worked on the bearings for a new gun at the bow. As the *Alabama* moved north into October, it got much colder. The crew took the temperature of both air and water every hour, watching for a sudden plummet that could mean ice in the sea. Iceberg season had ended a few months earlier, but a stray berg could show up anywhere at any time. The weather grew darker and meaner, cutting visibility and preventing Semmes's noontime observation of the sun. He could only estimate the ship's position within thirty or forty miles.

On October 3 the sky and their spirits brightened as they took two prizes in a single day. The *Emily Farnham* carried an English cargo, so she was released on bond. The capture of the *Brilliant*, bound from New York to London bearing Union wheat and flour, mushroomed into a larger event with rippling effects from ocean to shore and back again, pushing the *Alabama* to a new level of notoriety. When her captain, George Hagar, was brought into Semmes's cabin, he resisted the usual verdict. The *Brilliant* was a fine ship of 839 tons, only two years old. Hagar owned a one-third share in her, and he carried no war risk insurance. If his ship were burned, he said, he would be ruined. Surely his own countrymen would not so mistreat him. Finally he started to cry "like a child," a young *Alabama* midshipman noted with disgust. Semmes felt moved to see a brother captain in such unguarded distress; but he still fired the *Brilliant*. It was late in the afternoon, with a calm settling in, so the *Alabama* stayed nearby as she blazed into the night. In the morning a Prussian vessel, attracted by the spectacle, came up to investigate.

Hagar and his crew, transferred to the *Farnham* and then to another ship, arrived back in New York on October 16. The *Brilliant* was the first of the *Alabama*'s prizes owned by New Yorkers—so the local newspapers awarded her special attention. Hagar, angry and bereft, unburdened himself at length to the *New York Herald*. Claiming a daily circulation of over 100,000, the largest in the country and more than all the other New York dailies combined, the *Herald* also functioned as the semiofficial journal of record for New York's maritime interests. In a potent conjunction of wartime patriotism, commerce, and news, it ran two long front-page stories on the *Alabama* and the *Brilliant*, all of it told from the angle and bile of the embittered Captain Hagar.

"A Pirate on the High Seas," blared one headline. In his cabin, Semmes greeted Hagar "in the most pompous and overbearing manner," the *Herald* reported. Hagar, asked about his cargo, replied that some of it was under English ownership. "Do you take me for a damned fool?" Semmes shot back with a scowl. "Where are the proofs that part of your cargo is on English account?" Hagar submitted papers that lacked a consular seal, so Semmes rejected them and condemned the prize. "Captain Hagar says," the *Herald* continued, "that, however much Semmes may have had the appearance of a gentleman when an officer of the United States Navy, he has entirely changed now." His enormous mustache ("it is evident that it occupies much of his attention") required daily waxing by his steward. His men called him "Old Beeswax." Semmes therefore both looked and acted like a pirate, "a combination of Lafitte, Kidd and Gibbs, the three most notorious pirates the world has ever known."

The officers on the *Alabama* were "very dainty gentlemen," finicky about what they took in plundering a ship: only white sugar, never brown; just the finest kid gloves, of the purest white. According to Hagar, the midshipmen pillaged the linen closet, taking sheets, towels, and pillowcases, stuffing them into their clothing so they resembled soft feather beds. "These were all private stealings, no notice being taken of the theft when they arrived on board their own ship," said the *Herald*. "It was evidently fine fun for these rascals to plunder and destroy." They carried off the handsome new furniture for their own cabins and wardroom. One man passed Hagar with double armloads of booty and, smiling maliciously, gloated over the captain's sad fate.

Having insulted the manliness, integrity, and gentlemanly qualities of the men on the *Alabama*, the *Herald* leveled an even more serious charge: when Semmes caught a prize, no matter the time of day, he waited until nightfall to burn her, then lay nearby through the night, hoping that other Union ships would see the blaze, come up to help, and fall into his trap. Semmes was thus violating the most basic conventions of safety and courtesy at sea, cheapening another captain's generous concern. (Semmes had indeed burned the *Brilliant* at night, stayed in the vicinity, and when the Prussian ship approached in the morning he had boarded her. But Hagar and the *Herald* were inflating a single incident into a general pattern that did not exist.)

The reach and power of the *Herald* gave these stories a broad, enduring circulation. Reprinted all over the North, they changed the tone of contemporary coverage of Semmes and the *Alabama*. Previous newspaper articles had called him a pirate and criticized him for keeping his prisoners restrained in irons and left out on the exposed upper deck. ("The deck is more or less wet," Semmes wrote in his journal on September 19, "and the prisoners must have an uncomfortable time of it, but I have nowhere else to put them. We are closely stowed below with our own crew.") He was, in fact, angry that federal authorities had mistreated his purser from the *Sumter*, imprisoning him and shaving

Union propaganda against the *Alabama:* Semmes allegedly attracting another victim by burning a prize at night. (*Frank Leslie's Illustrated Newspaper,* November 1, 1862)

his head, and at first he aimed to balance that offense by handling his own prisoners roughly. But that vengeful phase passed, and he generally tried to keep his captives in reasonable food and shelter.

Hagar and the *Herald* attacked him personally, at sensitive places. The *Alabama* was cruising close to the United States, stopping many Yankee ships, and getting the New York newspapers on a regular basis. Indeed, the younger officers would complain if even three days passed with no fresh news. Semmes's clerk maintained an ongoing file of the *New York Herald.* Copies of the latest papers would pass down from the captain to the officers to the midshipmen to the sailors. (The sailors also liked to use them for cleaning brasswork.) Hagar's lurid version of events on the *Alabama* made them all furious. Dark vows of revenge were heard in the wardroom and gunroom.

Semmes was a Southern gentleman who thought of himself as a descendant of the old Cavalier aristocracy. Nothing mattered more to him than his bristling sense of honor. The *Herald* had depicted him as a prissy outlaw; duels to the death were fought in the South over much less. Yet he himself, after all, had once referred to privateers as "little better than licensed pirates." Any accusation of freebooting misbehavior cut him deeply because it remained an unhealed wound. He was still an honorable man. He was sure. What would his family think of him? "Do not believe," he wrote to Anne,

> the malicious and false reports (and nearly all of them are of this character) that you see in the Northern newspapers. You know the kind and humane disposition of your husband too well [indeed she did] to believe he can be the heartless tyrant he is represented. My prisoners are uniformly treated humanely, and sometimes, when they deserve it, kindly. I never permit them to be despoiled of their private effects, as they have represented. My crew is not a set of ruffians, but my ship is a well ordered and well disciplined man-of-war, and I make war according to civilized rules, and with far more mercy than my enemies.

Even here, in confiding to his wife, he still seemed to be trying— too hard—to convince both her and himself. Implicitly, if not consciously, he was addressing a larger audience. He was writing with a sense of history looking over his shoulder, needing to get it all down in case he was killed and left defenseless: "They abuse me in the public prints and call me a 'pirate'—a pirate because I am doing what they themselves are doing, destroying the enemy's property—no more. But I have no other feeling on this subject, than that of regret, and astonishment [actually he had sharper, stronger feelings] that people of a better class could so far forget decency, as to descend to such scurrility and abuse. This abuse of me will not help them, as I shall continue to do my duty to my country unto the end." That final statement, at least, was simply and literally true.

Discipline on the *Alabama* descended from Semmes to the first lieutenant, John McIntosh Kell. During the entire cruise, Kell almost never left the ship, even when she stayed in a port for weeks at a time. He was always there, patrolling the upper deck, noticing everything and responsible for every detail. When Semmes gave orders, they generally went to the "First Luff," as he was called aboard ship. Kell passed them on and made sure they were carried out. Unlike the captain, he was a tall, powerful man, about six feet two, lithe and well built and with an absolute foghorn of a voice. Nobody ever had trouble hearing a command from the First Luff. His face, topped by receding, wavy brown hair, was anchored by an extravagant mustache and an auburn beard that, over the course of the cruise, grew from his chest down to his waist; usually he kept it braided and tucked out of the way under his coat. When the *Alabama* was sailing in good order, Kell was amiable and even-tempered, gentle and kind. If something went wrong, or a man neglected his duty, Kell clicked into a quite different persona. The dark blue eyes hardened, the thundering voice rose and deepened, and his ample body and beard expanded in scary rage: like a shaggy Viking swinging a vengeful sword. He was, next to Semmes, by far the most important man on the *Alabama*.

A Georgian, Kell grew up on a farm near the ocean in McIntosh County, settled in the eighteenth century by his Scots ancestors. "I think," he later wrote, "being born almost within sound of the billows and in sight of the 'deep blue sea,' I had an innate love for it which grew with my growth." His congressman got him appointed a midshipman in the U.S. Navy in 1841. He loved the strict discipline and etiquette on a man-of-war, and the enduring brotherhood with his classmates. He served in Hawaii and in the Mexican War. In 1849, however, Kell refused to obey what he considered inappropriate, demeaning orders. At the court-martial, Raphael Semmes became his lawyer; both men liked the Navy but chafed at its mossbacks. "So far from being a mutineer," Semmes decided, "he had a high respect for discipline." Kell lost his case and was dismissed from the service, but then was reinstated two years later. When Georgia seceded from the Union in January 1861, Kell quickly resigned his commission and joined the Confederate Navy. Semmes took command of the *Sumter* a few months later and asked, at once, for the services of John Kell.

On that ship, and later on the *Alabama*, they made a peculiar team. They walked the deck like Mutt and Jeff, the little captain and the big luff. Semmes was usually alone in his cabin; Kell was up on the quarterdeck, talking, mixing, giving orders, and seldom out of contact with other people. At his table, pen in hand, Semmes wrote a fluid, articulate prose; Kell hated the act of writing and preferred oral discourse. Semmes, a Roman Catholic, adored the rituals and ceremonies of the mass; Kell, a pious Protestant, wished the ship could be run on true religious principles and disliked the "priest-ridden superstitions and

Six of the *Alabama*'s officers during the entire cruise. (W. S. Hoole Special Collections Library, University of Alabama)

top left: First Lieutenant John McIntosh Kell of Georgia, the First Luff

right: Chief Engineer Miles J. Freeman of New Orleans

bottom left: Lieutenant Arthur Sinclair of Virginia

top left: Master's Mate George T. Fullam of Hull, England

right: Lieutenant Beckett Howell of Mississippi

bottom left: W. Breedlove Smith of New Orleans, the captain's clerk

idolatry" of Catholicism. Not personally intimate, always formal and respectful to each other, they shared only a fierce Confederate patriotism and their common mission on the *Alabama*.

Of the five lieutenants under Kell, four were quite young men just recently promoted from midshipmen to fill out the *Alabama*'s complement of watch officers. Richard F. Armstrong of Georgia, only twenty, outranked everyone on board except Semmes and Kell. He commanded the Blakely forward pivot gun, the most effective weapon on the ship. Joseph D. Wilson of Florida, quick to anger, was sometimes vindictive toward enemy personnel who came within his reach. Both Armstrong and Wilson were veterans of the U.S. Navy and of the *Sumter*. Arthur Sinclair of Virginia, the son and grandson of U.S. naval officers, had served on the Confederate ironclad *Virginia* (*Merrimac*) during her epochal battle with the Union's *Monitor*. Irvine Bulloch of Georgia was the younger brother of James Bulloch, godfather to the *Alabama*. The only non-American in this group, John Low, was a British citizen living in Savannah when the war started. With some seafaring experience, he joined the Confederate Navy to serve his new country and was ordered to the *Alabama* in Liverpool.

The engineering department, under Chief Engineer Miles J. Freeman of New Orleans, was a separate domain. Freeman and his assistants had all moved over from the *Sumter*. The engineers, grimy but bleached with indoor pallor, toiled down below, in dark, smoky, often gruesomely overheated conditions. They only came up on deck for fresh air and sunshine, never to work. Tending the boilers, condenser, and engine, supervising the coal handlers and firemen, they represented the new industrial revolutions of the nineteenth century. The officers and sailors up on deck, all of them raised on sailing ships, were creeping anachronisms. The two worlds, above and below, shared no overlapping expertise, no common ground, and had little to say to each other. Though Semmes seldom deployed his steam propulsion, the entire ship depended on the precious freshwater from Freeman's steam condenser. Without that machinery and its keepers, the extended cruise was impossible. The captain, in a tacit admission of his own ignorance of the new technologies, generally left the chief engineer to his esoteric purposes.

The other principal players on board included, most notably, Lieutenant Beckett K. Howell of Mississippi. As the only Marine on the *Alabama*, he trained the crew at the manual of arms and close-order drill. He was also the brother-in-law of Jefferson Davis, president of the Confederacy—and, perhaps for that reason, was Semmes's apparent favorite among the officers. Master's Mate James Evans, a former pilot-boat captain from Charleston, South Carolina, could uncannily identify the nationality of ships at sea from afar. Proud of this expertise, when teased about it he would explode into a stuttering rage at any doubters. Master's Mate George T. Fullam, an Englishman from Hull, became the chief boarding officer. When the *Alabama* was hiding under a British flag, and conversing at close quarters with a potential captive, Fullam's English accent completed the disguise. The three young midshipmen were Edward M. Anderson of Georgia and his cousin, Eugene A. Maffitt of North Carolina, and William H. Sinclair of Virginia.

W. Breedlove Smith of New Orleans, the captain's clerk, filled a special niche. A graduate of the University of Virginia, cultured and sophisticated, he saw more of Semmes from day to day than anybody else. His cabin lay just outside the captain's door. When Semmes felt like talking, Smith could converse at his level. As clerk he supervised the ship's library, supplemented occasionally from prizes, and its file of newspapers and magazines, many with inflammatory articles about the *Alabama*. He was discreet, indispensable, and devoted to the captain. "Smith had a peculiar man to deal with in Semmes," Arthur Sinclair wrote later, "and probably few could so have understood and pleased him."

What distinguished these shipmates was their youth. Only Kell and Freeman were over thirty. As young men, they could more easily bear the physical demands of the long cruise. For the same reason they could tolerate the psychological costs as well. The generation of Southerners that matured in the 1850s had grown up on the sectional squabbles of the time. They had no memories of the United States as a single, united nation. Imbued with the zeal and moral simplicities of youth, they had always inhaled the air of Southern independence and the benefits of slavery. Leaping past their parents, in general, they believed sooner and more fervently in the Confederate cause; in fact Semmes's own children followed this pattern. Thus Midshipman Eddie Anderson, nineteen years old, wrote his father a fiery letter home from the *Alabama*, crowing over the burning of the first prize, the *Ocmulgee:* "As though she was calling down curses on the head of Abe Lincoln and his Cabinet, the disturber of peace and quietness and the principle cause of all our trouble. May he live long enough to be crushed to death under the Government which he now rules."

In a similar spirit, Lieutenant Richard Armstrong spurned Captain George Hagar's plea that they belonged to the same country. "We are nothing to each other as countrymen," Armstrong replied, as Hagar recalled it. "The North and South are now distinct races, with no feelings or interests in common. The people of the South are the only true representatives of the American race. You of the North have intermarried so much with the lower classes of Europeans that you have, in a great measure, if not altogether, lost your nationality, and are not worthy to be considered of the same people as ourselves." That bone-deep sense of ethnic and national superiority, dead sure and combative, could help sustain a man through long months of variable weather, boredom, loneliness, and absence from home.

On the other hand, the prevailing youth and inexperience of the lieutenants and midshipmen on the *Alabama* could also provoke discipline problems with the older, tougher sailors in the forecastle. During the fall of 1862, the skippers of captured ships brought back nearly unanimous impressions about this aspect of life on the Confederate cruiser. Discipline was "not very good," "very poor," "very slack for an armed vessel," and "very slack, more like that of a privateer—where it is every man for himself—than a regular man-of-war." "There was no discipline on board the steamer," another captain reported, most tellingly, "excepting when Captain Semmes or Lieutenant Kell was on deck." Another skipper agreed that the ship's officers "with the exception of the captain and first lieutenant seem ignorant of their sea-duties." Of course these Union loyalists were smarting under the recent loss of their vessels and were not inclined to praise the men of the *Alabama.* But the striking consistency of their reports—given independently, in different times and circumstances, some of them under oath—is revealing and persuasive.

On any ship, the line between officers and sailors, the quarterdeck and the forecastle, was a traditional bulwark not to be breached. On the *Alabama,* they were further divided by nationality and allegiance. The officers, almost to a man, were enthusiastic Confederates. The sailors, as Semmes confided to his journal, were drawn "from the groggeries and brothels of Liverpool." Citizens of Great Britain, mainly English and Irish, they had signed up for money and adventure, not to serve the Confederacy. As time passed they got their double pay and grog, as promised. But, as yet, they had still enjoyed no thrilling gun battles at sea, no blowout excursions on shore, and none of the expected prize money from captures. "Many of my fellows, no doubt, thought they were shipping in a sort of privateer," Semmes supposed, "where they would have a jolly good time and plenty of license. They have been wofully disappointed, for I have jerked them down with a strong hand, and now have a well disciplined ship of war."

The captain was isolated with his books and charts and solitary ways. He did not know—indeed chose not to know—many discordant details of life on his ship. That was Kell's job. "I have never seen a better disposed or more orderly crew," Semmes assured himself in his journal. "They have come very kindly into the traces." The grizzled old tars in the forecastle, muttering resentments about the callow young officers, knew better; but they kept no journals and left no record for history. Semmes truly believed that his boarding parties behaved properly on captured ships and removed no money or personal property, as he had instructed. The testimony of Union eyewitnesses, again, described a looser, more freebooting procedure. Semmes's men, officers included, often lifted rum and whiskey from prizes, smuggled it aboard the *Alabama*, and got satisfyingly drunk that night.

Stubbornly aloof from such matters, Semmes paced the deck by himself. It was a daily ritual that his men came to recognize, part of his thinking process as captain. He furrowed his brow and pulled at the famous mustache. Lost in his own private communion, he spoke to nobody as he walked up and down. His officers looked on, discreetly, wondering what he was ruminating about. Usually not even Kell or Armstrong, the two top lieutenants, knew where the ship was going or what the captain was planning. Arthur Sinclair, as sailing master, plotted their position on a chart each day. By stringing the positions together, he could guess about the general direction of the ship's course—but only guess.

After supper, in good weather, the sailors came out on deck. In their brief interval of leisure before eight bells at eight o'clock, they smoked, played checkers, told stories, and sang songs either sentimental or nautical. Sometimes they played instruments and danced. To the easy sounds of music and laughter, the ongoing tensions between the quarterdeck and forecastle floated away for a while. Up on the bridge, Semmes sat on a campstool and smoked his evening cigar, winding down and enjoying the scene below (on hand, but still at a distance). "The men feel no restraint from his presence—rather they enjoy it," Sinclair noticed. "In their way they love him and are proud of him, and he returns the sentiments—in his way."

THREE

For Money and Fighting

At some point in early October 1862, Semmes decided to attack New York City. Newspapers told him the city, far from the Southern battlefields of the war, was lightly defended. No Union ship patrolling the harbor claimed the combined speed and firepower of the *Alabama*. As far as anybody in New York knew, the Confederate cruiser was somewhere around the Grand Banks of Newfoundland, a safe distance away. Semmes planned to pass Sandy Hook on a dark night and steal into the outer harbor, then board a few unarmed merchant vessels and burn them after sending their crews onto the local lightship. For emphasis, he might lob some cannon shells into lower Manhattan, and then escape before dawn. By the time the enemy could mount any pursuit, the *Alabama* would be racing out to sea, covered by darkness. The captain's plan was startling and audacious—a single warship assaulting the busiest harbor in North America—but reasonably feasible, given the right weather and sleepy complacency among the Union watchdogs.

The ship turned to the west and south from the Newfoundland Banks, running down toward New York. On October 9 they caught a most problematic prize, the packet *Tonawanda*. Owned by the Cope Brothers line of Philadelphia, she was one of the sailing passenger ships that made routinely scheduled trips between Britain and the northeastern United States. As such she was carrying seventy passengers, most of them women and children—who presented Semmes with a dilemma. What should he do with them? He couldn't kill them, could not leave them out on his exposed deck, and had no room for them below. Yet he wanted to burn the *Tonawanda*.

The Union skipper, Theodore Julius, was ushered into his hearing before Semmes, Lieutenant Kell, and clerk Smith. He sensed some leverage. "I found that our women passengers were a great trouble to them," Julius said later, "and I built good hopes from that that we should get clear." While the captain pondered what to do, Smith took Julius forward to join the captured crews from two other recent prizes. The two men found they had a mutual friend back in New Orleans. Julius chatted up the clerk, trying to ingratiate himself. Later, when Semmes told him he would have to sleep on the exposed deck, Julius pleaded for a spot below. Semmes said he had no space, but Smith spoke up and suggested they could find room for him in the steerage. So it was done, with the captain deferring to his clerk. The troublesome women and children stayed on the *Tonawanda*. The ship and the other captured crews were released on bond a few days later: that is, Julius bound the Cope Brothers to pay the Confederacy $80,000, the assigned value of the ship and cargo, after the end of the war— assuming the South won.

The *Tonawanda* resumed her course to Liverpool. Semmes, in a foul temper after losing so plump a trophy, returned to his scheme for New York. He caught the *Lamplighter*, a Boston bark heading from New York for Gibraltar with a cargo of tobacco. The boarding party demanded liquor; the men from the *Alabama* drank some of it and poured the rest on the floor. The skipper, brought to his hearing, pleaded with Semmes to spare the ship. "I hope," Semmes shot back, "to be able to serve you a damned sight worse yet." The skipper offered a certificate of neutral ownership from the British consul in New York. Semmes waved it off. "The New York people are getting very smart," he concluded, "but it won't save you; it's all a damned hatched-up mess." The captain suspected a sly Manhattan deception. He ordered Kell to go burn the ship at once.

The weather had been growing dirtier for days, and Semmes's mood was probably not cheered by his usual dogging seasickness. On

The *Alabama* after releasing the *Tonawanda* on bond.
(*Illustrated London News*, November 15, 1862)

the morning after the *Lamplighter* bonfire, the sea and sky conspired in a hurricane. As the barometer plummeted, the men on the quarterdeck could see and smell it coming. Risking their lives, sailors climbed up the rigging to put the ship under very low sail; the masts, acting like long levers, exaggerated the motions of the pitching sea, whipping the sailors back and forth in extended, perilous arcs. They close-reefed the topsails and bent the main storm trysail into place. Lifelines were laid out across the deck, hatches clamped shut, and the quarterboats swung inboard on their davits and secured. All fires were extinguished except the binnacle light that illuminated the compass.

The wind suddenly accelerated in the forenoon. Kell, in twenty years at sea, had witnessed only one other storm of such ferocity. The surface of the ocean was churned into blinding sheets of foam and spray, like a dense, slanting snowstorm. Two men wrestled with the wheel; still it spun out of control and threw a sailor over its top onto the deck. The main topsail, fore staysail, and main stern staysail were shredded and blown away. The decks were knee-deep in water. A whaleboat near the stern was stove in, then vanished. Other parts of the ship, in particular the main yard (the spar that supported and spread a workhorse sail on the mainmast), were broken or destroyed.

Abruptly, ominously, the wind just stopped: as though some cosmic switch had been flipped. Semmes and his men now realized they were trapped in the vortex of a cyclone. In the brief calm, the *Alabama*—which had been heeled over so far that water was flooding in her gun ports—came back to vertical. The waves, no longer flattened by the wind, rose like pulsing mountains on every side. The ship rolled violently back and forth, the masts bending like willow branches. In the diminished atmospheric pressure of the vortex, the wave mountains jutted up into cones. With no wind to push them anywhere, they just bumbled around in random motions, jostling each other like drunks in a crowd. Semmes, ever the student of the ocean, thought it was the most remarkable spectacle he'd ever seen.

After thirty minutes, the switch flipped back and the wind returned, cutting off the tops of the waves. Again the *Alabama* heeled over. The men cowered under the bulwarks on the upper, windward side, trying to raise their heads, struggling for a breath. The ship sounded hurt, crying out, the large timbers groaning and creaking; at such moments of stress, as in chasing the *Dunbar*, she seemed most alive. They rode it out. A few men were hurt, but none seriously. Inspecting the damage afterward, they found a peculiar memento: a Gordian knot of a sail fragment and two lines, so entangled by so many winds that it had to be sliced away with a knife.

"I must capture another ship now directly," Semmes wrote in his journal, "to enable me to repair damages and replace my boats." He took three prizes in the next twelve days, raiding their supplies and then burning them. From a cache of newspapers, he learned that Union gunboats, sent on his trail, were heading toward the Grand Banks of Newfoundland.

"While they are running from New York," he mused, "I am running toward it." The captain told the officers about his designs on New York Harbor, and word passed down to the forecastle. Semmes typically kept such plans to himself; in this case, perhaps he divulged them as a morale enhancer after the cyclone and two months of increasingly monotonous cruising with no time on shore. In any case, his men relished the imagined pleasures of such a daring raid. On October 30, though, Chief Engineer Freeman reported that he was down to four days' worth of coal for continuous steam cruising. (The coal holds had not been replenished since leaving Terceira.) The *Alabama* was still 220 miles from New York. To sneak in and out of the harbor quickly, and then—if pursued—to flee at full speed for days afterward, Semmes needed the safety margin of more coal. The ship was also still crippled from the cyclone, and Semmes knew that so audacious a strike could only be prudently risked with everything in perfect trim.

Battered and depleted, Semmes had to drop his plan. "As coal was both fuel and water for me," he wrote to James Bulloch, back in Liverpool, "I could not afford to run it quite so close." He ordered the fires in the boilers banked and the propeller raised, and set a new course to the southeast, toward Martinique. There he was due to meet the *Agrippina*, his supply ship from the Azores, and her most welcome load of coal. The men on the *Alabama*, pumped up and then let down, were left gnawing on their disappointment. "We were considerably startled and annoyed," Master's Mate George Fullam regretted in his journal. "To astonish the enemy in New York harbour, to destroy their vessels in their own waters, had been the darling wish of all on board."

On the way to Martinique, the *Alabama* burned two especially succoring prizes. The *Levi Starbuck*, only five days out of New Bedford, was bound for a whaling voyage of thirty months to the Pacific. She was stuffed with fresh food and many kinds of supplies, all happily received. ("We were placed in irons," her second mate later told the newspapers, "and treated very fairly, considering they were pirates.") The *Thomas B. Wales*, six days later, was sailing from Calcutta to Boston. Her cargo of saltpeter, an ingredient in explosives, condemned the ship as contraband of war. The *Wales*'s main yard was the right size to replace that crucial spar lost in the hurricane. Her most useful booty, though, was human. From previous captures, Semmes had picked up occasional recruits to fill out his undermanned crew. The *Wales* yielded a bonanza of eight sailors and her second mate, an Englishman, all willing to sign up with the *Alabama*—"a prize more valuable than the prize itself," Semmes noted.

But she had passengers too, and Semmes, far at sea, had to take them aboard. "We are to be embarrassed with two females," the captain grumbled to his journal, "and some children, the master having his wife with him, and a passenger and wife. I shall bestow them upon the ward room, having a couple of staterooms vacated for them. Poor women! They are suffering for the sins of their wicked countrymen." After nearly three months of the cruise, they were the first alien intrusions on a very masculine domain. In the rough, crowded conditions of the lower deck, women dealing with the intimate details of everyday life were forced into an "awkward position," as Arthur Sinclair later put it. Kell made room for them by displacing a few lieutenants. For ten days the *Alabama*'s men tried to behave politely. Down in his cabin, Semmes could hear the overhead patter on the deck of small feet and happy children's voices at play. It reminded him of home. One morning, he woke to those domestic sounds, went back to sleep, and dreamed about his children.

On November 18 they reached Martinique. Anchoring in the harbor of Fort-de-France, Semmes put his prisoners ashore. The waiting *Agrippina* was sent on to a more isolated rendezvous, the barren island of Blanquilla, to the south. That night, the simmering discontents in the forecastle suddenly boiled over. The sailors had enjoyed no shore liberty since leaving Liverpool. They still had savored no combat at sea, and the prospective adventure in New York Harbor was dangled, then pulled back. Now the men could see the town of Fort-de-France and imagine the illicit sailorly delights that beckoned there, but they still weren't allowed off the ship. During the afternoon, local bumboats came alongside, selling fruits and other refreshments.

The men started drinking after supper, ventilating their grievances. Kell, on duty as always, heard a commotion and walked toward the forecastle. Somebody threw a belaying pin at his head, which missed. A few of the bolder men stepped forward and angrily berated the First Luff. When Kell ordered other sailors to seize the beraters, they refused. That act, spurning a first lieutenant's order, constituted a mutiny. Semmes, drawn by the noise, found a surly clump of half-drunken sailors by the foremast, egging each other on and defying the captain's authority.

The captain reached back for military discipline. He told Kell to beat to quarters, a call to muster that all hands had often practiced. The sharp sounds of drum and fife cut through the alcoholic haze. The men lined up at their battle stations by the guns. The officers were far outnumbered, but they were armed with pistols and cutlasses (as if preparing for battle) and the sailors were not. Semmes and Kell walked the deck fore and aft two or three times, inspecting the men, looking for drunks. They plucked out about twenty culprits and had them locked in irons. Placed in the gangway, the passage through the bulwarks, they were slapped with repeated buckets of cold seawater in their faces. At first defiant, roaring their contempt, they soon subsided, struggled for breath, and asked for mercy. For the other sailors, looking on, it was literally sobering. The mutineers, released from their shackles, quietly went below to their hammocks. The crisis passed.

The *Alabama* met the *Agrippina* at Blanquilla, a tiny coral protuberance with no human inhabitants except four Spaniards and their herds of goats and jackasses. For two and a half days, the sailors moved coal from one ship to the other, filling the *Alabama*'s bunkers. Semmes then, at last, let them go ashore. In the absence of bars and brothels, the sailors had to find amusement where they might. "We gave our crew liberty while we stayed here," Midshipman Anderson wrote home, "and allowed them Rifles to enjoy themselves with, but as soon as they landed, they forgot themselves, and commenced killing goats, jackasses, and everything else that they could come across. We all thought that it was very good fun, but it was good for all hands, that Captain Semmes knew nothing of it."

Shooting those animals blew off some steam. The Spaniards on Blanquilla were glad to see the sailors leave; "We were afraid of them," one said later. For Semmes, the tensions with his crew remained. They wanted prize money and they wanted real action: a pitched gun battle with the enemy, not just harmless warning shots at unarmed merchantmen. So did the captain. Pacing the deck, reading the newspapers, he came up with two schemes—one for money, one for fighting.

In these years before the transcontinental railroad, regular allotments of gold and silver from California and western Mexico came by ship from San Francisco to Panama, then across the isthmus to the Caribbean port of Aspinwall (later renamed Colón). From there, paddlewheel steamers took the precious cargo—worth up to five million dollars in a single trip—to the banking houses and U.S. Treasury office in New York. These steamers also brought passengers grown rich out west and their own private hordes of specie. The ships traveled virtually undefended, with no protection from the U.S. Navy. Stephen Mallory, the astute Confederate secretary of the Navy, recognized the golden apples waiting to be plucked. "The capture of one or two of the enemy's treasure and passenger ships," he noted in October, "would be a heavy blow to his credit at home and abroad,—far greater than the capture of an equal value of property in any other form." Semmes, on his own, saw it too. A million dollars in gold deposited in Europe, he figured, would buy some more fast cruisers like the *Alabama* to lay waste Union commerce.

The gold ships from Aspinwall steamed through narrow passages at the eastern or western tips of Cuba. Semmes knew he had a fine shot at flushing his quarry, squeezed into those straits. He decided to try the eastern route, which was slightly more direct from Aspinwall. Now trim and fully coaled, he sailed northwesterly from Blanquilla toward the Mona Passage between Puerto Rico and Hispaniola. In that busy crossroads, he thought he might also encounter an enemy cruiser. "I am looking for a California steamer," he told his journal, "and whilst I am looking for her perhaps I may find a fight." Not yet; through the Mona Passage, he turned sharply westward and ran along the northern coast of the island of Hispaniola. The *Agrippina* had delivered coal but no food. Running short of provisions, but still in good luck, the *Alabama* happily captured the bark *Parker Cook* from Boston, the first prize in three weeks. They took her pork, cheese, and crackers, then burned her.

In such crowded waters, with golden visions beguiling everyone on board and extra lookouts volunteering their services, Semmes was busy. The *Cook* was fired at ten o'clock at night. The captain turned in at midnight, late for him. He was called two hours later, went back to bed and fell sound asleep, then got an urgent summons from the officer on deck that a large ship was bearing down on them. Jumping into his clothes, he hurried up on deck and saw the intruder wending harmlessly to leeward. That day they encountered three ships, a Dutchman and two Spaniards. That night at ten o'clock, a dangerous-looking warship—lights blazing, under steam, with every studding sail set— loomed up fast behind them. Semmes summoned all hands to quarters, loaded the guns, and cleared the ship for action. The stranger, probably Spanish, passed by in peace. Semmes stayed up for hours. On the following night, the weary captain hoped for some unmolested rest. After undressing, about to lie down, he was called again. The suspicious steamer turned out to be an innocuous brig. Over the next nine hours, he was awakened three more times, all to no real purpose. "This night will answer as a prototype of a great many," he lamented.

From his faithful spies, the loyal Union newspapers, Semmes knew a steamer was scheduled to leave Aspinwall for New York on the first of December. If she went east of Cuba, the ship would arrive there on about December 4. The *Alabama* settled in to wait, backed up against the high headlands of Cape Maisi, trying to hide. When the captain retired that night, he left orders not to be called unless for a steamship; he slept through till morning. For two more days they watched and waited. "Several sail in sight, but I can not yet leave my station to overhaul them, lest my principal object should be defeated." The weather was clear and calm, with pellucid visibility. They could see the western end of Haiti, ninety miles away.

At midday on December 7, the lookout cried "S-a-i-l h-o!"— stretching it out for emphasis, the announcement they had all been waiting for. They saw a large paddlewheeler with two masts. The straight stem and the tall walking-beam engine, seesawing up and down between the paddle boxes, identified her as a Yankee. On the upper deck, awnings were hung out against the Caribbean sun. Under them were crowds of passengers, the women dressed in bright colors, with ribbons and streamers from their bonnets fluttering in the breeze. Groups of soldiers in uniform stood on the forward deck. Some of the passengers studied the strange ship through opera glasses. The *Alabama* looked like a friendly gunboat of the U.S. Navy, perhaps a protective escort.

On the Confederate cruiser, their initial elation was quickly tempered. The U.S. ship, the *Ariel* of the Aspinwall line, was approaching from the north. Instead of carrying gold *to* New York, she was probably bringing passengers and cargo *from* New York. Nonetheless Semmes ordered steam up, sails furled, and the propeller down. All hands were called to quarters, and a battery was loaded with shell and run out for action. "Everybody in the best possible spirits," Master's Mate Fullam noted, "and eager for a fray." The two ships headed toward each other and passed at close proximity. People on one could read the faces on the other. The *Alabama* came about and raised a Union flag; the *Ariel* also showed Union colors. When Semmes fired a blank cartridge and ran up the Confederate flag, the officers on the *Ariel* realized they had met the fearsome *Alabama*. They decided to run.

Both ships poured on steam. Dense clouds of black smoke coughed from their funnels. The *Alabama*, still not up to full power, started to fall back. Semmes ordered Lieutenant Armstrong to fire a shotted shell from the forward pivot gun toward the steamer's funnel; at the same moment, a trigger-happy gunner boomed an unauthorized broadside cannon of the *Alabama*. On the *Ariel*, a rapt passenger saw the smoke from the guns rising as the projectiles left the muzzles and whizzed and tumbled toward him. One whistled past the engine; the other hit the foremast, ten feet above the deck, nearly cutting it in half. Most of the startled passengers scurried below. Some ducked down behind the pine bulkheads of the upper-deck saloons—which would have provided no protection whatever, with the added risk of flying wood splinters.

The captain of the *Ariel*, Albert Jones, stopped his engine and lowered his flag. The boarding party from the *Alabama* found an armed contingent of 140 U.S. Marines, bound for San Francisco. The commander of the Marines knew that his muskets could not match the Confederate cannon, and that any such battle would only kill many civilians. So all those Marines had to surrender to a boarding party of about ten men. The boarders unlocked the ship's storeroom and took away $8,000 in Treasury notes and $1,500 in silver. Many of the five hundred passengers, meanwhile, expected to be robbed, or worse. Men hid their watches and money and rummaged anxiously through their trunks. Women were weeping and hysterical. For Semmes was a pirate, was he not?

A man from the *Alabama*, evidently Armstrong, stood back and tried to calm the situation. "Passengers, you're safe in our hands," he said. "You have no occasion to weep or be alarmed. What do you take us for? We are all honorable men; rest assured of that. Did anyone harm you as yet?" "You were near sinking the ship," someone pointed out. "That is only our duty," said the Confederate. "We make war on the sea, and the Yankees are our enemies." More weeping and cries of alarm. "We are gentlemen. Do you think we are ruffians who would attack the helpless, or do you imagine we are robbers? Have confidence in us and we will protect and not injure you. Not an article from

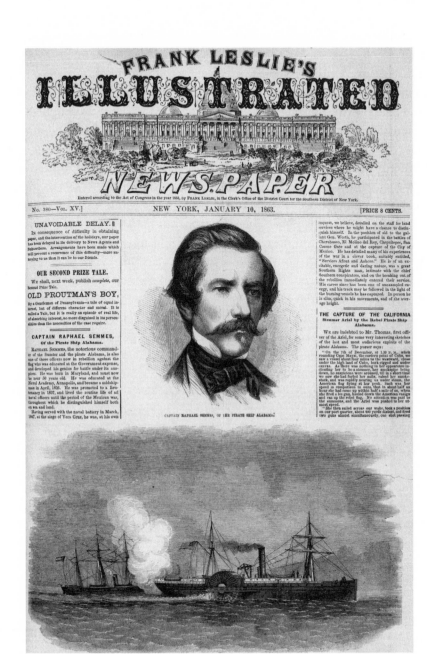

A Union comment: Semmes of "the pirate ship *Alabama*" capturing the *Ariel*.
(*Frank Leslie's Illustrated Newspaper*, January 10, 1863)

your baggage shall be taken from you." Armstrong was handsome and persuasive, sure of his charm. Tall and slim, resplendent in his gray Confederate uniform, sword, and sash, he did not look so dangerous. Shifting easily into a familiar mode of seduction, he started talking with the prettiest young women in sight. One asked if she might have a bright button from his coat as a souvenir of this perilous encounter. The frightened moods softened. Other women came forward. Off came the buttons, one by one, sacrificed in the hard line of duty.

For Semmes, the *Ariel* presented the same problems as the *Tonawanda*, but multiplied many times over. What could he ever do with five hundred passengers? The situation was so absurd that everyone relaxed into a good humor. The captors and captives mingled amiably on the *Ariel*. Captain Jones, taken onto the *Alabama*, was not confined. He walked freely around the upper deck and messed in the wardroom. For two days Semmes tried to devise some tactic for dumping the passengers and burning the *Ariel*, but nothing worked out. He was obliged to release her on a (potentially) lucrative bond of $260,000, the estimated value of ship and cargo. As the vessels parted company, the crewmen of the *Ariel* cheered the *Alabama*, and ladies fondly waved their handkerchiefs. Semmes's men watched their golden dreams fading away. "I was sorry we had to let her go," Midshipman Anderson wrote sweetly to his mother. "If I had had my way I would have burnt her, if I had to burn every soul on board of her."

Among the supplies taken from the *Ariel* were twelve cases of Drake's Plantation Bitters, a popular alcohol-laced patent remedy sold for every human ailment. Semmes, in a rare teasing whimsy, gave Captain Jones a letter to the Drake company for delivery in New York.

> Having procured one case while at the Island of Martinique, its beneficial effects in my hospital room and in curing the scurvy was such as to render it too desirable an acquisition to pass, particularly as it was evidently intended for the South, from the name Plantation. Rest assured, sirs, I trust you will not fail to freight each vessel likely to cross my path with the Plantation Bitters, and I will guarantee to place a case in the hands of President Davis before the 4th of March.

The notorious pirate's endorsement was featured in the next newspaper ads for Plantation Bitters.

Semmes now needed to disappear. News of the *Ariel*, his splashiest prize yet, would bring down a flotilla of chasing Union warships. His next plan—the one for fighting—depended even more than normally on surprising the enemy. "It is important," he told himself, "I should make the run I contemplate without being traced." He had to hide for a while, to avoid sightings and incitements. Then he could suddenly blaze forth where unexpected, taking his advantage in surprise. "I hope to strike a blow of some importance and make my retreat."

The *Alabama* turned south and west, ran along the northern coast of Jamaica, and dipped down farther to avoid the most heavily trafficked lanes off the western tip of Cuba. The crew must have been puzzled; why was the captain not positioning them to intercept enemy ships? A moderate gale blew in from the north. "The clouds look hard and wintry." Semmes took in sails while the gale persisted all day, tumbling the ship in a rough sea. "Weather cloudy and gloomy looking, and wind moaning and whistling through the rigging, enough to give one the blues. These are some of the comforts of seagoing." At night, the extended rolling motions kept waking him up. Water sluiced freely over the bulwarks, across the deck, and down the gaping ladderway—kept open for fresh air in the tropics—by Semmes's door.

They rounded the Yucatán Peninsula as closely as they could. Into the Gulf of Mexico, they again headed southwesterly and sneaked toward the uninhabited Arcas Islands, a hundred miles off the Mexican coast. Semmes had ordered the *Agrippina*, still not empty of coal, to meet him at this isolated place after their rendezvous at Blanquilla in November. Anchored off the Arcas, sailors again bent to the filthy, choking chore of pouring coal down the *Alabama*'s scuttles.

On the day before Christmas, the captain went ashore for the first time since leaving Liverpool on August 13. Over the next few days he walked the beach in the afternoon. Struggling through the soft sand, he looked for shells and watched sunsets and birds (black men-of-war and white gannets). Christmas Day inspired yearnings for his family and country. "They will live in history as a people worthy to be free, and future generations will be astonished at the folly and fanaticism, want of principle and wickedness, developed by this war among the Puritan population of the North." The crew, more intent on matters at hand, celebrated with an extra shot of grog.

While the coaling continued, Kell put other men to overhauling and setting up the topmast and lower rigging, and recaulking the seams of the upper deck, opening again under the hot tropical sun. Sweating away for day after day, tarring and painting, the men got restless. The chief boatswain's mate asked to return to England on the *Agrippina;* Semmes said no. A sailor got drunk, took his bag, and tried to board the supply ship; he was confined in double irons. Another man was triced up for insolence. "Constant cruising," Semmes admitted, but only to himself, "vigilance against being surprised by the enemy, salt provisions, and a deprivation of the pleasures of port so dear to the heart of the seaman are probably what most of them did not expect." To brace their spirits, Semmes revealed his plan for fighting.

The goal of his mysterious course was Galveston, Texas, over six hundred miles to the north. His usual newspaper sources had told Semmes that a large Union expeditionary force of 20,000 men was due to arrive in Galveston on about January 10. It was commanded by Nathaniel Banks, an incompetent political general from Boston, recently chased around the Shenandoah Valley by Stonewall Jackson. (An incompetent Bostonian: How could Semmes resist?) From Galveston, recently taken by Union forces, the Banks expedition planned to invade Texas. Because the bar off Galveston Harbor was only twelve feet deep, Semmes figured that the Union troop transports—perhaps fifty ships—would have to linger out in the open sea, clumsy and undefended, waiting to be landed. By mounting a night attack, the faster and well-gunned *Alabama* might riddle them with impunity. The arrant audacity of the plan recalled the captain's designs on New York Harbor: destroying an entire army with a single armed vessel.

They left the Arcas on January 5, 1863. Coaled up, in fighting trim, the *Alabama*—as her sailors liked to say—could do everything but talk. Working under sail but delayed by a calm, they approached Galveston at noon on the eleventh. Semmes intended to head for the Galveston lighthouse, take a distant look at the Banks fleet, then haul off and wait for nightfall before moving in to attack. Late in the afternoon, the lookout cried, "Land ho! Sail ho!" He saw not a harmless cluster of troop carriers but five steamers that looked like armed Union warships. One of them soon fired a shell that burst over Galveston. What could this mean? A Union gunboat would not be bombarding a city held by friendly forces.

By hiding out, Semmes had lost his normal sources of intelligence.

They had not caught a prize since the *Ariel*, more than a month earlier, and so had seen no recent newspapers. In that blank pause, a Confederate force had retaken Galveston. The Banks expedition had landed at New Orleans, hundreds of miles to the east. Semmes—suddenly understanding his situation, backing up, and rethinking—was now facing five enemy ships of war. One of them, the *Hatteras*, got up steam and started moving toward the *Alabama*. Semmes retained the precious advantage of still being unrecognized; his ship was thought to be far away, perhaps somewhere off Brazil. The captain of the *Hatteras*, Homer Blake, supposed he was investigating a harmless blockade-runner trying to sneak into Galveston.

At such moments, when an impending battle might take any number of unexpected directions, time slowed down in the tense clarity of life and death. On the *Alabama*, men of their own accord pulled out the cannon and got ready. Officers saw to their sidearms. Steam came up and the propeller went down. "Everyone delighted at the prospect of a fight," Master's Mate Fullam exulted. Semmes was supremely in his element, fencing with a mortal enemy at sea. He pulled off, hoping to draw the *Hatteras* away from the other Union vessels and so reduce the odds to one against one. He applied a little steam power, but not too much. The *Hatteras* followed, slowly, approaching with caution. The *Alabama*, always the chaser, was now being chased. Semmes wanted to look like the mouse but was actually the cat. Toward nightfall, about fifteen miles from the other Union ships and well out of sight, Semmes clewed up and furled his topsails. Calling his men to quarters, ready for battle, he turned back and moved toward the *Hatteras*. She kept coming.

Seconds ticked by slowly. The two ships closed on each other to about one hundred yards. Men strained and peered through the fading daylight, trying to recognize the other ship, guessing what that might mean.

Within hailing distance, someone on the *Hatteras* asked, "What ship is that?"

"Her Majesty's Steamer *Petrel*," Kell shouted, his thunderous voice enhanced by a speaking trumpet. He inquired about the other ship. The reply was not audible. Again Kell asked.

This time they heard, "This is the United States Steamer . . ." The name of the ship trailed off, but the "United States" was enough.

The *Alabama* was turned broadside to the *Hatteras*. Semmes asked

Kell if the men were ready. They were. A quiet moment before the explosion stretched out in taut expectation. Time stopped. Tell the enemy who we are, said Semmes.

"This is the Confederate States Steamer *Alabama!*" At the final word, the arranged signal, the starboard battery volleyed in unison. The guns barked together, their muzzle flashes lighting up the sky and water. In a minute or two, the guns of the *Hatteras* fired back. The two ships steamed ahead in parallel lines, locked in raking broadside fire, Confederate starboard to Union port. They were about equal in size, crew, and number of guns; but the *Hatteras* had no weapons as formidable as the *Alabama*'s two pivot cannon. "The conduct of our men," Fullam observed, "was truly remarkable. No flurry, no noise, all calm and determined."

It was now dark and moonless, but with enough starlight for reasonable visibility. Semmes stood on the horse block at the stern, on the weather side, raised above the ship's rail so he could see everything. Shells flew past him. "Give it to the rascals," he shouted. "Don't be all night sinking that fellow!" The enemy fired high, missing or hitting in harmless places, and low, opening six holes near the waterline, small and manageable. "Aim low, men," urged Captain Semmes. The *Alabama*'s gunners carved fatal wounds below the waterline of the *Hatteras*, tearing off sheets of iron. One shot disabled the engine ("I thought the wheel was coming into the engine room," the chief engineer said later). Another shell exploded the steam chest.

The battle lasted just thirteen minutes. The Union ship surrendered by firing two guns from her off, or starboard, side. The Confederate crewmen bellowed and cheered, exulting over a sea battle at last—and such an easy victory as well. The *Alabama* came up close to the sinking *Hatteras* and asked if she needed help. Yes; Semmes lowered his boats, and they picked up the last of the enemy crew just as the ship went down, bow first and on fire, about forty-five minutes after the surrender. Given the closeness of the fighting, no more than one hundred yards apart, and the repeated broadside volleys, casualties were remarkably light: one slightly wounded on the *Alabama*, two dead and five wounded on the *Hatteras*. John C. Cleary, a fireman, and William Healy, a coal handler, were killed. Five months into the cruise, after twenty-seven prizes, Semmes counted his first deaths.

On the *Alabama*, the sailors got extra rations of grog. "The main brace was spliced," Fullam noted, "with a very long splice indeed!" It was the first time in naval history that a steam warship had sunk another steam warship. In the Civil War, it marked the first (and last) sinking at sea of a Union warship by a Confederate vessel. Semmes and the *Alabama*, after taking so many unarmed merchantmen, had finally turned and fought an armed enemy gunboat—and destroyed her quickly. When the news reached the North, it raised the Confederate captain to a new level of threatening fame. "He does everything with a daring and a celerity that have rarely been surpassed," conceded the *Philadelphia Evening Bulletin*. "Cannot some one of our naval commanders show himself a match for the pirate? It is disgraceful."

FOUR

Impacts: North and South

In its early stages the Civil War was still a gentleman's conflict. Battles were fought between organized forces, duly appointed by the contending governments, that tried to preserve a traditional line between "military" and "civilian." As the war ground on, that distinction began to blur because almost all the hostilities took place within the Confederacy, in terrible land bloodbaths and naval battles along the Southern rivers and seacoasts. "With the South the war is primary," Ralph Waldo Emerson observed in 1862; "with the North it is secondary; secondary of course to their trade, then also to their pleasure. The theatres and concerts are filled as usual." Southern civilians, just by living among the fighting, inevitably started to absorb their own hard losses in lives and property. Caught in this inescapable erosion of innocence, the conflict lost its gentlemanly pretensions. It became a bleak prototype for the merciless total wars of modernity.

Raphael Semmes and the *Alabama* brought the war home to the Union. The captain had declared his own personal crusade against the civilian commerce of the enemy. In so doing he generally avoided the warships of the U.S. Navy; his quarry was not military. The first impact of Semmes's cruise was therefore the material and psychological disruption of civilian life-as-usual in the North. His planned attack on New York City, however bold and startling, would have merely extended this broader purpose.

When he burned the Boston bark *Lauretta* on October 28, 1862, Semmes once again reserved the prize's nautical instruments for himself. Captain Marshall Wells of the *Lauretta* asked to keep his telescope, which he said was a gift from a friend who had died. "No," Semmes replied, "I'm going to destroy all the property of the Yankees that I can, no matter what it is."

"It is very hard," offered Wells, as he soon recounted the exchange, "that masters of ships should lose all they are worth in this manner."

"Well, that may be," Semmes concluded. "But the innocent must suffer as well as the guilty." At the dawn of total war, nobody could still claim the polite shelter of innocence.

The notion was so preposterous: A single Confederate warship, not especially large or heavily armed, that would disrupt the seaborne commerce and domestic peace of one of the great powers of the earth? Impossible. As the earliest reports of the *Alabama*'s escape from Liverpool and then of her first captures trickled in, some crucial people remained unconcerned. An alarmed New Yorker asked Gustavus Vasa Fox, the assistant secretary of the Navy, if the city was safe. "The defence of New York Harbor," Fox insisted, "has been entrusted to the Army Engineers, who have been to work upon it for some sixty years, and who I think ought to be able to keep one steamer out." (Semmes might have tested this assurance had he not run short of coal and into a hurricane.) In Bermuda, Charles Wilkes—just appointed to command the U.S. Navy's West India Squadron—told his boss, Secretary of the Navy Gideon Welles, not to worry. "From the accounts I receive of her," Wilkes declared of the *Alabama*, "she has but little speed, and is generally believed it is the intention to run the blockade, instead of becoming a cruiser under the Confederate flag. . . . I do not believe she will prove any match for even one of our Gun-boats."

Wilkes was a distinguished fool, soon to serve as a hapless foil for Semmes's maneuvers around the Caribbean. Yet shrewder heads also nodded into a similar complacency. "Any of our three-masted schooners cannot only outsail her, but sail around her," announced the

Boston Traveller. "She is so long, and her masts so badly placed that she cannot be stayed, or in other words, cannot be brought round head to the wind, and she is very long in wearing, in being brought to upon the opposite tack by sailing before the wind." Americans were still building the finest sailing ships in the world; a squad of fast schooners, the *Traveller* suggested, would quickly catch the pirate.

Hamilton Fish, former governor and U.S. senator from New York, and a future secretary of state, was also fretting about Manhattan's safety. "Disabuse your mind entirely," Commander Henry A. Wise of the Navy's ordnance bureau in Washington assured him, "of any apprehensions regarding the appearance of such a vessel as the 'Alabama' in the waters near New York. Any one of the armed ferry boats now at the Navy Yard would make toothpicks of her in five minutes." John Murray Forbes, perhaps the canniest, most influential Bostonian of his time, dismissed the first local flutters about the Confederate cruiser. "Here on the coast," he wrote his friend Gustavus Fox, "we are subject to spasmodic attacks of the shakes—and just now our public is much concerned about the Alabama. . . . As the Alabama has now got <u>past</u> Nantucket I don't know but the spasm may be over."

In line with such gross miscalculations, the Union Navy's long pursuit of the *Alabama* was fecklessly intermittent, ill-considered, incompetent—and unlucky to boot. Circumstances admittedly did favor the Confederates. Gideon Welles and Gustavus Fox had to concentrate their naval resources on a porous Union blockade of three thousand miles of Southern coastline. The U.S. merchant fleet, which had doubled during the previous fifteen years, spread many unarmed prizes across the vast oceans of the world. The *Alabama* could pursue hundreds of targets; the Union Navy had, at first, just one. "What vexes me about this vessel," complained Rear Admiral Samuel F. Du Pont, "is that so few people know or understand what a needle in a haystack business it is to chase a single ship on the wide ocean—and the want of success is attributed to want of energy, enterprise, or skill and somebody is blamed."

But Welles and Fox committed and sustained a fundamental mistake. Instead of guessing where Semmes might strike next, they in general sent warships to places where the *Alabama* was last reported. Still some four decades before the advent of wireless telegraphy, it took weeks and even months to send messages from a ship at sea to Washington and back again. By the time a pursuing vessel arrived anywhere, Semmes had long since disappeared. In the North and South Atlantic, certain areas were well known to be crowded with merchant vessels at given times of year—such as Semmes's first two hunting grounds, the Azores in whaling season and the Newfoundland Banks after the fall grain harvests. Then, with the gruesome North Atlantic winter about to descend, and less traffic on the Banks, it was logical for Semmes to head down to the West Indies. The men on the *Alabama* were always puzzled (and grateful) that the Union Navy brass could not seem to anticipate such obvious movements.

Instead of informed speculation, Welles and Fox relied on rumors and wisps of intelligence, much of it mistaken. After the *Alabama* crept out of Liverpool in late July 1862, they heard she was bound for Nassau, a prime staging area for Confederate blockade-runners. On September 8, Welles ordered seven warships under Charles Wilkes to patrol around the Bahamas and Cuba, looking for the *Alabama*. Semmes was then three thousand miles away, plucking whalers near the Azores. A false report placed him in Havana, yet Wilkes did not move quickly; he was a veritable McClellan of the sea, slow to act, never satisfied with his forces or his preparations. His squadron finally pulled into Bermuda in late September, and into Havana on October 10, and of course found nothing. By then Semmes, after feasting off Newfoundland, was running down toward New York. Authorities there, upon hearing about his latest prizes, inevitably sent pursuers up toward Newfoundland. At some point, concealed by distance or darkness, Semmes and his stalkers quietly passed each other in opposite directions.

A third player entered the chase in the fall of 1862: the force of public opinion. All during the war, military events and public discourse at the homefront bounced off each other in dynamic, unpredictable ways, tangled into tight circles of cause and effect. Most Civil War historians, studying either the shooting or the homefires in relative isolation, have slighted this complex, reciprocal interplay. It was the first war fought under the full, revolutionary impacts of railroads, telegraphy, and high-speed newspaper printing presses. Communication during a war had never been so quick and widespread. In a democracy fueled by commercial interests and a recklessly free press, readers followed the latest military news every day. (At sea, Semmes learned whatever he needed to know from those captured Union newspapers.) The daily news and editorials provoked sharp public responses, which prodded the politicians, who took measures that made the next day's news and affected military strategies and events. This in turn made more news, beginning the cycle again.

At the start of the war, half of all the American merchant vessels engaged in foreign trade belonged to residents of Boston and New York. Those two cities also comprised the dominant commercial, political, intellectual, and publishing centers of the nation. Public opinion along the Charles and Hudson rivers therefore carried particular heft—and was self-interestedly attuned to the concerns of ocean shipping. In October the first news of the *Alabama*'s feats came in day by day, sometimes in clusters, shocking and unbelievable. "What if some fine morning she should make her appearance off Boston Light?" asked the *Boston Post*. "Have we anything with which to stop her?" The Confederate cruiser was not supposed to be where she was taking her prizes. And she kept moving. Captured crews came home to report that the men on the *Alabama* were confident they could outgun or outrun any ship in the Union Navy. The jittery public mood was inclined to believe it. "Whether the authorities at Washington realize the fact or not," said the *Post* on October 17, "this is getting to be very serious business. What security is there for the millions of property which Boston has at this moment afloat in the Atlantic?" A few weeks later, after yet more prizes and escapes: "This is galling—almost unbearable. It is a disgrace to our country that the career of this monster is not closed."

For New Yorkers, public opinion reached critical mass after the lurid stories told by Captain George Hagar of the *Brilliant*. "The terror of the ocean," cried the most widely read *New York Herald*, "commanded by that experienced and daring freebooter, Raphael Semmes," with a piratical crew worthy of Captain Kidd: "She is in all respects an ugly customer, and one that will destroy millions of property before she is caught, if she is caught at all." The *New York Times* feared she was "too swift" (and Semmes "too skillful") for an easy catching. The pirate himself, on his way to assault Manhattan, read his latest batch of newspapers. "The intelligence of our captures (as late as the *Brilliant*)," he happily noted, "seems to have created great alarm for the safety of commerce in New York." On October 21, at a special meeting of the New York Chamber of Commerce well attended by shipowners and shippers, the city's massed business interests recorded their weighty dismay and frustration—and sent alarmed resolutions to the Navy Department in Washington.

One day later, Gideon Welles dispatched two more ships after the *Alabama*, to the Newfoundland Banks and to Bermuda and Trinidad. Within ten days he sent three more, to Brazil, the Azores, and the coasts of Europe and Africa. Combined with Charles Wilkes's West India Squadron, the scattered posse soon consisted of a dozen Union warships, all burning coal and money in their desperate pursuit of a single Confederate cruiser. Captain Hagar, seeking revenge and spinning his tales, said he had heard that Semmes might be meeting an English supply ship at six possible locations from the Azores down to the Caribbean and up to Nova Scotia. Welles dutifully tried to cover them all. The Navy Department also announced two alluring dead-or-alive rewards for anybody who might nab the *Alabama*: $300,000 if she were sunk, and $500,000 if captured (which was twice what James Bulloch had paid for the ship).

On November 19 one of the Union's pursuing ships, the *San Jacinto*, pulled into Martinique, one of the six rendezvous points named by Hagar. And there, anchored in the harbor of Fort-de-France, was the *Alabama*. Semmes, on hand to be coaled by the *Agrippina*, had just doused his crew's near mutiny. His ship lay immobile and defenseless at anchor. The men on the *San Jacinto* recognized her, shouted in delight, and without orders ran to their stations and got their guns ready. Within the harbor, so near the town, naval battles were banned. But the scourge of Union commerce was sitting right there, helpless. Ralph Chandler, executive officer on the *San Jacinto*, implored Captain William Ronckendorff to ram and sink the *Alabama* at once—the legal consequences be damned. "Here is your opportunity," urged Chandler. "The ship is as strong as oak and iron can make her, and we can run that ship down before she can get her anchor."

"Captain," his deck officer agreed, "ain't you going to run over that ship and sink her?"

"No," demurred Ronckendorff, "I am not the man to take that responsibility." Legally correct and mindful of possible international ramifications, he passed up the Union Navy's best shot yet at the *Alabama*. Instead the *San Jacinto* moved harmlessly outside the harbor and waited.

Semmes thought about fighting the *San Jacinto*. But the Union ship had twice his gunpower and manpower, so he decided to wait for darkness and then run. He was spookily repeating himself. On the *Sumter* almost exactly a year earlier, in the similar nearby harbor of St. Pierre on Martinique, he had escaped the Union ship *Iroquois* at night by feinting a dash to the southern outlet, turning around, and racing out the northern end. Now, with the extra advantage of dark, rainy weather, he first ran toward the inner bay of Fort-de-France. Concealed by the high abutting land, he turned and slipped through the southern outlet to the sea. The *San Jacinto* patrolled back and forth all night, sighting nothing, and found the *Alabama* long gone in the morning. Poor Ronckendorff had to send an abashed report to Welles. "I could find out nothing of the future movements of the *Alabama*," he lamented.

A New York magazine paid tribute with a poem, "The Napping Captain."

> Over the stormy waters all night,
> Chafing and spoiling for glory and fight,
> Went the "San Jacinto," but never a sight
>   Did she get at the "Alabama."
> In grief did the Captain tear his hair,
> And wring his hands in a grim despair—
> He ought to have known it is wrong to swear,
>   But I fear that he whispered: "D——n her!"
>
> Now what shall we do with such fellows as these,
> Who hunt the Rebels upon the seas,
> Yet let them escape with marvellous ease,
>   To burn and ravage and plunder?

What, indeed, to do? Through the fall of 1862, the *Alabama* kept burning prizes, disappearing, and showing up somewhere unexpected. A ship at sea, west of Bermuda, heard eight heavy artillery shots—could that be the *Alabama*?—when she was actually off New York. Another ship reported her near Boston when she was 1,400 miles east of Florida. Again, when she was deep in the Caribbean, somebody was sure he saw her off the coast of Maine, about to invade the small and unstrategic town of Sullivan. Along with such false reports, the Navy Department was showered with schemes for snaring Semmes. In the main port cities of the North, merchants, shipowners, and marine insurance companies kept crying for redress. Newspapers poured acid criticisms on Welles's bewigged old head. "The undisturbed sway of the pirate Alabama overawes our commerce, destroys millions of dollars worth of property and disgraces the country," blared the *New York Herald*. Needing a scapegoat and a simple explanation, the *Herald* landed on Welles: he "did nothing to prevent her completion, nothing to keep her from putting out to sea, and has done nothing towards her capture"—so he should be fired for "culpable neglect of duty."

Under fierce pressures, Welles played his only trump. Cornelius Vanderbilt, the very symbol of New York's seaborne capitalism, had donated his eponymous steamship *Vanderbilt* to the Union cause. One of the fastest transatlantic liners, she had crossed the ocean at a brisk average speed of 13.75 knots. After being refitted as an armed cruiser at the Brooklyn Navy Yard in early November, she bristled with a pair of hundred-pound Parrott pivot cannon, fore and aft, and a dozen nine-inch Dahlgren broadside guns. Her oversized paddlewheels and exposed engine machinery left her vulnerable in a pitched gun battle. But the *Vanderbilt* was still the biggest, fastest, most formidable ship in the Union Navy—swifter and over three times larger than the *Alabama*, and with twice the firepower. Other U.S. warships, berthed next to her at the navy yard, looked like mere fishing smacks.

For the *Vanderbilt*'s first cruise, Welles sent her after the *Alabama*. "Your main object," he told her captain, Charles H. Baldwin, "will be the pursuit of that vessel." Hunt in the tracks of ships within the Gulf Stream, Welles ordered, east to the Newfoundland Banks and south to the Delaware Capes, and come into Boston, Bermuda, or New York for the latest news of the pirate's whereabouts. (Semmes was then far to the east, bound for Martinique.) Baldwin stayed out for three weeks and 3,600 miles. He collided with an English bark, burned up to one hundred tons of coal a day, and found no trace of his quarry. After refueling in New York, he set forth again. "I <u>do</u> hope we shall have better luck this time than the last," Baldwin wrote to Gustavus Fox. "This Ship is in capital order, and I think if we only have the luck to meet the rascal, you shall have no reason to complain of the account we give of him." The converted liner was admittedly a very expensive coal hog; "I am fearful our great expenditure of <u>coal</u> will frighten you," Baldwin warned. "She however is a <u>Big</u> Ship."

Semmes now was hiding in the Gulf of Mexico, on his way to Galveston. Baldwin trolled eastward to the Azores, coming up empty. Scratching for any news, he read a weeks-old report in a Boston newspaper that Semmes was sighted near Barbados. "I cannot but think I will at least hear of him there," Baldwin ventured. (Not meet or sink him—but maybe hear of him.) The *Vanderbilt* poked around the Caribbean, again came home for coal, and was sent after the *Alabama* yet again. Welles, with—as usual—no idea whatever of Semmes's location, ordered Baldwin to cover an impossibly vast search area bounded by New York City, Rio de Janeiro, the Cape of Good Hope, and Lisbon: in other words, most of both the North and South Atlantic.

Aware of his adversary's lurching incompetence, Semmes seldom worried about what Welles might do. But the *Vanderbilt* did concern him. From his captured newspapers, Semmes knew about the converted liner and her particular mission to sink the *Alabama*. If the two ships ever encountered each other, the Confederate commander might, by clever tactics or deceptions, compensate for their disparity in size. But he could never outrun the *Vanderbilt*—and so could not avoid a pitched battle that would find him gravely outgunned. When he caught the *Ariel* in December, Semmes pumped Captain Albert Jones for information. Just how fast was the big cruiser? What about her armament? The Union captain loyally declined to say. "The only ship that Semmes fears is the Vanderbilt," Jones reported when he got home. "He laughs at all the other ships we have."

Over the course of her first four months of cruising, though, the *Vanderbilt* caught nothing but the jealous attention of Commodore Charles Wilkes. As head of the West India Squadron, he was the earliest and most frustrated of all the naval officers sent after Semmes. "The first great and imperative duty of your command is the capture and destruction of the Alabama," Welles told him, again, in December. "You could perform no duty more acceptable to the whole country." Wilkes kept asking for more ships and men; if adequately supplied, he was certain, he would already have caught the pirate. "I am aware," he replied to Welles, "that the whole country is looking with the greatest solicitude for the capture or destruction of the *Alabama*, but with an inefficient force . . . it is utterly impossible." In particular, he said, the worn hull and boilers of his flagship, the *Wachusett,* forced him to stay near his base in Havana instead of out searching the Caribbean.

Baldwin brought the *Vanderbilt* into Havana in late February 1863. Wilkes outranked Baldwin; yet the junior officer commanded a much larger, finer ship. Wilkes coveted the expansive living quarters and left-over luxuries of the converted passenger liner. With the same arrogant, heedless impetuosity that had so marked his entire career, Wilkes decided to seize the *Vanderbilt* as his new flagship. "This is the vessel for me," he crowed to his wife. "She has the speed and all the appliances for the comforts I am entitled to." Over Baldwin's objections and Welles's explicit orders, Wilkes diverted the only Union Navy ship that Semmes feared from her assigned mission of hunting the *Alabama* to the routine, local pursuit of blockade-runners—from which, by the way, his share of the prize money was "filling his pockets," as Wilkes told his wife. With the *Vanderbilt,* he at last had a ship that matched his notions of his own greatness. The chase after the Confederate cruiser descended from simple incompetence to chuckleheaded farce.

Welles and Fox continued to send out more ships, hoping to overcome their strategic mistakes with sheer numbers. The pursuing force reached fourteen vessels, then eighteen. The bad news kept coming. "It is a sickening record," said the *New York Times,* "like sending a hawk into a flock of barn-yard fowls, or turning a wolf into a sheep-cote. The only business is to slay and eat." Semmes captured the large paddlewheeler *Ariel* despite her contingent of 140 Marines, and then easily sank the Union Navy's gunboat *Hatteras* off Galveston—"no one suspecting for an instant," wrote Rear Admiral David Farragut from his headquarters in New Orleans, "that the *Alabama* was in this part of the world." The Confederate cruiser and captain began to drift off into legend, seemingly uncatchable and impregnable, scaring adversaries into stacking the odds. "Look out for the *Alabama,*" Farragut warned a subordinate in Texas. "Direct the gunboats to keep two or three in company if possible. Then they could surely be a match for the *Alabama.*"

Yet no Union vessel except the now commandeered *Vanderbilt,* it was generally agreed, could equal the speed of Semmes's ship. "There is not in the United States, to be purchased for love or money," concluded the *New York Tribune*, "a steamer possessing the speed necessary to catch her, and at the same time the strength to fight her." And even the *Vanderbilt* was dangerously limited by her exposed machinery and paddlewheels. The *Alabama* was fast, well armed, able to stay at sea indefinitely under sail—and better designed because her machinery and screw propeller were safely buried below the waterline, protected from enemy gunfire. For decades, British shipbuilders had more quickly seen the advantages of propellers over paddles. "The English must certainly be far ahead of us in shipbuilding," one Union naval officer fretted to another. "We certainly have nothing like this, and the sooner, if it is all true, we go into the English market likewise the better."

With so much frustrated attention on the elusive *Alabama*, the diversion of so many ships, men, and resources was harming the most important mission of the Union Navy, its blockade of the Confederate coastline. "It is annoying," Welles wrote in his diary, "when we want all our force on blockade duty[,] to be compelled to detach so many of our best craft on the fruitless errand of searching the wide ocean for this wolf from Liverpool." Off the Cape Fear River in North Carolina, the local Union commander had to spend coal and scarce supplies on false reports of the *Alabama*, at the expense of his blockade duties. Off Port Royal, South Carolina, Samuel F. Du Pont was sacrificing both his warships and supply ships to the pursuit of the *Alabama*. "We are all feeling a good deal the confusion in our supply ships," he noted, "and long detentions—for we are out of a good many things—and badly off in our messes." A bit later, as the volume of blockade-running picked up: "We are out of provisions—living on the Army."

The Union Navy's success rate at stopping blockade-runners off the key ports of Charleston and Wilmington dropped from 27 percent in 1861–62 to 13 percent in 1863. In New Orleans, Farragut worried "that all our small blockaders will be gobbled up before we catch the fellow." At Key West, alerted by the capture of the Aspinwall steamer *Ariel*, the Union commander felt obliged to divert one of his finest gunboats to escort the gold shipments from Aspinwall in Panama; and Welles sent another ship south for the same purpose. Aside from all the strategic losses, these measures cost many hundreds of thousands of dollars, more than the value of the ships destroyed by the *Alabama*—all "to keep a whole fleet out looking after the slippery scoundrel," said the *Boston Post*, "like ten cats looking for a weasel in a hundred acre lot."

While these chases went nowhere, Semmes was invading the pocketbooks of Union civilians. The *Alabama*'s first prizes, the whalers taken off the Azores, had cost marine insurance companies over $63,000. The companies therefore tripled and quadrupled their "war risk" surcharges to 4 to 6 percent—beyond the usual marine rates of around 8 percent of the total value of vessel and cargo. Ship men believed they were already donating quite enough to the Union cause without these additional costs. An aggrieved meeting of merchants and shipowners in the major whaling port of New Bedford, Massachusetts, sent a bleating protest to the federal government, demanding some redress against the *Alabama*'s "atrocious and brutal" pillagings. "We are the more emboldened to urge our request," they said, "in view of the large contributions we have made during the rebellion, in officers and men, for the Navy of the Union. While we are manning the naval squadrons with thousands of our seamen, who are doing efficient service for the country, we ask that those who are pursuing their peaceful though hazardous calling may be reasonably free from piratical depredations." In time the added war risk reached as high as 10 percent—too steep for any prudent businessman. Thereafter it could make more sense to carry no insurance at all, daring a total loss.

The war was thus coming home to the North. After Semmes took the *Ariel*, gold shipments from Panama to New York—nearly $3 million each month at the start of the war—fell off, eventually by around 70 percent. Public confidence in the gold steamers plummeted. (In January 1863 a second Confederate cruiser, the *Florida*, started marauding in the same area.) Constricting the flow of specie affected key Union financial interests in New York and elsewhere; and the loot instead now went from San Francisco to England, mainly on British ships. Britons also profited from the steep rise in American war risk insurance. Instead of paying those exorbitant rates and still risking interception at sea, hundreds of Union shipowners sold their vessels into foreign ownership, especially British. Transferred from U.S. registry, they were then, perhaps, safe from the *Alabama*. In one transaction that became all too typical, a large American ship in Liverpool, loaded for home, was sold for half her value before she dared to embark. "The commerce between Liverpool and the United States," a London paper reported late in 1862, "is almost completely paralyzed."

At the port of Philadelphia, the value of exports in U.S. vessels fell from $8.8 million in 1862 to $3.4 million in 1864, while those in foreign ships zoomed from $2.7 million to $10.2 million. Other ports recorded similar declines. "Our commerce will soon be entirely in the hands of foreigners," wrote a well-connected Bostonian to Gideon Welles, "unless our trade is protected by every means within the power of the Government." The U.S. merchant fleet, sold away to avoid Semmes, was dealt blows from which it wouldn't recover until well into the twentieth century.

All these circumstances—the *Alabama*'s ongoing captures in unexpected places, the Union Navy's earnest but ineffective pursuit, and the various rippling, portentous impacts on Union commerce—created a prevailing uneasiness in the North, especially in port cities, which at times skirted a full-blown panic. Countermeasures seemed so useless, just inept flailings that accomplished nothing. In February 1863 the New York Chamber of Commerce again "resolved" against the *Alabama*—"which hurts Semmes," the *Boston Post* remarked, "about as much as Welles's measures." The *New York World*, a Democratic newspaper hostile to the administration in Washington, acidly suggested that Lincoln simply announce a proclamation abolishing the *Alabama*, just as he had recently abolished slavery by his unenforceable Emancipation Proclamation. As for the embattled secretary of the Navy, twitted the *World*,

> There was an old fogy named Welles,
> Quite worthy of cap and of bells,
>   For he thought that a pirate,
>   Who steamed at a great rate,
> Would wait to be riddled with shells.

Vanity Fair, a magazine of humorous commentary published in New York, took refuge in jests. It published an imaginary biography of Semmes's childhood as related by his old black mammy. He was born on a raft at sea and acquired his first name from the raffle by which his foster parents came to adopt him. At age four he started drinking applejack, and when he robbed a hen roost he would divide the chickens among his friends. He always did like to burn things; he stole gunpowder and planted a charge in his mammy's pipe, but she still loved him anyway. He also blew up a neighbor's dog. "He began to be dressy—he is a tremendous swell now, you know." He liked to embark in a canoe and harass the ducks on a nearby pond. At church, he stole marbles from the other boys and dissolved the congregation by putting cayenne pepper on a hot stove—inspiring a prediction by the parish fool that he "would grow up a man not to be sneezed at." Then, in serious conclusion: "And so he has: at least all our naval commanders appear to believe it."

One particular drawing published in *Harper's Weekly* suggested the mood of the North in the spring of 1863. It was done by the artist Winslow Homer, then on the magazine's staff. Captioned "The Approach of the British Pirate 'Alabama,' " the full-page illustration showed an officer and two sailors on a ship at sea, all peering and straining to identify a three-masted steamship looming out on the horizon. (The *Alabama* was a steamer with three masts.) Around the officer were grouped four women, pointing and beseeching, in various tense postures of fretful, unprotected feminine vulnerability. Sharpening the point, one woman held a baby; an older child cowered in the background. They all looked utterly helpless, just waiting for the terrible Semmes to pounce.

An odd story from Washington reflected the extent of Union interest in the *Alabama*—and how desperately people wanted some resolution. Semmes had been causing political storms for the White House; the capture of the *Ariel*, Lincoln's secretary John G. Nicolay had predicted, "will of course set all New York howling about the ears of the Administration again." In April the *Boston Saturday Evening Gazette*, a newspaper loyal to the Union, reported on a spiritualist séance at the White House. The medium, supposed to have marvelous "supernatural powers," was one Charles E. Shockle. On hand for the evening were the president and his wife, Secretary of the Navy Gideon Welles, Secretary of War Edwin M. Stanton, and two others. The session began, according to the *Gazette*, at eight o'clock. As Shockle summoned the spirits, they moved a few tables, swayed a picture of Henry Clay on the wall, and elevated two candelabra. Rappings were heard beneath Lincoln's feet. A discussion of military strategies followed, with pithy advice from Napoleon, Lafayette, and other dead authorities.

The séance, according to the article, moved on to one of the overriding issues of the day. "I wish," said the president, "the spirits would tell us how to catch the Alabama." The lights in the room were sud-

Winslow Homer's depiction of Union jitters over the *Alabama*.
(*Harper's Weekly*, April 25, 1863)

denly dimmed. An ocean scene appeared in the large mirror over the mantel: the *Alabama* at full steam fleeing another steamer in pursuit, with two merchant prizes burning in the distance. The image in the mirror then shifted to the *Alabama* at anchor below an English fort, with no visible signs of life on board. This picture disappeared, replaced by a statement in purple letters: "The English PEOPLE demanded this of England's ARISTOCRACY." It seemed to predict that British authorities would finally make up for the *Alabama*'s notori-

ous escape from Liverpool by taking her back. "It is not very compli-
mentary to our Navy anyhow," Lincoln observed. "We've done our
best, Mr. President," Welles replied. "I'm maturing a plan which,
when perfected, I think, if it works well, will be a perfect trap for the
Alabama." (This halting assertion sounded authentic, fitting the general public perception of Welles as vague and diffident.)

At a time when many serious people took spiritualism quite seriously, and Mary Todd Lincoln found comfort in contacting her dead
son Willie, the *Gazette*'s story was reprinted by scores of Union newspapers and accorded duly respectful attention. But a spiritualist newspaper in Boston, the *Banner of Light*, investigated the report and
concluded it was all a concocted hoax. (And a substantial breach of
journalistic ethics by the *Gazette*.) The alleged séance had not taken
place. In fact "Charles E. Shockle" did not even exist. The Union
pursuit of the *Alabama* would have to continue without supernatural
intervention.

For the Confederate States of America in the fall of 1862, good news
about Semmes and his ship arrived along with a general upsurge in the
South's military fortunes. The events of the war continued to unfold in
fluid, unpredictable ways; civilian moods shifted with the morning
newspaper's latest headlines. Rebounding from the dire circumstances
of the previous spring, Confederate forces achieved a remarkable
string of victories. Robert E. Lee had taken command of the Army of
Northern Virginia. Stonewall Jackson emerged from the Shenandoah
Valley as a universally acknowledged military genius. Together the two
Confederate heroes rescued Richmond from a Union threat and
pushed the enemy out of Virginia. After a bloody triumph at the second Battle of Bull Run, Lee even invaded the Union state of Maryland,
putting Washington and Baltimore at risk. A clouded Union victory at
Antietam was far outweighed by the loss of nearly 13,000 Northern
troops at the debacle of Fredericksburg. Out west, Southern troops
forged ahead in Tennessee and Kentucky. The South was moving, it
seemed, from defense to offense.

The *Alabama*, pushing this streak of Confederate success into an
unexpected realm, became a recurring wonder for the Southern media.
When the war began, some eight hundred newspapers were pub-

lished in the states of the Confederacy. At least half of them had expired by early 1862, killed off by wartime shortages of paper, ink, and subscribers. That still left a robustly independent press operating all across the South. The Confederacy had no real navy, hence no naval correspondents like those on Union warships who sent in their reports to Northern newspapers. Stories about the *Alabama* in general came to Southern readers secondhand and a bit later, reprinted from Yankee and British papers—but with Confederate headlines and commentaries.

As these reports accumulated, they raised Semmes up into the pantheon of Southern military heroes. The first wisp of Confederate news about the *Alabama* appeared in the *Richmond Examiner* of September 23: a mistaken story sent from Nassau that Semmes had battled with a Union warship at sea. Six days later, the *Charleston Mercury* printed a list of the *Alabama*'s top twelve officers. The *Augusta Daily Constitutionalist* reported in mid-October that the cruiser had acquired her former name, the *290*, from being 290 feet long; the *Savannah Republican* correctly noted instead that she was so designated as the 290th vessel built by the Lairds.

The first news of the *Alabama*'s whaling bonfires around the Azores reached the South from an account in the *London Shipping Gazette*, brought to New York by the crack Cunard liner *Persia* and published in the papers there. In celebration, the *Charleston Mercury* announced that it had on display—right here at its office, for just a few days—a rare (if outdated) photograph taken on the *Sumter* of "the great naval hero, Captain SEMMES, and of the brave officers under his command." A day later, the rival *Charleston Daily Courier* allowed that it had the photograph too. The *Alabama*, added the *Courier*, was of late "dealing largely in the oil and whalebone business."

From that blazing start, the Southern press tracked the rich and varied trail of the *Alabama*'s first five months and beyond. When the captain of a captured whaler reached home and complained of being placed in irons, the *Mobile Register and Advertiser* headlined the story "Retaliation at Sea—Bravo, Captain Semmes!" That was the innovation: the South, long besieged by the Union blockade and practically defenseless, was now fighting back in the new arena of the ocean. The Northerners might take comfort in their accusations of piracy and freebooting. "What a mighty difference it makes whose 'ox is gored,' " the Mobile paper commented on its local hero. "Off every Southern port for eighteen months past, Yankee cruisers have been picking up every boat or ship that bore Confederate colors, and confiscating them to their use. These are honest and gentlemanly sea warriors, but when Capt. Semmes turns the table on Yankee ships, Semmes is 'a pirate and a villain.' " Hence no loyal Southern newspaper should follow the prejudiced Northern practice of dismissing the *Alabama* as a mere "privateer."

Most white Southerners believed, with Semmes, that the United States had splintered into two irreconcilable cultures, the agrarian Cavaliers of the South and the industrial Puritans of the North. The Puritans were regarded as greedy and uncultured, interested only in money. For Confederates, the protests by the New York Chamber of Commerce over losses caused by the *Alabama* struck that ringing chord. "The sensitive nerve of their whole system is in their purses, and, when that is effectually pierced, the death agony is sudden," said the *Richmond Dispatch*, which claimed the largest circulation of any Southern newspaper. "If Northern commerce upon the ocean could be destroyed, or even to any great extent crippled, we should do the Lincoln empire more damage, at less cost, than by any land invasion of their territories."

Confederate papers gleefully reported on the cruiser's clever escape from the *San Jacinto* at Fort-de-France—"Semmes coolly slid out of port"—and on the Union Navy's clueless pursuit, savoring how a chasing enemy ship always seemed to arrive in any given port just after the *Alabama* had left. The *Vicksburg Daily Whig* listed the eighteen Union warships trying to find her and happily observed that her speed and the vast ocean made the task so difficult. "If Semmes survives the desperate chase the Yankees are making after him," said the *Charleston Mercury*, "he ought to be made an Admiral." Capturing the *Ariel*, the *Charleston Daily Courier* observed, "produced a profound sensation in New York commercial circles, and caused marine insurance to rise one hundred per cent. If a single vessel can do all this mischief, what might not a whole squadron propelled by steam do?" When the Union Navy's gunboat *Hatteras* was sunk off Galveston, the *Courier* proclaimed "another victory and achievement for the *Alabama* and the vigilant, persevering, energetic and ubiquitous SEMMES."

The Confederate government in Richmond was a democracy at war. Public opinion mattered, framing the often testy exchanges between the administration of Jefferson Davis and the Confederate Congress. In the absence of any real political parties, personalities became even more significant. President Davis had integrity and intellectual gifts of a high order, but he did not respond well to criticism. His two most persistent newspaper critics, the *Richmond Examiner* and the *Charleston Mercury*, ladled abuse on Davis and Secretary of the Navy Stephen Mallory. They had often demanded that Davis switch from defensive maneuvers and take the war to the enemy—exactly what Semmes was doing. Yet even the successive feats of the *Alabama* just gave the two papers another opening. "We and all the world," said the *Mercury*, "are finding out what we might have been doing these many months, and have not done, for the want of executive sagacity. Better late than never."

The *Examiner*, more broadly, saw the *Alabama* as starting a new dimension to the war. The South's military invasions of Northern territory had proven brief and ineffective—a quick tease of news that meant little. A better hope for final victory lay out at sea. "The Alabama at intervals electrifies the South by one of her daring and splendid exploits," the *Examiner* editorialized in January 1863, after the *Hatteras* sinking. "Glorious and gratifying as are the performances of the Alabama, they are in fact but reproaches to us, when we consider the splendid field of enterprise which she alone has dared to enter." A few more captures of Aspinwall steamers like the *Ariel* would consign all the Yankee gold to London—a crippling blow for Northern finances. And even more, said the *Examiner*, if the Davis administration had deployed an entire fleet of fast cruisers like the *Alabama*, the North would already have submitted peace overtures. Regardless of those nodding, plodding bureaucrats in Richmond, the strategic conclusion was obvious: "Captain Semmes is still demonstrating that the true theatre for Southern raids is the great ocean."

Carried to a reasonable conclusion, this new strategy would have redefined the Confederacy. Before the war the South had no grand maritime tradition like the North's; its waterborne commerce was restricted mainly to riverboats and coastal vessels. As the Confederate secretary of state, Judah Benjamin, conceded to George Moore, the British consul in Richmond, the South was particularly limited in its struggle to obtain adequate resources by the lack of an oceangoing fleet. Raphael Semmes and the *Alabama* constituted, at first, almost the entire effective force of the Confederate Navy. If the South were to attain its independence and assume a place among the sovereign nations of the world, it would need a respected presence on the deep ocean. The *Alabama* thus bore both immediate strategic tasks and wider implications for the future of the nascent country.

A poem published in a Richmond newspaper, "The Sea-Kings of the South," by Edward C. Bruce, addressed that double-edged role. In this great age of occasional poetry, verses routinely adorned any public ceremony and overflowed the pages of newspapers and magazines. Especially in a culture of limited general education like the South—where the illiteracy rate among whites was three times higher than in the North, and libraries and newspapers were proportionally underutilized—the oral, performing aspects of poetry took it beyond the limitations of print and reading. "Like all people much given to talking," declared the *Southern Literary Messenger,* the intellectual voice of the South, "Southerners, as a people, are little given to reading." Though written down, poetry when recited in public reached people who couldn't or didn't read and could be carried by memory to other events, from ear to mouth to ear, and thereby spread beyond the printed page.

Bruce, a writer and portrait painter in Richmond, began his poem with a bow toward the landbound military heroes of the South. Then a turn:

> But a ruggeder field than the mountain-side—a broader field
>   than the plain,
> Is spread for the fight in the stormy wave and the globe-
>   embracing main.
> 'Tis there the keel of the goodly ship must trace the fate of the
>   land,
> For the name ye write in the sea-foam white shall first and
>   longest stand.

This was a heretical notion, given the South's venerable military traditions of fighting on land. Bruce, writing in March 1863 with the latest exploits of the *Alabama* fresh in his mind, envisioned a naval future for the Confederacy.

> Oh, broad and green is her hunting-park, and plentiful
>   the game!

From the restless bay of old Biscay to the Carib' sea she
    came.
The catchers of the whale she caught; swift *Ariel*
    overhauled;
And made *Hatteras* know the hardest *blow* that ever a tar
    appalled.

She bears the name of a noble State, and sooth she bears
    it well.
To us she hath made it a word of pride, to the Northern
    ear a knell.
To the Puritan in the busy mart, the Puritan on his deck,
With "Alabama" visions start of ruin, woe, and wreck.

The poem's rolling cadences were well suited to public performance, easy to recite and pleasing to hear. "Verse is stronger than
prose," declared the *Richmond Examiner*, "and history is powerless in
competition with the popular ballad." A prevailing culture of oral
discourse—what the historian Drew Gilpin Faust has called "southern
orality"—was also fed by topical songs. During the war, the publication of popular sheet music and songbooks increased markedly in the
South, faster than any other type of publishing. Songs, like poems,
were written down and set in print—but then were performed in par-
lors and theaters, on marches and around campfires, and broadcast by
memory and repetition, with no need for literacy or the mediation of
paper and ink. They embodied public opinion in oral form.

A rousing song to Semmes, "The Alabama," was written by
E. King (words) and Fitz William Rosier (music) and published in
Richmond.

Our home is on the mountain wave,
    Our flag floats proudly free;
No boasting despot, tyrant, knave,
    Shall crush fair Liberty.
Firmly we'll aid her glorious cause,
    We'll die, boys, to defend her;
We'll brave the foe where'er we go,
    Our motto, "No Surrender!"

Then sling the bowl, drink ev'ry soul,
   A toast to the Alabama;
What e'er our lot, through storm or shot
   Here's success to the Alabama!

And so on, for three other verses and the chorus, intended by the song-writers to be sung "with majesty" to a stately, ascending melody in 4/4 time. The music itself sounded like an invocation, building upward toward something larger.

In these three forms—newspapers, poetry, and song—news of Semmes and his ship penetrated to the farthest inner reaches of the Confederacy. To pick one example among many: on a large cotton plantation in rural northeast Louisiana, some thirty miles from Vicksburg and far from the Atlantic Ocean, a young woman named Kate Stone nonetheless took pleased note of the *Alabama* in her diary. In a time of swelling Confederate hopes, Semmes's repeated brilliant naval feats for an agricultural, inward-facing nation exploded its traditional definition of military success and leaned hard into a wider, beckoning future.

At the Navy Department in Richmond, Stephen Mallory was already working toward the next level. In the winter of 1863 he sent drafts for $2 million to James Bulloch in Liverpool, with urgent instructions to seek contracts for four more fast commerce raiders just like the *Alabama*. "Push these ships ahead as rapidly as possible," he told Bulloch. "I deem them of the utmost consequence to our cause."

FIVE

Impacts: Anglo-America

Concurrent with these impacts in the North and South were international effects of the gravest kind, unplanned and unexpected. The
British origins of the *Alabama*—the ship, supplies, ordnance, crewmen,
and even a few of the officers—precipitated a tightening crisis in
Anglo-American relations that threatened to push the two nations into
yet another war. During this period when the battle for the Union was
going so poorly, a new shooting conflict between the United States and
the mightiest military power in the world would have ensured the triumph of the Confederacy. The North, already stretched to the brink
of defeat by the South, could not have withstood two such wars at
once. In these diplomatic affairs the *Alabama*, once again, spun off out-
comes seemingly beyond the capacity of a single ship roaming the
boundless ocean.

Today, after the Anglo-American alliances of two world wars and
other conflicts, and after massive cultural exchanges between the two
nations, it is difficult to recover a proper sense of just how much the
United States and Great Britain disliked each other for most of the
nineteenth century. Two bitter wars (the Revolution and 1812) were
followed by decades of ill-tempered squabbles over boundaries and

fishing rights, commercial and political rivalries, and endless rounds of mutual insults and provocations. In some ways it was a family quarrel between two nations so similar, yet so different. United by their common language, history, religions, and literature, the younger wayward child inevitably challenged the older mother country; the similarities themselves generated competition. Each party looked across the ocean and saw its own image, but with many irritating deviations that needed fixing.

The dreadful carnage of the American Civil War forced the people of Britain to choose sides. In general, liberals, religious dissenters, and the working class favored the Union, while conservatives, the Church of England, the aristocracy, the press, and most professionals and intellectuals supported the Confederacy. Over the years, historians have nicked at the corners of these alignments, but the broad patterns remain essentially intact. Those Britons who had always disapproved of the United States greeted the war with a certain malicious schadenfreude over the misfortunes of their upstart American rival. The conflict seemed to demonstrate the perils of headlong democracy.

Britain in 1861 was a quite limited democracy; among a total population of 22 million, only one million men had the right to vote. The gilded governing classes feared that democracy in the American style might spread its infections across the ocean. As Lord Richard Lyons, the British ambassador in Washington, summed up the difference in 1861, the United States was controlled by mediocre politicians, "men in general of second rate station and ability, who aim at little more than divining and pandering to the feeling of the mob of voters"; while in Britain, "a few statesmen decided what was for the interest of the community, and guided public opinion by their superior wisdom, talents, and authority." Therefore, it was hoped, the disintegration of the daring American experiment in democracy might check its toxic threat to infect other nations with extreme republicanism.

Yet even a determined populist like Charles Dickens, a noted friend of the underdog and skeptic toward entrenched authority, found reasons to line up with the Confederacy. Early in the war he expected a short conflict and stalemate that would leave two independent nations. As the killing ground on, he came to define the underdog in the war not as the slaves yearning for freedom, but as the plucky Confederacy standing up to a much stronger bully. "Slavery has in reality nothing on earth to do with it," he decided. "The North having gradually got to itself the making of the laws and the settlement of the Tariffs, and having taxed the South most abominably for its own advantage," was simply asserting its unchecked power. Neither side cared about the rights of black people. "For the rest, there is not a pin to choose between the two parties. They will both rant and lie and fight until they come to a compromise; and the slave may be thrown into that compromise or thrown out of it, just as it happens." So, Dickens concluded, let the Confederacy go and the bloodletting stop—and he was echoed by many other prominent British writers and intellectuals.

The Liberal government of Prime Minister Henry John Temple, Lord Palmerston, sympathized with the South but pursued an official policy of overt neutrality. The foreign secretary, Lord John Russell, defined the war in the fall of 1861 as "one side for empire, and the other for independence." *The Times* of London, the unofficial mouthpiece for Downing Street, also sided with the Confederacy. *The Times* was not the largest newspaper in London—the rival *Telegraph* claimed a daily circulation of 200,000 against 60,000 for the *Times*—but it was by far the most influential paper in Great Britain, indeed in the entire world. It endorsed the middle course adopted by Palmerston and Russell in 1861: acknowledging the Confederacy as a belligerent, which gave its ships and soldiers international acceptance and the right to enter British ports around the world for supplies and repairs, but still withholding full diplomatic recognition as a sovereign nation. In the hairsplitting realm of international relations, that distinction mattered.

The U.S. minister in London, Charles Francis Adams, felt beset and friendless. "There is, throughout England, a great deal of warm though passive sympathy with America," he wrote home. "But there is likewise an extraordinary amount of fear as well as of jealousy. And it is these last passions which have pervaded the mass of the governing classes." He toiled at what seemed a hopeless task, of representing his country and limiting British support for the Confederacy. At the same time, like many other cultured citizens of the eastern United States, he regarded Lincoln as a Midwestern bumpkin, vulgar and unfit for the presidency. Lincoln had risen from the least accomplished background of any president of the nineteenth century, and he was elected in 1860 only because of multiple party splits. Now Adams had to defend a leader in whom he had no confidence whatever. "He has never raised himself to the level of his position or of the emergency," Adams confided to his diary; in his "incapacity" and "honest incompetency," the president was a disaster. Adams himself was unqualified for the dreary but necessary social demands of his ministry. Even his admiring son Charles later described his manner as "chill and repellent." Making the obligatory rounds of London society, bored by all the gossip and empty forms, he was not a success. "I cannot well suit myself to this sort of company life. It is formal, constrained and idle," Adams regretted. "I am always glad to get back to my own room and even the cares of my public situation."

In November 1861 the ever-blundering Charles Wilkes ignited the first Anglo-American crisis of the war. On patrol south of Cuba, chasing Semmes and the *Sumter*, Wilkes heard that two Confederate commissioners to Europe were leaving Havana for England on the British mail steamer *Trent*. Wilkes stopped the *Trent* at sea, removed the two Confederates (James M. Mason and John Slidell) on his own dubious authority, and took them to jail in Boston. For so arrantly flouting British sovereignty on the ocean, Wilkes was lionized at home and barbecued in Britain. The Lincoln administration at first endorsed the seizure. "I fear the North to be utterly mad, and war to be unavoidable," wrote Charles Dickens. "They will of course do the wrong and the insane thing. . . . I am sick of hearing people rely on their 'common sense.' As if, as a country, they possessed such an article!" At the U.S. legation in London, young Henry Adams—spending the war as his father's private secretary—gauged the furious British response and tumbled into despair. "I consider that we are dished, and that our position is hopeless," he told his brother Charles. "This nation means to make war. Do not doubt it."

The two governments lobbed paper volleys back and forth. On the edge of another war, Secretary of State William H. Seward decided to blink and release Mason and Slidell. Semmes, then in Gibraltar with the *Sumter*, regretted the end of the crisis. "The whole British nation," he wrote to a Confederate colleague, "were so badly frightened in their late quarrel with the Yankees, and have been so delighted to get out of it without a war, that I am afraid we shall never bring them up to the mark again." The brief hope of a war-making alliance with British power drifted away. "So goes the world," Semmes shrugged. "Well, thank God, we are independent of them all, and can whip the Yankees without their assistance."

Mason and Slidell finally reached Southampton in late January. They found an active Confederate lobby in Britain, pumped up by the threat and the vindicating resolution of the *Trent* affair. The lobby was centered in Liverpool (James Bulloch's base of operations, and where the *Alabama* was being built). The city's connections with the American South went back to the late eighteenth century, when it served as the principal British port for the transatlantic slave trade. Many Liverpool merchant fortunes were drawn from that traffic in human beings. During the Civil War, the booming port on the river Mersey became the main nexus for Confederate blockade-running, bringing in cotton and taking out munitions and other supplies. Presiding over this thriving, illicit business was the merchant house of Fraser, Trenholm and Company, established in Charleston, South Carolina, in the early 1800s. The firm's Liverpool branch, managed by Charles Prioleau of Charleston, outfitted the local blockade-runners and functioned as the secret money dispenser and headquarters for the Confederacy in that part of England.

James Spence, a Liverpool merchant, was the South's most effective British publicist and organizer. Though his business interests and friendships inclined him toward the Yankees, he said, he wrote a polemical book, *The American Union*, in just fourteen white-hot weeks in the summer of 1861. He had no prior experience at writing for publication. Issued that fall, the book went through four editions in six months and helped shape British discussions of the war. A critique of democracies, it argued that tariffs, not slavery, were the true cause of the conflict, and that the South had the right to secede. "It has been very generally read in the educated circles of this country," James Mason reported, "and attracts great attention." Advertised by his book, Spence gave lectures, wrote for *The Times*, and organized Southern Clubs in Liverpool and other cities. His sincere advocacy was good business for him as well: he prospered by investing in Liverpool blockade-runners and, after Mason's endorsement, the Confederate government appointed him its paid financial agent for Great Britain.

In London, the seat of power, a picaresque Southerner of Swiss origins named Henry Hotze published his weekly newspaper, the

Index, as a journal of Dixie propaganda subsidized by the government in Richmond. (The Union, by contrast, had no counterpart anywhere in Britain.) Hotze ran pieces by established English writers, such as Percy Gregg of the *Saturday Review*, and planted many articles and editorials in friendly British newspapers. "A great success," wrote a correspondent for the *Mobile Register and Advertiser* about the *Index*. "The focus and rendezvous of Southerners in London. It is a seminary of Southern intelligence, and a school of Southern writers, not for its own columns, but for the other London papers. The cause of the South now engages some of the ablest pens in London." Hotze and the *Index* of course celebrated the exploits of Raphael Semmes on both his ships.

Semmes spent a few weeks in London in May 1862, between the *Sumter* and the *Alabama*. One day, as he was sitting in his room at Euston Square reading the American news in the *Times*, an Anglican minister named Francis W. Tremlett was brought in and introduced. "I have come to take the Captain of the *Sumter* prisoner, and carry him off to my house, to spend a few days with me," Tremlett announced. "You shall come to my house, stay as long as you please, go away when you please, and see nobody at all unless you please." Even the shy, solitary Semmes could not resist such an invitation. The Tremlett home in Belsize Park, a quiet neighborhood of London, became his favorite refuge in England, then and later. A native of St. John's, Newfoundland, forty-one years old in 1862, the Reverend Tremlett had been vicar of St. Peter's Church for two years. He founded an organization that urged a speedy end to the war; it distributed 20,000 copies of his sermon deploring "the Fratricidal War in America." The household in Belsize Park, known as "the Rebels' Roost" for its frequent hospitality to visiting Confederates, also included Tremlett's mother and unmarried younger sister, Louisa. All were ardent Southern partisans, well connected to local allies of the South.

Of these, the most powerful was William S. Lindsay, a wealthy shipowner and member of Parliament. Visiting the United States in 1860, he had met Semmes in Washington and been impressed by the American's versatile talents. ("How can a nation fail to be great," he later reflected, "which possesses such men as Raphael Semmes.") James Mason brought Semmes to call on Lindsay in London in May 1862, and the acquaintance ripened into a useful friendship. Lindsay's embrace of the Confederacy hurt his businesses; he lost about three thousand pounds a year in commissions with Union shipowners. "My interests were entirely with the North," he recalled. "All my personal friends, and all my business friends held views entirely different." But he sympathized with the South, "a brave and down-trodden nation," and wanted to stop what he regarded as a terrible, useless war. Lindsay always denied the persistent rumors that he owned blockade-runners; his loyalties, he insisted, had nothing at all to do with money or self-interest. "A man of highest consideration here," Mason wrote of Lindsay, "and of weight in Parliament. He is deeply in earnest." Mason, as the Confederacy's representative in London, stayed for weeks at a time at Lindsay's fine home in Shipperton on the Thames.

The Confederate lobby pressed the Palmerston government to offer the South either formal recognition or British diplomatic mediation to end the war. In July 1862 Lindsay introduced a motion in Parliament for recognition: an action of dangerous possible consequences. (If it passed, Secretary of State Seward ordered Adams, he should end his mission in London and prepare for war.) On July 19, Lindsay rose in the House of Commons and changed his motion from recognition to mediation. The debate continued for almost eight hours into the night. Palmerston listened with his eyes closed and hat pulled down, seemingly asleep. At 1:30 in the morning, the ancient prime minister— seventy-seven years old—stood up, tottered a bit, and then delivered an incisive summary of the proceedings that wound up by arguing against mediation. That closed the debate; Lindsay withdrew his motion.

During the following week, the government decided not to stop the *Alabama* from leaving Liverpool despite compelling evidence that she was a warship for the Confederacy, built and equipped in defiance of British law. Taken together, these two actions were a balancing act, tipped first toward the Union, then toward the Confederacy: in sum, another exercise in the government's declared policy of overt neutrality. In the still-roiling wake of the *Trent* affair, Palmerston and Russell could not appear to be shoved around by the Lincoln administration. So, well hedged by excuses and tiny legal niceties, and played against Palmerston's refusal to extend mediation to the South, the *Alabama* was allowed to escape.

Once again, events on the battlefield shaped political decisions. The surging tide of Confederate victories in the summer of 1862 made the war look unwinnable for the Union; so many thousands of deaths for nothing, it seemed. British public opinion shifted even more toward the South. American visitors to England that summer found virtually no support for the Northern cause. Semmes, stopping in Liverpool on his way to take command of the *Alabama*, concluded that nine-tenths of the civilized world were lined up with the Confederacy. "England, in particular, always friendly to us," he wrote home to his daughter Electra, "is becoming more and more our friend as she perceives with what determination and fortitude we carry on the war. . . . Liverpool, if we except some few houses engaged in trade with the Northern States, is a secession city, out and out."

Cruising into this volatile moment in Anglo-American relations, the *Alabama* flashed like a match struck in a room full of gunpowder. At a time of dwindling Union prospects, here was an uncatchable warship— entirely British except for most of her officers—unfairly allowed to sneak out of a British port, and now pillaging Northern commerce on the high seas with devastating impacts at home that kept spreading and metastasizing. The first news of Semmes's whaling bonfires reached London in late September. Ten days later, Chancellor of the Exchequer William Gladstone delivered a speech in Newcastle that soon became notorious. (Over the summer he had met with Henry Hotze of the *Index*, who found him sympathetic, and had read James Spence's *The American Union*.) "We may have our own opinions about slavery," said Gladstone, "we may be for or against the South; but there is no doubt that Jefferson Davis and other leaders of the South have made an army; they are making, it appears, a navy" (a bow toward the recent news of the *Alabama*); "and they have made what is more than either— they have made a nation." Therefore, "we may anticipate with certainty the success of the Southern states so far as regards their separation from the North." In that sequence, the *Alabama* was the clincher that pushed Gladstone to his declaration of nationhood and certain victory for the Confederacy.

Through the fall and winter of 1862–63, Charles Francis Adams peppered Lord Russell at the Foreign Office with protests and warnings about the *Alabama*, demanding compensation for the Union losses. He included detailed affidavits from the owners and captains of

THE ILLUSTRATED LONDON NEWS.

No. 1177.—VOL. XLI.]   SATURDAY, DECEMBER 6, 1862.   [TWO SHEETS, FIVEPENCE

CRIMES OF VIOLENCE IN THE STREETS.

THE uppermost topic of the week—that upon which conversation has been more general, and though more in earnest, than any other—is the frequency and the frightful audacity of crimes of violence in the streets of the metropolis. London has been almost as panic-stricken by prowling gangs of ticket-of-leave men as though a score of tigers were known to be at large. No man out of doors feels sure of his life. In broad daylight, in the most public thoroughfares, at times and in places the most unlikely, men are suddenly throttled or knocked on the head and rifled of any valuables they may chance to have about them. It is as if we had been, by some magical art, thrown back into the middle of the last century, and made the denizens of some Italian city infested with bravos. For aught we can tell, death may be lurking for us under any one of the gateways we have to pass. No one, when leaving his home in the morning for his place of business, is secure against being lodged in an hospital before night, maimed for the remainder of his days. Fear, of course, exaggerates the danger; nevertheless, the danger is real, and exists in fact as well as in fancy. Such a state of things has taken the town by surprise. For a brief interval people have been fairly staggered. Everybody is arming himself with some deadly weapon. There is a momentary tendency—only momentary, we hope—to throw away as useless and deceptive the lessons which it has taken us more than a century to learn, and to regret that our laws are not as savage as they were before Romilly laboured to tone down their harshness or Howard to soften somewhat the intolerable cruelty of prison discipline. The impulse, however, is probably as exceptional as the crime which has excited it. Neither the one nor the other is likely to outlive many weeks.

Taking it for granted, as surely we may consider ourselves entitled to do, that this exceedingly disagreeable and disconcerting phenomenon will speedily disappear, and that the very extravagance of the evil will ensure its quick suppression, it yet remains for us, as a practical people, to search for the causes which have conduced to the eruption. The ugly symptoms are, no doubt, bad enough in themselves; but it were wise, nevertheless, to look at them as protests against some remoter and deeper wrong latent in the body politic. We are not disposed to controvert the position that crime, like disease, occasionally takes an epidemic form; that it is sometimes wayward in its course; or rather, is governed in its forms of manifestation by unaccountable fashions. To some extent, perhaps, we may be at a loss to assign reasons for its sudden outbreak in this or that particular form, or may set down its prevalence under any special guise as due, in part at least, to that imitative propensity which plays so powerfully upon criminals as upon any other portion of the population. But we may reasonably infer that, underlying this law, which more or less is universally operative, there must be some more specific causes to the combined action of which this alarming type of epidemic crime may be pretty clearly traced; and, if so, the mere suppression of it should not content us; for crime, like disease, has always some lesson to impart, and will be apt to reappear again and again, until that lesson has been learned and reduced to practice.

Before proceeding to consider the proximate causes which appear to us to have prepared the way for the singular outbreak, the virulence of which has put the whole metropolis on the *qui vive*, we shall offer a remark or two upon somewhat that lies back of them, partly inherent in our system of law, but rendered still more remarkable by magisterial administration. Whether it be owing to the keen appreciation of property by the British people, to their predominant commercial habits, or to remoter antecedent circumstances, the fact is undeniable that crimes against the person are not dealt with by English law with anything like the severity which is systematically meted out to crimes against property. It is, we think, still less to be denied that our police magistrates, especially in London, ordinarily intensify, by their administration, this serious defect of our criminal code. The ruffian whose ferocious temper has maimed his victim for life, or who, in the indulgence of his brutal passion, has given the bodily constitution a shock from the effects of which it can never recover, commonly escapes with a lighter penalty than the dishonest but often needy wretch who feloniously appropriates to his own use goods to the value of £5 belonging to another. It is almost impossible to read a column or two of police reports without being struck with the ridiculously low appraisement which the magistrates ordinarily put upon the features and limbs of her Majesty's subjects, and with the small legal sacrifice at which brutes in the human form may indulge their barbarity upon the persons of others. Now, whilst such continues to be the case—that is, so long as the laws and their administrators make so light of offences against

A sympathetic English perspective in the fall of 1862, pairing Semmes with Stonewall Jackson as the Confederate heroes of the moment. (*Illustrated London News*, December 6, 1862)

ships destroyed by Semmes and his British craft. Adams did not expect any satisfaction then, but he was building a case for later. "It is very manifest," he told Seward in October, "that no disposition exists here to apply the powers of the government to the investigation of the acts complained of, flagrant as they are, or to the prosecution of the offenders. The main object must now be to make a record which may be of use at some future day." Russell, responding in the elaborate, muffled language of diplomacy, denied any past mistakes or current responsibility for Semmes and his ship.

The drumbeat of *Alabama* news kept pounding unchecked in the North: more captures, more escapes, panic and bafflement. Swelling frustration about the Union Navy's failure to catch the Confederate cruiser spilled over into anger at Britain. "But for the material support given by the British to the rebellion, it would have been over long ago," said the *Philadelphia Evening Bulletin*. "She is fooling us with avowals of neutrality, while she is virtually in alliance with the rebels." "If this craft be not a British pirate," asked *Harper's Weekly*, "what would constitute one? . . . The ruin of this country has evidently been the one object nearest the heart of the British Government." At the Navy Department in Washington, Gideon Welles and Gustavus Fox also blamed their problems on the British. In his annual report, in the section treating the *Alabama*, Welles invoked the sinister names "England" and "Great Britain" fifteen times in five paragraphs. "It is our weak point," Fox argued to the editor of the *Boston Traveller*, "long dreaded and difficult to guard against, where a great nation like England lends her aid to our enemies."

Caught between anger at home and stonewalling in London, Adams had to contend with the sharpest crisis in Anglo-American relations since the *Trent* embarrassment. "The subject which presses most upon me just now," he noted in December, "is the controversy with this Government about the Alabama." He kept hammering away, sending protests from the New York Chamber of Commerce and itemized bills from marine insurance companies. He was just punching a soft, billowing British pillow. "Her Majesty's government entirely disclaim all responsibility for any acts of the Alabama," Russell replied, again, "and they had hoped that they had already made this decision on their part plain to the government of the United States." ("I wonder what Great Britain would say," Adams mused to an influential friend in

Boston, perhaps trying to plant a strategy, "if we resorted to reprisals for the damage done by permitting the departure of the Alabama.")

Aside from the ongoing quarrel about the British provenance of the ship, the startling feats and clever escapes devised by Semmes underlined—once more—the incompetence of the Union military against the apparent mastery of the South. For any British officials contemplating the possibility of an imminent war with the North, that strategic distinction was only reassuring. "It suits well with the brilliant achievements of their land forces," an English military journal sneered in December, "to find the Federal cruisers cautiously giving the one armed vessel of the Confederates a very wide berth." It was surprising, Russell confided to Lord Lyons in Washington, that "with so large a Navy as the United States boast of having, they should not be able to capture, or drive off the seas near their own coast, a single and unsupported vessel such as the Alabama, armed with no more than a few guns, and with a complement of no more than 140 men." Surprising indeed. This further proof of Union ineptitude made victory over the South seem even less likely—and therefore, along with the Alabama's irritation of Anglo-American relations, again encouraged British intervention in a war the Union evidently could not win.

Meantime two new sea monsters were rising at Birkenhead, hidden underneath covered sheds. Commissioned by James Bulloch, designed by Henry Laird, and under construction at the Laird shipyard, they came from the same men who had produced the Alabama. Though these new ships were called "the Laird rams," that name rather missed the point. The bows did taper to iron rams; but three other features made the ships seem uniquely formidable. They were clad with layers of iron plates, five inches thick on the sides, thinning out to two inches at the ends. The armament consisted of two revolving armored turrets, eighty feet apart, with two guns each. And the ships were designed to be seaworthy, twice the size of the Alabama, with two powerful engines, twin screws, and sturdy sailing qualities that would let them roam the ocean at will.

In the spring of 1863, neither the Union nor Confederate Navy mustered any ironclads that could bear the rigors of the North Atlantic Ocean; indeed, the Union's famous Monitor had recently sunk in a gale off Cape Hatteras. If the new Laird ships were, on the precedent of the Alabama, soon released from Liverpool—which seemed more than likely—they might cross the ocean and scatter the Union blockade, even invade Northern ports with impunity. Lincoln's Navy had no vessel, not even the *Vanderbilt*, to match their fearsome panoply of iron skins, armored firepower, and vast oceangoing range.

Desperate circumstances called for desperate measures. Earlier, when urged to acquire fast war steamers in Britain for the Union Navy, to match the *Alabama*, Gustavus Fox had declined on principle. "We cannot leave the home market," he explained; "to do so would be to follow Semmes' path." The looming dangers of the Laird rams overcame any such scruples. Fox sent two influential, interested shipping merchants, John Murray Forbes of Boston and William Aspinwall of New York, to England on a secret mission to buy the rams away from the Lairds. To outbid the Confederates, they carried bonds worth ten million dollars to secure a loan of half that value, one million pounds, from the London banking house of Barings. This was over ten times the contracted price that Bulloch was paying. "You must stop them at all hazards," Fox told Forbes, "as we have no defense against them. Let us have them in the United States for our own purposes, without any more nonsense, and at any price. . . . It is a question of life and death."

Historical events in retrospect look more tidy and inevitable than when they were lived. From a distance, with the secret documents revealed and the divergent versions told and retold by the leading players, and all the sources sifted and compared, the broad patterns and necessary turning points seem clear. The choices look obvious. The dust has settled, usually onto the grubby hands of the historian who is rooting through the archives or peering at dim old microfilms. But historians usually come to understand that almost nothing is truly inevitable in human events. Nearly any episode might have turned out quite differently given variant twists of luck, chance, or contingency. Accident and coincidence often play more telling roles than intentional choices or human will. And always there are roads not taken, leading to later forks and other roads not taken.

This essential unpredictability of history must be borne in mind in order to understand the manifold impacts of the *Alabama*. The winter of 1862–63, the period of the greatest feats for Semmes and his ship, was also the lowest point for the Union in the Civil War. Victory for the North never looked farther away or less possible. The November elections brought Democratic successes and a thumping vote of no confidence in the administration. Northerners were exhausted by all the losing battles and bloodshed, with the end not only nowhere in sight but actually receding from view.

Final victory for the Union could only take the form of an overwhelming triumph, defeating all the Confederate forces on land and sea and breaking the resistant will of an insurgent populace spread across a huge territory of 750,000 square miles. The South was fighting a defensive war for survival, with the tactical and motivational advantages of holding an interior position. "Our men must prevail in combat," wrote John B. Jones, a clerk at a government office in Richmond, in his diary that March, "or lose their property, country, freedom, everything,—at least this is their conviction. On the other hand, the enemy, in yielding the contest, may retire into their own country, and possess everything they enjoyed before the war began." Defending their homeland, repelling invaders, "the armies of the South will fight with Roman desperation."

The eventual outcome of the war was not at all inevitable. While the North needed to win, the South only needed not to lose: a forced stalemate in which the North grew tired of fighting, and dying, and let the Confederacy go its own way after a negotiated peace. The visible signs during that grim winter for the Union pointed toward such a stalemate. British consuls in America, already tilted toward the Confederacy, thought they saw it coming. "The subjugation of the South will ere long be seen to be impracticable," George Moore reported from Richmond, "for the spirit of determination to resist to the last is universal. . . . The reconstruction of the Union I consider an impossibility." The merits of such a reconstruction might well be debated; but as a matter of feasible strategy it was simply unattainable. "The Confederates are resolved," Lord Lyons agreed from Washington, "to accept no terms short of an unqualified admission of their independence. The majority of the people of the North are weary of the war. . . . There is no longer even a semblance of unanimity in the North."

On many levels, Semmes and the *Alabama* encouraged hopes for a standoff. Along with destroying Union commerce, stampeding the merchant fleet into foreign ownership, and diverting limited naval resources from the blockade, they exerted a psychological impact on the North that chipped away at its will to keep fighting. Invading both Northern enterprise and home front morale, the Confederate cruiser seemed to be everywhere yet nowhere, too swift to be caught, a phantom and a pealing alarm bell in the night. Semmes was in fact just smarter, more adroit, than any Union commander sent after his disappearing wake. For the Confederacy at home, the *Alabama* expanded its concept of nationhood and spread military success into a novel arena of warfare. The salty air that was blowing out of Union hopes was blowing into Confederate aspirations. Many people in Richmond were expecting peace within three months.

In Great Britain, James Bulloch was working toward building four more versions of the *Alabama*. The Laird rams promised, if released on the precedent of the *Alabama*, to shred Union naval forces and drive the North toward capitulation. Given the bitter Anglo-American frictions over the suspicious escape and ongoing captures of the *Alabama*, the friendly government in London might still extend its recognition or mediation to the South. Or the United States and Britain might even fall into their third war in less than a century. Charles Wilkes was, after his typical fashion, arrogantly bumbling around the Caribbean, offending the local diplomatic missions of Mexico, Spain, France, Denmark, and—especially—Great Britain. (The *Trent* villain was lodged in London's throat.) "We are indeed drifting towards the iron bound coast of England," agreed Thurlow Weed, Secretary Seward's shrewd old political operative, after an informal diplomatic mission to London that winter. "I too for some time have seen that we shall inevitably clash with that power. We cannot stand any more *Alabama*s."

SIX

The Turncoats

Semmes needed to run. The cannon fire of the *Alabama*'s battle with the *Hatteras* on January 11, 1863, had lit up the night sky. Men on the other Union warships at Galveston, fifteen miles away, could hear the guns booming and see high flares of the muzzle flashes. Semmes knew they would get up steam and come to investigate. After rescuing 118 officers and men from the *Hatteras*, and watching her sink, Semmes doused all the lights on his ship and took off. "We are very much crowded with prisoners," he wrote in his journal, "but every one seems to be doing well."

Under both steam and sail, reaching for speed, they headed southeasterly across the Gulf of Mexico, back to the Yucatán passage. A moderate gale blew in, right in their faces, slowing them down. For three days the *Alabama* fought the adverse winds and currents, losing about three miles an hour and burning off precious coal. With no pursuers in sight and fuel running low, Semmes decided to bank the fires in his boilers and raise the propeller. He hove the ship to under single-reefed trysails, on a starboard tack. Two days of difficult sailing through gales and rain, under a "dull, hard-looking sky," brought them to the narrowing channel off Yucatán. They got through that bottleneck safely. Needing to rid himself of all those enemy prisoners, and expecting a friendly welcome at the British colony of Jamaica, Semmes ordered a straight course into Kingston.

The *Alabama* anchored on January 20. "Her arrival at this port has caused the greatest excitement," wrote the Kingston correspondent for a Liverpool newspaper, "and hundreds have been down to look at a vessel which has made such unprecedented havoc in the ranks of her enemies." The famous captain went ashore to see the local British commodore, Hugh Dunlop. Semmes was given permission to land his prisoners, take on coal and provisions, and repair six shot holes near the waterline. "The necessity of the repairs was obvious," Dunlop noted. But he urged the Confederate, in the interest of British neutrality, not to tarry long. "If I remain here one hour more than can be avoided," Semmes agreed, "I shall run the risk of finding a squadron of my enemies outside, for no doubt they will be in pursuit of me immediately." He could never, even in this apparently safe harbor, lower his guard and escape the tension and worry over the next ship on the horizon.

But for five days, until shipwrights finished fixing the damage, Semmes and his men enjoyed their first extended holiday since leaving Liverpool almost six months earlier. An English friend, a minister named Fyfe, came on board and invited the captain to visit his home in the mountains behind Kingston. Leaving the ship under the ever-watchful command of First Lieutenant John Kell, Semmes and the Reverend Fyfe rode out in his carriage from the hot, dusty town. For ten miles they wheeled along a fine natural road, lined by palm trees and giant cacti, passing well-maintained rural homes and farms, green valleys and forests. It felt so cool, quiet, and secluded: such a marked and sudden contrast to life on the *Alabama*. At the foot of the mountains, they switched to horseback and bridle paths and climbed through changing levels of plants and trees. They wound up at Fyfe's home—an exact duplication of an English country house, down to the proper shrubs and flowers. Semmes could glimpse his ship at anchor far below, looking like a distant seabird. He slept well that night, on sweet-smelling sheets, and woke to a chorus of songbirds. Lulled and beguiled, he spent another day in the mountains, making social calls and being celebrated. A party in the evening even included pretty women (of whom he always took keen, appreciative notice, especially after long months of monotonous masculine company).

Back down in Kingston, he learned that friends had announced he would give a speech at the Merchants' Exchange at noon. He stood on a table to address the curious crowd. "Gentlemen," he began, "we have been oppressed—I say oppressed—and we bore it, and bore it, till we could bear it no longer, and we have commenced to fight, and will fight to the bitter end." The audience—"Hear, hear!"—urged him on.

Thank you for your cordial sympathy, and the same kind welcome that I found in England. For we are all of kindred blood and interests.

When the Southern states desired to sever themselves from the North, what more did they do than follow the original example when, as a colonial possession of England, America fought for and gained her liberty? [Hear!] No, they were not rebels; they were fighting for the great cause nearest the heart of every man, and especially an Englishman's [cheers], for the same liberty for which Englishmen themselves fought till the glorious event of Magna Charta.

The entire world would benefit from Southern independence, Semmes predicted. With no tariffs or trade barriers, the South could buy silks from France, broadcloth from England, and even onions and pails from the Yankees. (And, more to the point, Southern cotton could flow unimpeded to British textile mills. An alliance of the two nations would nurture both liberty and commerce, ideal and real.)

The *Alabama*'s sailors were meanwhile enjoying their own kind of liberty. Fresh from the pounding excitement of sinking the *Hatteras*, bulging with unspent monthly wages, they descended on Kingston for their first real shore leave of the cruise, in a seaport town that offered all the usual sailors' pleasures. With Semmes away in the mountains, even the thunderous Kell could not keep them in line. They roared around Kingston, drinking at will and picking fights, yet still embraced by the local residents. They were Confederate heroes in a Confederate nest. "It is impossible to describe the hospitable welcome we received," Master's Mate George Fullam wrote in his journal. "Every one placing their houses at our disposal . . . all expressing a most hearty encouraging sympathy for our cause." Eight sailors liked Kingston so well they deserted the ship and stayed on. Three others tried to join them, leaping overboard into supply boats, but were chased down and hauled back to their duties.

Two other deserters came, months later, to assume surprising roles in the diplomatic fencing between the United States and Great Britain. John Latham, a fireman from Liverpool, was tired of shoveling coal down in the hot, choking boiler room and wanted to go home to his wife. Unacquainted with the ship's history and connections, he couldn't reveal much. But Clarence Randolph Yonge could. A true Confederate from Savannah, sent to Liverpool and employed by James Bulloch at the Fraser, Trenholm office during 1862, and then the trusted paymaster on the *Alabama* from the start of her cruise, Yonge held a position of real responsibility. At a time when the British provenance of the ship was being disputed between London and Washington, he knew the background and inner workings of the *Alabama*, down to the names and origins of every man on board. Coming into Kingston, he had written a long, chatty letter to a friend in England, proudly recounting the battle with the *Hatteras* and cheering for the *Alabama*, "a name that causes Yankee hearts to quake, whenever and wherever her name is pronounced." He apparently believed in the Southern cause.

Clarence Yonge, though, was a man of no principles, selfish and ruthless. He had left a wife and child in Savannah. Sent ashore in Kingston with money to pay the ship's bills, he instead got drunk and squandered the purse on various amusements. Kell forcibly brought him back to the ship. Semmes gave Yonge a curt, angry hearing and dismissed him from the Confederate service. Set adrift in Kingston, he courted another woman—who was perhaps of mixed race, white and black—and, without deigning to mention his wife back in Savannah, married her too. Eventually Yonge took all her money and made his way to Liverpool. There, broke and running short of options, still picking at the scabs of his anger and craving revenge against his former shipmates, he decided (for a fee) to tell the Union authorities in England everything he knew.

At sea again, coaled and repaired, the *Alabama* headed east. At 10:30 in the morning of the first day out, they found a handsome, freshly painted bark lying helpless and becalmed. Her tapering masts and white cotton sails marked her as a Yankee: the *Golden Rule*, bound from New York to Aspinwall. Semmes showed his U.S. flag. The quarry answered with their own U.S. flag, whereupon Semmes ran up his true colors and pounced. The enemy crew was obliged to help transfer some preserved meats, clams, lobsters, crushed sugar, candies, and sweetmeats (all luxuries welcome on the *Alabama*). The booty included a box of India rubber dolls, seemingly of no interest to Semmes, that cried when squeezed. According to the Yankee captain's report, the ferocious pirate—described as "a mere skeleton of a man"—amused himself by sitting on deck and squeezing the dolls to make them cry. It could be seen, depending on one's loyalty, as either charming or sadistic. The *Golden Rule* was torched late that afternoon.

The roistering sailors, now sober, still looked terrible. Their adventures in Kingston had left them with blackened and reddened eyes, broken noses, dirty clothes, frowsy hair, and matted beards. The captain inspected them with his usual fond contempt for their wayward habits. "Sick list largely increased," he scolded in his journal, exasperated but not surprised, "from the dissipation of my vagabonds on shore. It will take me at least a week to get the rum out of them, and to try the more vicious by court-martial." The relentless shipboard regimens of hard physical labor and regular sleep, with regulated portions of grog, gradually cleared their eyes and heads. The ship's bell tolled the watches and the familiar routines snapped into place. Old Beeswax and the First Luff again took control of their childlike charges.

(Though not entirely, then or ever. Two months later, Semmes caught two ships from Boston, the *Nora* and the *Charles Hill*. Half a dozen of their crewmen agreed to join the *Alabama*, replacing most of the losses in Kingston. Before the two Boston vessels were burned, though, lifted bottles of liquid contraband were smuggled onto the *Alabama*. "Several of my rascals have gotten drunk as usual," Semmes recorded, "when they can get liquor on board the prizes, which they do sometimes, in spite of all precautions, and these are sometimes my best men, who can be trusted with everything but whisky." Sailors were still sailors.)

A day after the *Golden Rule*, the *Alabama* burned another prize, the brig *Chastelaine*, and kept moving eastward. After landing the crews of these two prizes at Santo Domingo, they crept through the Mona Passage, between Puerto Rico and Hispaniola. This strait was, again, left unguarded by the Union Navy. Semmes's quick flight from Galveston had succeeded; his chasers as usual had no idea where he was. During the month after sinking the *Hatteras*, the *Alabama* was reported near Havana, and off Bermuda, and at the Cayman Islands northwest of Jamaica; furthermore, she was certainly in the Mediterranean Sea or headed for the Eastern Hemisphere, into the Indian Ocean. All these reports were fanciful. It took three weeks or more for hard news of the Jamaican sojourn, and then of the *Golden Rule* and *Chastelaine* bonfires, to reach Northern cities. "It is high time Semmes was sent to the bottom of the sea," said the *Boston Post* after these tidings, "or the bottomless pit, or hanged at the yard arm of some American war vessel. But where is the man to catch him?"

By then Semmes was once more loose in the Atlantic Ocean. From the Mona Passage he turned due north and slowly made his way up to the vicinity of the thirtieth parallel, about a thousand miles east of Florida. Working under sail to save coal, he encountered wildly variable winds. A whistling gale blew through one night, agitating the brackish bilgewater so much that its fumes blackened metals and paintwork and disturbed the captain's delicate sleep. The wind then practically disappeared for five days, holding the ship to a puny total of just 180 miles over that time.

"A gloomy Sabbath upon the sea," Semmes recorded, "bringing naturally to the mind thoughts of home and family and the possible termination of the war." A week later, on the second anniversary of his resignation from the U.S. Navy: "I have more and more reason, as time rolls on, to be gratified at my prompt determination to quit the service of a corrupt and fanatical majority." (Actually his decision was not prompt but cautious and delayed; he was projecting his current zeal back to early 1861.) "The politicians had become political stockjobbers, and the seekers of wealth had become knaves and swindlers; and into these two classes may be divided nearly the whole Yankee population."

Now he was taking the war to stockjobbers and swindlers. For the third time, he settled into a busy crossroads of ocean traffic, where the most popular shipping lanes converged and he could simply sit and wait for pigeons to come to hand. Any sailing ship bound from the West Indies to Brazil had to beat far to the east along the thirtieth parallel of latitude, into the fickle winds called the "variables," in order then to venture south and eventually maneuver around Cape St. Roque at the northeastern corner of South America. Toward the end of February, Semmes reached the busiest "crossing" at the intersection of thirty degrees north latitude and forty degrees west longitude. There, at midocean, U.S. ships plying the rich Asian trade, bound to and from Cape Horn, usually passed in thick clusters. In ten days, the *Alabama* overhauled and boarded thirty-one ships that looked like Yankees. But only five were actually Yankees; Semmes burned three of them, bonded one, and ransomed one. It was apparent that Union skippers and shipowners, at least, had realized they might avoid the *Alabama* by skirting the busiest shipping lanes. Nobody at Gideon Welles's Navy Department, it seemed, could deduce the corollary: to catch the pirate, go patrol those same lanes.

A prize taken on March 2, the *John A. Parks* of Hallowell, Maine, yielded enemy newspapers to the tenth of February. From them the men on the *Alabama* learned that the Confederate cruiser *Florida* had run the blockade out of Mobile in January. The news was over six weeks old—but still most welcome. "We have thus doubled our means of destroying the enemy's commerce," Semmes noted. The *Florida*, also built in Liverpool under James Bulloch's supervision, had escaped England in the spring of 1862; delayed by yellow fever and other problems, she was finally starting to make captures. The *Jacob Bell*, burned on February 12, was valued with her cargo at $1.5 million: the plumpest trophy of the entire war, it turned out, for the Confederate Navy. For the Union cause, the *Florida* meant another British pirate out marauding the ocean. "England is so much grieved at our domestic troubles," cracked a punster in Philadelphia, "that she gives vent to it in *fitting private teers.*"

Semmes turned the *Alabama* to the south and set a course for Brazil. His British coal tender, the *Agrippina*, was supposed to meet him at the Brazilian offshore island of Fernando de Noronha. On the long pull southward, the men changed from winter clothes and layers of blankets at night into summer whites and bare feet. Approaching the equator, they passed out of the trade winds and heard thunder rolling for the first time in months. It sounded welcoming and familiar, like the soft, warm breezes bathing their faces. Under a rainy calm the officers and men alike played around on the deck like ducks, paddling barefoot in the gentle downpour, waiting for the wind.

On March 23, in this amiable tropical mood, they caught a U.S. whaling schooner, the *Kingfisher* from Fairhaven, Massachusetts. "Must say that I was treated well," reported her veteran captain, Thomas F. Lambert, when he got home. "Captain Semmes gave me all my nautical instruments." (This was a startling departure from Semmes's usual practice.) "With him I had but little conversation." (Quite usual.) "But he appeared like a perfect gentleman, and his language was such." Lieutenant Kell seemed the same, and the cruiser's young midshipmen did him many small favors during his twenty-three days as a guest of the Confederacy. "Although Capt. Semmes burned my vessel and caused me great loss," Lambert concluded, "yet I have no reason to call him a bad man or pronounce such epithets upon him as many have done. I can only speak for myself."

A few days later they stopped and boarded an English bark, the *Chili*. At first, taking their typical approach, they pretended to be Yankees. Concluding that the bark was indeed English, they continued the masquerade; no point in revealing the whereabouts of the *Alabama* if it wasn't necessary. The men of the *Chili*, in a helpful spirit of Anglo-American friendship, said they'd heard the dreaded *Alabama* had whipped a Union vessel twice her size—so they warned their new friends not to fight her should they meet. (The Confederates must have struggled to maintain straight faces.)

In turbid, squally weather, under lowering black clouds, the *Alabama* crossed the equator for the first time on March 29. They chased a distant sail for a while but lost her in the murky conditions.

On April Fools' Day, Clarence Yonge presented himself at the U.S. legation in London. He was not unexpected. Thomas H. Dudley, the vigilant U.S. consul in Liverpool, had from his mysterious espionage sources secured a letter and other papers relating to Yonge, which he had sent along to London. Charles Francis Adams therefore knew about Yonge's behavior in Kingston and his bigamous second marriage. The U.S. minister in London was still interested in the lapsed Confederate. "He said that he would cheerfully testify to anything he knew," Adams wrote to his boss in Washington, Secretary of State William Seward. "He seems not to be wanting in intelligence or ability to tell the truth when he has a mind to. . . . Possibly he might be made useful in spite of the circumstances which necessarily impair confidence in his permanent fidelity."

Adams asked the secretary of the legation, Benjamin Moran, to have Yonge swear an oath of allegiance to the United States. Moran—who had been serving in London for years and was not easily impressed—found Yonge to be "a young man of rather good manners," twenty-nine years old, talented, and of well-developed perceptive faculties. "He took the oath," Moran recorded in his copious diary, "and then talked freely of the exploits of the pirate. I expressed myself very strongly against her and her crew, and thus drew from him the fact that he still had a good deal of the rebel in him." Why, then, was he now turning for the Union and against the *Alabama*? "The result in a measure of empty pockets and partly a matter of revenge," Moran supposed. "Still, he is a slippery fellow." Adams authorized Dudley to assume charge of the turncoat. After taking a long deposition from Yonge, probing his memory for any relevant details about the *Alabama* and her cruise until Kingston, Dudley brought him back to Liverpool and placed him on a modest retainer of five pounds a month—enough to live on, but not to book passage, yet, on a steamship to America.

Yonge's deposition, a crucial document in the history of the *Alabama*, confirmed similar sworn statements by three other men with links to the cruiser. One of them, Henry Redden, helped take the ship from Liverpool to her fitting-out at the Azores in August 1862, but then instead of signing on for the cruise had resisted Semmes's recruiting speech and returned home on the *Bahama*. Redden gave Thomas Dudley a deposition on September 3. Five months earlier, he said, he had shipped as boatswain's mate on a vessel then known as the *290* lying at Laird's dock. When the ship crept out of Liverpool at the end of July, a "Captain Bullock" was aboard. (At the time, James Bulloch's connection to the ship was still not proven.) Redden described the diversionary party of Laird ladies and gentlemen, the stealthy voyage to the Azores, and the arrival there of an English bark with guns, ammunition, and coal. Then Semmes joined them on another ship with forty sailors, two cannon, and two safes full of money in gold. Redden recounted the dickering between Semmes and the crewmen, and the inflated enticements he offered. "When we left the Alabama," he said, "she was all ready for fighting, and steering to sea. I heard Captain Semmes say he was going to cruise in the track of the ships going from New York to Liverpool, and Liverpool to New York." (Perhaps this was an intentional feint by the captain: actually he first trolled around the Azores in whaling season, then went on to the transatlantic shipping lanes off the Newfoundland Banks.)

Redden provided the Union authorities their first detailed account, under oath, of the *Alabama*'s initial month at sea. He also added to the mounting evidence of British collusion and responsibility for the ship. At the legation in London, in the crossfire of Anglo-American tensions, Benjamin Moran heard the boatswain's mate's story and could barely contain himself. "She is now at her hellish work under the pious, honorable, and spotless British flag," he sputtered in his diary. "To all intents and purposes she is a pirate, built, manned, armed, and fitted out from England. . . . And if we some day don't make these canting hypocrites pay for the vessels this British pirate may destroy, I shall lose all faith in the justice of Providence."

Another witness, George King, a sailor from Liverpool, never actually set foot on the *Alabama*. According to his deposition of September 27, 1862, he was hired by a man named Barnett on August 12 "to go on a secret expedition," perhaps to run the blockade on the *290*. "Asked where they were going to, and was told they were going to have some fun; that was all he was told." At midnight, concealed by darkness, he was taken aboard the *Bahama*. They sailed for the Azores at six o'clock that morning. "As soon as we got there Captain Semmes told us the 290 was a confederate gunboat, and was going on a three years' cruise; that every vessel she took or destroyed would be valued, and one-half go to the confederate government and the other half to the crew of the gunboat."

King listened to the recruiting pitch but was not persuaded. "I and about eight others refused to go when we found what the 290 was going for." From the *Bahama*, King watched the transfer of large guns and ammunition and the installation of machinery for the two swivel cannon. He could tell who was in charge ("Saw Captain Bullock superintending the fitting and arming the gunboat 290") and where everything came from ("The three vessels flew the British flag all the time the 290 was arming, and until the Sunday we left her outside Terceira Bay"). At one o'clock that day, men on the *290* lowered the British flag and raised a Confederate banner at the peak and a St. George's Cross at the foremast: the flags themselves proclaiming an alliance of London with Richmond. King then returned to Liverpool with Bulloch and Redden on the *Bahama*.

The motives of Redden and King for giving these depositions remain unknowable. They were British subjects, providing information of potential harm to their country's diplomatic interests. Perhaps they were unsophisticated seafaring men, not aware of the implications of what they were saying; or perhaps they, like most members of the British working class, were opposed to slavery and the Confederate cause and wished to help the Union. Both men had refused to join the *Alabama*. Thomas Dudley probably paid them something for their testimony—though it seems no hard evidence of such an exchange has survived. Dudley's sleuthing activities in Liverpool were, by their nature, shadowy and concealed.

A third witness was John Latham, a fireman on the *Alabama*. He deserted the ship in Kingston in January 1863 and made his way home to Liverpool. His deposition was given to Dudley a year later. In early August 1862, he said, he signed on to the *Bahama* "for a voyage to Nassau and back." They left at midnight, stopping in the river Mersey to pick up Bulloch, Semmes, and others. After a few days at sea, they were told the real destination was the Azores. "Captain Bullock, on the passage out, and after we arrived at Terceira, used arguments to induce us to join the Alabama." During the transfer of supplies and ordnance, Semmes and Bulloch went back and forth between the ships. Semmes gave his recruiting speech on the *Bahama*, followed by a further plea from the Englishman John Low, soon to become fourth lieutenant on the *Alabama*. Low came on board the *Bahama* in his uniform, Latham testified, "endeavoring to induce the men to come forward and join, and he succeeded in getting the best part of us. I was one who went at the last minute."

Latham provided a crew-level perspective on the cruise, including one detail that was kept from the captain. When the *Alabama* took the brig *Dunkirk* on October 7, they caught a sailor named George Forrest, who had deserted from Semmes's former command on the *Sumter*. Semmes could have hanged him as a deserter; instead the captain told Forrest that he might retain him in service through the war at no pay, but that if the sailor behaved himself he would get the same wage and prize money as the other men. But Forrest was incorrigible, taking a lead role in the near mutiny at Martinique in November.

According to Latham, Forrest "was frequently punished by having his hands and legs fastened to the rigging, the punishment being known as 'the spread eagle,' and he would be kept in this position for four hours at a time, and this was done at least twenty times." Finally he was locked in irons, both arms and legs, and left at the desolate island of Blanquilla, far from the mainland of Venezuela. The sailors and firemen of the *Alabama*, talking it over in the forecastle, evidently sympathized with their spread-eagled shipmate. They raised a purse of about seventeen pounds, "unknown to Captain Semmes, which we gave him [Forrest] in the hope of its being some inducement to a vessel to take him off."

Latham's wage was seven pounds a month. A note authorizing a monthly half-pay stipend for Latham's wife, Martha, was drawn on Fraser, Trenholm and Company of Liverpool—proving that Confederate firm's link to the *Alabama*. The note was signed by Semmes, Clarence Yonge as paymaster, and Breedlove Smith as captain's clerk. (When he got back to Liverpool, Latham called at the Fraser, Trenholm office for the balance of his wages; "they declined to pay me, and denied all knowledge of the ship.") Latham also testified to another British connection: the coaling rendezvous at Blanquilla with the supply ship *Agrippina*, which was "flying the British flag and loaded with coals from Cardiff." Along with Redden and King, Latham helped draw the many lines from the *Alabama* back to the Confederate British and the British Confederates.

The turning of Clarence Yonge, though, was the real coup. The paymaster simply knew more than the sailor, the fireman, and the boatswain's mate put together. Yonge was surely a drunken scoundrel; but he could clean up and seem plausible, whether at the U.S. legation in London or later when testifying in court. He presented the smooth surface of an expert, calculating confidence man. His letters to Thomas Dudley, now in Dudley's collected papers at the Huntington Library in California, were written in a graceful, flowing hand, correct as to spelling and grammar, and with occasional ambitious literary flourishes. When Semmes threw him off the *Alabama*, Yonge took away some materials that documented his functions as paymaster. (A pocket-sized account book listed, among other matters, liquor and clothing disbursements to the officers and crew; the items billed to the captain included buttons, an ornament, two undershirts, and two pairs of drawers.) These documents established a tangible, undeniable basis for the song Yonge was now singing.

Yet Yonge's greatest contribution to the Union cause was his selective, vengeful, self-serving memory. His main deposition was sworn at a judge's chambers in Chancery Lane, London, on April 2, 1863. Yonge said nothing about his earlier life or his wife and child in Savannah. He arrived in Liverpool, he said, in March 1862 on the steamship *Annie Childs* from Wilmington, sent over for the specific purpose of acting as paymaster on the *Alabama*. From a desk at the Fraser, Trenholm office, he paid the monthly wages of the Confederate officers waiting to serve on the *Alabama*. James Bulloch had come to England to build two cruisers for the Confederate Navy "with the understanding that he was to have command of one of the vessels. I have heard him say so; and I have learned this also from the correspondence between him and Mr. Mallory . . . which passed through my hands." As to the disputed contract for the *Alabama*, "I have seen it myself. I made a copy from the original. The copy was in the ship. It was signed by Captain Bullock, on the one part, and Messrs. Laird on the other. . . . The ship cost, in United States money, about two hundred and fifty-five thousand dollars. This included provisions, &c., enough for a voyage to the East Indies, which Messrs. Laird were, by the contract, to provide."

Before the ship was launched, Yonge went over to the Laird shipyard in Birkenhead and boarded her with Bulloch. He also saw the Lairds at the Fraser, Trenholm office.

> I have not the slightest doubt that they perfectly well knew that such steamer was being built for the southern confederacy, and that she was to be used in war against the government of the United States. When the vessel sailed from Liverpool she had her shot-racks fitted in the usual places; she had sockets in her decks, and the pins fitted which held fast frames or carriages for the pivot guns, and breaching bolts. These had been placed in by the builders of the vessel.

The ship was obviously not intended for peaceful trade.

The *Alabama* sailed from Liverpool on July 29, three or four days sooner than expected. "The reason for our sailing at this time, before we contemplated, was on account of information which we had received that proceedings were being commenced to stop the vessel." After boarding, one of the Laird brothers gave Yonge £312 in British gold, the balance remaining from various purchases—beds, blankets, tinware, knives, and forks—that he, as the builder, had made for the ship. Yonge and all the other officers understood the purpose of the vessel and her contemplated cruise, and when they left on the pretended party excursion they knew they were not coming back.

Yonge supplied additional details about the fitting-out at the Azores. The *Agrippina* was nominally owned by Sinclair, Hamilton and Company of London, but actually belonged to the Confederacy. Yonge gave exact descriptions of the guns and ammunition transferred to the *Alabama*, all the way down to the rifles, pistols, and cartridges. The cannon were manufactured by Fawcett, Preston of Liverpool. The bulging war chest of £20,000 was equally divided between British gold sovereigns and bank bills. In his speech on the *Alabama*, Semmes held out generous financial rewards, "at the same time appealing to them, as British sailors, to aid him in defending the side of the weak."

As paymaster, Yonge prepared two sets of articles: one for men shipping for a limited time, the other for the duration of the war. Of eighty-four men who signed up at the Azores, all but three joined for the entire war. In his six months on board, from recording and dispensing their monthly wages Yonge came to know the men by name and background. "There were not more than ten or twelve Americans," he estimated. Aside from one Spaniard, all the rest were British. From memory, Yonge could list the names of twenty-five officers and sixty-two petty officers, sailors, and firemen who were on the *Alabama* when he deserted. Until Yonge's deposition, to outsiders most of these men were blanks, anonymous and stateless. Now they gained significant identities.

In every sense, at every level except that of Semmes and the top tier of officers, the *Alabama* was a British ship, and James Bulloch was, beyond dispute, a Confederate agent operating illegally in Britain. Whatever his motives, Yonge knew his facts and told the truth. The layered significance of his sworn testimony—legal, political, and diplomatic—was apparent. Charles Francis Adams at once sent copies of the deposition to Seward in Washington and to Russell at the Foreign Office in London.

Dudley took steps to protect his prize witness, both from the Confederates in Liverpool and, probably, from his own self-destructive tendencies. The Union consul dispatched Yonge to the rural outskirts of Sheffield, about sixty miles east of Liverpool, and—to occupy his time—encouraged him to start writing an *Alabama* memoir. "I am finally domiciled in this place," Yonge wrote Dudley nine days after signing his deposition, "which in that portion where I am is more like a country village than a city, being nearly out of the incorporated limits." In two days, he promised Dudley, "I will commence my manuscript of the cruize of the Alabama, and will send to you when finished." The paymaster's memoir never got written. Clarence Yonge stuck around, doing no work, waiting for his monthly five pounds from Dudley.

The *Alabama* was running short of coal. Her bunkers had not been filled for over two months, since her stop at Kingston. Even with the propeller raised and, as usual, proceeding under sail power alone, the ship still had to burn coal to condense fresh water. The condenser was—in the best circumstances—pushed hard to produce the needed supply; and under a tropical sun the men needed even more water. At the end of March 1863 two prizes yielded some coal, but not much. The *Agrippina* was supposed to meet them with another load of fuel at Fernando de Noronha. But her captain, known for drinking and talking too much in seaport bars along the way, was not considered reliable. What if he didn't show up at the appointed place and time?

As commander of the *Alabama*, Semmes was tenacious, experienced, and endlessly resourceful and imaginative. And he was lucky. On April 4, a few degrees south of the equator, the lookout cried, "Sail ho!" at nine o'clock in the morning. The stranger, a handsome, tall ship of Yankee design, took off. The chase lasted all day. Just before sunset, the quarry showed a U.S. flag. With darkness closing in and the ships still a couple of miles apart, Semmes lowered a boarding party in a whaleboat; because the wind was abating, a crew of oarsmen could move faster than the *Alabama* under sail. After reaching her at ten o'clock, they wore the prize around and brought her back under the lee of the cruiser.

She was the *Louisa Hatch* of Rockland, Maine, bound from Cardiff to Ceylon with, if you please, a thousand tons of the finest, clean-burning Welsh coal. Such an impossible coincidence seemed providential—"a godsend in mid-ocean," as John Kell put it— bestowing not just more coal than they could use, but exactly the right kind for their line of work. "It was the very quality that we preferred," Lieutenant Arthur Sinclair noted, "being nearly smokeless, not likely to attract the attention of our prey when out of our sight, and free from the dust and smut which we disliked so much on our decks." Semmes decided to bring the *Hatch* along to Brazil, where coal could fetch seventeen dollars a ton. After a few days of groping through thick weather and worrying about losing his prize, Semmes got up steam and took the *Hatch* under tow. He tried to start coaling at sea by sending boats back and forth; but a coal-laden boat could not be safely warped against the *Alabama* while she was still steaming ahead, no matter how slowly. Then the abrupt strains of stopping and starting broke the towlines. After losing a night's sleep in all the commotion—the captain liked to guard his slumber—Semmes called it off until they came into Fernando de Noronha.

On April 10 they reached the island, a solitary volcanic upheaval 225 miles off the Brazilian coast. Like the *Alabama*'s previous coaling venues at Blanquilla and the Arcas, it was isolated and thinly populated, lightly policed and readily manipulated by an assertive attorney–sea captain with a lawbook in his hand. The governor of the island, a major in the Brazilian Army, was at once impressed by his illustrious visitor. The cruiser's outlaw reputation was no impediment because Fernando de Noronha was a penal colony, inhabited by one thousand of Brazil's most distinguished felons. With no means of escape, they were allowed to roam the island in contained freedom.

Semmes sent his respects to the governor, who suggested an exchange of supplies (fresh meat for wine, flour, sugar, and coffee) and invited the captain to his residence. Semmes found the governor and his family at breakfast; among the party were an old German forger and his pretty blond daughter, who was keeping her father company during his sentence. (The forger was a gentleman, explained the governor, not a common criminal.) After breakfast Semmes was presented to some of the local gentry who had come to meet him. He chatted and smoked with a polite, well-dressed group of murderers and forgers.

The governor then took him on a horseback tour of the island, up to the summit and through a dense forest to a coconut plantation, under intermittent drenching showers. Riding along, stopping for grapes, they discussed slavery and racial mixing in Brazil; the governor's wife was "a sprightly, bright mulatto," Semmes had noticed. "The governor expressed himself our very good friend," wrote the diplomatic captain in his journal. The governor sent him a turkey accompanied by a bouquet of roses from the mulatto wife. "The roses were very sweet," Semmes allowed, "and made me homesick for awhile."

The feeling stretched across a few days. Off the ship, in another man's family circle, among flowers and trees, he always started thinking about the home and family he had left behind. He had not seen them for over two years. "The island, after the rain, is blooming in freshness and verdure, and as my eye roams over its green slopes and vales, looking so peaceful and inviting, I long for the repose and quiet of peace in my own land. I do not think it can be far off." With many other Southerners in the spring of 1863, he was hoping, even expecting the war to end soon.

The *Alabama* hung around the island for twelve days, waiting for the *Agrippina*, but she never appeared. The *Louisa Hatch* now seemed even more heaven-sent. To speed the loathed chore of coaling, Semmes tried lashing the two ships together. But with no protected harbor, so far out at sea, the waves were too rough. The *Alabama*'s forechannels, the horizontal external timbers at the bow, were crushed, and the main topsail yard was lost. So the ships were separated and the sailors started lugging boatloads of coal from the *Hatch*. During five days of baking heat and humidity, sweating and swearing, they poured 280 tons down the coal scuttles. Just after they finished, as if on cue, two U.S. whalers came by. It took the *Alabama* more than an hour to weigh anchor and get up steam, but she quickly caught them both. Semmes sold some of the *Hatch*'s leftover coal to a Brazilian schooner. He then burned all three prizes and got permission to land their 106 prisoners on Fernando de Noronha.

In a celebrating mood, the officers and sailors of the *Alabama* went ashore for their first liberty since Jamaica, three months earlier. The island lacked bars and brothels—but it had plenty of fish, turtles, game, and fruits. After dreary months of seafaring meals dominated by beans, hardtack, and salted meat, the men happily foraged and gorged themselves without the harmful excesses of Kingston. It was the best time since the start of the cruise. Five sailors from the prizes, watching the frolic, were persuaded to join the *Alabama*—bringing her to a full complement at last. "We have had a glorious outing, are fat and saucy, and ready for spoils," Arthur Sinclair wrote. "We are departing in the best possible order for business."

Their visit left harder repercussions. The U.S. minister in Rio de Janeiro, James Watson Webb, heard a report that Semmes and the governor had been "mutually polite—exchanging visits, and driving out together," and that Semmes had "bought everything of which he stood in need, and landed his prisoners" and had improperly seized the two whalers within Brazilian territorial waters. Webb protested to the Brazilian Ministry of Foreign Affairs that the governor, in a clear violation of neutrality, gave "countenance and support to the pirate." The ministry agreed and the governor was abruptly removed from office. Six days after the *Alabama* left the island, the Confederate cruiser *Florida* encountered a much frostier reception. The new governor arrived and asked the captain of the *Florida* to leave at once.

Semmes kept heading south, toward the Brazilian port of Bahia. Fully coaled and crewed, he could finally achieve his ambition, thwarted aboard the *Sumter*, of patrolling the high-traffic sea-lanes off the northeast coast of Brazil. In ten days they snatched four prizes. Among the passengers were, alas, some women and children, never welcome in the tight, manly quarters on the lower deck. But the fourth of these captures, the fine clipper *Sea Lark* on May 3, became a particular coup. A relatively large ship of 973 tons, she was bound from Boston to San Francisco with a lavish load of general cargo. Her skipper, W. F. Peck, tried an evading tactic, but the breeze was light and the *Alabama* was faster under sail. When Semmes came up showing U.S. colors and fired his warning shot, Peck at once brought his ship by the wind and surrendered. "They put my officers and crew in irons, and I was forbidden to speak to them," Peck said later. "They took our chests, trunks, and so much of the cargo as they wanted, and then set the ship on fire." The hold yielded many plush articles. John Kell put the combined value of the ship and cargo at $550,000: the richest prize the *Alabama* ever took.

Crowded with over one hundred prisoners, Semmes anchored in the harbor of Bahia on May 11. It was then the second-largest city in

Brazil, with a substantial British presence and all the shore delights a sailor might want. The *Agrippina* was supposed to come there, too, after the earlier rendezvous at Fernando de Noronha had fallen through. The *Alabama* waited for ten days. The local residents were friendly and curious. "Visitors innumerable coming on board," Master's Mate Fullam recorded. "The most unbounded hospitality and kindness shown, with every mark of sympathy for all." The British officials of a local railroad gave the *Alabama*'s officers an excursion, and an English merchant named Ogilvie threw a fancy ball and supper. Buoyed by Anglo-Confederate amity, Semmes sent a preening progress report to James Bulloch in Liverpool. "We are having capital success," he wrote. "That 'little bill' which the Yankees threaten to present to our Uncle John Bull, for the depredations of the *Alabama*, is growing apace, and already reaches $3,100,000."

But while the people of Bahia, especially those of British descent, were welcoming, the local government was not. Alerted by the change of governors at Fernando de Noronha, under scrutiny from the Ministry of Foreign Affairs, the president at Bahia urged Semmes to stay for only three or four days. When he lingered on, the president registered his displeasure and ordered Semmes to leave within twenty-four hours. Semmes, still waiting for the *Agrippina*, held him off by arguing about coaling, then finally departed on May 21. The tardy tender at last pulled into Bahia ten days later. Her captain sold his coal, loaded a cargo, and returned to London. Those two missed connections, at such a distance and unrewarded cost, helped persuade Bulloch to stop trying to keep his cruiser supplied with coal. "The *Alabama*," he later wrote, "was therefore left to look out for herself."

Semmes and his ship were once again alone at sea, and now even more so. During the month after leaving Bahia, they cruised down to the twenty-fifth south parallel, southeast of Rio de Janeiro, taking only six prizes. With U.S. ships avoiding the sea-lanes and Yankee shipowners selling out to foreign buyers, the ranks of enemy vessels bearing enemy cargoes were thinning out. Aboard the *Alabama*, morale was probably starting to deteriorate. That hedged statement must be tentative because of certain gaping holes in the historical evidence. The crowded forecastle, the most discontented section of any ship, inevitably generated the fewest records for historians. Sailors did not, in general, keep journals or write memoirs. The officers up on the quarterdeck did, but they knew only their own section of the vessel. Like any mandarins of a governing class, they tended to project their own attitudes onto everyone else at hand.

The extensive historical literature on the cruise of the *Alabama* has been written mostly from the readily available internal sources, mainly the shipboard journals of Semmes and Fullam (later published) and book-length accounts written after the war by three officers of literary inclinations. External sources—the impressions and recollections of visitors who were brought aboard, willingly or not—have been relatively slighted, in part because they are located in less accessible places such as newspapers, manuscript collections, and obscure government documents. If the internal accounts may be criticized as overly parochial and self-serving, the external versions are limited by their negative biases in the opposite direction. But these two perspectives, considered together, offer a broader sense of the complete story than the standard secondary works by historians.

As the *Alabama* roamed the coast of Brazil during the spring of 1863, the officers and passengers on her Union prizes eventually made their ways home and told lurid stories for Northern newspapers. These unfriendly, even embittered accounts shade and darken events as they were described in the ship's internal sources. The *Nora* of Boston, taken on March 25, was bound from Liverpool to Calcutta with a cargo of salt. Frederick Adams, her first officer, said he and sixty other prisoners were forced to huddle on the open deck in a space twenty feet square. They were fed "wormy biscuit and half rotten pork" taken from a captured whaler that had been at sea for four years. The crew of the *Alabama* seemed undisciplined and inept. As for the ship, "She was dirty, never in what a sailor calls a shipshape condition, and there was about as much wasted by the men as they consumed." Plundered prizes supplied plenty of everything from cheese to coal. "While the prisoners were starved, the pirate crew had an abundance, and waste was the rule. The armament of the ship and the small arms of the men were alike in a slovenly condition, and neither were in proper condition for use."

The *Gildersleeve* of New York, burned on May 25, was taking coal from Sunderland, England, to Calcutta. When her skipper, John McCallum, was brought before Semmes's court, he argued that his cargo should come safely under English ownership. But the captain, as judge, found no compelling legal evidence. "Sir," he said, "your vessel is worth over sixty thousand dollars. Your coal is not worth twenty thousand dollars. I will burn your vessel." Semmes took McCallum's chronometers and nautical instruments, all that he owned of value on the ship. Perhaps nudged by that loss, McCallum reported that discipline on the *Alabama* was "of the worst description, as bad as none at all. The men are a hard looking lot—of all nationalities. Captain Semmes is a small man, with a red nose covered with pimples. His first officer [John Kell] is a big, burly man, with ample beard, wearing old cowhide shoes with the toes out, dirty linen, etc. The sailing master, an Englishman [George Fullam, the master's mate], is the most decent looking man in the lot."

The *Amazonian* of Boston, sailing from New York to Montevideo with a cargo of general merchandise, provoked Semmes on June 2 by resisting capture. During a seven-hour chase, the *Alabama* fired one blank warning shot, then a second, but Captain Winslow Loveland of the *Amazonian* would not give up. Finally an earnest shell from the rifled pivot gun, even at a distance of over four miles, made him surrender. That left the pirate, according to a passenger's account, in a prickly temper. Semmes treated Loveland "with great scorn—told him he could not expect any favor, being from Boston; no bonds would be taken; the vessel must be burned. The captain was sent to sleep on deck, and to mess with the motley crew of that and another vessel." The passengers were handled more kindly, though one was restrained in irons and all were considered as prisoners of war. "There seemed to be no want on board the Alabama. Many articles lay around in sad waste and confusion, such as curiosities of every kind, parrots, albums, ornaments, musical instruments." Two boxes of books, sent for a Yankee clergyman in Buenos Aires, were opened on deck, with each man from the *Alabama* free to help himself. The passenger was left with a general impression of squalor, greed, and disorder—like conditions on a pirate ship.

Toward the end of June, Semmes finished his maneuvers off Brazil. The quarry was becoming ever more elusive; he wasn't taking many prizes. He also assumed that news of his operations and his extended visits to Fernando de Noronha and Bahia had by then reached the Navy Department in Washington. Gideon Welles, awakened again, would surely be sending more gunboats after him, maybe even the feared *Vanderbilt*. Semmes needed to go hunting somewhere else— somewhere he hadn't been yet.

In a London courtroom on June 23, Clarence Yonge testified in the case of the *Alexandra*, another privateer built in Liverpool for the Confederate Navy. The Palmerston government, apparently shifting the policy it had defended in the squabbling over the *Alabama*, had seized the ship in April before she could be fitted out. The ministry then charged the overt owner of the *Alexandra* with violating the relevant statute, the Foreign Enlistment Act. At the trial, Yonge was brought forward as a witness for the prosecution to demonstrate the possible consequences of letting such an Anglo-Confederate weapon loose on the ocean. By a tangled sequence of twists, the Confederate turncoat was testifying for the British government, against a Confederate defendant, in the ultimate interest of the United States—and of Clarence Yonge, of course.

Guided by the attorney general, Sir William Atherton, for the prosecution, Yonge went over the same ground as his deposition of April 2. He described his work for James Bulloch in Liverpool, Bulloch's various roles as a Confederate agent, and their shared room at the Fraser, Trenholm office. He received money in that office, he said, which he later paid out on the *Alabama*. He recalled the guns and munitions transferred at the Azores from the *Bahama* and *Agrippina*. He again recounted the cruise and Bulloch's instructions, his job as paymaster and how he made out wage allotments for the cruiser's men to the order of Fraser, Trenholm. In summary, he testified to the past collusions between British and Confederate interests that might, if repeated, send the *Alexandra* as well to fight against the United States.

On cross-examination, an attorney for the defendant picked at Yonge's obvious vulnerability, the questions about his character.

Have you left your wife and children in Savannah?

"May I ask a question, whether I am obliged to answer that question?"

Do you object to answering it?

"I have an objection to answer."

The judge—Frederick Pollock, the lord chief baron of the Exchequer—asked what his objection was.

"I do not see what my own family affairs have to do with the case."

Pollock explained that witnesses could be asked whether they in the past had conducted themselves creditably as men or husbands or fathers, or in any other way. The attorney prodded Yonge about his wife in Liverpool.

"I left her there."

Did you also leave your wife and two children in Savannah?

"I did not." (Literally true; the con man knew the courtroom subtleties.)

One child? (The attorney understood the game too.)

"One child."

You were in James Bulloch's employment when you came to England?

"I was in the employment of the Confederate government."

You are now a spy for the United States government?

"I am not."

In their employment?

"I received no employment from the United States government or anybody else." (Not formally, though Thomas Dudley was secretly sending him five pounds a month.)

Before the *Alabama* sailed from Liverpool, were you in touch with the United States government?

"I was not."

When did you first meet Mr. Adams, the American minister?

"In this year; the latter part of March, or the first of April."

Did you give him valuable information about the *Alabama*?

"I gave to the United States officials what I suppose went to Mr. Adams; I made certain statements to them."

You are not a secessionist now?

"I am not at any rate."

At Kingston, when the *Alabama* started out of the harbor, did you drop overboard and go ashore?

"Not exactly."

What was it exactly?

"Several hours before the ship sailed I left her."

And you then became a Northerner?

"Anything you choose to say."

In Kingston, did you marry a mulatto woman who now passes as your wife in Liverpool?

"I did not."

Did you marry a woman who now passes as your wife in Liverpool?

"Yes, I did."

And in Liverpool, did you go live with someone other than her?

"I went away."

Did you leave your wife in Liverpool destitute?

"She was not particularly destitute. I do not know what you call destitute. . . . Her mother was with her, who had plenty of money."

While on the *Alabama*, did you decide to leave the Southern states?

"I had not made up my mind to leave the Southern states, but I had made up my mind to leave the *Alabama*."

Did you come to England in order to contact Mr. Adams?

"After I came I made up my mind what course I would adopt."

Do you have an appointment in the United States service?

"I have not."

Did you expect to make money for your assistance to the Union?

"I asked no questions. When I went to the United States minister I asked no questions."

And he told no lies in court, though at times he avoided complete truths. At the U.S. legation, Charles Francis Adams was not hopeful about the outcome of the *Alexandra* case. "The ministry are feeble and vacillatory," he wrote in his diary, "whilst the commercial interest is pushing and decided. Nothing will move England but an idea of our power." Lord Chief Baron Pollock, in sending the case to the jury, gave such tilted, prejudicial instructions that the defendant won a quick verdict. The government was ordered to return the ship to her owner—and thus to the Confederates.

"The enemy of course are jubilant," John Murray Forbes, in England on his secret mission to buy the Laird rams, wrote home to Gideon Welles, "but if the result brings the Government to a sense of its responsibilities they may be too <u>early</u> in their rejoicing." (Forbes was characteristically astute.) While the case was appealed, the *Alexandra* stayed harmlessly in Liverpool. The more serious question of the Laird rams remained undecided, indeed as yet unaddressed.

Clarence Yonge, perhaps again needed as a witness during the appeal, was obliged to stay in Britain. His keeper, the U.S. consul Thomas Dudley, stashed him in Dublin for a while. A month after his testimony in the *Alexandra* case, Yonge thanked Dudley for his regular five pounds and for the book that Dudley gave him in London, "which has served not only to occupy my mind but has afforded much valuable information." He was playing his role, so smoothly, and playing Dudley as well: presenting himself as the U.S. consul would have liked to see him. "I am very much pleased with Dublin, and the many places of resort in its vicinity. The weather continues very cool. I am, thank you, in excellent health." Could Dudley, if without inconvenience, send him a New York newspaper? And, by the way, how long would he have to stay put in Dublin? "I can then make arrangements," he explained, very dignified, "for the proper disposition of my time."

In the entire saga of the *Alabama*, Yonge was the anti-Semmes. While the captain forsook home and family in order—as he saw it—to defend his invaded country, Yonge turned against his sworn patriotic duty, deserted two wives, and cared only about himself. Semmes spent hard, lonesome, dangerous years at sea, enduring sleepless nights and recurring seasickness, losing weight and wearing down. Yonge took his safe and subsidized ease in Dublin, happy to enjoy "the many places of resort" and quite concerned about the "proper disposition" of his time. Semmes lived for his principles; Yonge lived without any. Yet for both men there remained tugging moral ambiguities, which became clearer later on.

SEVEN

Cape Town Zenith

In the summer of 1863, Raphael Semmes and the *Alabama* were approaching the first anniversary of their cruise. The hunting ground off the coast of Brazil had become barren and dangerous, with too little prey and soon—probably—too many Union predators. The captain had to make what was always his most elemental yet complicated decision: Where to go next? In deep-thinking mode, he paced the deck and tugged on his mustache. As usual, he kept his own counsel; the other men could only watch and await his orders. He reached back to the earliest cruising scheme for his ship. In 1861, Stephen Mallory and James Bulloch decided to build a cruiser that would operate on the other side of the world, off Indonesia and Southeast Asia: a lush nexus of Yankee shipping far from any enemy gunboats. The builder's contract between Bulloch and the Lairds included a stipulation for enough provisions for a voyage to the East Indies. When Semmes, in Nassau in June 1862, learned of his appointment to command the *Alabama*, he wrote to Mallory that "I think well of your suggestion of the East Indies, as a cruising ground," and hoped to be there by that fall. Now, returning to the original design, he decided to cross the South Atlantic Ocean, round the Cape of Good Hope, and proceed across the Indian Ocean to the Far East.

As he contemplated this long passage, both Semmes and his ship were worn. At sea, he had to keep his fires banked in case an emergency required sudden steam power. Since the boilers could only be cleaned when cooled, that prevented regular maintenance and left them corroded and encrusted with scale (the stubborn mineral residue of evaporating water). Some of the tubes had begun to leak, spewing hot water into the hold and making the machinery less efficient. On the outside of the hull, below the waterline, accumulating plants and organisms grew into a thick, shaggy overcoat that impeded the flow of water and hobbled the fast cruiser. "Our ship has certainly got to be very dull under canvas," Semmes fretted on June 15, "for with a press of sail, and the wind a point free, she has made to-day but 8 knots. The consequence is that a stern chase has become a forlorn hope with us." The vessel's legendary reputation for speed, her sharpest weapon to inspire fear and despair in the enemy, was at risk.

After almost a year on the *Alabama*, and two years since he ran the *Sumter* through the blockade off New Orleans, Semmes felt old and tired. Never a man of robust physique, he had evidently become even skinnier on the uncertain diet and certain seasickness of long cruising. Among his recent captives, the captain of the *Golden Rule* had seen "a mere skeleton of a man"; the first officer of the *Nora*, "a little weazen, white bearded man of about sixty years of age" (he was fifty-three). The red nose covered with pimples described by the captain of the *Gildersleeve* suggests that Semmes may have suffered from acne rosacea, a condition that can be aggravated by heat, wind, sunlight, and stress—all common on the *Alabama*. Even his Confederate naval uniform, according to a report sent from Brazil to *The Times* of London, was "not improved by exposure."

So neither captain nor craft was trimmed for the voyage that stretched so far ahead. In late June, a turbulent sea and half a gale blew in from the east, tossing the ship around and rendering Semmes uncomfortable once again. "The fact is," he confided to his journal, "I am getting too old to relish the rough usage of the sea. Youth sometimes loves to be rocked by a gale, but when we have passed the middle stage of life we love quiet and repose." He noted, without any delight, the second anniversary of his escape on the *Sumter*. "Two years of almost constant excitement and anxiety," as he summed them up: contending with all the normal perils of the sea, weather, shoals, and coasts, plus the wartime strains of chase, battle, capture, and escape, plus the challenge of governing the "senseless and unruly spirits" among his officers and crew, plus the diplomatic bother of disagreeable officials in foreign ports. No wonder he felt tired! "All these things have produced a constant tension of the nervous system, and the wear and tear of body in these two years would, no doubt, be quite obvious to my friends at home, could they see me."

At least he was still lucky. Under way for the Cape of Good Hope, he asked for an inventory of the sea bread (hardtack) on board. Informed they had just thirty days' worth, he limited daily consumption to only half a pound per man. Soon he learned that even that inadequate store of hardtack was inedible, infested by weevils. "The bread supply is imperative," he noted; so they had to turn around and head back toward Rio de Janeiro, 825 miles away, for another stock. After five days of hard sailing, still a long way from Rio, they caught the *Anna F. Schmidt*, bound from Boston to San Francisco with general merchandise including such useful items as clothing, medicine—and bread. "Such Boston bread, biscuits, and crackers, and all so fresh and good!" John Kell recalled in smacking gusto. "We helped ourselves hugely (with thankful hearts) and burned her." Well supplied and ever fortunate, the *Alabama* again turned eastward.

The course ran roughly along the thirtieth south parallel. On the long haul to the Cape of Good Hope, they were alone for most of the time. Sixteen days passed without the sight of a sail on the horizon. The lookouts peered and strained and squinted, but said nothing. For a month they took not a single prize—the longest fallow period since the previous winter, when Semmes was hiding in the Gulf of Mexico before his approach to Galveston. As on that occasion, they now remained in isolation from the outside world, locked in a self-contained bubble at sea, neither making nor getting any news.

Back home, the war—so far as they had learned—had continued to go well for the Confederacy. The Union Army had endured a miserable Valley Forge winter of poor shelter and food, with soldiers dying of scurvy in unheated tent hospitals. "Dark blue days," wrote the New York diarist George Templeton Strong. "We are in a fearful scrape, and I see no way out of it." The parade of inept Union commanders marched on. Lincoln could not find the right man for his keystone Army of the Potomac, thus encouraging the loud chorus of doubts about his own leadership. "The country is wonderfully demoralized," Rear Admiral David Farragut wrote to Gustavus Fox. "I do not know what to make of it—we do not fight." Out west, Braxton Bragg's Confederate forces pushed into Kentucky, and Grant's repeated assaults on the Mississippi River stronghold of Vicksburg were turned back. All across the South, the Yankee invasions of the Confederate homeland had not broken the civilian population, but instead had actually stiffened its will not to lose. Lee's army, the pride of the Confederacy, pulled off a brilliant victory at Chancellorsville in early May. Prodded on by success, seizing the offensive, Lee next prepared to invade Pennsylvania.

Diplomatic relations between Washington and London remained testy, reviving Confederate hopes for British recognition or intervention. Charles Francis Adams kept hearing reports of new enemy warships under construction at British shipyards. "The temper of our people is already roused enough," he wrote in his diary, "by the constant annoyance created by the ravages of the gunboat 290." His counterpart in Washington, Lord Lyons, sent a similar report back to London: the "predominating feeling" there, he wrote, was exasperation over the *Alabama* and her descendants. At this delicate moment, a third Confederate cruiser, the *Georgia*, escaped British authorities in April and went hunting. She took five quick prizes in the South Atlantic. "A day of reckoning must come," warned the influential *New York Herald*. "Where one of our vessels is destroyed by these British pirates we will sink and burn a hundred English vessels. We are not a nation to submit tamely to disgrace and insult." Adams kept firing protests that Russell at the Foreign Office kept deflecting. The U.S. minister, angry and frustrated, sensed an explosion coming. "No man can delude himself," he wrote home in late April, "with the idea that this post will be anything else than purgatory just now. I have always felt as if I were sitting on the mouth of a volcano."

The most threatening Anglo-Confederate weapons, the Laird rams, were almost ready at Birkenhead. The secret guerrilla mission of John Murray Forbes and William Aspinwall to buy the rams for the Union had failed; the two men did not meet a friendly reception, especially after *The Times* revealed their plans. "It was indeed socially a very chilly climate that spring in London," Forbes recalled. "Our best friends, with a very small circle excepted, were only with us in feeling." Adams launched another round of protests and affidavits, but without much hope of blocking the newest, scariest British additions to the Confederate Navy.

The swelling Confederate tide, stretching from London to the Mississippi River, even reached into Raphael Semmes's own family. His independent wife, Anne, had begun the war as a loyal Unionist. While her husband went Confederate, she took their two daughters and youngest son and stayed for a while with his brother, Samuel, in Cumberland, Maryland; then they settled with her Spencer kinfolk in Cincinnati. Samuel and the Spencers also lined up with the Union, thus reinforcing her allegiance. At some point, Anne's daughter Anna—fourteen years old in 1861—was taken out of her convent school in Philadelphia to join them. (As late as November 1862, the Northern press reported that "a daughter of the pirate Semmes is now at school in Philadelphia," but the item was probably out of date by then.)

From the start of the war, however, compelling circumstances pushed Anne to switch sides. Her two oldest boys fought for the South. Spencer Semmes, who was practicing law in New Orleans, enlisted as a second lieutenant in a Louisiana regiment of the Army of Tennessee. Later he was promoted to captain and major. Oliver Semmes, after resigning from West Point, was also appointed a second lieutenant. He served with distinction in various units in Mobile, New Orleans, and Baton Rouge. During combat, he was taken prisoner in April 1863 while commanding a gunboat in southwest Louisiana. Two months later, as he and other imprisoned officers were being transferred to a Delaware prison, Oliver spearheaded a revolt that overpowered their guards at Hampton Roads, Virginia. He then led the escaped prisoners safely through the dense Dismal Swamp to Confederate territory in Richmond. From there he eventually rejoined his command.

The younger Semmes children were also blazing secessionists. Electra, a particular favorite of her father's, was a pretty, headstrong girl of eighteen when the war began. She juggled her abundant beaus with the fickle insouciance of a proper Southern belle. Semmes, doting but not uncritical, urged her not to neglect more earnest pursuits. "I am glad that you have devoted yourself to a course of profitable reading," he wrote her from Liverpool in August 1862. "Educated women have many advantages over the uneducated. An ignorant young beauty may have her brief hour of conquest, but the foundations of happiness in after life must be laid on a more solid basis than mere personal attractions." That summer one of the Semmes daughters, probably Electra, shouted out her allegiance by attending a wedding in Newport, Kentucky, arrayed in a large scarf that resembled the Confederate Stars and Bars. "Secession Impudence," snapped a Cincinnati newspaper.

Anne and her children lived with one of her many brothers. In their Unionist household, they would have seen the *Cincinnati Daily Commercial*, the pro-Union newspaper in town. The *Commercial* extended full coverage to the exploits of the pirate Semmes. She may have come to feel pride in her husband's feats and fame; but occasional items reported in the *Commercial* were more worrisome: the rewards of $500,000 for the *Alabama* if taken and $300,000 if sunk, a false rumor that she was captured, the eighteen Union warships in pursuit, and a story from Jamaica that the *Alabama* was "severely riddled" while sinking the *Hatteras*. Moreover, Semmes's gathering notoriety, the challenge and rebuke that he represented to the Union cause, made Anne's life in Cincinnati less agreeable. Newsboys gathered outside her house, shouting fake extras: "All about the capture of the pirate Semmes!" With her distant husband and oldest sons engaged in deadly combat against the North and her other children also in their camp, with most of the war news favoring the Confederates, and feeling besieged even in her own hometown, Anne converted her loyalty. The family was finally united for the South.

At sea, Raphael wrote home when he could. Seeking intelligence about the pirate, the Union authorities in Cincinnati watched Anne's mail and, at least once, searched her house and baggage. A few letters from Anne somehow reached her husband. The Navy Department in Richmond sent her an occasional allotment of his salary; but it was erratic and insufficient, and she worried about money. Writing from the Arcas Islands in January 1863, preparing to assault the Union troopships he expected to find off Galveston, Raphael apparently responded to a discouraged letter from Anne:

> You must be of good cheer, and bear the evils of separation from your husband, and the other calamities of war, with chris-

tian resignation to the will of the Almighty, and with fortitude. Good will no doubt finally come out of this probation to which, for a wise purpose, we are being subjected. We shall be made better men and women by it, and have our thoughts turned to more serious subjects, than formerly. Cherish, and console our dear children, and set them an example of self sacrifice, and endurance. . . . The war will not last always, and I hope a merciful Providence will permit us all to meet again.

As to money, Raphael wrote that from Martinique, in November, he had sent her a draft by way of his agent in Liverpool. He hoped she had received it by then. But in general, "You must practice economy, my dear wife, both for its own sake, because it is a virtue, and because we are not rich. You know I derive no benefit from the prizes I capture. We cannot sell them, as our enemies do theirs, because our ports are blockaded, and foreign powers refuse us entrance into their ports for the purpose. Unless the government shall make me some compensation, I shall come out of the war as poor as when I went into it." As a husband, he did not let himself indulge much warm, understanding sympathy for Anne's war-widowed travails at home. Think about more serious matters, Raphael urged, consider the children, and be more thrifty. He had a war to fight.

So did Anne. During the winter of 1863, with the news drifting so badly for the Union, muttered fears were expressed in Cincinnati about unnamed "traitors" and "terrible dangers" in their midst. And there, living among them, were the wife and children of the notorious pirate Semmes. A new local commander, Ambrose Burnside, issued a draconian order in March that anyone committing unfriendly acts— such as expressing support for the South—could be shot. In that harsh spirit, Anne and her children were abruptly ordered to leave town for enemy territory.

A lieutenant, kind but vigilant, escorted them by train to Philadelphia and Baltimore, then south by boat to the James River under a flag of truce. Anne had to pay the traveling expenses, which she thought excessive, and relinquish a box of brandy, quinine, and other medicines. Nearly cashless, they reached Richmond in late April. Raphael's cousin Thomas J. Semmes, a leading member of the Confederate Senate, maintained a famously hospitable home in the secession capital. (The cousins had grown up in the same home in Washington.) Anne got to see her sons Oliver, still recovering in Richmond from his escape, and Spencer, who was granted leave in June to go visit his family. The mother and her six children, all pulling in patriotic unison, were briefly together again—missing only the absent captain, then on his way to the Cape of Good Hope.

In all this turmoil of dislocation and uncertainty, Anne was vulnerable to a shady character who called himself Frank Lacy Buxton. They were introduced by "a very estimable lady of Virginia." His real name was actually William Saunders. An Englishman, he had deserted his wife and two children and reinvented himself in the United States. (Saunders and Clarence Yonge would have recognized each other.) After stealing from various employers in New York and Philadelphia, "Buxton," in the early, free-form stages of the war, became both a field correspondent for the *New York Tribune* and a spy for the Union. In fact he was a brazen double agent, feeding dubious intelligence to both enemy camps. Eventually detected, he was locked up in the Old Capitol prison in Washington.

Released with the help of Lord Lyons, the British ambassador, Buxton was paroled on condition that he remain north of New York City. Instead he went south to Richmond and landed, once again, on his agile feet. He seemed to have plenty of money, flourishing sterling bills, and he spoke vaguely of distinguished Buxton relatives in England. Anne Semmes was fooled—along with most of Richmond society, it seems. The Englishman, worldly and persuasive, agreed to accompany the family as they returned to their home in Mobile that summer. Anne no doubt hoped that such an adroit masculine presence would smooth their unpredictable journey through the war-ravaged South. Buxton harbored his own unspoken motives—which included the comely eldest daughter. Electra also believed the impostor, and more. In yet another Anglo-Confederate alliance, she and Buxton got engaged to marry in the fall of 1863.

Anne's husband, Electra's father, was so far away. After a dull crossing, the *Alabama* reached the southern tip of Africa on July 29. Instead of heading directly into Cape Town, where Union warships might be waiting, Semmes made land at Saldanha Bay, sixty miles up the west coast. In that sheltered anchorage, he reconnoitered the situation and set his men to overhauling the ship. The rigging and machinery needed repairs, and the hull had to be caulked and painted, inside and out: routine maintenance after months at sea. While Kell took charge, the captain went ashore and set foot on the African continent for the first time. "A gloomy, desert-looking place," he noted, "the shore composed of sand and rock, without trees, but with green patches here and there." A few farmhouses and fishing huts were visible. A group of officers went hunting, bringing back rabbits, pheasants, and small deer, all eaten with relish.

Semmes let some of his sailors loose. They somehow managed, even in such barren territory, to find diverting trouble. "Three of them have run off," the captain regretted, "and the rest have behaved so badly in getting drunk that I have stopped their liberty. One of these fellows drew a revolver on a master's mate. The fact is, I have a precious set of rascals on board—faithless in the matter of abiding by their contracts, liars, thieves, and drunkards." Thus the judgment handed down from the captain's cabin. From the perspective of the forecastle, by contrast, the men were indirectly venting their opinions about the *Alabama* after a year. Only one sea battle, long stretches of cruising, not much liberty on shore, and—especially—none of the promised prize money in their pockets: the dangled lures that had persuaded them to sign on were not being delivered. The crew's misbehaviors, though surely inevitable and traditional for seafaring men, yet implied more than just the random unleashing of confined animal spirits. They were also a kind of labor protest, however inchoate and inarticulate: acted out instead of spoken.

During the week at Saldanha Bay, Semmes and his men got an early sense of the reception that was awaiting them in Cape Town. Even here, thousands of miles from the American Civil War and their own previous exploits, among people who spoke no English and had no stake in the war, they were famous and admired. Taking a walk on shore, Semmes met Dutch farmers in a four-horse wagon, in from the country to see the *Alabama*. They brought the captain a wild peacock. A ship came up from Cape Town with letters from merchants offering coal, supplies, and expressions of goodwill. Over the next few days, more Dutch farmers arrived in country wagons and on horseback, bearing presents of ostrich eggs or feather plumes, to tour the ship. Semmes, as always, noticed the women: "plump, ruddy Dutch girls, whose large, rough hands and awkward bows, or courtesies, showed them to be honest lasses from neighboring farms, accustomed to milking the cows and churning the butter." Young men hefted the hundred-pound cannon shells, and young women—the captain noted—examined the mustaches on the ship's officers.

Cape Town, the capital of Cape Colony, a British possession since 1814, was primed for the cruiser's arrival. For days the city knew the *Alabama* was coming. (Semmes had requested permission for repairs he could not undertake in Saldanha Bay.) The Anglo-Dutch city had no sheltered harbor; Table Bay instead was open to the sea, with long vistas out toward the north, west, and south. The setting was dramatic, presenting white beaches and eighteenth-century Dutch manor houses, clusters of buildings on a narrow coastal plain backed into the sudden sheer granite of Table Mountain shooting up 3,500 feet, and Semmes could not have contrived a more theatrical entrance. As the ship approached Table Bay from the north on August 5—cue the quarry—the bark *Sea Bride* of Boston appeared from the south. She was newly painted, with tapered spars and white sails: an apparent Yankee. They were about five miles offshore, shortly after noon, in fine weather with clear visibility. The sea was smooth and transparent. The drama unfolded under perfect conditions.

In Cape Town, a newspaper reporter was walking along Adderley Street. A man on horseback galloped wildly by, shouting, "The *Alabama* in sight, in chase of a Yankee bark!" The reporter asked, "Where, where?" But the horseman was gone, the repeated news trailing after him. Rumors flew around that the *Alabama* had fired a broadside into the bark or sunk her or burned her or run her aground, or perhaps all of these. Shops, warehouses, and counting houses quickly emptied, with people not knowing where to go, but drifting toward the thickest crowds, shouting and screaming. Horses and cabs rattled up to the highest vantage points on Lion's Hill and the Kloof Road. But the best seats were back down the hill, past the Round House to a spot near Brighton. The reporter, pursuing his story, rushed downhill.

The few who got there in time saw a quick chase. Concealed under a British flag, the *Alabama* fired a warning shot, then another. The skipper of the *Sea Bride* might have saved himself by running into neutral water closer to shore. Instead he tried to escape to sea and was soon caught. From the land, it appeared that Semmes was even toying with his prey, letting her draw off a short distance, then getting up steam again and pouncing. The *Alabama* circled all around the *Sea Bride*, coming within twenty yards and taking a careful look, then raising the Stars and Bars and sending a boarding party. Knowing he could not take the prize into Cape Town, Semmes was going to burn her right away. The boarding party scattered tar barrels and piles of ammunition and got ready to apply torches; but then Semmes signaled them to wait. The *Alabama* came into Cape Town like a triumphant athlete who, having defeated his opponent, turns toward the crowd to bathe in his ovation.

"As we approached," John Kell wrote to his wife, "it was really wonderful to behold the people congregated on shore, the hillsides covered with an excited populace." When the ship came to anchor, it was besieged by a motley fleet of boats and boaters requesting permission to come aboard. "Hundreds crowded on board," Kell recorded. "Their enthusiasm was beyond description and their hearty welcome and sympathy expressed for our cause was truly gratifying." Disregarding the finer niceties of British neutrality, they shouted three ringing cheers for the *Alabama*. Ladies waved their handkerchiefs from opened windows of the villas at the bottom of the hill. Many people stood on the roofs of houses along Strand Street. All the jetties into the harbor were thronged, and the uniformed rowing clubs put to sea at double time. The captain of the *Sea Bride*, Charles F. White, accepted his surprising loss. "What can't be cured must be endured," he told an interviewer. "I had not the remotest idea of a capture at this end of the world. I never supposed that she was in this direction."

For a reporter from the *Argus*, Semmes proudly reeled off a list of the year's harvest. One ship, the bark *Conrad* from Philadelphia, was taken off Brazil on June 20. Semmes renamed her the *Tuscaloosa*, after a town in Alabama, and made her a tender to his own ship (and an unofficial cruiser). Equipped with two guns and a small crew of fifteen, she was currently anchored nearby. The *Alabama* had bonded nine prizes bearing neutral or troublesome cargoes. One—the *Sea Bride*—was to be sold. Forty-three others had become bonfires. Thus fifty-four captures in all: more than one a week since the previous September. The total value of vessels and cargoes, the captain estimated, was $4.2 million. Though he did not make the claim, his ship was already the most effective commerce raider in the history of naval warfare.

S C E N E S   O N   B O A R D   T H E   A L A B A M A.

FROM PHOTOGRAPHS.

CAPT. SEMMES' SECRETARY.   MR. BULLOCK, MASTER.

CAPTAIN SEMMES.

MR. MACINTYRE KELL, FIRST LIEUTENANT.

A full-page English report on the *Alabama* at Cape Town; the two men in the
top picture, here misidentified, are Lieutenant Arthur Sinclair and Lieutenant
Richard F. Armstrong; at the bottom, Kell's middle name was actually McIntosh.
(*Illustrated London News*, October 10, 1863)

"There is but one subject of talk—the Alabama," a newspaper reported the next day. "She is, according to the opinion of Cape Town, the only ship in the world, and Captain Semmes is the only hero in the world. Everybody who had not boarded the ship and shaken hands with the Captain, touched his coat, heard him speak, or even just caught a glimpse of him over the heads of the crowds that pressed around him, is a nobody." The day was declared a universal holiday, with most work suspended. The *Alabama* was jammed from the bow to the horse block, above and below. Women in crinolines and hoop skirts brightly clogged the tight passageways. Fielding waves of questions and opinions, the captain bantered back. "You are a native African, are you not?" he asked a Cape Town belle. Yes, she was. "Well, do you know that the southern slave states have passed a law prohibiting the importation of native Africans; but I suspect they'd make an exception in your case." Flirting in wartime, jesting about the slave trade: Semmes, at ease, was revealing himself.

In two years at sea that included many friendly receptions, he had never encountered anything on this scale. Though harried and pulled in diverse directions by so many enthusiasts, he remained affable and cordial. "Take a seat if you can find one," he told a man from the *Advertiser and Mail* who had squeezed into his cabin. "Ours is a working, fighting ship, and we have not much room to spare for ease or pleasure." Like most people meeting the infamous pirate for the first time, the reporter was surprised by what he saw. The gray uniform looked old and stained, buttoned up close to his throat, with battered shoulder straps and faded gold trimmings. The hero himself seemed tired:

> At first sight Capt. Semmes does not come up to the idea which every one involuntarily forms of any celebrated character. He has nothing of the pirate about him—little even of the ordinary sea-captain. He is rather below the middle stature, with a spare bony frame. His face is care-worn and sunburnt, the features striking—a broad brow with iron-gray locks straggling over it, gray eyes, now mild and dreamy, then flashing with fire as he warms in conversation.

The reporter thought he looked "somewhat older" than his fifty-three years.

The captain puzzled over why the British government had not yet extended recognition or intervention to the South. Russell, he said, leaned too far toward the North, and Palmerston was simply a cold politician without any real sympathies. Expanding into a topic, Semmes pointed a bony finger and smacked his lips with emphasis. Turning to his cluttered cabin, he gestured wonderingly at the flowers and other gifts left for him that day. "My own countrymen," he said, "would not have done as much for me, or anybody else. They are not fond of hero-worship; you English are a strange people."

The remark suggested a bedrock humility, as though he did not deserve all this fuss. His private report on the day's events, in a letter to Anne on August 8, conveyed the same proud but bemused distance from such commotion:

> I am sure our excellent President Davis never had a more crowded levee than I had in my cabin from 9 o'clock in the morning to 3 o'clock in the afternoon. . . . The ship was packed, from stem to stern, and there was a constant <u>jam</u> in my cabin of men and women—officers and officers' wives, judges and lawyers and their wives and daughters, and Tom, Dick and Harry besides, all pressing forward to shake hands with me and to beg my autograph! Was not that a predicament for a modest man to be placed in! Indeed, they nearly tired me out with demonstrations of kindness.

(Just for the record, though, he did enclose his most fulsome newspaper clippings for his wife's admiration.)

It was his first letter to Anne in three months, since the stopover at Bahia in Brazil. That letter went to Cincinnati, but he had since learned about the order by "the Yankee brute Burnside" that forced them to leave. Not knowing where they might be, he hoped they were safe with friends. "I feel now practically what is meant by 'times that try men's souls,' but we must not give way to weakness," he urged. "We must school ourselves to these trials like Christian philosophers. We must be brave men and women for our country's sake, and trust all the rest to God." As for the cruise, "I have every reason to be satisfied with my success against the enemy. I believe I have rendered as good service to my country as I could possibly have rendered in any other direction, and the world is kind enough to talk of me in a friendly spirit, and to put a higher estimate upon my labors than I think they deserve. If I estimate them by the abuse which the Yankees heap upon me, they are certainly very great."

All these circumstances—the well-anticipated arrival of the famed cruiser, the staged and witnessed capture of the *Sea Bride*, and the fervent welcome by Cape Town, all within the context of so much recent war news favoring the Confederacy—brought the cruise of the *Alabama* to its zenith. As a colonial outpost at the bottom of the world, far away from the main arenas of Western history, Cape Town was inevitably dazzled by such a famous visitor from the faraway American war. The residents, in their own quarrels with the colonial administration in London, could sympathize with the South's struggle against a larger, more powerful adversary. The recent Union consul in Cape Town, Thomas MacDowell, had embarrassed his country by drunken sprees in the streets and unpaid debts that had plunked him in jail. The contrast between the recalled consul and the noble captain, standing for their two nations, was striking. "There is hardly a man now living and moving within the realm of Christendom," declared the *Advertiser and Mail*, going for broke, "who has a better prospect of hereafter passing into a hero and becoming the principal character of an epic poem or drama than Captain Semmes of the *Alabama*."

Such extravagances were not unanimous in Cape Town. Some of the Dutch residents, accustomed to resisting British authority, held out against the flood of British enthusiasm for the Confederate visitors. "The ship is nothing more than a well equipped pirate," insisted a Dutch paper, the *Het Volksblad*, "and her captain is simply a decent, competent, modern sea-rover, who hasn't done any more than hundreds of other captains have done: Why then regard him as a hero and the greatest man of goodwill to visit Table Bay?" But this was a solitary dissent in a whooshing wave of adulation.

So many visitors came aboard, day after day, that the men wished they had printed answers to the usual questions, to be posted around the ship. The officers were invited to parties, balls, and country outings at the lush Constantia vineyard a few miles outside town. The sailors, finding old shipmates among the British ships in the bay, ran their own excursions to the bars and whorehouses in the east end of town. Two of the *Alabama*'s men even burst into print: the *Advertiser and Mail* published George Fullam's shipboard journal, covering the first year of the cruise, and a poem by the sailor Frank Townshend, poet laureate of the forecastle, about the sinking of the *Hatteras*.

The advent of the *Alabama* also generated a durable oral tradition among the indigenous Cape Malays. They composed a folk song in tribute, a headline crossed with an erotic lullaby. Translated from the Afrikaans:

> Here comes the Alabama, the Alabama comes o'er the sea,
> Here comes the Alabama, the Alabama comes o'er the sea,
> Girl, girl, the reed-bed girl, the reed-bed is made-up for me,
> On which I can sleep.

And on through other verses. It was sung well into the twentieth century, beyond a time when anybody was still alive to remember the momentous visit.

Still, Cape Town was a British port, and in the legal spirit of neutrality the Confederate cruiser was not supposed to linger. After four days of celebrations, landing prisoners, taking on coal and provisions, and repairing boilers, the feted *Alabama* steamed out of Table Bay. She went down to the Cape of Good Hope, rounded it, and turned northward into the military base at Simon's Bay. In this sheltered harbor, more protected than the waters off Cape Town, the crew again bent to its chores. The men replaced copper sheathing at the waterline, repaired the engine, and kept on caulking. At Simon's Town, Semmes was given a private dinner by Rear Admiral Sir Baldwin Walker, the commander of British naval forces at the Cape. The colonial governor for Cape Town joined the party. The British officials had to abide formally by the letter of neutrality—but they did not trouble to hide their real sympathies.

Six days passed in Simon's Bay. The sailors became drunk and snarly, of course, and Semmes put the worst of them in irons. Twenty-one men deserted the ship. A photographer came aboard to take pictures of the officers in various poses. (A photograph of Semmes leaning jauntily on a pivot gun, with Kell standing in the background, became the most evocative image of the captain and his ship.) Semmes dispatched a Yankee sewing machine, taken from a recent prize, to his friend Louisa Tremlett in London. He had hoped to include some choice tea, he added, but had snatched no tea ships lately. "We have had a reasonable degree of success, however," he admitted to Tremlett, "and are touching the enemy on two of his most tender spots—we are wounding his <u>vanity</u> and depleting his <u>purse</u>."

The mail steamer from England arrived with yet more good news: Lee had invaded Pennsylvania. If he succeeded, the war might soon be over. Such surging hopes coincided nicely with the final highs of their visit. On August 15, with her repairs finished, the *Alabama* returned to sea. She was headed back to the Cape of Good Hope, then would troll up the west coast for a secret rendezvous with the captured *Sea Bride*.

At that moment, the Union warship *Vanderbilt* arrived at the mid-ocean island of St. Helena, some 2,200 miles northwest of Cape Town.

The most familiar image of the captain and his ship, taken by a Cape Town photographer in August 1863: Semmes leans casually on the aft pivot gun with Kell, as always, backing him up. This photograph has been copied and recopied so many times that it has lost resolution; no clear, sharp print seems to exist.
(Naval Historical Foundation)

The ill-favored, consistently stupid Yankee pursuit of the *Alabama* suddenly turned lucky. The biggest, fastest, most coal-hungry vessel in the Union Navy, the only enemy that Semmes feared, was finally getting closer to the *Alabama*. It was just an accident, the coincidental upshot of a comical series of events. Six months earlier, in February, the doofus Rear Admiral Charles Wilkes had seized the *Vanderbilt* as his personal toy. Having already enraged British diplomats by his creation of the *Trent* crisis in 1861, Wilkes and the *Vanderbilt* then careened freely around the Caribbean in the spring of 1863, ruffling international protocols. In England, the U.S. emissaries John Murray Forbes and William Aspinwall pleaded with the Navy Department to remove Wilkes from his command. "Everything he does," wrote Forbes, "hits twice as hard in irritating John Bull as the same thing done by anybody else." "Every Englishman," Aspinwall agreed, "thinks that his appointment was a taunt to them intentionally made." Aside from these needless diplomatic affronts in a region of many British colonial missions, Wilkes had—unilaterally and selfishly—taken the *Vanderbilt* off her assigned task of chasing the *Alabama*.

Gideon Welles at last bestirred himself in June. He dismissed Wilkes and restored Charles Baldwin as captain of the *Vanderbilt*. In the interim, Semmes had roamed from the thirtieth north parallel down to the thirtieth south parallel, from Florida to Brazil, hunting and burning at will. Baldwin was ordered, again, to find and destroy the *Alabama*. "Detaining you in the West Indies has been a fatal error which has led to a great public loss," Gustavus Fox told Baldwin. "Chart according to your best judgment in pursuit of the rebels even if it be to the uttermost parts of the earth, and may success attend you."

So down to the perennial question: Where was the *Alabama*? The latest reports of captures placed her off the coast of Brazil. The *Vanderbilt* reached Fernando de Noronha on July 4 and learned that Semmes had left there over ten weeks earlier. Hearing that the *Alabama* had stopped at Bahia, Baldwin headed in that direction—but was diverted by a credible rumor that the cruiser was expected soon at the island of Trinidad, off the northeast coast of Venezuela. "You may believe, sir," Baldwin reported to Welles, "we lost not a moment in getting to the island, and with the hope that at length fortune was kind. We had to steam against strong S.E. trade wind and large sea, but arrived there the fourth morning at break of day; but nothing was to be seen.

I attempted to land, but the surf was too great." (Three buts in two sentences.)

Furthermore, Baldwin explained, his boilers were worn, in constant need of patching, and so thin they could no longer be scaled; a leak had recently scalded a fireman. Such inefficient boilers were burning more fuel than ever. Only Rio de Janeiro might provide enough coal to fill the *Vanderbilt's* yawning bunkers. Because of her paddlewheels, Baldwin went on, the ship could not well proceed using sails alone. Under a robust trade wind, the paddleboxes acted like fixed transverse sails, pushing the *Vanderbilt* off course to leeward. She therefore had to steam constantly, devouring coal. With all her size and power, the ship was also crippled, wasteful, and technologically obsolete.

They reached Rio on July 14, almost out of fuel. The enlistments of forty of the crew would expire in August, and of seventy-five more in the next few months. "I can only hope that success may crown our efforts," Baldwin reported, "before the state of our boilers, etc., shall render it necessary for the ship to return." The last sighting of the *Alabama* placed her slightly east of Rio on June 17. The information was almost a month old, and not definite. It did suggest the *Alabama* was heading eastward, maybe. Baldwin thought about running up to Bahia, where Semmes had been. But, as the Yankee explained his decision, the weather was better, with lighter trade winds than expected, so he instead headed eastward for St. Helena. He could refuel there, perhaps; or if not he might still, with economy, turn around and reach Bahia. On this whimsical basis, the crucial decision was made.

The *Vanderbilt* came into St. Helena toward the evening of August 15. The U.S. consul delivered important news: both the *Alabama* and the newest Confederate cruiser, the *Georgia*, were seen off the Cape of Good Hope in late July. A day later, a Danish schooner brought a confirmation: the *Alabama* lay off Simon's Bay on August 2. The two reports were the freshest, most substantial news of the cruiser that Baldwin had yet heard. He had only six hundred tons of coal on board, along with another hundred tons in bags that were packed for protection around the exposed machinery on the upper deck. Still, he had to go. Within forty-eight hours of arriving at the island, he set forth for the Cape—but fresh trade winds blew him back. Three days later, after some limited coaling, he started again.

Bucking hearty trade winds from the southeast, burning forty-six tons of coal a day and still making only a bit more than seven knots, the *Vanderbilt* reached Simon's Bay at one o'clock in the afternoon of August 30. The *Georgia* had left just eighteen hours earlier; another near miss. The *Alabama* had disappeared. Semmes was hiding at Angra Pequena (also called Lüderitz Bay), about six hundred miles up the west coast. He had gone to that isolated spot, over which no European power claimed jurisdiction, in order to sell the *Sea Bride* to a Cape Town merchant. In the absence of any recognized law, the sale could not be considered illegal. (The lucky merchant got a bargain for £3,500, about a third of the ship's value. It was the only prize that Semmes ever managed to sell.)

The transaction completed, on August 31 the *Alabama* started working back down the west coast. Semmes did not know the *Vanderbilt* was waiting at Simon's Bay; Baldwin did not know the *Alabama's* location or course. The two ships were close, and getting closer, but groping in the dark. Semmes had his own machinery problems. The condenser, after producing undrinkably salty water for two weeks, stopped working entirely. Though he had loaded up with 1,500 gallons in Angra Pequena, the captain had to limit his men to a daily half gallon each. The hunting off the coast continued poor as well. "We are on the Yankee track," he noted, "but see no Yankees. They no longer pursue the beaten road." As hunters, they had spooked their game and become the victims of their own success.

The *Alabama* poked along through days of light winds and calms. Then a gale blew in from the southeast, sending the ship off course to the west. "We had a rough, ugly night of it, with a continuance and even increase of the gale and a short, abrupt sea, into which the ship occasionally rolled and pitched with violence, frequently thumping my cot against the beams overhead and awaking me." Water leaked in through the propeller well and cabin deck. The gale continued the next day, tossing the ship about. All aspects were dreary and uncomfortable.

The slow passage down the coast, however tedious and unsettling, may have saved the *Alabama* by delaying her arrival. The *Vanderbilt*, loaded with 904 more tons of coal, departed Simon's Bay on September 11. She hung around the Cape for days, waiting and hoping for Confederate prey. The *Alabama* belatedly reached the vicinity. Both warships were hunting and hovering, biding their time. One night at around ten o'clock, in thick weather and poor visibility, the watch on the *Alabama* heard a nearby vessel strike four bells. Arthur Sinclair, peering through his night glasses, saw "a very large steamer, looming high out of the water, and lying, like ourselves, in a loafing attitude." (The *Vanderbilt* was a very large steamer that rode high.) The men on the *Alabama* hushed and whispered, so as not to tip their presence. Someone hurried down the stern ladder to rouse the captain. By the time Semmes came up on deck, the other ship had disappeared into the night.

The escape, if such it was, punctuated their descent from the zenith. The *Alabama* came into Simon's Bay on September 16. Semmes finally learned—surely with some alarm—that the formidable Yankee gunboat had been nearby for the past two and a half weeks. "He thinks the Vanderbilt much too heavy for him," the *Argus* reported after a talk with the captain, "that the Vanderbilt has very much greater speed than the Alabama, and that it will be impossible for him to get away from her." (Semmes didn't know about her disintegrating boilers.) If it came down to a pitched battle, he said, he would try to avoid a broadside; instead, turned at a right angle to the Yankee, he would aim for her vulnerable machinery with his stern Blakely pivot gun. "He says that if he has to fight, he will do his best." The mouth of the bay was sixteen miles wide. Given that much maneuvering room, Semmes guessed that if blockaded he might, even with less speed, still reach open water on a dark night and run from an overmatched fight.

Learning that the *Vanderbilt* had swept up all the coal in Simon's Town, Semmes sent off to Cape Town for another supply. Kell had the ship heeled over on her side so they could reach the copper sheathing around the blowpipe, three feet below the waterline, which needed replacing. To replace the twenty-one sailors who had deserted, however, was more difficult. After a year's service at sea, it was the forecastle's most resounding wordless protest yet—fanned, to some extent, by the cajoling enticements of money and freedom from the resourceful U.S. consul in Cape Town, Walter Graham. To replenish his ranks, Semmes had to reach far down to the trashy denizens of a waterfront flophouse—hungry, bleary, and almost shirtless—and pay the conniving landlord exorbitant fees for his alleged trouble.

On September 24, urgent telegrams from Cape Town warned

Semmes that the *Vanderbilt* was still lurking nearby. With the moon nearly full, and fearing a blockade by the Yankee that might hold him in Simon's Bay until the next dark of the moon, the captain ordered steam and weighed anchor shortly before midnight. A gale blew under a clear sky and bright moonlight. The only clouds lay low, as white and motionless as snow banks, on top of the surrounding mountains and highlands. Beneath that serene, illuminated canopy, the waves of the bay churned and broke, sometimes crashing onto the men on the upper deck. It was so quiet up there and so agitated down here: the two halves of the scene not fitting together. The spectral white light of the moon showed every object, revealing but distancing, clear and cold. The scene looked strangely unreal. And where was the *Vanderbilt*?

The *Alabama* headed due south for two days, running from the Yankee, and then settled eastward into the southern expanse of the Indian Ocean. Captain Baldwin of the *Vanderbilt*, guessing wrong, had already turned up the southeastern coast of Africa toward the island of Mauritius. His boilers, as ever, needed more patching; and now his starboard drive shaft was cracked and might break if pushed too hard. "In my present crippled condition," he regretted, "I shall have to go along slow and nurse the shaft as much as possible." Semmes and the *Alabama* had gotten away again.

EIGHT

The Track of Fire to Singapore

When news of the *Alabama*'s maneuvers around the Cape of Good Hope reached New York, it inspired a dime novel. *The Track of Fire; or, A Cruise with the Pirate Semmes* was written and published in the fall of 1863. The author listed on the title page, "Captain Wheeler, U.S.A.," was a pseudonym for one Leon Lewis, which may also have been a pseudonym. The genre of dime novels, launched in 1860 by the Beadle brothers in New York, marked a recent innovation in American publishing, raucously popular and lowbrow. The Beadles put out one book a month, pocket-sized, about one hundred pages long, bound and printed cheaply, and without undue attention to spelling or proofreading. Aimed mainly at young people, costing just ten cents, they were particular favorites of Civil War soldiers in the field. The books, fitting well into knapsacks, killed off many boring hours in camps and could be readily passed around and then discarded. Within four years the Beadle dime books had sold five million copies, an average of over 100,000 for each release: staggering figures for the publishing industry of the 1860s. During its short, fleeting life, a dime novel reached far more readers, and different kinds of readers, than the more ambitious mainstream books of the time.

The Track of Fire, for all its shabby modesty, is nonetheless a vivid historical document, suggesting how Semmes and the *Alabama* were perceived in the North after one year of the cruise. The story begins with the cruiser off Cape Town. "The history of Capt. Semmes," writes the author, whoever he or she was, "his personal characteristics, etc., are too well known to the world at large to require mention in these pages." In cahoots with his villainous adjutant, Lt. Murlick, Semmes buries $60,000 in captured gold and silver somewhere near Table Bay. "We can't be expected to risk our lives for nothing," says the captain. Then they leave for the Bay of Bengal, their next hunting ground. (Not a bad guess; the author knew as much about Semmes's actual course from Cape Town as, say, Gideon Welles.) "The East-Indian route shall be a perfect *track of fire*," the pirate gleefully predicts, "illuminated by the conflagration of the ships we capture!"

Semmes burns a prize at night to attract other prey—"his usual *modus operandi*." This heartless ploy, first described by Captain Hagar of the *Brilliant* in the fall of 1862, is sheer fiction; but it fits a piratical profile. Another Yankee ship, the *Ocean Cloud* of Boston, comes along and tumbles into the trap. When dealing with his captives, the captain is tersely unconcerned: "I never allow any whining to effect me." He dispatches the crew of the *Ocean Cloud* in irons to his dreaded "prison-hold" below. This grim, crowded chamber—"as famous, in its way, or rather *in*famous, as the Libby prison, at Richmond"—is dark and filthy, dank and poorly ventilated, with no berths, beds, blankets, or skylights. "The air in this living grave was fetid and feverish, and the prisoners fairly reeked in this close confinement." No appeal from such punitive conditions will move the cruel buccaneer. "I can't help that," he shrugs. The actual cruiser harbored no such prison hold, though the book's pungent description hardly overstates the reality in the sailors' squalid forecastle on the *Alabama*—or any other oceangoing ship of this period.

The plot of *The Track of Fire* runs to dime-novel conventions of an evil villain (Murlick), a noble hero (Captain Willis of the *Ocean Cloud*), a fair maiden in peril, and a long-lost son. At the end the hero inevitably saves the good guys. Yet the notorious pirate, in effect twirling his storied mustache, gets away. His famed collection of captured instruments, the scalps displayed on his wall, includes 211 chronometers, no less. "The subsequent career of Capt. Semmes can

A Union depiction of the alleged "prison-hold" on the *Alabama*'s lower deck.
(*Frank Leslie's Illustrated Newspaper*, November 22, 1862)

be traced [by] the attentive reader through the daily papers. Whether
he will yet be captured by the active cruisers of the U.S. Government
remains to be seen." Even inside the alternate universe of dime novels,
where things always turn out well, the captain and his ship are still triumphantly uncatchable.

WOLF OF THE DEEP

· · ·

They seemed more formidable from a far, uninformed distance. Despite all the parties and celebrations at Cape Town and Simon's Bay, all the press clippings and flowers tossed his way, Semmes could not shake the heavy, dragging feeling of recent months. He still felt too old and worn out for the relentless demands of the *Alabama*. The warmth and ease of his receptions ashore actually made sea life that much less tolerable. During the final weeks of trolling around the Cape of Good Hope, gale winds and choppy seas again brought up hard memories and his latest meal. "I am supremely disgusted with the sea and all its belongings," he keened to his journal. "The fact is, I am past the age when men ought to be subjected to the hardships and discomforts of the sea. Seagoing is one of those constant strifes which none but the vigorous, the hardy, and the hopeful—in short, the youthful, or, at most, the middle-aged—should be engaged in. The very roar of the wind through the rigging, with its accompaniments of rolling and tumbling, hard, overcast skies, etc., gives me the blues." A few days later: "No sail in sight! Mustered the crew. How tiresome is the routine of cruising becoming!"

In mid-September, about a week before departing Simon's Bay, he learned—two months after the fact—of crushing defeats of Confederate forces at home. Lee's army, beaten at the defining Battle of Gettysburg, had retreated back into Virginia and recrossed the Potomac River. After months of resistance, the vital Mississippi River outposts of Vicksburg and Port Hudson had fallen to the Union, splitting the Confederacy and cutting off its internal lifeline. "Greatly discouraged by the news from home," Semmes worried. "Our poor people seem to be terribly pressed by the Northern hordes of Goths and Vandals." The South had reached its high-water mark and was settling into a long, stubborn descent. Semmes, like most of his compatriots, was far from ready to concede defeat. "We shall fight it out to the end, and the end will be what an all-wise Providence shall decree." But the clustering bad news, overlaid on his unshakable shipboard blues, left him disheartened as he turned toward the longest leg yet of the *Alabama*'s cruise.

The passage would demand all his resources and will. The course ran about five thousand miles: eastward along the thirty-ninth south parallel across the southern Indian Ocean, and then north to the East

Indies, to the Strait of Sunda, between the islands of Java and Sumatra. "A weary, monotonous, and boisterous voyage," as Arthur Sinclair remembered it. An occasional prize would have broken the dreary monotony and offered welcome news and supplies (perhaps canvas and twine for the sailmaker, cordage and naval stores for the boatswain, lumber for the carpenter, provisions and tobacco for the sailors, and charts and another chronometer for the captain). On two previous occasions, the *Alabama* had gone prizeless for a month. Now, after taking the *Sea Bride* at Cape Town back on August 5, they went three months—three long, blank months—without a single capture.

Within the tight, contained world of the ship, more isolated by the extended voyage and poor hunting, the daily routines of cruising provided the only structure for the successive sameness of days. The new sailors, dragooned from the lower depths of the Simon's Town waterfront, had to be raised up to—or at least near—the standards of man-of-war discipline. The *Alabama* was repainted and her metalwork repolished. Two new master's mates stepped right into their duties: Maximilian von Meulnier and Julius Schroeder, both officers in the Prussian Navy, had recently been shipwrecked near Table Bay while on a private tour of the world. Drawn to serve on the famous Confederate cruiser, they asked Semmes for positions. Along with their strict Germanic notions of shipboard discipline (welcome on the quarterdeck if not in the forecastle), von Meulnier spoke several languages—useful in boarding parties—and Schroeder beamed forth a genial personality that made him a sunny favorite among his shipmates.

A day usually began with the thudding, raspy sounds of holystones being hauled across the upper deck, removing the daily residue of salt spray and other debris. The heavy, flat stones, with ropes attached at each end, were dragged back and forth across the wet, sanded deck. Sailors loathed this unavoidable dogwork. Smaller stones, for cleaning in tight places around the masts and guns, were called prayer books because men used them on their knees. Once scoured, the deck was flooded and scrubbed with dry swabs, then scraped dry with leather squeegees. All these tasks were slogged through before eight bells and breakfast, after which the deck became too busy for unobstructed cleaning.

On a routine day, with no sails in sight, Semmes generally kept to himself in his cabin. He spoke mainly to his devoted clerk, Breedlove Smith, and his equally faithful steward, Antonio Bartelli, who guarded the august proprieties of his station and reserved the choicest foods for the captain's table. (Bartelli also served as barber to all the wardroom officers, taking special pleasure in brushing and plaiting John Kell's extravagant beard.) Having no social peer on board, Semmes typically dined by himself—which suited his solitary habits. "I was the Commander," he would explain, "and therefore . . . more or less isolated socially from the rest of my officers."

Up on the quarterdeck, Kell ran the ship. In any weather, at any time of day or night, under any circumstances, the First Luff was reliably there, watching and snapping orders. It is not clear when, if ever, he slept. "How I used to hate him," Midshipman Edward Anderson wrote later. "He used to make us youngsters stand around, and after we were made lieutenants we thought ourselves as important as he. It was duty, first, last, and always, with our first officer, and no boyish nonsense either, except in our frolics ashore on off duty days." "You were kind and good to us all," a gunner's mate later told him, "but we sure had to mind you and I'm glad of it." The men *knew* Kell, saw and felt him as a roaring, implacable presence in their lives every day, and granted him various proportions of fear, respect, and affection. One sailor later anointed him as "the only man we fellows on the berth deck would fight or go to hell for."

Kell's constant preoccupation was the delicate, complex dance between the wind and his sails. From his elevated position on the horse block at the stern, he scanned the sky and sea, smelled the wind, and guessed what was coming. Semmes told him what course to take. Kell then decided whether to approach it directly or tack to one side or the other, as the wind shifted in power and direction. For the First Luff this all meant steady, subtle adjustments in making and shortening sail. He gave orders to the boatswain, Benjamin McCaskey, who blew his whistle to summon his mates, who passed the commands down to the sailors, who sprang up into the rigging to furl or unfurl the canvas. They had performed these tasks so many thousands of times, on the *Alabama* and other ships, that the process was crisp, automatic, without wasted motions or—usually—any dangerous mistakes.

At noon, another ringing of eight bells, the captain emerged to shoot the sun. The sailing master aimed his sextant and reported the latitude. "Make it so, sir," Semmes replied, and then went below to calculate the ship's position and enter it into his journal. Boatswain

McCaskey and his mates piped the men to dinner: the major meal of the day, brightened by grog. The sailors filed around the grog tub, downing on the spot their cherished tot of rum and water, then ambled forward in their peculiar side-to-side sailor's gait, rubbing their stomachs in appreciation. Seated on the forward deck, legs doubled under them, they cut off a chunk of salt beef or pork with their sheath knives, balanced it on a slice of hardtack, and washed the meal down with tea or coffee. They ate quickly, silently, in order to leave time for a smoke before the boatswain's whistle called them back to work.

In the evening, with the time varying according to the latitude and hour of sunset, Kell ordered the sails reduced for the night hunt, under the low canvas of single-reefed topsails. The familiar commands went down the chain: All hands reef topsails, stand by the topsail halyards, haul out the reef tackles, and haul up the buntlines. Aloft, topmen; man the boom tricing lines, take one snug reef, haul out to leeward, lay in, down booms, lay down from aloft. The men descended to the deck quickly, like circus aerialists zipping down a rope. More orders: Man the topsail halyards, tend the weather topsail braces, overhaul the reef tackles and buntlines, hoist away the topsails. When the weather braces were hauled taut, the ship was trimmed and secured for the night.

And finally to the most welcome command: All hands splice the main brace. The men happily lined up for their second turn of the day at the grog tub. After a light evening meal, they settled into the relaxed dog watch, the allotted leisure time before eight bells at eight o'clock. In the unhurried rounds of yarns, games, and songs, certain individuals—their personalities well defined and understood by this point in the cruise—generally took the lead. Among the deserters at Cape Town was the Irish fiddler Michael Mahoney ("one of our greatest losses," Semmes recorded). But the party still included Master's Mate James Evans, the resident yarn spinner, and two amiable Britons, Master's Mate George Fullam and Assistant Engineer Matthew O'Brien, both adept at contriving sports and cheering people up. An informal glee club might sing into the evening—"Dixie," "Bonny Blue Flag," old plantation songs, or pop ditties from Liverpool—and the more adventurous sailors might essay the latest dances, learned from the hired girls in Cape Town.

The forecastle, like most of the Confederacy, was overwhelmingly an oral culture. The officers partook of the ship's library, maintained by Breedlove Smith; it included volumes on permanent loan from captures. Arthur Sinclair, seeking a quiet place to read, would take a book aloft in good weather. Straddling a topsail yard, he leaned back against the mast and found a haven above the tumults below. But the sailors, many of whom were illiterate, lived on steady oral discourses of commands, songs, stories, and even poetry. Frank Townshend, an English crew member since the start of the cruise, had composed a poem about the sinking of the *Hatteras* in January 1863. Jangled in rhythms and eccentric in rhymes, it is the only surviving literary artifact from the *Alabama*'s crewmen.

> Off Galveston, the Yankee fleet secure at anchor lay,
> Preparing for a heavy fight they were to have next day;
> Down came the Alabama, like an eagle o'er the wave,
> And soon their gunboat Hatteras had found a watery grave. . . .
>
> The sun had sunk far in the West when down to us she came;
> Our Captain quickly hailed her, and asked them for her name;
> Then spoke our First Lieutenant—for her name had roused
>   his ire—
> "This is the Alabama—now, Alabamas, fire."
>
> Then flew a rattling broadside, that made her timbers shake;
> And through the holes made in her side the angry waves
>   did break;
> We then blew up her engine, that she could steam no more,
> They fired a gun to leeward, and so the fight was o'er. . . .
>
> And now, to give our foes their due, they fought with all
>   their might;
> But yet they could not conquer us, for God defends the right;
> One at a time the ships they have to fight us they may come,
> And rest assured that our good ship from them will never run.

Freeze that scene. The sailor poet, reciting his verses to a group of his peers, relives again their favorite, most exciting memory of the cruise: the moment when they were most united for the cause, "for

God defends the right." All of them facing sudden death at sea, but then relieved by the delivering exultation of a complete and nearly bloodless victory; so many fierce gusts of emotion crammed into such a brief, intense moment. And now, cruising toward the East Indies, the mellowing evening runs along amid laughing conversation and sentimental, heart-tugging music about faraway homes and families. Semmes and his officers look down from their quarterdeck in benign approval. The captain savors his nightly cigar, and his unshared worries drift away with the smoke. Everything seems properly stowed, in good order for the night.

Yet the scene is deceptive. As the *Alabama* sailed into the second year of her cruise, the ship's company—always fractious—was splintering apart. The festering grievances within the forecastle (not enough battles or liberty, and no prize money at all) remained unaddressed. The extended period at sea without captures left the men bored and restless. Over the next few months, the sailors came close to mutiny.

At sea again, the *Alabama* charged across the Indian Ocean, driven onward by a nearly constant gale from the northwest. In just under twenty-five days they reached the hundredth meridian, due south of the East Indies, making a total of 4,410 miles at a daily average of 178 miles—quite fast for a steamship under sail power alone. "I presume this run has seldom been beat," Semmes guessed. Even with her worn copper sheathing curling in strips and her bottom fouled, the *Alabama* was still relatively swift. But the speed came with an unavoidable loss of comfort. For day after day the ship ran before the wind, rising and falling on the long, majestic swells of the Indian Ocean. Descending those waves, running downhill at a scary pace, the helmsmen struggled to keep the ship from swerving to port or starboard and thus turning broadside to the overpowering forces of wind and water. The tiniest loss of control might have proven fatal. On four occasions the steady gale cranked up to a cyclone; the ship's main timbers groaned and creaked, bending and twisting, and water leaked through the tortured seams, soaking the captain's bookcases and the bedding in the wardroom.

As they turned north toward the equator and the Indies, the wind fell and the temperature rose. For nineteen days they saw no other sails. The absence of prizes became more dire when the paymaster reported they had run out of butter, coffee, and beans—even though he had paid for three months' worth of those precious commodities in South Africa. Someone had evidently cheated them. The sudden change in climate, the blanketing heat and humidity, made the captain sick. "As usual, when not well," he reflected, "my thoughts turn despondingly toward my home and family." Again reminded of the long separation, now stretching more than two and a half years, he wondered whether he would ever see them again. "These are the real sacrifices which a naval officer makes to his country."

On October 26, a passing English bark told them a Union Navy gunboat, the *Wyoming*, was patrolling the southern entrance to the Strait of Sunda. David S. McDougal, the commander of the *Wyoming*, was not looking for the *Alabama;* he thought the Confederate cruiser had returned to the Atlantic after departing Simon's Bay. But McDougal was deploying the obvious strategy that Gideon Welles should have pressed from the start, of hanging around the major ocean crossroads. Semmes saw it at once ("This is the first time I have found a pass guarded by the enemy"). He knew the *Wyoming* was a fair match in size and firepower for his own ship. "I have resolved to give her battle," he decided. Supposing that the enemy would anchor near the island of Krakatoa, just west of the strait, he hoped to spring a surprise attack at night under a bright moon—though the start of the rainy season made the night sky subject to sudden, random changes.

For the next ten days they cruised outside the strait, getting reports about the *Wyoming* but not finding her. Late in the afternoon of November 6, the long prize drought finally ended as they caught the rakish bark *Amanda* of Bangor, Maine, bound from Manila to Queenstown, Australia, with a cargo of sugar and hemp. After taking sails, cordage, and provisions (perhaps including some greatly needed butter, coffee, and beans), they burned her that night under a dirty rain. A nearby British ship, attracted by the bright blaze surrounded by the murky darkness, came up to investigate. "It was one of the finest sights I have seen at sea," that ship's captain observed. "Though, as we were close to the unfortunate bark, it was as light as day, all outside the halo of her light was doubly dim and black." The skipper of the *Amanda*, Isaiah Larrabee, later reported that "the crew of the 'Alabama' seemed to be dissatisfied with their long cruize and uncertainty of obtaining their prize money, but order was preserved on board."

Under steam power, watching for the *Wyoming*, picking their way carefully, they passed through the Strait of Sunda into the Java Sea. Within a few hours they caught a rich prize, the American clipper *Winged Racer* of New York. Relatively large at 1,767 tons, and quite beautiful, she was one of the most celebrated Yankee ships running between New York and San Francisco; now she was heading home from Manila with hemp, sugar, indigo, pearl shells, and cigars. "We thought the *Winged Racer* too handsome a ship to burn," Kell recalled, "but what could we do?" According to George Cumming, the clipper's captain, the boarding party demanded liquor and got drunk at once. They took coal, oil, provisions, and other supplies, pitching the articles into the boats so carelessly they caused leaks that required bailing. Cumming asked to keep a telescope that was lying on his skylight, but was told to leave it for the bonfire. Unlike Captain Larrabee, he was appalled by what he saw during his stay on the *Alabama:* "a most disorderly set of fellows, apparently under no discipline whatever, and the officers comparatively ragged."

A day later, sailing to the northeast toward the Karimata Strait off Borneo, the lookout spotted a sail off the port bow. She looked to be a Yankee. Semmes had just ordered his boilers banked and propeller raised; but with the prospect of a chase, the firemen and engineers kept steam power available. The careful fencing began. The *Alabama* raised U.S. colors. The Yankee ship, the *Contest* of New York—another famous clipper—did the same. She was bound from Yokohama for home with cotton, tea, and other merchandise. Semmes fired a warning shot and put up the handsome new version of the Confederate flag, the cross and stars on a white field, obtained in South Africa. Instead of surrendering, the *Contest* unfurled topgallant and topmast studding sails—and ran for her life.

They were about four miles apart, in a fresh breeze. The *Alabama* poured on sail and steam but could not close the distance. Her bow seemed heavy and out of trim, plowing too deeply into the oncoming waves, so Semmes ordered his crew and some of the forward guns aft to the quarterdeck. With their weight shifted, the bow rose and the ship picked up speed. Aboard the clipper, a passenger, William Nevius of New York, watched the brisk chase in fretful admiration. The legendary Confederate cruiser lay to windward and far astern. "She had all sail set and steam up," Nevius noticed, "and presented a beautiful appearance." It was an ocean race between two thoroughbreds, an exciting sport with grave consequences. Both ships crammed on every sail they could carry. Men on the cruiser crowded to the rail to relish the spectacle, like fans at a horse race. The *Alabama* luffed up for a moment, for better aiming, and boomed a shell that fell well astern of the quarry.

The contest for the *Contest* was not decided until the wind died. The clipper, dependent on sails alone, began to slow down. Semmes ordered his scale-encrusted boilers pushed to their limits; his engineers warned of an explosion. From about a quarter mile away, the *Alabama* threw another shell, aimed with more harmful intent. William Nevius heard it whizzing overhead between the clipper's foremast and mainmast. At that sensible moment, after a thumping race of ninety minutes, Captain Frederick Lucas of the *Contest* decided to give up. He shortened sail, came to the wind, and hove to. "We had never captured so beautiful a vessel," Arthur Sinclair recalled. "She was a revelation of symmetry, a very race-horse. A sacrilege, almost a desecration, to destroy so perfect a specimen of man's handiwork." In a rare display of respectful seafaring tribute, many of the Confederate officers came on board to inspect her before the especially cruel bonfire. John Kell admired an elegant set of Japanese hand-carved ebony armchairs "that it seemed a shame to burn," he wrote, "they were so beautiful. We made the night brilliant."

Nevius, who had been ill, was treated kindly on the *Alabama*. Lieutenant Beckett Howell gave up his berth to the sick man, and Nevius messed with the wardroom officers, eating the same privileged fare as Semmes. His general sense, though, was of a pirate ship, sloppy and undisciplined, and not a proper naval vessel. The leader of the boarding party was "a most rascally and seedy looking individual," Nevius wrote, "with a sword at one side and a pistol at the other." Captain Semmes was "villainous in appearance. He keeps much to himself and is on deck very little." And down in the forecastle, "The crew is composed chiefly of the offscourings of the English service, and is in quite an insubordinate condition."

James Babcock, the first officer of the *Contest*, was even harsher after being held on the *Alabama* for a week. He later reported:

> Crew much dissatisfied, no prize money, no liberty, and see no
> prospect of getting any. Discipline very slack, steamer dirty,
> rigging slovenly. Semmes sometimes punishes, but is afraid to

push too hard. Men excited, officers do not report to captain, crew do things for which would be shot on board American man-of-war; for instance, saw one of crew strike a master's mate; crew insolent to petty officers; was told by at least two-thirds of them that will desert on first opportunity. Crew all scum of Liverpool, French, Dutch, etc.

The officers up on the quarterdeck looked besieged, armed for protection from their own sailors.

Officers on duty have cutlass and revolver; never saw Semmes in uniform; puts on sword at muster. Have given up small-arm drill afraid to trust crew with arms. While on board saw drill only once, and that at pivot guns, very badly done; men ill disposed and were forced to it; lots of cursing.

Earlier in the cruise, external sources from the *Alabama*'s prizes had given similar reports of disorder and poor discipline. Yet no such witness had ever been as caustic and detailed as James Babcock. His testimony, considered along with the other recent evidence from captured men on the *Amanda*, *Winged Racer*, and *Contest*, implied that conditions on the *Alabama* were deteriorating markedly. Something had happened—perhaps at the Cape of Good Hope, or during the uncomfortable, monotonous passage across the Indian Ocean. A dangerous set of long-simmering complaints was heating up, edging close to an explosion. Semmes and his young officers were nearly losing control of their ship.

The *Alabama* lingered for a few days in the Java Sea, hoping to avoid the *Wyoming*, which Semmes supposed would have taken off to the north. In a gesture of reconciliation to his crew—a tobacco bribe—the captain ordered some of the choice cigars from the *Winged Racer* handed out to the sailors. Refusing to be bought off so easily, still wanting their promised prize money, the men contemptuously threw the cigars into the ocean. Semmes considered the gesture mutinous. He had the three apparent leaders of the cigar protest arrested and confined for a court-martial. Among them was Frank Townshend, author of the fervently loyal poem about sinking the *Hatteras*; the angry disaffection among the crew had even reached him.

Semmes, in his usual shipboard role as both prosecutor and judge, punished the poet and another sailor severely for their "mutinous and seditious conduct" with reduction to the grade of ordinary seaman, loss of three months' pay, and solitary confinement in double irons, for a month, on bread and water. Their locked-up examples, the captain hoped, would "bring the disorderly to their senses." Still, the penalty for mutiny and sedition could have been worse, from being spread-eagled in the rigging to banishment and even death. After fifteen months of the cruise, facing the hardening resentments in the fore-castle, perhaps Semmes was indeed—as James Babcock perceived—"afraid to push too hard."

Under sail, running short of coal again, they passed carefully through the Karimata Strait on November 18. It required deft seamanship during a northwest monsoon; such conditions sometimes forced a sailing ship to waste a month tacking back and forth before squeezing through the narrow passage. The *Alabama* ran along the northwest coast of Borneo into the South China Sea. They spent two desultory weeks in a wide counterclockwise arc from Borneo toward the coast of Indochina. The waters were unfamiliar to Semmes, full of concealed dangers and unpredictable currents. Drifting fifty or sixty miles a day in dead calms, with the sails slapping idly against the masts, they sighted no Union vessels—and, in any event, lacked the coal for a chase. The weather continued jangly and frustrating. After tedious days of no wind at all, a monsoon blew in with too much.

The flurry of three quick captures in early November was followed by another long dry spell. Without the periodic diversions of chase and prize, the men could think too much about what they were missing. "We must have constant bustle and excitement," wrote Arthur Sinclair, "to smother our rising thoughts of the far-off land we love so well." Sinclair wondered how the captain still bore the relentless burdens of carrying all their lives on his skinny shoulders. At any hour of day or night he could be seen bending over the maps in his cabin, or up on deck, checking the soundings of those poorly charted seas. More rugged than he looked, he was also more frayed than he dared acknowledge. "Our captain begins to show the wear and tear of weary months of watching, thinking, and anxiety," Sinclair noticed. "True, he can go below at desire, be at all times comfortable as to dress, and has no watch to keep; but these privileges are more than offset by the irregular sleep and hours, grave responsibilities, and disadvantage of more than twice our age."

They had now been at sea continuously for over two months since departing Simon's Bay on September 24. Semmes decided to stop at the island of Condore, about sixty miles off the southern tip of Indochina. "My ship required overhauling and repairing," he later reported to the Navy Department in Richmond, "and my crew needed the refreshment and quiet of port." Condore offered the kind of island sanctuary that the captain favored: a pliant local government liable to be impressed by a famous visitor, fresh food and water, good hunting and fishing, but few illicit pleasures for his men. The French colonial administration, which had recently taken control of the island, seemed unfriendly at first. The French officials had heard, and believed, that Semmes murderously burned his prizes with all hands still trapped on board. Once advised otherwise, they became more cordial.

The *Alabama* stayed at Condore for twelve days of repainting and general recuperation. Semmes had time to look around, finding gradual renewal in the inevitable play of his unbounded curiosity. He watched a group of baboons, "these caricatures of humanity," as they sat on the beach and studied the ship carefully. When a boat from the *Alabama* landed, another group of younger baboons started frisking around, but an older one called them back from danger to the dense forest. An island locust trilled a high, piercing whistle almost as loud as a railroad locomotive's. The ship's hunters brought back an ugly East India bat that measured over three feet from wingtip to wingtip, and a lizard nearly six feet long. An officer shot a monkey that died like a human, bringing his hands to his wound and voicing plaintive, accusing cries; his monkey comrades buried him in the sand. Somebody found a peculiar tree product, long, thin, and dark, that looked exactly like a fine Havana cigar. It was neither fruit nor seedpod but woodlike; Semmes as amateur naturalist could not imagine its intended function.

Isolated from any news since leaving South Africa, the captain perused a supply of French newspapers that were over two months old. The war news from America was not encouraging. "We see nothing in them of any more Confederate cruisers being fitted out," Semmes fretted. "We feel almost as if we had been abandoned by our Government in this matter. What can the Secretary of the Navy be about?" On the other side of the world, as far as they could possibly get from home and compatriots, they were quite alone. Singapore, the nearest major port, was two days from Condore by fast steamship. On December 14, Semmes figured that the regular mail steamer had brought news of his presence on the island to Singapore by the twelfth. If an enemy warship like the *Wyoming* was then nearby, and was alerted, trouble could arrive at Condore at any moment.

On his own, by himself (as always), he had to decide where to go. After about seven weeks of cruising around the East Indies, he had taken only three prizes. The weather was often hot and oppressive, the winds wildly varying, the coal supply not reliable. What was the point of sticking around? "A lengthened cruise would not be politic in these warm seas," Semmes told his journal. "The homeward trade of the enemy is now quite small, reduced, probably, to twenty or thirty ships per year, and these may easily evade us by taking the different passages to the Indian Ocean." The coasting trade among Chinese ports, or to Calcutta or Australia, would carry only neutral cargoes forbidden to the *Alabama*. "There is no cruising or chasing to be done here, successfully," he continued, "or with safety to oneself without plenty of coal." British colonial ports by law could only provide him coal every three months; and the ports of other nations' colonies, given the predictable vigilance of Yankee consuls, would probably refuse him. So he decided to recross the Indian Ocean and return to the Cape of Good Hope; then he might go back to the coast of Brazil. But the deteriorating state of his ship dictated its own conditions. Her copper-sheathed hull and worn-out boilers required major overhaulings. For such elaborate repairs, demanding special supplies and machinery, he needed a friendly port somewhere in Europe. But where?

His immediate need was coal. Without it he could not condense water or outrun a Yankee gunboat, or perhaps even catch a prize. The British colonial port of Singapore, across the China Sea to the southwest, was his best coaling chance; and any enemy warship recently there was probably heading up toward Condore. With luck they would pass each other unseen at sea. Under sail, with fires lit but banked, the *Alabama* left the island on the morning of December 15. "Our young officers," the captain recorded, "who had had so agreeable a change from the cramped ship to the shores and fruits of Condore, with their guns and their books, had become so attached to the island that they left it with some regret." At the opposite end of the ship's social order, the two culprits from the cigar mutiny—imprisoned during the entire sojourn at Condore—were finally released from their month in solitary.

After fitful sailing through ugly, cloudy weather, they reached Singapore on December 21. Their reception recalled the *Alabama*'s first visit to Cape Town, four months earlier. News of that occasion, along with the three prizes recently taken around the Strait of Sunda and rumors of the cruiser's impending arrival, primed the local reception. The *Wyoming* had indeed been recently on hand, but she had departed in early December. So Singapore was, for the moment, safe. Semmes moored his ship in the New Harbour at the docks of the Peninsular and Oriental Company, the major British steamship line that ran between Asia and Europe. The P&O was not supposed to sell coal to a Confederate warship—but did so anyway, at a quite reasonable price.

On the twenty-third the ship was opened to curious visitors. "The *Alabama* once seen will not be readily forgotten," the *Straits Times* reported. "She has the air of a dare-devil craft that would hesitate but little to test her strength against a much larger enemy." The man from the *Times* was struck by her long, low dimensions, especially the "extreme narrowness" at midship. For this public display, it seems, the crew had cleaned and shined her up. "Everything on deck is in splendid order and of the very best material. Her engine-room is also a picture of neatness."

Of course the observer's perceptions were skewed by his particular blinders. Where captured Yankees wanted to see dirt and chaos, the sympathetic reporter wished to find neatness and order. "Whatever may be our impressions when we sedately view the mission of the *Alabama*," he decided, "it is impossible in the presence of the little craft not to be momentarily carried away by an enthusiastic sympathy for her cause." When the reporter mentioned the South's declining prospects in the war, Semmes was yet unbowed. "It is no matter," he shot back, "that flag"—defiantly pointing at the Confederate ensign overhead—"never comes down."

All classes of Singapore society made their way to New Harbour, three miles by road from town. Even the local Asian populations, usually not concerned with any matter outside their ken, came to behold the famous cruiser. They aptly called her *kappal hantu*, the ghost ship. The officers proudly pointed out four scars from the battle with the

Hatteras: under the main anchor chains, low and just in front of the foremast, on the deck near the middle starboard broadside gun, and through the funnel. These residues of the fight, now almost a year old, were still obviously well cherished on board as evidence that the *Alabama* did not merely prey on unarmed merchant ships. The man from the *Times*, aware of recent reports that doubted the crew's loyalty, saw "no sign of impatience, much less of insubordination." The officers were "all fine men, and seem enthusiastic in the service on which they had adventured." But one note of caution: "Some of them admitted to me, however, that the capture and destruction of merchantmen had begun to lose its excitement." In such a cheery report, that discordant admission suggested other, darker strains, not to be acknowledged out loud.

Semmes ventured ashore to explore. In a city of around 100,000 Chinese and Malays and only 1,500 Europeans, he was astonished by the bustle of the free port. Asian products flowed in booming quantities through the port to Europe. "The business is almost exclusively in the hands of the Chinese, who are also the artisans and laborers." Money was plentiful. The streets were clogged with buffalo carts and taxis for hire. "The moving multitude in the streets comprises every variety of the human race, every shade of color, and every variety of dress." The men with dark skins looked most impressive in their white flowing mantles and impeccably clean turbans. He saw only one woman out in the streets. At the trading house of Whampoa, Semmes watched the owner working his "Chinese calculating machine," an abacus. The captain asked him to multiply a four-digit number by a three-digit number, which he did in a flash. Semmes also visited a shop that prepared opium. ("It pays an enormous license.") In the jungle just outside town, he was told, Bengal tigers killed about ten people a week.

Anchored at Singapore were twenty-two Yankee ships, laid up by news of the *Alabama*'s captures near the Sunda passage. With their masters afraid to leave port, they couldn't attract buyers or cargoes; so they just lay there, rising and falling on the tide, slowly rotting away. "The enemy's East India and China trade is nearly broken up," Semmes reported to Richmond. "Their ships find it impossible to get freights."

A party of officers from the *Alabama* repaired to the principal hotel in Singapore, drawn by its billiard tables, bowling alley, and oddly American bar and mixed drinks. A group of marooned Yankee skippers invited the Confederates to join them: hunter and prey raising friendly glasses together. They shook hands and began drinking. A Yankee proposed a toast, a bit too pointed, that landed on the Southerners as an insult. Thoroughly lubricated, the amiable encounter suddenly exploded into a fistfight. Declaring a rough-and-tumble victory, the Confederates bolted for their ship, leaving behind some property damage. Their cab was closely pursued by the police. The boozy brawl passed into shipboard lore, to be retold amid laughter and exaggerations.

NINE

Running Down

They departed Singapore on the day before Christmas. Coaled up and with renewed good luck, the *Alabama* moved into the Strait of Malacca, running northwesterly between the Malay Peninsula and Sumatra. To cap this eventful year of 1863, they took three prizes in three days. The *Texan Star* of Boston had been sold just fifteen days earlier to a British buyer; though transferred to Burmese registry as the *Martaban*, she still looked unmistakably Union and carried a Yankee skipper and mates. When boarded by the *Alabama*, the skipper— Samuel B. Pike of Newburyport—refused to leave his ship for a hearing before Semmes. For the only time on the cruise, the captain had to come to the prize. Not pleased with such an insult to his authority, he arrived in a foul humor. Pike asked him to be seated; Semmes snapped, "I *shall* sit down!" The proffered documents about the recent sale did not persuade him. "I am not to be humbugged," he warned, "with any sham papers—you ought to have a certificate of sale. I shall burn your ship!" Pike protested, but Semmes ended the conversation after three minutes. (Late that night, following the bonfire, Pike—as Semmes told the story—admitted the ownership transfer was fraudulent.)

Two days later, still in the Malaccan passage, they burned the

Sonora of Newburyport and the *Highlander* of Boston, both discovered at anchor early in the morning. The two top officers on the *Sonora*, Captain Lawrence Brown and Chief Mate Isaac Colby, later wrote detailed accounts of their encounter with Semmes and his ship. The *Sonora*'s black boatswain saw her first. "Good Lord!" he shouted. "That is the *Alabama!*" The cruiser approached within fifty yards under British colors and stopped. The men on the *Sonora* heard a whistle, then saw the British flag replaced with the Confederate Stars and Bars. The armed boarding party came alongside. Before climbing up the rope ladder, the boarding officer asked, "What ship is this?" Her name in large gilt letters was directly in front of him, on the side of the ship. "Can't you read?" offered Captain Brown. The encounter, begun badly, slid downhill from there.

Lieutenant Richard Armstrong asked Brown to come meet with Semmes at once, but the Yankee refused. He therefore witnessed the chaotic scene on his ship. Four or five boats arrived from the *Alabama*, bringing sailors to remove food and other supplies. Brown observed that the men were out of control:

> They entered the cabin and searched around, feasting on what they could find to eat and drink; taking everything they could hide upon their persons. They soon stripped the cabin of the valuable things it contained, and one of them told me they were not allowed to do so but their officers would not say anything as they had first pick. . . . They emptied several bottles of wines that they found, and seemed to have turned their morning call into a first class picnic.

At times they bickered among themselves like children, disputing who saw something first and could therefore claim it. "The whole affair was of rather a ridiculous, undignified nature."

With his ship about to be torched, Brown was finally rowed away. The men in the boat seemed undisciplined, reclining at ease, already smoking cigars and pipes. They told Brown they would like to quit the *Alabama*, but Semmes still owed them ten months' pay and all their prize money. (Ten more sailors had deserted the ship in Singapore, trading their elusive paydays for freedom.) On the cruiser, "there seemed to be little order on board, more like everybody for himself."

The entire ship looked dirty, the guns in particular. Semmes bade Brown good morning and extended his hand; the Yankee said good morning back but refused to shake hands. Semmes "stared at me and looked as though he would like to hurt somebody." They went down the aft ladder to his cabin. The captain's cap and clothing seemed worn. He had a bright red face, Brown noticed, and "was very much excited and nervous for a captain, as though he trusted no one but himself." Semmes threw his cap onto the table, glared at the Yankee, and did not invite him to sit down. (No handshake, so no courtesies.) They sniped back and forth, annoying each other. "You can clear out," Semmes finally said. "You are the most impertinent man I have dealt with." Brown accepted this, he later insisted, as a compliment. The *Sonora* and *Highlander* were ignited before noon.

Clear of the Strait of Malacca, again in the Indian Ocean, they headed west toward Ceylon and the southern tip of India. Semmes was still at low ebb. Facing the unknowable future without spirit or relish, he steeled himself for the long trek back to the Cape of Good Hope. He sentenced three of his sailors, caught in sailorly misbehaviors at Singapore, to various punishments. ("I never touch a port but the rascals give me trouble.") On New Year's Day, 1864, the captain could only muster a weary look back: "Alas! another year of war and toil and privation has passed over me, leaving its traces behind." So much for the illustrious cruise of the legendary ghost ship, her red track of fire and manifold impacts, toying with hapless Yankee pursuers far in her churning wake. The internal and external perspectives on the *Alabama* again did not match up.

Nothing much happened for two weeks. The relentless routines of life at sea clicked into place. On January 8, just south of Ceylon, they stopped an English bark bound from Mauritius to the Bay of Bengal. Remaining under disguise, they coyly pretended to be a Union gunboat in search of the *Alabama*. "It won't do," the bark's master warned them; "the *Alabama* is a bigger ship than you, and they say she is iron plated besides." (Wrong on both points.) The Englishman's latest news of the Confederate ship, more than three months old, placed her still back at Simon's Bay in South Africa.

On January 14 they burned their first prize of the new year, the *Emma Jane* of Bath, Maine, bound from Bombay in ballast. When her captain, Francis C. Jordan, came ashore in Bombay two weeks later, his account confirmed the reports of chaos and disorder given by other captives of the *Alabama* over the last few months. He said that Semmes, without examining the ship's papers, simply declared, "Captain, I am going to burn your ship." After inspecting the Yankee's nautical instruments, he found them unworthy of his collection and threw them overboard. The *Emma Jane* was torched.

"While she was burning," according to the *Bombay Times of India*,

> the officers of the *Alabama* were shouting and crowing, and doing all they could by word and gesture to distress Captain Jordan and his wife. They amused themselves in tearing up Mrs. Jordan's silk dresses to make pocket-handkerchiefs for themselves. Captain Semmes is described as a small man, of unpleasant visage, coarse manners, and foul tongue, the very type of a Southern slave driver. His officers seem to maintain their position by terror, being constantly armed cap-a-pie, with swords, daggers, and revolvers. The petty officers told Captain Jordan that they were determined to seize the ship, and were watching for an opportunity . . . that none of them ever gets wages or anything else, and would desert if they could get a chance.

The ship herself was filthy and no longer fast under sail. Her steam machinery was so disabled, said the *Bombay Times*, that the engine could run for just an hour at a time. As for the crewmen, "While in dread of their lives from the officers, there is no discipline among them. They curse and swear at each other boisterously all day, and frequently fight like fiends; while their night orgies are described as frightful. Indeed, the vessel is described as a floating hell."

Another local newspaper account, in the *Cochin Chronicle*, also drawn from interviews with the Jordans, reported that Semmes was "a careworn and anxious man, with great taciturnity and austerity of manners and yet at times capable of much courtesy and affability." He allowed Mrs. Jordan to engage him in sharp debates about the war and the Confederate cause, granting her floor space and a freedom of expression he might not have tolerated from a male captive. He was still a steadfast Southern patriot. Yet the captain's wife sensed his creeping exhaustion, the leaden weariness after so many months far from home and family: "There seems to be little doubt, however, of his great anxiety for the termination of this unhappy internecine war." If the war ended, he could go home.

West of India, they sailed into the Arabian Sea for a long, gradual descent toward the east coast of Africa. The wind favored them at the height of the northeast monsoon with clear skies and gentle, steady breezes. For twelve straight days, the *Alabama* skimmed along without having to lower a studding sail, day or night. Semmes had never experienced a finer stretch of weather, even on his home waters of the gulf coasts of Alabama and northern Florida in summertime. Pulled out of his pressing circumstances, the captain once more found simple pleasures in watching the sea and sky and deeply inhaling the soft, balmy air. "The sky was of the deepest blue," he sang to his journal, "the 'trade clouds,' piled in fantastic fleeces, reflected the golden light of the sun, and the deep-blue sea was just moved enough by the breeze to roughen its surface, and thus to increase its hue and to give a pleasant motion to the ship." As the sun set, cloud masses above the western horizon sometimes took on extraordinary architectural shapes of domes, spires, and colonnades, all lit up by bright shades of green, purple, orange, violet, and gold. Watching the colorful show as he crossed the Arabian Sea, and reaching for a characteristic historical reference, Semmes thought of old Araby's ancient cities of spices and pearly grottoes.

They stopped occasionally along the way, but essentially it was one long haul of two months and no prizes. After crossing the equator for the third time, the *Alabama* ran south-southwesterly, roughly parallel to Africa's east coast, on the course down to the Cape of Good Hope. On February 9 they reached the Comoro Islands, at the northern end of the passage between Mozambique and Madagascar. Semmes hoped to surprise some Yankee whalers, which often anchored there for supplies, but news of his operations off South Africa had apparently driven them away. The captain, presented with another new place, went ashore to study it. The land and vegetation were beautiful, the human inhabitants and their buildings mostly squalid. As a Muslim outpost, the island offered no illicit delights to the *Alabama*'s sailors; so Semmes sent them on liberty without worrying about their return. "My vagabonds on shore looked rueful and woe-begone," he noted. "Nature had no beauties for them, and there was no liquor to be had. If I were to remain here long, I should make it a practice to send them on shore for punishment." Even so, four of the restive crewmen took off for the hills. The truants were pursued, retrieved, and court-martialed for their desertions.

They sailed on down the coast, through weeks of tedium relieved only when a sailor was pitched overboard from the head. In that precarious position, exposed at the rail, anyone was vulnerable to the ship's motions. Another seaman, Michael Mars, threw himself and a wooden grating into the water and rescued the man. But the dreary passage to the cape, without any relieving excitements of capture and plunder, did not improve tempers on a vessel that was already pulling apart at the seams, both wooden and human. On March 4 the captain marked the latest sad anniversary. "It is three years to the day since I parted with my family in the City of Washington," he wrote, "on the day on which the great republic of Washington was humiliated by the inauguration as President of a vulgar, third-rate politician." For three years Semmes had been waging virtually uninterrupted war against the Lincoln government, which he regarded as an illegal usurpation of the historic American democracy. "These three years of anxiety, vigilance, exposure, and excitement have made me an old man, and sapped my health, rendering repose necessary, if I would prolong my life." Semmes was sounding a new note: that the cruise had to end not just because he felt tired, or missed his family, or believed his mission fulfilled. He had to get off the *Alabama* to save his own life.

After reaching the Cape of Good Hope on March 11, they trawled around the area for nine days, still taking no prizes. They came into Cape Town for coal and supplies and were again received warmly; yet it felt anticlimactic measured against the extravagant receptions of seven months earlier. That zenith in August 1863, with its theatrical capture of the *Sea Bride*, seemed a terribly long time ago. Since then both the war and the ship had deteriorated, and the captain was perceptibly losing vitality. They spent just four full days in Table Bay—and then were back once more in the South Atlantic, heading northwesterly toward the distant midocean island of St. Helena.

At sea, Semmes finally had time to peruse the file of newspapers collected in Cape Town. It was not pleasant reading. "The Yankee

Government and people," he responded, "and along with them the English press and people, or a greater portion of them, seemed to have jumped suddenly to the conclusion that we are beaten, and that the war must soon end by our submission. Mr. Lincoln has even gone so far as to prescribe the terms on which our States may reenter the rotten 'concern.' " From his distant vantage, thousands of miles away, getting news that was already months old, Semmes as yet could not imagine a Confederate defeat. "Verily, the delusion of these people in the matter of this war is unaccountable. No power on earth can subjugate the Southern States." As he mulled the prospects, though, he could not stifle new doubts creeping into the edges of his speculations. "If," he allowed, "contrary to all human calculation, we should be subjugated . . ."

During 1863, the year that for Semmes and the *Alabama* began in the Gulf of Mexico and ended in the Strait of Malacca on the other side of the world, the Civil War had gone through a revolution. Lincoln's Emancipation Proclamation took effect in January 1863. It only purported to free slaves in those states that remained in rebellion; yet it transformed the Union war effort, imparting a moral dimension by recasting the conflict as a crusade to end slavery. The proclamation also marked Lincoln's growing mastery as president. Always personally opposed to slavery, for political and strategic reasons he had earlier claimed only to be fighting to restore the Union. The events of the war now allowed—and required—him to become more himself, to take a bolder stand against human bondage. Leaving behind the initial blunders of his presidency, he was maturing into the Lincoln of history.

In Great Britain the friends of the Confederacy could no longer frame the combatants as a plucky little chap standing up to a bully. Virtually all classes of British society detested slavery. When James Spence, the South's most valuable English publicist and organizer, started urging emancipation, he was shunned by the Confederate agents in London. Former apologists for the South such as Charles Dickens could not still insist that the war had nothing to do with slavery. At the U.S. legation in London, young Henry Adams greeted the shifting tides. "The Emancipation Proclamation," he confided to his brother Charles, "has done more for us here than all our former victories and all our diplomacy. It is creating an almost convulsive reaction in our favor all over this country." Many public meetings cried for emancipation and union. In Parliament and within Palmerston's ministry, any remaining chance of recognition of the Confederacy or intervention in the war drifted away. "The emancipation movement is coming to our rescue," John Murray Forbes reported from London that spring, "and the people are with us and are moving in their strength."

To be credible the proclamation needed solid Union military success: the righteous cause backed by the terrible swift sword. As Charles Francis Adams had perceived during the *Alexandra* trial, "Nothing will move England but an idea of our power." Finally, six months after the proclamation was issued, Union forces managed double triumphs at Gettysburg and Vicksburg. The beleagured, ill-led Army of the Potomac at last achieved a real victory; "I did not believe the enemy could be whipped," wrote a former corps commander. The loss of Vicksburg, after grinding, bloody assaults and repulses, dealt an irrevocable blow to Confederate hopes in the Western theater. These military victories, extended by the occupation of Chattanooga in September, helped secure Republican wins in state elections that fall as loyal voters endorsed the double-edged Lincoln policy of abolition and union. The distant battlefields, once again, swayed politics back at home.

With Lee's army driven from Pennsylvania and the Mississippi River in Union hands, those sectors of British opinion that remained unmoved by "sentimental" objections to slavery had to recognize military realities. "I think our Govt. grows colder and colder every day," mourned William S. Lindsay, the South's most influential advocate in Parliament. Even the editors of *The Times* of London started to shift away from the Confederacy. The government in Richmond, giving up on any more pointless diplomatic minuets with the British, recalled James Mason from his post in London. "England is too rich to be generous," Semmes decided. "The sordid pursuit of gain has stifled all her nobler qualities, and she is cowering beneath the Yankee lash like a whipped spaniel."

Within the South, politicians and opinion shapers assumed brave public faces, hoping to shore up popular support for continuing the war. No panic, no defeat. They weren't beaten, not yet. In private, though, at dinner parties and in the candor of a diary, it was impossible not to fall into gloom. "Yesterday we rode on the pinnacle of success,"

Josiah Gorgas, the chief of Confederate ordnance, wrote in his journal after Gettysburg and Vicksburg. "To-day absolute ruin seems to be our portion. The Confederacy totters to its destruction." Such bad news after so long a run of good news seemed disorienting. How to explain it? Many observers wondered about Jefferson Davis; perhaps the strains of his presidency and recurring poor health had affected his mind. "I have never actually despaired of the cause," wrote Robert G. H. Kean, head of the Bureau of War, in his diary, "priceless, holy as it is, but my faith in the adequacy of the men in whose hands we are, is daily weakened. . . . The prospect is very gloomy. Men of the most hopeful temper are getting discouraged, and I believe nothing will arouse the spirit of the people fully without a change in the cabinet."

After the series of defeats on land, some Southerners turned with forlorn hope to the war at sea. The *Richmond Dispatch*, the largest Confederate newspaper, again urged the relative impact, at little cost, of attacking the Union fleets on the ocean. "If we had only twenty Alabamas and Floridas upon the seas," the *Dispatch* declared that fall, "we could make the Northern cities howl, and cause the Stars and Stripes to trail ignominiously the waves of every sea." But the *Florida*, after taking twenty-five prizes in eight months, was laid up for repairs in August 1863 at Brest in France and would not capture another Yankee until the following spring. The *Georgia* had proven ineffective and ill suited for cruising, with only nine captures in seven months, and had limped into Cherbourg for overhauling. The *Tuscaloosa*, the *Alabama*'s tender, was seized by British authorities in Cape Town after just two prizes, which both had to be bonded instead of burned. James Bulloch's attempts to build four more ships like the *Alabama* had foundered on money problems and stiffening British resistance to arming the Confederacy. "We are alone in this war," the *Dispatch* had to concede a few weeks later. "The rest of the world is not only not for us, but it is positively against us. There is no port in the world into which our cruisers can conduct and dispose of a prize. There is no ship-yard in which we can build a ship."

The showdown drama over the most formidable Anglo-Confederate vessels, the Laird rams, played out amid one of the strangest episodes of the entire war. Though the evidence of this bizarre plot has been available to researchers since the 1920s in the well-plumbed papers of Gustavus Fox at the New-York Historical

Society, it has not previously been revealed. Fox, as assistant secretary of the U.S. Navy, had sent John Murray Forbes and William Aspinwall to England in the spring of 1863 on a secret mission to buy the rams for the Union Navy. The Yankees were thwarted. During the summer, Charles Francis Adams in London grappled with Lord Russell at the Foreign Office, trying to stop the rams by legal and diplomatic arguments. The Yankees were not hopeful of success.

Secretary Fox became desperate. He was therefore receptive when a seedy character named Isaac Oakford came to his office in Washington that summer. Of erratic fortune, Oakford was originally from Philadelphia, a promoter of various schemes, and acquainted with Benjamin Moran of the U.S. legation in London. He hit Fox with a daring, even breathtaking proposition: if provided enough money, he would go to England and arrange for the Laird rams to be burned at their docks in Birkenhead.

An official of the U.S. government should not have facilitated such a major crime against British private property; the shipbuilder still owned the vessels until they were at sea. "I told him the Department could not go into that business," Fox recalled a year later, "but I saw no reason why merchants and insurance people should not." So he gave Oakford introductions to two substantial Boston ship merchants, John Murray Forbes and George B. Upton. (Semmes had torched Upton's ship *Nora* a few months earlier, and Forbes was still yearning to block the ironclad rams.) Forbes and Upton handed Oakford $5,000 for his vigilante bonfires. Such a large sum, bestowed by such men for such an errand on such a dubious agent, demonstrates just how frantic the Union effort to halt the rams had become.

In August, Oakford sailed to Liverpool in grand style on the *Persia*, the finest Cunard liner of the time. "I will stop the ships by some means," he wrote to Fox. "I have done more in a week than all your representatives and agents have done in a year." He had improved the policies of *The Times*, he said, and furthermore had persuaded all the leaders of the government to mend their ways. Russell, well prodded by Adams and responsive to the improving Union prospects in the war, finally seized the rams on September 8, ending the crisis. Oakford of course took full credit. "I have had no easy job," he assured Fox, "and feel quite satisfied with my diplomacy." A few months later, having squandered the $5,000 on nothing useful, he showed up at Fox's office, beaming in triumph. The secretary, by then embarrassed over his enabling role in the scam, called Oakford a scoundrel and a swindler and told him to go away.

In his own mind, Semmes had not gone to war to defend slavery. As he tried to decide what course to take in the early months of 1861, he barely mentioned the South's peculiar institution. A political moderate and military patriot, he did not at first endorse secession, and after it happened he did not expect a war. Events pulled him along. He buckled on his sword, he claimed, to defend his home and section against a Yankee invasion of Puritans and barbarians. It was a noble revolution

PUNCH, OR THE LONDON CHARIVARI.—November 14, 1863.

NEUTRALITY.

Mrs. North. "HOW ABOUT THE *ALABAMA*, YOU WICKED OLD MAN?"
Mrs. South. "WHERE'S MY RAMS? TAKE BACK YOUR PRECIOUS CONSULS—THERE!!!"

An evenhanded English comment on British neutrality.
(*Punch*, November 14, 1863)

for freedom and democracy, he believed, in the honored tradition of the old Revolution of 1776.

The war in fact was always about slavery, and Semmes knew it. At his home in Mobile, he owned three household slaves. He regarded the institution as a benevolent two-way contract. In his memoir of the Mexican War, he described the free, impoverished people of Mexico as less fortunate than American slaves, who lived in relations "more or less of mutual regard; the master bestowing upon his slave the kindly feeling which is naturally inspired by those who are dependent upon us, and the slave, in return, regarding himself as a member of his master's family, and more or less identified with his interests." Semmes was conventionally racist for his time, no worse than most white Americans. Even white abolitionists in general regarded blacks as hopelessly inferior and childlike. Semmes believed that blacks, incapable of running their own lives, needed the structure and guidance of slavery. As he sailed around the Caribbean and Brazil on the *Sumter* and *Alabama*, he saw confirming signs of the failures of what he called "free niggerdom." Anywhere slavery was abolished, he maintained, free blacks had reverted to indolent savagery because "niggerdom will not work sua sponte [voluntarily]."

Early in the war, visiting Brazil on the *Sumter* in September 1861, he defined the shared cause of these two slaveholding nations. A local official told him he could purchase coal and supplies, but no war munitions. "I then stated to him," Semmes recorded in his journal, "that this war was in fact a war as much in behalf of Brazil as of ourselves; that we were fighting the first battle in favor of slavery, and that if we were beaten in the contest, Brazil would be the next one to be assailed by Yankee and English propagandists. These remarks were favorably received." Two months later, at Martinique, the *Sumter* was boarded by local politicians, "to whom I explained," he noted, "the true issue of the war, to wit, an abolition crusade against our slave property." Again, "they listened with much appearance of gratification."

Semmes not only spoke for slavery. Both his ships included slaves in their crews. The *Sumter* left New Orleans with a young slave, Ned, who served as the captain's steward and body servant. Semmes described him as happy and docile, a cheerful favorite with his fellow crewmen. Yet only two months later, the contented slave deserted the ship in Surinam. Semmes blamed the interference of the U.S. consul;

but perhaps Ned was not as docile as he appeared. The *Alabama*, manned from Liverpool, had no slaves in her initial crew. Two months into her cruise, however, the captured *Tonawanda* yielded among its booty a black youth from the slave state of Delaware. David Henry White, about seventeen years old, was taken despite protests and assigned to duty as a waiter in the wardroom officers' mess. The *New York Herald* ran the story under an outraged headline: "The Pirate Steals a Colored Boy from the Tonawanda." Also characterized by Semmes as cheerful and willing, White remained with the ship and received the wages of his station. Snatched as a slave yet paid as a freedman, he did not try to escape despite many later chances in foreign ports.

Slavery was the sinister underside, not always apparent, of the *Alabama*'s cruise. When she stopped at Kingston, Jamaica, in January 1863, the newspapers edited by and for white people reported Semmes's fervent speech at the Merchants' Exchange as a paean to freedom, linking the Southern cause to a traditional English quest for liberty that went back to the Magna Carta. A local black paper, the *Jamaica Watchman*, recounted a different speech: "This lover of slavery . . . said that before the war broke out in America the slaves were a contented people throughout the Union; they were well cared for, fed, clothed, and in every respect better provided for than any other of their class on the face of the earth." Southerners, he said, were "fighting for the protection of their property," not just for their own independence. "Captain Semmes is striving to perpetuate slavery in America," the *Watchman* concluded, "and it is impossible that he can be rid of the feeling when he is the hater of the Negro race here, as he is on the soil of Alabama."

The Emancipation Proclamation merely confirmed what Semmes already believed about the North's designs on Southern property and institutions. It made him only more determined to pursue the war to the end. At Cape Town in August 1863, he sputtered about "the rant of white-chokered negrophilists, who believe that we Southerners are a set of heathen slave-drivers, pirates and cut-throats." Early in 1864, at the Comoro Islands, he was asked whether he was fighting for the side that upheld slavery. "Yes," he replied, "we belong to the country where the black man is best taken care of in any part of the world." It was an ironic response given that his interrogator was a dark-skinned black

African. "Oh," the man assured him, "we are slaveholders here; being Mohammedans, we have no prejudices that way. Our only trouble is that we can not get slaves enough for our purposes."

Raphael Semmes was a moral paradox. Although a slaveowner, he was not deeply invested, financially, in slavery. He operated from a clear, unselfish set of principles, and denied himself comforts and even his health to serve the cause. Yet that cause, as Ulysses Grant later remarked, was one of the worst for which a people ever fought. Semmes thus took the wrong actions for high, principled reasons. Clarence Yonge, the brazen anti-Semmes, wound up with the Yankees in the Civil War—but in assuming that allegiance was selfish, deceiving, and unprincipled. He took the right actions, ultimately, for the wrong reasons. So who in the end was more admirable?

A reasonable answer, though laden with these complicated ironies of motive and outcome, is self-evident. Semmes, by defending slavery in a nation committed to individual rights and democracy, put himself on the wrong side of history. Neither he nor any other true Confederate, then or now, can escape that judgment. When seen against the grand scope of Western history and its finest achievement, the endless struggle for freedom and self-determination, the cruise of the *Alabama* deserved to end in defeat.

TEN

Cherbourg

Semmes played out his hand. Departing Cape Town on March 25, 1864, he set a northwesterly course toward the ocean outpost of St. Helena. There the lookouts saw no prey, and the weather was stormy and fickle, so the *Alabama* turned due west and made for the coast of Brazil. Once a rich hunting ground, the area now yielded just two prizes, both taken in late April: the guano ship *Rockingham* of Portsmouth, New Hampshire, and the *Tycoon* of New York, bound for San Francisco with a general cargo. Wherever the *Alabama* went, the pickings were sparse; Yankee ships were either hiding in port or sold into foreign ownership. Semmes and his men had succeeded all too well.

A cache of recent newspapers from the *Tycoon* prodded the captain once more to finish his mission and go home. Into his journal he pasted a clipping that announced the marriage of his elder daughter, Electra, in February. Evidently from a Southern or British paper, the clipping explained that the bride's eminent father was "now abroad for the benefit of the Confederate naval health." The ceremony, officiated by the Roman Catholic bishop of Mobile, took place at the family's home in the city. Though Semmes often mentioned his wife and children in his journal, noting the many missed anniversaries and long separations, he recorded no comment about Electra's wedding. It was perhaps too painful that his favorite daughter, just turned twenty-one, had married a man he did not know, had not met or approved. So he said nothing at all. "May the gallant rover come home in good time," the newspaper notice hoped, "and in peace to see his family and friends."

At some point in the previous year, while Anne Semmes and her children were staying in Richmond or after their return to Mobile that summer, Electra had gotten engaged to the English con man (and sometime journalist and double agent) who called himself Frank Lacy Buxton. He was smoothly persuasive, an accomplished pretender, and the family bought his lines. Aside from Electra's coquettish beauty, he was no doubt drawn to the fortune that he imagined her father was piling up from his captures at sea. In September, however, Confederate authorities in Mobile warned the Semmeses of Buxton's multiple levels of shadiness. Anne went to the British consul at Mobile, Fred J. Cridlund, and asked him to consult her husband's most influential friend in England, the shipowner and active member of Parliament William S. Lindsay. "Much doubt exists with regard to Mr. Buxton," Cridlund told Lindsay, "and he is accused of being an impostor and a Lincoln spy and a bogus correspondent of some London paper—and though unknown to him he is under surveillance here. Now Mrs. Semmes is not disposed to believe any of these charges against Mr. Buxton nor is the daughter to whom he is engaged. The wedding which was to come off this year is now postponed." After making inquiries, Lindsay wrote Anne that no one in England—including his alleged relatives—had heard of a Frank Lacy Buxton. With that nudge, and just in time, the impostor was unmasked.

Very quickly, perhaps on the rebound, Electra became engaged to someone else. Her new beau, Pendleton Colston, came from a distinguished Baltimore family. A lawyer, he spent the war in Mobile serving as a judge advocate for the Confederate Navy. (As an attorney from Maryland involved with naval affairs, he may have reminded Electra of her father.) Raphael's cousin B. J. Semmes, visiting the family in Mobile in January, approved of Colston—"a very clever and promising man"—but wondered about the fiancée's notorious inconstancy: "I liked him very much and it is a match that will please Raphael if Electra will hold to her engagement."

In common with the rest of the Confederacy, Mobile was suffering from dire wartime shortages and inflated prices. Union raids into Mississippi and Alabama were reducing local food supplies. Yet the city was still well fortified, behind a bay considered too shallow for large warships; Consul Cridlund regarded Mobile as "one of the safest places in the Confederacy." Social life went on as usual, at times with oddly lavish spending and people taking dangerous risks under the looming prospects of death and ruin. According to Cridlund, reporting to the Foreign Office in London, "lying, blasphemy, drunkness, gambling, licentiousness and robbery have become the order of the day." Given the war's uncertainties, the fashionable attitude seemed to be live now, spend now. B. J. Semmes attended a lush wedding and ball in Mobile for which the bride's gown and trousseau cost $10,000—excessive even in Confederate currency. "Electra was certainly the handsomest girl in the room," cousin B.J. informed his wife, "and in fact the Semmes party generally was the best looking." A few days later, Anne threw an indulgent twenty-first birthday party for Electra, with an elegant dinner that turned the house upside down.

Such extravagance would not have delighted Raphael Semmes if he had known about it. (At that moment he was crossing the Arabian Sea and contending with a mutinous crew.) But he would have welcomed the sudden transformation of his party-girl daughter. Just before her marriage to Colston, Electra fell victim to an epidemic of smallpox spreading through Mobile. Her entire body was thickly covered with horrible lesions. Then came an inexplicable miracle, understood by the family as divine intervention: in one hour she was cured, and two days later, at her wedding, she showed no mark of the disease. Not previously pious, she suddenly embraced the faith of her father. "She had been recd into the church and is very devout," B. J. Semmes wrote in astonishment. "She is very much changed."

When Captain Semmes ran across that newspaper article two months later, he learned none of these important details. He was missing the most significant turns in his beloved daughter's life. His son Spencer was also recently married, to a distant cousin from Georgia, and his Uncle Ben—the mindful foster father who taught him the habit of serious reading, to whom Semmes dedicated his Mexican memoir—had died at seventy-four. Along with all his other reasons, now, for leaving the *Alabama* behind, the captain needed sharply to get home.

Gaily along the rebel came,
Under the flag of the cross of shame;
Knight of the handcuff and bloody lash,
He twirled the point of his red moustache,
And swore, in English not over nice,
To sink our Yankee scum in a trice. . . .
Semmes has been a wolf of the deep
For many a day to harmless sheep;
Ships he scuttled and robbed and burned,
Watches pilfered and pockets turned.

(FROM A UNION POEM BY GEORGE H. BOKER, 1864)

The *Rockingham*, taken on April 23, broke the longest drought of the cruise: three months and nine days without a prize. After the *Tycoon*, three days later, the *Alabama* had no more luck at all. Semmes headed north, crossing the equator again on May 2. They caught the friendly northeast trade winds after the usual preamble of calms mingled with thunderstorms. Near the great ocean crossroads at the thirtieth parallel of north latitude, Semmes tried to overhaul two likely prospects that were showing British colors—but they easily outran the once swift cruiser. "Our bottom is in such a state that everything passes us," the captain exasperated. "We are like a crippled hunter limping home from a long chase." Two days later, two more ships hove into sight on the same course as the *Alabama*—but skipped away. "The lame hunter continues to be beaten." Many of the ship's beams, crafted from uncured timber by a shipbuilder that specialized in iron hulls, were splitting and failing. The copper sheathing continued to strip off below the waterline, and the decks were leaking copiously, dampening the captain's cabin and adding serious inches to the normal daily rise in the bilgewater. The *Alabama*, still months from her second anniversary at sea, was coming apart.

The ship required major servicing in a European port. With Great Britain closing down to the Confederacy, Semmes decided to try France. The government of Emperor Louis Napoleon had sympathized with the Confederacy, at times, and nearly extended formal recognition to Richmond. Semmes's two cruising mates, the *Florida* and the *Georgia*, had recently found refuge in French ports. Bearing toward France, the *Alabama* passed near the Azores, where Semmes had first caught sight of his beautiful new cruiser twenty-one months earlier, long ago, back in August 1862. There the untried *Alabama* was equipped and declared a warship of the Confederate Navy, and there she lit her first bonfires: ten Yankees in just two weeks. Now Semmes and his men found no quarry to slow their progress toward the English Channel. They arrived on June 10, greeted by a typically dense channel southwester. That night, Semmes made an extraordinary, prescient, yet ambiguous entry in his journal: "And thus, thanks to an all-wise Providence, we have brought our cruise of the *Alabama* to a successful termination." Did he mean the end of the vessel's initial cruise? Of his own presence on the ship? Of the *Alabama's* entire history at sea and war?

Early on the following afternoon, they entered the port of Cherbourg, about seventy miles across the channel from the southern English coast. Semmes applied to the local authorities for permission to land his prisoners and start repairs. The French official regretted that Semmes had not chosen a commercial port, such as Le Havre, where private docks were available. Cherbourg, a naval station, had only military facilities, and the French government now preferred not to service a ship from an active belligerent in the war. But the decision was delayed for several days, in the languid French manner, until the emperor should return from his holiday in Biarritz.

The fame of the *Alabama* meant that her presence in Cherbourg could not remain a secret. In fact, rumors from her brief sojourn at Cape Town that she was next headed for France had already reached Union agents in Europe. In late April, Charles Francis Adams had reported that the ship was expected in a French port "probably to refit, and discharge some of her men who feel as if they had been in her long enough." An *Alabama* rumor, for once, got it right. Within hours of her arrival at Cherbourg on June 11, the U.S. vice consul at the port cabled the news to the U.S. minister in Paris, William L. Dayton, who at once sent a telegram to the Union gunboat *Kearsarge*, patrolling off the Dutch port of Flushing. Dayton had earlier protested to the French minister of foreign affairs over the port facilities extended to the *Florida* and *Georgia*. "The character of this vessel is so obnoxious, and so notorious, that it is possible they may exclude her," Dayton hoped. "The arrival of the Alabama will spread universal dismay among American shippers in these seas and all engaged in American trade."

The *Kearsarge* had been chasing Confederate cruisers, and not finding them, for years. The elusive figure of Raphael Semmes ran all through her history. She pursued the *Sumter* near Gibraltar, and the *Alabama* after her debut around the Azores. Hoping for better results, the Navy Department replaced the ship's first commander with a new man, John A. Winslow, and told him to get the *Alabama*. After hearing about Semmes's capture of the Panama steamer *Ariel*, a fireman on the *Kearsarge*, William Wainwright, wondered in his journal, "Shall we never have the pleasure of running across this terror of our merchant-men if we could only have the pleasure of comming in contact with her once I dont think she would destroy any more defenseless merchant-men." The sailors and firemen on the *Kearsarge*, like their counterparts on the *Alabama*, craved action and prize money. But instead they mostly got everyday routines and leads that went nowhere.

In the spring of 1863, off the Azores, the *Kearsarge* encountered a recent Yankee victim of the *Alabama*. "We was unable to gain any information of the Capt. Semmes," Wainwright noted, "so we put to sea once more." Two months later, at the Madeira Islands, the U.S. consul came aboard and told them a Confederate steamer was reported at the Canary Islands, three hundred miles away. "The great trouble with us being after Privateers every time we see smoke away we go to see what it is," Wainwright wrote. "So we are off again on another wild goose chase." A few days later, they just missed a blockade-runner. "We are always behind."

Captain Winslow and the *Kearsarge* spent the fall and winter of 1863–64 patrolling the English Channel, assigned to snatch the *Florida* and the *Georgia* when they emerged from their repairs at Brest and Cherbourg. The two ports were over two hundred miles apart, pro-tected by irregular coastlines and the foggy vagaries of channel weather. "I do not think we have a shadow of a chance of capturing either of them," a *Kearsarge* officer wrote home. "How can it be ex-pected that we can take care of these two vessels?" Indeed, both Con-federate cruisers did escape, and the Union gunboat was blamed for not intercepting the enemy.

When the *Kearsarge* went to London for repairs in late March, her men were acting cranky and unhappy with their captain. Benjamin

Moran of the U.S. legation visited the vessel at the Victoria Docks on the Thames. "Much dissatisfaction with Capt. Winslow exists in the ship," Moran noted. "One of the gentlemen openly said he was either a traitor or an imbecile. . . . They stated the ship needed no repairs and that there was no need to bring her to London. In fact, all that she required was a little scraping to free her bottom." Instead of being laid up for insufficient reasons, they implied, the gunboat should have been out hunting Confederate cruisers. Both Winslow and his men had something to prove—to each other, and to the dissatisfied Navy brass in Washington.

They returned to their dreary sentry duty in the channel, seemingly too far from any actual military activity. In early June another restless *Kearsarge* fireman, Charles Poole, heard real news of the war at home. "I wish that we could be doing something for its cause," he wrote in his journal, "but the prospect looks rather poor at present." Four days later, Poole picked up his journal but drew a blank; "Nothing to mar the dull monotony of life on a man of war." The engineers and firemen fell to the eternal chores of men at sea with time on their hands: they painted and cleaned, shined and polished, inventing small tasks just to be occupied. "I must say," Poole yawned, "that we have got the best looking Engine Room in the US Navy."

On Sunday, the twelfth of June, the *Kearsarge* was steaming off Flushing, near the border between Belgium and the Netherlands, when Winslow received Dayton's telegram that the *Alabama* had pulled into Cherbourg on Saturday. The most coveted enemy prize was now within his territory—offering a chance for fame and redemption. The captain told the boatswain to call all hands to muster. The men lined up in a rush on the quarterdeck, wondering why. Winslow shouted out the good news: They were ordered to Cherbourg to stalk the *Alabama*! The boatswain's mate, an enthusiastic young Irishman, called for three cheers to the success of the *Kearsarge*, and three more cheers for the captain. All were bellowed forth, and the suddenly unified ship's company, released from tedious months of dithering, zoomed into action. "I for one," Charles Poole wrote in his journal that night, "am willing to give up most everything to get the Pirate Alabama off from the ocean." They weighed anchor that night. The *Kearsarge* stopped at Dover in the morning to pick up a new trysail and topsail—which might be needed in an ocean chase—and then expected to reach Cherbourg on Tuesday. In the forecastle, many bets were placed about whether the *Alabama* would actually be there.

Sunday in Cherbourg was cloudy and cool. Semmes, suffering from a cold and fever, was glad that just a few visitors came on board to see the famous cruiser. He ordered the usual Sunday muster and inspection of his crew. Late in the spring of northwestern France, it was the middle of strawberry season, and the berries were large and luscious. After two and a half months of salted meat and hardtack, the men welcomed sweet milk and butter, and fresh beef and mutton from local farms. With the *Kearsarge* tearing across the channel, bearing down on them, they at least were eating quite well.

On Monday, learning that his naval superior, Samuel Barron, was in Paris, Semmes sent him a report about the *Alabama*. "She will require to be recoppered, refastened in some places, and to have her boilers pretty extensively repaired, all of which will detain her a couple of months." If given permission to enter the dock at Cherbourg and start the repairs, he expected to grant his crew extended shore leave, "many of them being in indifferent health, in consequence of their long detention on shipboard and on salt diet." His officers would expect the same privilege. After the ship, crewmen, and officers, he brought up the captain. "As for myself, my health has suffered so much from a constant and harassing service of three years, almost continuously at sea, that I shall have to ask for relief." In plainer English, he was resigning from the *Alabama*. He wanted to go home.

But later that day, advised that the *Kearsarge* would soon appear, he had to change his plans for both the ship and himself. The Yankee arrived at midmorning on Tuesday, the fourteenth. She entered the Cherbourg harbor—where hostilities were outlawed—and steamed slowly past the *Alabama* at anchor. The men on both ships took long, wary, curious, appraising looks at each other. "She is a fine looking steamer, about our tonnage," noted Ezra Bartlett, acting master's mate on the *Kearsarge*. "We have now had a sight of all the Confederate cruisers and I hope we will have a chance to take this one, the most <u>formidable</u> and notorious of them all." The vessels were remarkably similar: long, low, narrow, and black, wooden-hulled, with three masts, a single funnel, and steam machinery driving a screw propeller. The *Kearsarge*, a bit smaller, carried more crewmen, but the differences were not significant. In total firepower they were roughly equivalent:

the *Alabama* mounted eight guns, the *Kearsarge* seven, but the Yankee had two big Dahlgrens that threw solid shot, eleven inches in diameter and 160 pounds, larger and more penetrating than any of the Confederate's metal.

Without anchoring, the *Kearsarge* steamed through the harbor and took up a position beyond the breakwater. On two previous occasions, both at Martinique, when the *Sumter* and *Alabama* were trapped by Union gunboats, Semmes had slipped away with clever maneuvers at night. But now his ship was crippled and slow, and the enemy was fresh from her overhauling in London, with a clean hull and sound boilers. Even if Semmes did elude the *Kearsarge*, he would just find himself at sea again, low on coal, needing repairs, with nowhere to go and his crew more restive than ever. If he remained at Cherbourg, laid up for months with his officers and crewmen scattered to points unknown, an entire squadron of Yankee warships might assume positions off the breakwater, all lusting for the glory of sinking the *Alabama*. In that situation he would merely be waiting around for a too predictable outcome.

Semmes had just one more option: come out at once and fight. As he thought it over, that became his obvious choice. Other Yankees had called him a prissy coward, a pirate who just burned harmless, unarmed merchant ships, who ran from battles and had only sunk the *Hatteras* by deception and surprise. He thought of himself as a cavalier and a gentleman, with a Southerner's bristling code of honor, which, if insulted, had to be avenged. He was also exhausted, his ship worn out, his men near mutiny. Having done their work so well, they could no longer find enough Yankee vessels to burn. The cruise was finished, one way or another. He yearned for his home and family. If Semmes could defeat the *Kearsarge*, it would balance all his outstanding accounts and end the cruise, already the great naval feat of the war, in triumph. And the two ships were evenly matched; the odds were fair. Suppose his men were able to board and subdue the *Kearsarge* in close, hand-to-hand combat. Then he might switch ships, go back to sea in an already refurbished vessel, and leave the worn *Alabama* behind to be repaired. He—or another commander in his place—could then turn those powerful Union cannon back on the Yankees.

The captain called the First Luff down to his cabin. "Kell," he said, "I am going out to fight the *Kearsarge*. What do you think of it?" They talked it through, dwelling on the dangers of the eleven-inch Dahl-grens and the uncertainty of their own fuses and gunpowder after twenty-two months at sea. In recent target practice on their prize the *Rockingham*, a third of the shells had failed to explode. "I saw his mind was fully made up," Kell recalled, "so I simply stated these facts for myself. I had always felt ready for a fight, and I also knew that the brave young officers of the ship would not object, and the men would be not only willing, but anxious, to meet the enemy." Semmes clinched his decision by pointing out to sea, toward the U.S. flag at the peak of the Union gunboat. "I am tired," he said, "of running from that dirty rag!" The hare was turning on the hound.

Like a gentleman arranging a duel, Semmes conveyed his plans to a second, the Confederate agent in Cherbourg. "I desire to say to the U.S. consul," he wrote on Tuesday, "that my intention is to fight the *Kearsarge* as soon as I can make the necessary arrangements. I hope these will not detain me more than until to-morrow evening, or after the morrow morning at the furthest. I beg she will not depart before I am ready to go out." Instead of full repairs, he advised the French officials, he now only wished to fill his coal bunkers. Given the battle's uncertain outcome, he sent to shore the paymaster's last payroll along with five bags containing 4,700 British gold sovereigns (almost half the original supply from the start of the cruise) and the sealed ransom bonds from the prizes he had not burned.

Out beyond the breakwater, the *Kearsarge* steamed back and forth, keeping watch. Her men were hopeful and excited, though not convinced the pirate would really come out and fight. Semmes had a reputation for avoiding combat. "What glory for us eh?" Ezra Bartlett wrote to his brother. "Now our two years and a half of hopes and expectation are about to be realized in a fair contest with Semmes, the man we first started after. . . . Semmes is a tricky man and may try another 'Hatteras' game on us, but not so successful a one I think."

> Fearlessly the seas we roam,
> Tossed by each briny wave;
> Its boundless surface is our home,
> Its bosom deep our grave.
> No foreign mandate fills with awe
> Our gallant-hearted band;

We know no home, we know no law,
  But that of Dixie's land. . . .
We do not fight alone for gain,
  So far from native strand;
But our country's freedom and its fame,
  And the fair of Dixie's land.

(FROM A CONFEDERATE POEM BY ALEX H. CUMMINS, 1863)

"My crew seem to be in the right spirit," Semmes reflected in his journal on Wednesday, "a quiet spirit of determination pervading both officers and men. The combat will no doubt be contested and obstinate, but the two ships are so equally matched that I do not feel at liberty to decline it. God defend the right, and have mercy upon the souls of those who fall, as many of us must." On the *Kearsarge*, Captain Winslow returned from an errand ashore with the welcome news that the enemy would indeed soon emerge for battle. He ordered his men to quarters, had the guns loaded, and cleared the ship for action. He knew Semmes from the Mexican War; they had briefly been shipmates, even messmates. Winslow told his crew that the Semmes he knew was a brave man who would deliver as promised. "I want to catch Semmes," the Yankee wrote his wife, "for old friendship's sakes."

But his deadlines passed, Wednesday evening and then Thursday morning, and still the *Alabama* did not come out. "Well there is no signs of the Alabama showing herself to day," wrote William Wainwright of the *Kearsarge* on Thursday, the sixteenth, "so all our precaution amounted to nothing. But then it is well enough to be ready. In case of she should try to play any game on us. . . . It is my candid opinion that he will try to give us the slip some dark night." A sudden alarm called all hands on the *Kearsarge* to repel boarders; in less than two minutes, every man had his weapon and was at his station, ready for action. The harbor pilot, afraid of being drilled in the ensuing crossfire, asked for his boat and rushed to escape—to the guffawing amusement of the crew. "Every man is confident of our ability to handle the Alabama," explained the *Kearsarge* fireman Charles Poole, "and hoping that she may give us a trial to see who is the best." Any private fears were stifled or at least unexpressed. On both ships, the men longed to start shooting, to prove at last their doubted mettle. Within the harbor, the *Alabama* continued to take on coal. Everyone kept waiting.

On the *Alabama*, the men were also practicing boarding techniques in case the battle came down to such close quarters. Whatever qualms they may have felt were muffled under joking and teasing. "Banter is the order of the meal hours," Arthur Sinclair noticed. When the captain announced that any personal valuables could be placed in the ship's safe to be sent ashore, Lieutenant Joe Wilson said that all he owned was his guitar, and he would keep it on hand to maintain their spirits. They lightly twitted the wardroom waiter, the black slave David White, about his courage; ever amiable and cooperative, he just smiled back at them. On shore leave, the officers loaded up at Cherbourg's cafés—because, as Wilson mordantly put it, they needed to be fattened for the slaughter. Under the prospect of sudden death, time passed slowly, abstractly, though at times vividly.

To Semmes, the most precious object on board was his shipboard journal—his own daily record of the cruise, reasonably candid and private, and the basis for the memoir he was probably planning to write if he survived the war. After almost two years, the journal filled two folio-sized bound volumes, a bit worn and stained, with the daily entries written in ink in the captain's graceless but legible hand. On Friday, to his great joy and relief, he placed his journal with a suitable caretaker. An English publisher, C. Warren Adams of the London firm of Saunders, Otley and Company, had heard that the *Alabama* was at Cherbourg. He crossed the channel, picked his way through layers of port officials and gendarmes, and got to Semmes. The captain loaned the journal and other ship's papers to Adams with the implicit hope of quick publication. Even if the ship and captain went down together, at least their records would survive and surface. The last words of the final journal entry, on Thursday: "Coaling ship. Some lady visitors on board. The enemy's ship still standing off and on the harbor."

In London on Friday, at the parsonage in Belsize Park, Semmes's best friends in England—the Reverend Frank Tremlett and his sister, Louisa—sat down to dinner with the Confederate naval officer Matthew F. Maury. While they were at table, a Confederate agent arrived from Paris with the startling news that Captain Semmes was going to fight the *Kearsarge* off Cherbourg "if she met his approval." (That made it seem up to the captain; in reality he had little choice.) In

Paris, the local Confederates felt so sure the great Semmes would prevail, perhaps by boarding the *Kearsarge* and converting her to another cruiser for the South, that they mused about the right officers for this next addition to their navy.

At Cherbourg, at about eight o'clock on Friday evening, the steam yacht *Deerhound* came to anchor after a short trip from the Channel Island of Jersey. She looked like a miniature version of the *Alabama*, a little sister, and that was not a coincidence: she was designed by the same naval architect, Henry Laird, on the same model as the *Alabama*, and was built in 1858 at the same Laird shipyard in Birkenhead. One of the first steel-hulled yachts in England, she was acquired in 1859 by John Lancaster of Wigan, Lancashire, a wealthy mining engineer and coal magnate—and a Confederate sympathizer. In 1862, while the *Alabama* was still under construction at the Lairds, the *Deerhound* returned to the shipyard for lengthening and a more powerful engine. For a while, then, both vessels were lodged at Birkenhead. When the *Deerhound* appeared at Cherbourg on Friday night, they already had a shared history that was about to turn murky.

John Lancaster and his family, on a holiday cruise through the channel, had left the yacht that morning for a two-day sojourn into the French countryside. The *Deerhound*'s captain, Evan Parry Jones, arriving in Cherbourg on Friday, heard at once about the impending battle. According to the later testimony of three members of the *Alabama*'s crew, officers from the *Deerhound* came on board the Confederate cruiser at various times during Saturday. Boats went back and forth between the two vessels, perhaps carrying more valuables to the *Deerhound* for safekeeping. Brent Johnston, a quartermaster on the *Alabama*, later recalled that visiting sailors had the name *Deerhound* in gilt letters on their caps. But Johnston knew nothing about the purpose of these visits, if indeed they amounted to anything beyond the usual public interest in the celebrated cruiser.

On Saturday, a young Englishwoman named Alicia Maria Falls—a daughter of the British consul for Normandy and Cherbourg—joined a party that visited the *Alabama* in the morning. Her blazing contempt for the Yankees on the *Kearsarge* and her hope they would soon be sunk amused Semmes; his daughter Electra was of about the same age and spirit. "He was a very quiet, silent man," Falls wrote years later, "with a face full of determination, wearing at that moment an anxious expression." He called her "little girl," though she was an adult. He asked if she had visited the *Kearsarge* as well. She indignantly said no. "You know the *Kearsarge* says the *Alabama* is afraid to fight her," the captain jested. "Do you think I look afraid?" She did not. A friend of Falls invited Semmes to dine on his yacht, but the captain, pleading his duties, declined.

At nine o'clock the previous night, on the *Kearsarge*, a false report that the *Alabama* was coming out to fight had roused the Yankees, then let them down once more. On Saturday they heard, yet again, that the battle would finally take place on that day—or maybe the next. "Well we are ready for him any time he feels like showing himself," William Wainwright groused to his journal, "and I hope he wont keep us waiting much longer. For we are getting tired of waiting for him. I begin to think the same as a good many others. That he don't intend to come out. Not in the day time anyway."

Semmes finally decided at some point on Saturday. His coaling and other preparations were completed; in one final act of prudent foresight, his treasured collection of chronometers from prizes—about sixty-five in all—was transferred to another English yacht at Cherbourg, the *Hornet*. The weather had been dark and cloudy for days, but Sunday promised the bright sun and improved visibility that he wanted for battle. In addition, Sunday had been a lucky day for the *Alabama*: the day on which she was commissioned at the Azores, the day she caught the *Ariel* and sank the *Hatteras*.

On Saturday evening, strolling around the square in Cherbourg, Alicia Falls again ran into her hero. "Have you heard that all is settled?" Semmes asked her. "To-morrow we fight." The *Kearsarge* had heavier guns, he said, so he hoped to board her. If they could manage that feat, they would win. "He was very grave," she remembered, "very quiet." She, realizing that the morning might leave Semmes and his men dead or captured, started to sob. "Little girl," he said, "you are crying." On the eve of the battle, he perhaps again thought of Electra.

At ten o'clock that night, John Lancaster and his family arrived in Cherbourg by train and went to the *Deerhound*. The town and yacht were buzzing with the impending battle. Lancaster intended to embark for Southampton, but his children—two grown sons and a younger son and daughter—wanted to stay for the spectacle. A sailor on the yacht heard one of them plead, "Oh, pa, do let us see it." The parents were outvoted, and they remained in the harbor. On the *Alabama* and *Kearsarge*, and the *Deerhound* and *Hornet*, all hands settled down for the night. A historian must wonder what they thought about as they lay in their bunks and hammocks.

> In Cherbourg Roads the pirate lay
> One morn in June, like a beast at bay,
> Feeling secure in the neutral port,
> Under the guns of the Frenchman's fort;
> A thieving vulture; a coward thing;
> Sheltered beneath a despot's wing.
> But there outside, in the calm blue bay,
> Our ocean-eagle, the Kearsarge, lay;
> Lay at her ease on the Sunday morn,
> Holding the Corsair ship in scorn.

(FROM A UNION POEM BY THOMAS BUCHANAN READ, 1864)

Sunday, the nineteenth of June, dawned bright and mild, with just a slight overcast. The sea was calm, the surface smooth. The setting for the battle was ideal. People in town moved to the quays and breakwater and higher locations, the upper stories of buildings and the heights above Cherbourg, for a better look at what they hoped was coming. The regular weekend excursion train from Paris brought about 1,300 more spectators; expecting just a pleasant holiday at the shore, they were instead treated to a free performance of deadly combat at sea. The *Alabama*'s two German officers, Maximilian von Meulnier and Julius Schroeder, who were heading home on leave, hurried back from Paris and arrived in time to rejoin their ship. Another Confederate naval officer in Paris, Terry Sinclair, reached Cherbourg at eight o'clock and was allowed to come aboard—but not to remain, by the captain's agreement with French officials, because he had no prior connection to the ship. (Sinclair noticed the general state of wear on the *Alabama*: "The officers, including Semmes, looked rough, jaded and worn out. The men were rough-looking, but a fine set of fellows.")

John Kell had his ship ready. The decks and brasswork were scrubbed and shining. Sand was spread around to absorb blood and prevent a slippery deck, and wooden tubs were filled with water. On the lower deck, the surgeons laid out their instruments. The sailors were dressed in their muster uniforms, as though for a Sunday inspection, and the gun crews stripped to the waist. The boatswain and his mates blew their whistles to call all hands aft. Semmes mounted a gun carriage and addressed his men for the first time since the ship was commissioned at the Azores. He was characteristically terse: You now have another chance to fight the enemy, the first since the *Hatteras*. You have sailed the world, sinking and driving away half the enemy's commerce. Your illustrious name must not now be tarnished by defeat. Defend the flag of your young nation. Go to your quarters.

The *Alabama* was heavily loaded down with coal, to help protect the steam machinery and to present a lower target. Semmes had decided to fight with his starboard battery, so he had moved guns across the deck from the port battery. Their unbalanced weight gave the ship an awkward list to starboard. Semmes did not trust his powder and fuses, weakened by long exposure to ocean dampness and steam from the freshwater condenser, located adjacent to the powder magazine. So his strategy was to fire the first shots and get the enemy leaning backward, avoid the impact of the powerful Dahlgrens, then run up close to the *Kearsarge*, grapple and board her, and secure a quick victory that left him in control of both vessels.

At nine o'clock, Captain Jones of the *Deerhound* took his vessel out of the harbor, beyond the breakwater to where the *Kearsarge* was waiting. The yacht then turned around and came back in, running near the *Alabama*. To some observers it appeared that the two vessels exchanged signals. At 10:30 Semmes told Kell to get under way. The Confederate cruiser moved toward the Yankee, where some of the crew had just assembled for Sunday service. Captain Winslow was turning the Bible's pages, looking for his text, when the lookout shouted, "Here she comes!" The congregation dissolved at once. The *Kearsarge* turned and steamed out into the channel; Winslow wanted to make sure the battle took place well beyond the French three-mile limit. The *Couronne*, an ironclad warship of the French Navy, was patrolling the scene for the same reason. The *Deerhound* followed behind at a prudent distance.

At about seven miles from shore, the *Kearsarge* turned back toward her pursuer. The two ships closed on each other. The *Alabama* suddenly sheered, turned broadside, and opened fire from a mile away.

The battle off Cherbourg; the two ships are circling each other, starboard to starboard, both under steam with sails furled. (*Illustrated London News*, July 2, 1864)

The men on the *Kearsarge* could see the shells flying and bursting overhead; perhaps the Confederate gunners were overcompensating for their ship's starboard list. The Yankees waited till they reached the range they wanted, a thousand yards, and then fired to better effect. Semmes tried to come closer, but the *Kearsarge*—with a cleaner hull and stronger boilers that produced more power—was faster, more agile, and thus could dictate the dance. The two ships settled into a circular pattern around a common center, broadside to broadside, that seemed to a sailor on the *Kearsarge* like two flies crawling around the rim of a saucer. They fired steadily, gradually drawing in the circle, across a distance that ranged from nine hundred to four hundred yards. By degrees the Confederate fire tapered off while the Yankees' came more thickly.

From the shore, the fight looked like two boxers circling each other and jabbing from a distance. At a Catholic church on a hill above Cherbourg, the first gunfire interrupted morning mass; the priest adjourned the service, and everyone went out to look. Though their flags could not be discerned from land with the naked eye, the ships identified themselves by the exhaust from their funnels. The *Alabama*, burning Welsh coal, was nearly smokeless while the *Kearsarge*, using coal from Newcastle, burned thick and black. The sound of the gunfire echoed across the channel and far into England, nearly all the way to Bristol. Just outside the range of the cannon, Lancaster and Jones kept the *Deerhound* distant enough for safety, but close enough for possible service.

The fighters turned through seven circles, booming away. The eleven-inch shells from the Dahlgrens tore heavily into the *Alabama*'s bulwarks, slicing them away in sections, the wood splinters flying wildly and cutting jagged wounds into flesh. The aft pivot gun, one of the two main Confederate weapons, took a direct hit, killing or wounding all of its crew except the compressor man. On the *Kearsarge*, a shell from the Blakely cannon ripped through the aft quarter, a terrific explosion that shook the entire ship. Overall, the *Alabama* fired less accurately; her gunnery practice had been restricted by limited supplies of ammunition and, toward the end of the cruise, by the crew's mutinous spirit. Now that long neglect was exacting lethal consequences.

The men on the *Kearsarge*, well drilled in combat, fired and loaded without haste, almost casually. "We all laughed and talked thro the fight," wrote William Cushman, the chief engineer, "and were perfectly cool." The most damaging shell came through the bulwark below the main rigging, wounding two sailors and a gunner. Another shell pierced the funnel, exploding inside, but Cushman's steam machinery remained intact. Another zipped through the engine room skylight and fell into the water on the other side. Across the deadly circle, Semmes stood on his horse block, the elevated position at the stern that gave him the best view of the battle. "Confound them," he said of the Yankees; "they've been fighting for twenty minutes, and they're as cool as posts." A shell splinter zinged through the air and wounded the top of his right hand, a painful but not disabling injury. He had the quartermaster bind and sling the hand, and stayed at his post, giving orders. Blood was now pouring out on his ship. Bodies and pieces of bodies littered the deck.

The Confederate ammunition was, as feared, degraded and not reliable. Explosions from the *Alabama*'s guns sounded muffled and

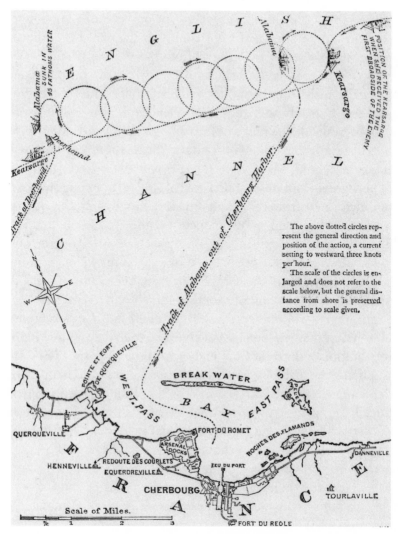

A schematic drawing of the battle.
(*Battles and Leaders of the Civil War,* 1887)

dull, with thick puffs of smoke like heavy steam; those from the *Kearsarge* cracked clear, sharp reports that burned off into a thin vapor. Shells from the *Alabama* at times just bounced off the enemy's wooden side. One crashed through the counter at the stern and lodged in the rudder post, but failed to explode. Another slammed into the rail just forward of the fore pivot gun; the impact raised the gun and carriage but, again, the shell didn't explode.

The big Dahlgrens did most of the damage to the *Alabama*. An eleven-inch shell crippled the rudder, making the ship nearly uncontrollable. Another broke in at the waterline, entered the engine room, and exploded. The *Alabama* trembled along her entire length, as though recoiling from that shot to the heart. The fatal hole near the waterline was big enough to swallow a wheelbarrow. When the ship rolled, waves poured in; as she settled, the volume increased. The rising water snuffed out the fires under the boilers, cutting off steam power and disabling the pumps. Without fire and steam, the ship was literally powerless.

There was only one recourse: run for the shore, now nine miles away, and get back within the three-mile limit, where the combat would have to stop. At noon the *Alabama* set fore-and-aft sails, but Winslow—recognizing the tactic—moved inshore of his enemy and cut her off, firing full batteries at close range as he went. Taking more water, disabled and helpless, the *Alabama* began to sink. The ship settled perceptibly at the stern. Semmes asked Kell to go below and assess the damage. He reported that she would founder in ten minutes. As the

One of the *Kearsarge's* Dahlgren cannon during the battle.
(*Battles and Leaders of the Civil War,* 1887)

Alabama lay bleeding, the Yankees threw volley after volley at her, raking her entire length with no return fire, reaching for the coup de grâce.

In the final, desperate moments, intentions and signals became confused. Semmes ordered the colors struck, but at the same time two last shots—*bang bang*—were fired, unauthorized, from the forward section as a stubborn, mistaken gesture of defiance. Infuriated at this apparent duplicity, the *Kearsarge* responded with another volley of five shots, provoking in most of the Confederates a bitter suspicion of Union treachery after they had already surrendered. Two men on the *Alabama* raised a white flag. The guns subsided. Kell ordered all hands to abandon ship, to leap overboard to escape the possible suction when she went under. Only two of the *Alabama*'s lifeboats remained intact. One, commanded by George Fullam, was sent to the *Kearsarge* with the Confederate wounded.

The *Alabama*, still with her sails set, drifted idly away. At about ten past twelve, only seventy minutes into the battle, her bow rose into the air and the stern went under. "We had hardly got warmed up," noted William Cushman on the *Kearsarge*, almost disappointed, "and were expecting to fight several hours." The mainmast of the *Alabama*, riddled during the fight, snapped in two. As the stern settled, the ship struggled upward into a nearly vertical position. For an instant she lingered there. Then, like a steam pile driver descending, she plummeted straight down and disappeared. "I took my last look," William Wainwright recorded, "at a little past twelve of the far famed Alabama the boast of England the Pride of the Confederate Navy and the terror of American Merchantmen."

The *Deerhound* came up from behind the *Kearsarge*, on her way to the men struggling in the water; Lancaster asked if they could help the Yankees. "No," he was told. "But for God's sake do what you can to save them!" The *Kearsarge* had only two boats still usable after the fighting. Both vessels lowered their available boats. Fullam brought his wounded to the *Kearsarge* and announced the surrender of his ship. He asked if he might go rescue more men; with permission, he picked up additional shipmates—but took them to the *Deerhound*, not back to the Yankee. On the *Alabama*, just before the end, Semmes had removed his boots, heavy pants, and vest, but left on his woolen uniform coat. He was last seen in a small group at the stern that included his faithful steward, Antonio Bartelli, the steadfast Kell, and a couple of others.

The final moments of the *Alabama*, as drawn soon afterward by an eyewitness, Robert Lancaster, son of the owner of the *Deerhound;* while the *Kearsarge (at left)* stands by, the *Deerhound* approaches the foundering ship. (*Illustrated London News,* July 2, 1864)

She has gone to the bottom! the wrath of the tide
　　Now breaks in vain insolence o'er her;
No more the rough seas like a queen shall she ride,
　　While the foe flies in terror before her! . . .
Her country's lone champion, she shunned not the fight,
　　Though unequal in strength, bold and fearless;
And proved in her fate, though not matchless in might,
　　In daring at least she was peerless. . . .
And as long as one swift keel the strong surges stems,
　　Or "poor Jack" loves his song and his story,
Shall shine in tradition the valor of Semmes
　　And the brave ship that bore him to glory!

(FROM A CONFEDERATE POEM BY MAURICE BELL, 1864)

The water was cold—biting and numbing. Kell swam a few yards away, then turned to watch the *Alabama* sink. He thought about asking the men near him to raise three cheers for the grand, departed cruiser.

But he saw dead men floating around him, and felt a deep sadness, so he decided against it. It was no time for cheering. His own shipboard journal went down with the ship.

A boat from the *Deerhound*, looking for survivors, approached the First Luff. An *Alabama* crewman already in the boat recognized Kell from his lavish beard, spread out and floating on the water. He was pulled into the boat. There, to his immense relief, he saw Semmes lying on the stern sheets, looking pale and nearly dead. The captain opened his eyes and extended his hand. Kell asked if he was hurt. "A little," he said. A launch from the *Kearsarge* came near. At Kell's suggestion, Semmes lay flat in the boat, out of sight. Kell disguised himself by donning a crew cap with the *Deerhound* name and taking an oar. The Yankees asked whether Semmes was saved. "He is drowned," Kell said, and it worked. Their boat made for the *Deerhound*. Once aboard, Semmes implored Lancaster and Captain Jones to head directly to the British safety of Southampton, just across the channel. Agreed; the yacht turned northward and ran off at top speed. Lancaster later acknowledged that he wanted to help the Confederates escape.

As the *Deerhound* hurried away under full steam, the men on the *Kearsarge* could not believe what they were seeing. The officers, Lieutenant Commander James Thornton and others, urged Winslow to heave her to, even to prod her with gunfire, but Winslow refused. Surely, he said, a captain of an English yacht would not skip away with the Union's prisoners. And the *Deerhound*, furthermore, had women and children aboard. "Had I deemed him mean enough to have done it," Winslow wrote his wife a day later, "I would have opened my guns on him." In her sudden flight, the *Deerhound* left men still in the water: a final act in the widening, mean-tempered breach between the officers and sailors of the *Alabama*. Most of the survivors that day were picked up by boats from the *Kearsarge* and other harbor craft that hastened to the rescue—and not by the runaway yacht.

The *Deerhound* reached Southampton and landed forty-one men from the *Alabama*. The roster of the saved at once looked suspicious: the two top officers (Semmes and Kell) and twelve other wardroom officers, eight petty officers, five firemen, and fourteen sailors. How, in a supposedly random, unplanned, purely humanitarian act of kindness, had Lancaster and Jones managed to save such a high proportion of the Confederate officers, especially the commander and the first lieutenant? All the principal parties on both the *Alabama* and the *Deerhound*, then and later, denied any prearrangement. But it seemed impossible that, in the terror and confusion of the battle and sinking, such an outcome could have happened just by chance. The rescue may have been arranged at a lower level, by junior officers on both vessels, so their superiors might later sincerely deny any private scheme. The weight of the circumstantial evidence suggests, in any case, that those boats passing back and forth in Cherbourg harbor on the day before the battle were conveying more than just curious visitors. A plan was evidently hatched, if the *Alabama* went down, for men from the *Deerhound* to find the key Confederates in the water.

By Sunday evening the human costs of the unequal battle became clear. The *Kearsarge* sustained only minor damage and three wounded men (one of whom died three days later). The *Alabama* lost nine killed in action, sixteen drowned or lost afterward, and one man who died of his wounds on the *Kearsarge*. Among the twenty-six Confederate dead were just one officer (the assistant surgeon, David Llewellyn), the steward Antonio Bartelli, and the slave waiter, David White, freed at last. With her twenty-one wounded, the *Alabama* took forty-seven casualties in all—almost a third of the ship's company. "It is the proudest moment of my life," Ezra Bartlett of the *Kearsarge* wrote his brother that night, "and I would not have missed it for untold gold. . . . Their officers say that the slaughter among them was perfectly terrible." Midshipman Eddie Anderson, lightly wounded by a flying splinter, remained in the frigid water for nearly half an hour. "The Yankees were very tardy in rendering us assistance," he wrote home to a friend, "and if it had not been for an English Yacht, I would have drowned."

Semmes and Kell spent Sunday night at Kelway's Hotel in Southampton. On Monday, lacking any clothes except what they were wearing, they went to see a tailor in town. The tailor, duly impressed, took them to his private apartment and gave them cake and wine. After the fitting, the two men found a crowd gathered outside, blocking traffic. Police had to clear a path back to their hotel. Late that afternoon, James Bulloch and Francis Tremlett arrived on the train from London for a reunion and full report. Bulloch, the *Alabama*'s grieving father, now had to sort through her postmortem affairs. The Reverend Tremlett, no less distressed, came to invite his friend Semmes back to Belsize Park for peace and recuperation.

. . .

In the immediate aftermath of the fight, Semmes was criticized by some Confederates for starting, and losing, the battle. To defend his conduct, he contrived a specious explanation for the defeat: he had learned after the fact, he said, that the *Kearsarge* was ironclad. More than a year before the fight, her men had protected the vulnerable midship section with sheet anchor chains, hung over the sides in bights and covered with boards painted black. Other Union vessels were adopting the same protection. From a distance, this armor was not apparent. During the battle with the *Alabama*, at least two of her shells slammed into the wood-covered chains and bounced off.

Yet the chains shielded only one-quarter of the entire length of the *Kearsarge*, leaving ample wooden hull for the Confederate gunners. The *Alabama* was sunk because of her inferior powder, fuses, and gunnery, and—in particular—because of the crushing force of the two Dahlgren cannon. The chains were largely irrelevant. Later on, after passions cooled, three of the *Alabama*'s officers—Arthur Sinclair, Breedlove Smith, and Francis Galt—admitted that they had heard about the armored midsection before the battle, but Semmes had decided to proceed anyway. Only William Cushman, of all the *Kearsarge*'s men, later maintained that the chain armor made any difference by stopping a one-hundred-pound shot; but he had placed the chains himself, and presumably wished to claim their benefits. "Semmes knew all about it," Sinclair later insisted, "and could have adopted the same scheme."

To reach for such a dubious—indeed, false—excuse did Semmes no credit. During the first weeks after the battle, as he remained in Southampton tending to the funereal details, he went through private tortures of shock and guilt. He was finally off the *Alabama*—but at such a cost. After three years of brilliant, consistent success, his final decisions were now being doubted. "He was very much worn and jaded," Kell recalled. "Disappointment, too, had naturally broken his brave spirit, and he was greatly depressed." His right hand was swollen and painful, and he could not use it for writing. In his three years at sea, he had suffered only one prior injury, when a fall down the ladder to his cabin as the ship was rolling left him with a bruised side. Now he was wounded physically, and worse, emotionally.

Editorial comments by the British press were comforting. "He paralysed the commerce of a great nation," declared the *Manchester Guardian*. "The career of the Alabama was so wonderful and romantic, the effect of her crusade against the enemies of her flag was so extraordinary. . . . Any other ship in her place would have been taken long ago; but the Alabama was the Alabama, and Captain Semmes was her commander. She seemed to bear a charmed life." It was by any measure one of the great achievements of naval warfare. In twenty-two months and 75,000 miles of cruising, the *Alabama* burned fifty-two Union ships, sank one, bonded nine, and variously disposed of three others: sixty-five captures in all. By their own estimates, the men of the *Alabama* seized over five million dollars' worth of enemy shipping. Beyond those numbers, Semmes had affected the Union blockade, Confederate morale, Union morale, Anglo-American relations, and the current and future prospects of the U.S. merchant fleet. A few weeks after the battle off Cherbourg, the *New York World* printed a list of over nine hundred Yankee ships sold into foreign hands, mainly British, since 1860. The *Alabama* was the main reason. In achieving so much, Semmes combined amazing tenacity, imagination, and shrewd tactics as a sailor and strategist with a long run of recurrent good luck. That consistent blend of skill and fortune kept the *Alabama* hunting.

Leaping on the historical moment, in just six weeks Warren Adams and his publishing house produced *The Cruise of the Alabama and the Sumter: From the Private Journals and Other Papers of Commander R. Semmes, C.S.N.*, in two stout volumes and 846 pages. The first and last chapters were written by the English poet and novelist George Meredith. As yet in the early, scuffling stages of a notable career, Meredith worked for Adams as a reader and adviser. Like so many other British intellectuals, he was a Confederate partisan; "The *Alabama*'s sunk," he noted after the battle, "and my heart's down with her." Though Semmes took no part in the book beyond the loan of his journal, the two volumes, well printed and richly illustrated, were a handsome tribute. Meredith in his chapters praised the lost cause ("for the defence of southern liberty"), the captain ("as little the hungry fire-eater which many of his admirers suppose him to be, as he is the Black Pirate of the New York press"), and the defeated cruiser ("a vessel whose renown, short as her career has been, may challenge that of any ship that has spread a sail upon the waters"). At Cherbourg, "It would have been glorious for her to have won, but it was not disgraceful that the day went against her." After selling well in Britain, the book came out in New York only a month later.

A committee of British naval officers raised, by public subscription, a fund to replace the sword that Semmes had thrown into the sea just before his ship sank. The new sword was custom-made, costing about eight hundred dollars, with an elaborate gold scabbard that was enameled and jeweled and adorned with the national emblems of Britain and the Confederacy. Above the flags of the two nations was the hopeful motto "Peace and friendship," invoking an alliance that in fact was withering away. An Englishwoman of high degree, Lady de Houghton, gave the captain an enormous Confederate flag that she had sewn from the plushest silk. Semmes dined at the London home of John Laird, a friendly member of Parliament and father of the men who designed and built the *Alabama*. And the captain's valuable collection of chronometers, arrived safely on the *Hornet*, awaited his disposition.

Such gestures of English adulation helped soothe the sting of his bloody defeat. In early July, finished with his responsibilities in Southampton, he relaxed into the embrace of the Tremletts in Belsize Park. They understood his need for rest and quiet, his aversion to noisy social rounds and commotion about his exploits. Amid the flowers and shrubs of a midsummer London garden, he finally unwound after three hard years at sea.

Over the next three months, some sort of romantic connection, impossible to define precisely, grew between Semmes and Louisa Tremlett. She was in her late twenties, never married, not pretty, of slightly equine features. The most ardent of Confederates, along with her brother, she had known Semmes since his brief visit to London in May 1862. From the Cape of Good Hope, in August 1863, he sent her a sewing machine captured from a prize. She followed his career with the *Alabama*, worried about him, heard about the impending battle with the *Kearsarge*, worried even more, heard that the *Alabama* was sunk, and then—after an anxious interval—learned that the captain was saved. At last he, a wounded hero, came back to her home, sad and defeated, needing her care and sympathy, and stayed awhile.

When he arrived at Belsize Park in July 1864, Semmes had not seen his wife, Anne, for three years and four months. For almost two years on the *Alabama*, he had known only the distant company of

Semmes in England after the battle with the
Kearsarge. (W. S. Hoole Special Collections
Library, University of Alabama)

rough men. In short visits ashore, he always took appreciative note
of the attractive women and flirted with them whenever he could. But,
so far as the discreet record shows, he had not been on terms of
intimacy—either emotional or sexual—with any woman in all that
time. And now here was Louisa, adoring and unattached (and sixteen

years younger than Anne). She picked flowers from her garden and spread them around the house. They played croquet together, the newly fashionable outdoor amusement for both men and women. She gave him a ring, which he wore next to his wedding band.

Their later letters, most of which have survived, include cryptic words of endearment. Addressing her as "my <u>dearest</u> Miss Louisa," he called himself "a swain" and referred to "my <u>two</u> <u>families</u>, my English, and my American family." She wrote, in overt reference to his gift of the captured sewing machine, that "stolen fruits are always sweetest." It may be that he became in some way her stolen fruit; and perhaps she was his belated retaliation for Anne's affair and child back in 1847— which also happened under the dislocations of war.

Menaced by Union agents in London, they decided to run away. Charles Francis Adams had noticed the inexplicably high proportion of officers among the men saved by the *Deerhound*. As he wrote in his diary after reading Captain Winslow's report, Adams suspected "a formal purpose" on Lancaster's part "to aid and abet the escape of Semmes and the rest of his crew"—another instance of the "strong tendency of the English to intermeddle with us." Upon giving up his ship, Adams believed, Semmes should have surrendered to the *Kearsarge* instead of fleeing to England. In an official protest to Lord Russell, Adams demanded that British authorities hand the captain over. "By all the rules of honorable warfare," Winslow agreed in a published interview, "he is now my prisoner."

On July 30, Semmes, Louisa, her brother, and three of their friends fled for almost seven weeks on the Continent. The captain traveled under an assumed name with his initials, Raymond Smith, and a false passport obtained by the Reverend Tremlett. Semmes gave Louisa a tiny ivory diary, only one inch by two inches, in which she recorded their stops. Later he remembered "when we made the swift journey together, and I lugged your carpet-bag for you, as a labor of love." They went through Belgium, had a "delightful day at Waterloo," and spent three days at the resort town of Spa, with music, walks, and agreeable drives. Then to Cologne and up the Rhine to Heidelberg and Baden Baden, "perfection of art and nature," and on to Zurich and the Swiss lakes, crossing the mountains to Lucerne in a carriage. On the fifth of September they took a train from Geneva to Paris, "where we remained a week and <u>did</u> the city." It was the captain's first visit to Paris. The contrast with Semmes's arduous, ascetic, solitary life on the *Alabama* could not have been more dramatic, and it showed in his general health. In Paris he met with his flag officer, Samuel Barron. "I never saw him looking better," Barron wrote in his diary, "or indeed so well."

On September 15 the rest of the party left for England. Semmes remained in Paris for a few days longer, perhaps preferring the more discreet safety of traveling alone after the conspicuous company of his English friends. While he stayed on, Semmes received a letter from his faithful clerk, Breedlove Smith, in Liverpool, asking for instructions. "My movements will be so uncertain for some weeks yet," Semmes wrote him, "that I think you had better not wait longer for me, but make the best of your way home by the first opportunity that offers."

Semmes proceeded to take his own advice. Returning to London later in the month, he left his sword, flag, and journal for safekeeping with the Tremletts—a deep measure of his trust in their household. He said his farewells to Louisa and Frank. Not willing to risk the blockade and the potential consequences of being caught by the Yankees, Semmes booked passage on a steamship to Havana. From there he planned to enter Texas by way of the Mexican port of Matamoros, and then on to Mobile. He embarked on the third of October. At last, leaving one family for another, he was on his way home from the war.

ELEVEN

Afterward

The terrible years after the war exemplified an occasional tendency in United States history: to win a war but botch the peace. The most tragic, consequential instance of this sporadic failure was the Civil War—the conflict that killed far more Americans than any other, that to a unique degree ended in bitter victory for some Americans and bitter defeat for the others. In its tangled aftermath, the re-United States desperately needed rare wisdom and patience from the next generation of leaders. Instead it got careless corruption, vengeance, and incompetence from nearly everyone, North and South, white and black, presidents and Congress, Radicals and Redeemers. Their mistakes ensured that the Civil War would continue indefinitely in other forms, far longer than any other American war, with all the complex, unresolved legacies that stalk us down to the present.

Groping his way through revolutionary times, Raphael Semmes was no wiser than most of his contemporaries. The *Alabama* was sunk; the captain came ashore. Ratcheting down from the intense focus of those two years at sea, he could not for long disengage the ferocious, stubborn will that sustained him through the cruise. He kept fighting the war in other ways. Deprived of his ship and guns, he deployed his pen and voice. In adjusting to peacetime civilian life, Semmes conceived many new plans for himself. He tried various occupations and wrote another war memoir. Through it all, he was in effect still standing on the horse block of the *Alabama*, chasing down another Yankee ship, snapping orders to Lieutenant Kell. Declining to let go of the war, Semmes could neither recognize nor admit defeat. So raise the mainsails and stoke the fires, and let her rip.

The steamer from England arrived at Havana in late October 1864. From there Semmes took another ship across the Gulf of Mexico to Matamoros, a Mexican seaport town on the Texas border. By an irony that Semmes appreciated, this vessel was a small Yankee schooner—recently transferred to English ownership in order to escape the Confederate cruisers. Semmes was still traveling under the name of Raymond Smith, bearing the false passport used in his flight to the Continent. The passage across the gulf was punishing; Mr. Smith was confined with fifteen other passengers in a modest cabin for ten very long days. His worst shipboard blues from the *Alabama* must have come flooding back. On shore at last, he crossed the Rio Grande into Brownsville, Texas. "I felt a strange thrill," he noted, "as I placed my foot again upon my native land; all the more dear to me for her agony of blood and misery." He had been away for almost three and a half years.

The last leg of his journey took four weeks by stagecoach and horseback. At stops along the way, the local citizens came out to see the famous commander and shake his hand. For the first time, probably, he came to appreciate how deeply the *Alabama*'s impact had penetrated even into the farthest reaches of Texas. When his stagecoach entered a town, he received a salute of artillery. Hotels welcomed him for free, and crowds gathered in the street, expecting a speech. Semmes smoked cigars, drank mint juleps, and sampled the ambiguities of notoriety. At Shreveport, Louisiana, he rested for a few days in a hospitable mansion, then traversed 140 miles of appalling roads to meet up with his son Oliver, a major in command of a Confederate battalion below Alexandria. Father and son crossed the Mississippi, controlled by the enemy, at night. They reached Mobile in mid-December.

Raphael and Anne had not seen each other since March 1861. For three years and nine months, their only contacts were by occasional correspondence subject to long delays and unpredictable deliveries. She followed the cruise of the *Alabama* through newspaper reports—which were typically sensationalized, frightening, partisan, and unreliable. At some point her daughter Anna joined the family from her exile in Philadelphia. They moved from Washington to Cincinnati, were then ordered by Union authorities to Richmond, and finally returned to the family home in Mobile. Anne and Electra endured the private shock and public embarrassment of being deceived and courted by an English impostor. The two oldest boys, Spencer and Oliver, spent the war as officers in the Confederate Army, and the youngest child—Raphael Jr., only fifteen years old—was already a midshipman in the James River Squadron in Virginia. Spencer and Electra were both recently married.

For the family, much had happened in almost four years. After all that, after the captain's perilous service at sea and, in its aftermath, his apparent romance with Louisa Tremlett, Raphael and Anne were now alone in a room, facing each other. No record of that moment beyond a bland note that everybody was in good health, not the slightest hint of what happened and how it went, was written down at the time, or later. One may imagine that they needed a period of decompression, of simply becoming used to each other's presence again. One may also imagine that they took refuge in the polite formalities of middle-class Victorian marriage, at least at first. Raphael characteristically barricaded his real emotions behind a cheerful, imperturbable façade. Anne apparently did not; and if they wished or managed to unbend into their truly felt responses, it was presumably her doing. But perhaps that never happened, and the prudent formalities remained safe and sufficient. The family was reunited. They were still married. Though Mobile Bay had been taken by Farragut's naval forces in August, the city itself was still in Confederate hands. The Semmes household might resume some sort of normal family life.

Not yet. The captain telegraphed news of his arrival to the Navy Department in Richmond. "When ready to come on," the reply directed, "regard this as an order to report to Department." Semmes quite reasonably believed that he had already completed his duties for the war. After just two weeks in Mobile, which included Christmas and New Year's, he set out for Richmond—expecting that, with his naval services terminated, he could return home soon. The overland journey provided Semmes a shocking, punching, repetitive experience at first hand of the long war's domestic ravages. Day after day, he saw ruined plantations and the burned remains of sawmills, sugar mills, saltworks, and grist mills. Renegade bands of drunken soldiers pillaged through houses, insulting the people and stealing whatever they wanted. (Rather like a boarding party from the *Alabama*, especially in the latter phases of the cruise.) Liberated slaves roamed the countryside, larcenous and starving. Even the most loyal Confederates were demoralized, convinced the war was lost. Semmes saw cynical speculation and profit-taking, and Southern soldiers as drunk and debauched as the worst of his own sailors.

At stops along the way, when dragooned by local citizens, Semmes delivered cheerleading short speeches. He said many things that he knew were not true. In Columbia, South Carolina, on January 11, he declared that his tour of the interior of the Confederacy had revealed "material resources greater than he expected; and our croakers [doubters] more numerous." Europe was still friendly, he insisted, especially England. At every port during the cruise, furthermore, he was cordially received. They were not yet defeated; he pointed toward "the finer prospect ahead that should encourage us to do and dare to the last." In Charlotte, North Carolina, two days later, he reported that the South still bustled with workshops, factories, and internal improvements. The prevailing gloom and hopelessness, he said, were "totally uncalled for," and "the prospects of the Confederacy are as bright now as they ever were. . . . All that is required now is a cheerful spirit, and a united, determined effort." After traveling the entire breadth of the Confederacy and grasping the overwhelming extent of the destruction and despair, he could not, early in 1865, have truly believed what he was saying. He was merely performing a public duty, fighting on till the end.

Indeed, that became his assignment for the rest of the war. In Richmond he was promoted to the rank of rear admiral, had dinner with Jefferson Davis, stayed overnight at Lee's quarters, and was granted an honorary seat on the floors of the Confederate Congress and Virginia legislature. The honors were heady and richly earned. But instead of returning home, Semmes was ordered to take command of the James River Squadron, a broken-down fleet of three ironclads and five wooden ships that guarded the water approach to Richmond. An Irish visitor to his flagship—intrigued by the chance to behold "Semmes! Semmes!"—found him "looking as hard and determined as flint." For seven weeks the admiral went through the pointless motions, lightened only by weekly visits with young Raphael. "Dreary, weary, lonely," he confided to his inevitable journal. "A man is a man indeed who stands the utter laceration and breaking of his heart."

Bad news rained down: Charleston and Wilmington evacuated, Columbia burned, Mobile threatened, Sheridan rampaging through the Shenandoah Valley. "The Vandals seem to be swarming every where." Still, he only surrendered to doubts in the privacy of his journal. "We have plenty of men," he assured Frank Tremlett, "and resources to fight the war on to a successful conclusion, if our people remain firm, and I think they will." Here he was addressing not his trusted friend, but a British ally of potential influence. "I am fortunately of a sanguine disposition," he admitted. "I never despair." If only the politicians would do more fighting, he mused, and less talking . . .

On the second of April, Lee abandoned Richmond and Petersburg. Semmes was ordered to scuttle his fleet and take his remaining men to the new Confederate outpost of Danville, Virginia. The admiral had his orders, so he kept moving on. At Danville he was assigned the rank of brigadier general and told to reorganize his force as an artillery brigade in the remnant of an army commanded by Joe Johnston. The admiral, now general, had Raphael Jr. assigned to his staff. Lee surrendered his army at Appomattox. The war was over. But Semmes was told to take his men to Greensboro, North Carolina. On the way, desertions brought his command down to about 250 men. Finally, seventeen days after Appomattox, Johnston came to terms with Sherman. Paroled at Greensboro, Semmes at last lay down his arms.

The father and son set out for home on foot and horseback, accompanied by a few officers, a baggage wagon, and "servants." Once again Semmes got a close look at the ravaged South, now annealed by the finality of official defeat. They foraged for food along the way, finding wild fruit and berries, occasionally bartering with local farmers for cornbread, eggs, and milk. Though they passed through the many blooming, singing beauties of a Southern spring, it was surely the saddest journey of Semmes's entire life. For four weeks and eight hundred miles, they traversed an imploding social catastrophe that was only getting worse.

At Montgomery, Alabama, they boarded a steamboat for the trip down the Alabama River to Mobile. A correspondent for the *New York Times* on the boat reported that Semmes "looked mad and ragged." He had no money to buy meal tickets, so the steamboat captain gave him some. "The country is ruined," Semmes said. "Southern gentlemen are utterly reduced to poverty by these cruel invaders—there is no hope left." As to the cause of it all, "the negro was happy in a state of slavery—freedom as understood by the negro is worse than slavery in any form, and the Yankees will find it so." How could a wise God have allowed this to happen? "The defeat of the South," Semmes ventured, "with a cause so just, is a deep mystery that wears the appearance of God being against the South, but that could not be a fact for the reason that the sacrifices and devotion of the Southern people were so sincere and so religious."

Baffled and weary, feeling deserted by his faith in God and country, and perhaps angry about his commanded but impotent services during the final throes of the Confederacy, Semmes reached Mobile in late May. It was his second and final homecoming of the war, nearly six months after the first.

According to the story later passed down in the family, when he reached home Anne was out in the vegetable patch, hoeing with three former household slaves. The social revolution of Reconstruction had begun. Under Union control since April, Mobile was an occupied city. The slaves were freed; new arrangements between the former owners and chattels were still being worked out. The wartime excesses of fancy parties and high living yielded to plain, hard living. With Lincoln dead, the new administration of Andrew Johnson might treat the defeated white South mercifully. Johnson was himself a Democrat from Tennessee. But, so soon after the war, everything remained vague and in motion.

Within days of arriving home, Semmes wrote to his English friend Lindsay about joining the Brazilian Navy. He felt stateless and rootless with the Confederacy gone and its lands controlled by invading criminals. About five thousand former Confederates did immigrate to Brazil following the war; it still allowed slavery and offered abundant cheap land. But for Semmes it was just a passing notion, one of many. He needed, at once, to earn a living. He thought about starting an import-export business in New Orleans, or a monthly steamship line from New Orleans to England. He considered selling whiskey or insurance or dairy products. He mused about offering himself to the navies of Argentina, Turkey, or Greece. Or perhaps he would return to sea, in command of a British steamer, or retire to the country and become a farmer. The transient variety of these plans testified to the chattering dislocations within his psyche. On the *Alabama*, he was supremely in his element and knew exactly what to do. In the new world of the South, as he approached his fifty-sixth birthday, he was lost.

Semmes passed the summer idly. Because of the disputed circumstances of his rescue and escape at Cherbourg, his legal status remained undefined. Though excluded from President Johnson's amnesty proclamation because of his prior naval service, his status as both admiral and general, and his warfare on Yankee commerce, he could have petitioned for a special pardon. He refused to do so as a matter of pride and undefeat: he had committed no crime, after all. Meantime he could not practice law, and he was broke. "I came out of the war as poor as when I went into it," he wrote to Lindsay in August. Though he had done Britain the huge favor of destroying U.S. enterprise on the ocean, the British government had kept him poor. If Russell had let him bring his prizes into British ports, he told Lindsay, "I should have been worth a million of dollars." So be it; "I have ten years of vitality in me yet, and God willing I will yet strive to recover my lost fortunes. Country, I have none." His captured chronometers were sold in England for three thousand dollars, only half of what he expected, and even so he dutifully shared half the proceeds with his top officers.

After the bloody fratricidal war, reconciliations had to take place on many levels, from the national government on down to families and households. As the country split open in 1861, Semmes's only sibling, his brother, Samuel, chose the Union side in his free-labor town of Cumberland, Maryland. Raphael was "disappointed and mortified" over his brother's defection; "even our own blood relatives fall away from us," he lamented. For four years the brothers, very close since childhood and the early deaths of their parents, stayed out of touch. In August 1865, Raphael—unwilling to make peace with the Yankees—

decided at least to offer peace to his brother. "You have been frequently in my thoughts during our unfortunate struggle," he wrote to Samuel. He had not inquired about Samuel's conduct during the war, knowing that whatever he did would have been honorable. For himself, he had taken the only course "which a faithful Southern man could pursue, and maintain his self-respect." He had no regrets, made no apologies; "yet my name will probably go down to posterity in the untruthful histories that will be written by bigoted and venal historians as a sort of Blue Beard or Capt. Kidd." The war had left him impoverished, and he did not know where to go or what to do. "We have become old men," he concluded. "We have both had our troubles, but the chain of affection which binds me to you remains unaffected by the cares of the world, and is as bright now as when we slept in each other's arms."

Samuel quickly replied. Once the war began, they were not as divided as they seemed. "My own course has been a neutral one," Samuel explained. He opposed secession, but after the Emancipation Proclamation—"the fiendish spirit of abolition"—and Lincoln's assumption of emergency war powers, he no longer supported the administration. Lincoln was merely "the weak tool of a party," Samuel insisted, with "none of the elements of a great man in his character." After his misrule, "I can never again feel proud of my country." So the Semmes brothers emerged from the war in partial agreement. "Your course in taking part with the Southern States," Samuel told Raphael, ". . . has never affected my love for you as a brother." He had often worried "whilst you have been all the time facing dangers the most varied and appalling." Now the war was over, and they were brothers once more.

Anne Semmes, worried again about money, tried to remain cheerful and not let her husband see her fret. She appealed to her brother Henry, the former mayor of Cincinnati. "But I am afraid," she wrote to Electra, "they are too Yankee and bitter to do any thing to oblige me or mine." Friends in Mobile, she said, were also reluctant to help because they feared Yankee disapproval. She went on, unburdening herself to her eldest daughter:

> I have lost all faith in man, and begin to realize the hollowness of all mankind. I am sorry to admit that I begin to detest the meanness and cringing people of the South, as much as our

enemies the Northerners; even your precious Father, who is such a patriot and scarcely speaks ill of any one, is very much disappointed in the Alabamians: and says if he had twenty thousand dollars, he would [leave] the country and never put foot in it again; I think it is so hard after four years of such hard labor, that he is now reduced almost to poverty.

They had to leave their rented house, which now cost $150 a month, and move to a humbler place four miles west of town.

Semmes spent the fall in legal limbo, wondering if he would be arrested and thrown to a Yankee mob. He felt like a fugitive waiting for a knock at the door. With his sense of history, he recognized that he was living through an epochal change, the shift from the South's old slave-based labor system to some new form. Caught in such upheaval, he reached back to something familiar (though with no apparent enthusiasm): he obtained a license to practice law in Mobile. Semmes and his eldest son, Spencer, opened an office on North Royal Street as "Attorneys at Law and General Collecting Agents." After a month, and no fees yet received, Semmes remained typically hopeful. "I think," he ventured, "we shall be able to take hold of a fair share of the practice of our one-horse city."

The knock at the door came on the evening of December 15. As Semmes was relaxing with his family, a Marine detachment surrounded the house and he was arrested, charged with illegally escaping Union custody after surrendering his ship at Cherbourg. The order was issued by the admiral's old pursuer Gideon Welles, still the secretary of the U.S. Navy; Welles had finally caught him. Yet Semmes was imprisoned more for political than for legal reasons. During the winter of 1865–66, the president and Congress were settling into a historic showdown over the control of Reconstruction. Johnson wished to restore the rights and authority of the defeated Southern whites; the Radical Republicans in Congress preferred to punish those whites and instead to protect the rights of the freed slaves. To stave off its Radical critics, the Johnson administration needed, on occasion, to seem punitive toward former Confederates of particular notoriety.

Thus the arrest of Semmes. John A. Bolles, the Navy Department's solicitor and judge advocate, participated in the legal maneuvers of the case. "No name connected with the Rebel service," he wrote a few years later, "unless that of some spy, 'bushwhacker,' or guerilla of the grossest criminality, was so generally detested as that of Raphael Semmes. Harsh epithets were heaped upon him, not only by sailors and master-mariners, and merchants whose ships and goods had blazed under his torch, not only by 'sensational' reporters and editors, but by some of our gravest writers and highest dignitaries." Through his feats at sea, his escape on the *Deerhound* to England, and his unpunished life in Mobile after the war, Semmes epitomized Confederate defiance even in defeat. He offered the White House both a symbol and an example. "I told him I thought it a good opportunity to show that he was ready to bring criminals to trial," Welles wrote of Johnson in his diary. "Here was a case which belonged to him specially and no one else. Hence if he ordered Semmes to trial the country would be satisfied that he was sincere and discharging his duty towards the worst Rebels."

Semmes celebrated his first Christmas after the war under armed guard, on a steamship bound from New Orleans to New York. From there he was taken to the Marine barracks at the Washington Navy Yard. His son-in-law, Pendleton Colston, a Baltimore lawyer, visited him in early January. The circumstances were not too unpleasant. After being kept in a small room, then another small room, he was lodged in better quarters just above the gate to the navy yard. A servant took care of his cell and served the meals that he picked from a local restaurant. "His health is good," Colston reported to Anne Semmes, "and he is the same philosopher there as elsewhere, even cheerful." After a month he was allowed to walk in the enclosed barracks yard— his first exercise outside his cell. He noticed that groups of Marines, scattered around the yard, turned to stare at him, their prize prisoner. The days passed in confined routine: meals, newspapers, reading books of law and history, working on his legal pleadings. "I have ever found," he wrote in his prison diary, "when in trouble that the best remedy is to chain down the imagination in its flights and set reason at work."

His case stalled amid disagreements among the president, the cabinet, and the Navy Department about the charges and proper jurisdiction for a trial. Johnson, to Welles's impatient annoyance, kept urging delays and another legal opinion from the attorney general. Anne Semmes came to Washington, was allowed to visit her husband, and besieged the president with personal calls and appeals. After losing Raphael for virtually the entire war, she could not abide the prospect of another long separation. The administration, immersed in its quarrel with congressional Radicals over the extension of the Freedmen's Bureau, lost interest in the case. "The President said he had some doubts," Welles noted in early April, "but wished to get rid of the subject, for Semmes's wife was annoying him, crying and taking on for her husband. The President has a gentle and kind heart, melted by woman's tears." They had finally decided to try Semmes by a military commission—but then the Supreme Court in its *Milligan* decision ruled against the authority of such commissions. Welles gave up and released his prisoner after holding him for almost four months.

The experience left Semmes another grievance against the Yankees. When he returned to Mobile, a Confederate crowd cheered him at the waterfront. He again took up the ongoing puzzle of how to make a living, running through a series of brief sallies and failures. Riding the enthusiasm of his triumphant delivery from prison, he was elected a judge of the probate court in Mobile; his two opponents withdrew to leave the vote uncontested. But President Johnson, perhaps needing to balance the political impact of Semmes's release, ordered that he could not hold any public office because he remained unpardoned. ("Are we to be handed over to our enemies," Semmes wondered, "bound hand and foot?") He bought a one-third interest in a Mobile newspaper, the *Gazette*, and became its editor; but the paper failed two months later for lack of support. He next tried teaching at a college in Louisiana, the ancestor of Louisiana State University; but the work didn't suit him, and he missed his family.

In early 1867 the leading newspaper in Memphis, the *Bulletin*, offered him the generous salary of $5,000 to become its editor. Again he ventured into what he called "the drudgery of a daily press." For a time he seemed to have found the right mooring. At a fair in Memphis in June, he presented a U.S. flag to a popular Mississippi River steamboat. It seemed odd, he said, "to restore, as it were, the Star Spangled Banner to the mast-head of the merchant ship, from which, in times gone by, I have so often caused it to descend. But such are some of the revolutions of history." He had never fought, he insisted, against the institutions of his country. Now the war was over, they were beaten, and all Americans again had only one flag. "That war has left many and ghastly wounds," he said. "Let us of the South do our part, by closing them with a tender and gentle hand, so that no scars may remain to remind us of the conflict."

That sounded conciliatory—but only on the white South's terms. In Congress, Radical Republicans seized control of Reconstruction over Johnson's veto. They divided the old Confederacy into five military districts subject to martial law and shifted much of the franchise from white to black voters. At an election in Memphis in August, Semmes watched the procession of freedmen coming to vote. "We scanned the countenances of the dusky voters," he wrote in the *Bulletin*. "Childish curiosity and simplicity, stolid indifference, blank ignorance, wretchedness and crime were the main characteristics. . . . We turned away sick at heart." Under the new Radical regimes, the admiral—and most of the white South—dug himself in against the war's outcome. He was back on the *Alabama*. "The Caucasian, in the State of Tennessee, has passed under the rule of the African," he declared. "The Yankee is avenged; he has thrown down the Southern man, and raised up the negro in his stead." His unreconstructed politics cost him another job. The owners of the *Bulletin* disagreed with his editorial policies of urging states' rights and resisting federal power. By the fall of 1867 he was back in Mobile, where Spencer had maintained their law practice.

With some desperation, but also with an intellectual need to explain and justify himself, he embarked on a lecture tour—at first near home in Alabama, and then through Tennessee and Kentucky. Though he disliked the travel and the nightly contending with unpredictable audiences, the lectures paid well and spread his version of the war. In January he spoke to an audience of about three hundred in Covington, Kentucky, across the Ohio River from Cincinnati. He came out on stage dressed in baggy trousers and an old-fashioned vest and black frock coat. "His whole appearance," wrote a reporter, "is quite the reverse of any preconceived ideas as to what either a sea captain, 'Admiral,' or any other sea-going notable would look like." His eyeglasses dangled from a cord. He looked haggard and worn, the face wrinkled, the dark, unkempt hair swept back from his forehead and falling straight behind his ears. The waxed mustache remained his most distinguishing feature. "The expression of his countenance," another reporter decided, "in repose or in speaking, can not be called pleasing; it is rather sinister, and that is made emphatic by a habit of squinting his eyes and contracting the muscles about the mouth into rigidity."

After moving the reading stand toward the gas lights to one side, so he could see his manuscript, he spoke for over two hours, often departing from his text for improvised digressions. "We are one people," he said, "of one blood, almost of one household," so we must agree on the true history of the war, "calmly and without prejudice." His purpose was "the vindication of my course on strictly historical grounds," without reference to politics or polemics. The South had simply followed the precedents of the American Revolution, declaring independence and making war as a de facto government against the restraining nation. His own actions were as legitimate as those of John Paul Jones. He recounted the history of the *Alabama;* when he recalled her commissioning and raising the Confederate flag at the Azores, he got the loudest cheers of the evening. He became most emotional in describing the battle off Cherbourg. In passing, he explained ocean currents, the foolish habits of sailors, the nature of the Gulf Stream, and the origins of ocean storms. He noted that he still had the ransom bonds from those captures he had not burned. "If any gentleman in this audience wishes to invest in them," he said, "I will sell him some cheap," and the crowd laughed.

At times he stepped from behind the podium and unconsciously assumed a sailor's stance, spreading his legs wide so he looked like an inverted *Y.* Thrusting his hands deep into the pockets of his breeches, swaying backward and forward, lost in his discourse, he occasionally withdrew one hand and plunged the thumb into the armpit of his waistcoat or into the vest pocket. "With a little more animation," one of the reporters concluded, "Mr. Semmes would not be a bad lecturer." Though not a polished performance, it was still effective; and his Southern audiences, there and elsewhere, were reliably curious to behold the legendary commander—even if his looks were, as usual, disappointing.

The sufficient success of his lectures encouraged Semmes to write a memoir of the war. After retrieving his *Alabama* journal from Frank Tremlett, the admiral spent most of 1868 immersed in book writing. It was the logical, almost inevitable next step for him. His memoir of the Mexican War had sold well and drawn praise from all quarters, North and South. During his Civil War service, the journals he kept on the *Sumter* and *Alabama* often read as though they were intended for early publication, as the captain seems to be explaining himself with a larger audience in mind. The quick two-volume book drawn from his journals and published in London after Cherbourg did not satisfy him. He wanted to produce his own apologia—to make money, and to leave a conspicuous, permanent record of the rage he still felt over the war's outcome.

Memoirs of Service Afloat, During the War Between the States was published late in 1868 by Kelly, Piet and Company of Baltimore. The title notwithstanding, Semmes conceived it as more than a war memoir, as a "book of the sea, and of adventure, independently of the ship or the writer." So he digresses freely through 833 pages, departing from his narrative for three pages on ocean currents, five on cloud rings, five more on gyratory storms, and eleven on a sailor's constant focus, the fickle ocean winds. No matter where he is cruising, and what else is taking place, he always keeps all his senses open to "the wonders and beauties of nature." On these levels the book has a timeless, classic quality, conveying the tang, terror, mystery, and exultation of life at sea. Semmes is fascinated by the structural marvels of the coral organism, "that patient little stone-mason of the deep," and the shifting kaleidoscope of the ocean sky, especially at sunset. When the *Alabama* arrives at a port, the captain goes ashore and reports on the strange land and people. Life on the cruiser herself is inevitably inward and even claustrophobic, but these larger aspects offer space and relief to the memoir, often welcome, and connections to wider worlds.

Semmes begins his book with eight chapters on the historical background of the war. The founding constitutional principles of the United States, he argues, had been perverted, mainly by New England Puritans. In their "gloomy asceticism of character, and an intolerance of other men's opinions quite remarkable," they seized control of the national government and imposed crushing taxes and tariffs on the South. The two sections diverged into incompatible cultures, Puritan and Cavalier, creating a replay of the English Civil War. "Whilst the civilization of the North was coarse, and practical, that of the South was more intellectual, and refined." The North had no sincere objections to slavery, but merely used the issue as a cynical excuse for expanding its power. (This overview of events has not stood up well to later historical understanding. Intellectual life was freer and much more robust in the North. The English Cavaliers were Roman Catholics, like Semmes, while the white South was overwhelmingly Protestant, especially Baptist and Methodist—those two most un-Catholic of Protestant denominations. And nobody was more puritanical in his personal habits and religious beliefs than Stonewall Jackson, the greatest Confederate martyr-hero.)

Semmes does not reach the *Sumter* until page 93, and the *Alabama* until page 400, nearly halfway through the book. Once at sea, the narrative consists essentially of excerpts from the journals with the author's later elaborations and digressions. Semmes takes recurring liberties with the purported excerpts, changing the wording, adding sentences, and altering details. Many of these changes are simply to improve the story—"a woman" becomes "a beautiful woman"—and the plain language of the journal is elevated into literary flourishes. The size of the Union force supposedly at Galveston in January 1863 is raised from fifty ships and 20,000 men to one hundred ships and 30,000 men—making the captain's intended raid that much more daring. As to onboard discipline, "we never had any trouble about keeping the most desperate and turbulent characters in subjection."

Semmes therefore does not mention the cigar mutiny of November 1863 or the crew's bristling restlessness during the latter part of the cruise. He insists that boarding parties were never allowed to bring alcohol or personal booty back to the *Alabama*—"if such license had been permitted, disorder and demoralization would have been the consequence"—but many external sources contradict this. (Isolated in his cabin and by his own willful inattention, he may never have known the true extent of the looting.) Semmes does not include his boarding strategy for the battle with the *Kearsarge*, perhaps because it failed, or the week he spent in Paris at the end of his flight to the Continent, perhaps because that might have seemed too self-indulgent while the Confederacy was bleeding and burning.

In his most serious rewriting of the journal, Semmes overturns his actual understanding, early in the war, of slavery as the cause of the conflict. In August 1861, while coaling the *Sumter* at a port in Venezuela, he fell into conversation with an English sea captain. According to the *Memoirs*, he explained that slavery had little to do with the war. "The canting, hypocritical Yankee cares as little for our slaves, as he does for our draught animals," he recalls saying. Slavery was only a pretext for robbing the South and extending the Yankee empire. "We are, in fact, fighting for independence." Semmes had recorded none of these alleged statements in the journal entry for that date. He could not have remembered them, word for word, seven years later; they were just his retrospective wisdom masked as contemporary insight. Instead, in journal entries later in the fall of 1861, he had written "that we were fighting the first battle in favor of slavery" and "the true issue of the war" was "an abolition crusade against our slave property." But Semmes tellingly does not allow these candid admissions into his book. On this most consequential point, he denies and twists his own clear historical record.

Yet *Memoirs of Service Afloat* is one of the finest, fullest works by a major participant in the war. Of the principal commanders, North and South, perhaps only Farragut, Sherman, Mosby, and Rosecrans could match Semmes's intellectual range and interests. In the *Memoirs* he presents quotations in Latin, French, and Spanish, all without translations, assuming that any intelligent reader would understand them. He sprinkles the narrative with brief snatches from the Bible, Shakespeare, Francis Bacon, Walter Scott, Horace Greeley, Tocqueville, the English poet James Montgomery, the Confederate poet Father Abram Ryan— and his favorite poet, Lord Byron, with eleven quotations. Considered simply as a piece of writing, the book is far deeper, wider, and better written than—for example—the much more famous memoir by Grant. (But Grant's side won the war, and history gets passed down by the winners.) Like most autobiographies, it is a testament, presenting the best aspects of the author as he wished to be remembered. It sold fairly well, reaching ten thousand copies after less than a year, and kept selling.

In the politics of the late 1860s, it was an act of war. Written during the most Radical phase of Reconstruction, when the white South felt besieged by scalawags, carpetbaggers, and blacks asserting their rights as free men and women, the book screamed one long cry of wounded but unvanquished pride. It surely did nothing to help reconcile the former enemies. "The shameless record of a most inglorious and deplorable career," declared *Putnam's Magazine* of New York. "We have no patience with Admiral-Captain Semmes and his gasconading book. . . . There never was a meaner, more ungallant enterprise than that of the ship-scuttling skipper of the British pirate Alabama." The war continued.

As he slowly settled into his post-1865 life in Mobile, Semmes pulled away from Louisa Tremlett. Their correspondence has survived in scattered collections in the Semmes Family Papers at the Alabama state archives in Montgomery, and at the Museum of the Confederacy and the Virginia Historical Society, both in Richmond. These letters record the natural course of a wartime romance, inspired and enabled by unique circumstances, that inevitably cooled off with distance and the relative normality of peace and a return home.

At first he was more ardent. After departing England in early October 1864, he sent her three letters before he reached Anne and their family more than two months later. "My dearest Miss Louisa," he wrote from Brownsville, Texas.

> I am writing to you my dearest friend, under a kind of high pressure, and with a head somewhat muddled by excitement. . . . Be sure to write to me yourself very often (I must at least have letter for letter, and you now owe me three). You will always be to me as now, very, very dear, and one of my greatest pleasures will be, my correspondence with you, until the Fates so will it that I shall see you again. . . . So love to mama and brother Frank, and a thousand loves to yourself.

She didn't write back. Perhaps she doubted the propriety of addressing a letter to him at home. But he only stayed in Mobile for two weeks before leaving for Richmond and the final, sputtering days of the Confederacy. "My dearest Miss Louisa," he wrote in March from his James River Squadron. "Here I am, my dear friend, about as forlorn a swain as you could well imagine, away from both my English and my American family." He hoped the war would end soon so she could visit him in America, as they had discussed. "I think my wife is a little jealous of you, I have talked about you so much since my return. There now, there is a compliment for you." (Anne knew about her, he was saying, so she was cleared to write to him.) During a possible visit at Mobile or London, "you shall see how charmingly Madame will greet you, as her husband's faithful friend and ally in the glorious cause of the Confederacy." He recalled the poppy she had picked at Water-loo when they ran away to the Continent. After a separation of six months, "your image is as firmly photographed upon my memory as ever. . . . Do not forget your promise, my dear friend, to let me hear from you occasionally."

Prodded and assured, she may have quickly sent back a reply that did not survive the chaos of that spring. In any case, the first extant letter from Louisa to Raphael was written the following October. The tone was friendly and admiring, but more guarded than his letters. Lord Palmerston had just died amid a grave Anglo-American crisis over Yankee demands for British compensation for damages caused by the *Alabama* and other Confederate cruisers built in Britain. "You see what trouble," she wrote, "you have brought upon the nations! You must not depreciate your own importance after this." Frank would send his journals to Mobile when it seemed safe enough, and she had assembled his ship photographs into an album to include with the package. "Love to all your belongings," she signed off, "from all here."

He wrote back at once, briskly and rather impersonally, dwelling on politics and his own legal situation. The right of self-government in the South, he feared, was forever gone. He was just waiting around, wondering what the Yankees would do to him. "I spent the whole of last summer in enforced idleness, and to a man of my active habits you may imagine how almost insupportable this was." Though excluded from the president's amnesty proclamation, and perhaps soon to be imprisoned, he had decided not to immigrate to another country. The war, after all, was still not over. "The end is not yet. God governs the world by moral laws which cannot be broken with impunity."

A month later, the Marines came and took him away. Yet again he was deprived of both his families. During his four months in captivity, Anne came to Washington, pressed for and received permission to visit him, wore down the president with her tearful pleas, and helped secure her husband's release. In jail, helpless beyond the legal pleadings he composed, he especially needed her love and advocacy. Her loyal, indomitable support must have reminded him of their mutual bond, tested but enduring, and of everything they had gone through in twenty-nine years of marriage. The whole prison experience, so humiliating and emotionally distressing, drew him back to his wife.

The dynamic between Raphael and Louisa shifted. She became more intent on maintaining the correspondence, he more diffident about it. In the fall of 1867, she chided him for not answering her letter of more than a year earlier. "You are much oftener in our thoughts," she wrote, "than we seem to be in yours—but then we have so many reminders (beside memories) constantly before us which puts us almost daily in mind of you." She still had the Confederate flag sewn by Lady de Houghton and the sword given to him after Cherbourg. "Your sword," she wrote in an unconscious sexual image, "I dust and rub carefully every now and then. . . . It stirs up all those old 'proclivities' and makes ones heart burn again." The sword, rubbing, stirring up, heart burning: presumably she did not fully understand what she was conveying.

On a lecture tour, just after his appearance in Covington, Kentucky, in January 1868, he wrote back. Away from home, away from Anne, he might call up the old feelings. "My dear Miss Louisa," he began. (His salutations had shifted from <u>dearest</u> to dearest to dear.) He apologized for not writing for so long. "You do not know," he offered, "how near to you your sprightly letters draw me, reviving in my memory your well remembered features and the kindly expression of your eye." He was pushing it, trying to recover those months at Belsize Park and on the grand tour. "Your image is as warmly and affectionately cherished as ever, and you do not need to be told how warmly and affectionately that was. I constantly endeavor to cheat myself . . . transporting myself in imagination to the 'Parsonage,' and to the mountains of Switzerland when you cheered with your bewitching presence a few weeks of my toilsome life, and restored me to comparative youth again." The reverie passed; he thought of Anne.

> Indeed my dear, good wife is quite jealous of you, when she hears me speak of your many attractive qualities, and especially when I playfully show her your ring, on the same finger, side by side with her own—the diamond which you remember. When she talks of my allegiance, I tell her that we states-rights men have been bred in a school which teaches that a man may owe two allegiances at once—both of the heart and yet not interfering with each other.

Her response to this fond, jesting, elusive letter was silence. She may have felt toyed with; after sending nothing for too long, he came back with all his guns blazing. It was well intentioned, probably, but not quite believable. She finally replied over eight months later. They exchanged a few more letters, cooler in tone, restricting themselves to less personal matters. "I am making a comfortable living," he wrote in the fall of 1869, just turned sixty, "and am growing in domestic honors, as well as in years." It was his final letter to her. "He has quite cut me now," she mourned early in 1871. "I have not heard from him for more than a year. I have a great mind to write him a stinging, impudent letter." He never returned to England. She never visited America or got married. The Tremletts, sister and brother, lived out their lives at the parsonage in Belsize Park.

Relinquishing the memory and fantasy of Louisa may have helped him leave the war behind. Other circumstances of the early 1870s pushed him along. Across the South, white Redeemer governments were gradually retrieving political control. In Alabama, outbreaks of white violence against blacks and their Republican allies led to the election of a Democratic governor in 1870. Nothing had more agitated the ex-Confederates than the specter of black political power. ("The people of the South will not submit to negro domination," Semmes had assured Louisa Tremlett. "We will exterminate the race first.") With the gradual ending of Radical congressional oversight, Southern blacks were left in the angry, vengeful care of their former owners. The system of American apartheid was locked into place, by law and by custom, to remain undisturbed for nearly a century. Sacrificing the black South allowed the reconciliation of white Confederates with white Yankees; in the cruel balancing of that moral equation, blacks were the tragic, helpless losers. Old fighters like Semmes could lower their weapons at last.

The long-festering squabble between the United States and Great Britain over the *Alabama* and other British-built cruisers was also finally resolved. During the war, Charles Francis Adams had built a detailed legal case, protest by protest, for later demanding compensation from the British government for all the destruction and added war costs caused by the *Alabama* and her sisters. The arguments then went on for years after the war; to recover the damages, some American politicians wished to annex Canada. This threat of annexation helped push the Canadian provinces toward federation and independence from London in 1867. The rippling impacts of the cruise of the *Alabama* thus included, at one or two removes, the founding of Canadian nationhood.

The American and British governments, after feuding and fussing for most of the previous hundred years, now had compelling economic and diplomatic motives to get along. Both sides wanted to settle "the *Alabama* claims," as they were called. By the Treaty of Washington, signed in May 1871, Britain expressed regret for the damages caused by the cruisers and agreed to pay compensation. A five-nation tribunal in Geneva—the first major international tribunal, an important precedent—ordered Britain to pay $15.5 million to the United States for the havoc wreaked by the *Alabama* and two other cruisers. Of this total, the largest share, $6.75 million, was assigned to Semmes's ship. For him, the *Alabama* claims quantified and codified his historical significance. Though he would never agree that Britain was in any sense responsible for his actions, the case proved that he was a legitimate naval commander, not a pirate, engaged in a real war, not a mere rebellion. As a novel judgment in international law with long implications, the decision preserved his ship's name in history on yet another level.

In the summer of 1872, a remarkable two-part article appeared in the *Atlantic Monthly*, the literary, abolitionist voice of Semmes's detested New England. Titled "Why Semmes of the Alabama Was Not Tried," the article was written by John A. Bolles, the Navy Department lawyer partly responsible for the arrest and jailing of Semmes back in 1865–66. With the war now receding, Bolles had only praise for the man he had once aimed to punish. "He was, probably, beyond all other men who had been trained in our navy, the man to carry out the 'destructive policy,'" Bolles declared. "I had no sympathy with those persons, official or unofficial, who denied courage and gallantry to Semmes." Early in 1866, seeking witnesses for a possible trial, Bolles had placed advertisements in the major newspapers of the seaboard states. He heard from people with knowledge of thirty-six of the *Alabama*'s prizes. "Very few of these letters," Bolles concluded, "accused Semmes of either cruelty or unkindness." Instead they presented him as "by no means the guilty monster" so generally perceived in the North. It did seem to Bolles that Semmes should not have escaped after surrendering at Cherbourg, and then should not have later resumed Confederate war duties; but after the war, "it was scarcely worth while to bring him to trial for these offences." So, given certain political and legal circumstances at the time, he was released.

That article, written by Semmes's former prosecutor for Boston's favorite magazine, epitomized the warming trend of sectional reconciliation. In the same spirit, after reading the article, Semmes sent an astonishing letter to the editor of the *Atlantic*. He wrote:

> Mobile, and Boston are situated on different parallels of latitude, and perhaps this is all the difference between them. Men's opinions are what circumstances make them, and if the people of Boston had been born in Mobile, and the people of Mobile in Boston, there can be little doubt, that they could have reciprocally exchanged opinions. This reflection should moderate our human pride, and teach us charity. The difference of opinions of the two peoples, born of the difference of parallels of latitude, brought them into conflict during the late war. There are signs that the bitterness of feeling produced by that conflict is passing away.

After arguing for years from strict notions of immutable principle, of simple right and wrong, he now could step back and blame the war's bloody divisions on mere caprices of birth and geography. If born in Boston, he might have become an abolitionist!

The war was over; he was off the *Alabama*. "For the last few years I have been leading a very quiet life," he wrote Frank Tremlett in 1872. "The Yankees have, at last, ceased to abuse me, or indeed, even to speak of me." In his early sixties, he served as city attorney for Mobile and maintained an adequate law practice. Friends and admirers subscribed to a fund that bought the Semmeses a fine two-story brick house on Government Street. A small boy down the street later remembered "the Great Admiral," as they called him, walking home every evening, "very erect and impressively commanding of presence." He always wore a naval cloak over his shoulders, even in hot weather, that flashed a bright red lining. "It used to fascinate me, that red lining," the boy recalled. "Everything else about him was so dark and somber that the carmine lining seemed to shriek out." The neighborhood boys would line up and salute him, and Semmes would gravely respond by removing his hat in a gesture of benediction.

In the spring of 1874, almost ten years after the sinking of the *Alabama*, he spoke at the unveiling of a monument to the Confederate war dead at Magnolia Cemetery in Mobile. A local detachment of the U.S. Army contributed a floral arrangement that Semmes formally accepted. "It comes from the victor to the vanquished," he said, "in a spirit worthy of our age, and of our history, and is indicative that the strife between brethren is over." He spoke with great earnestness, emotionally, out of character. In the future, he predicted, there would be no more North and South except as a friendly, generous rivalry. "As between soldier and soldier, at least, the war between the States is at an end."

Early in 1877 he started suffering chronic intestinal problems. "I think I am improving a very little," he told Anne, but probably he wasn't. In August a meal of bad shrimp seemed to lead to ptomaine poisoning. On his deathbed he remembered the night his father died, so many years ago. At another moment, he imagined that he was back on the *Alabama*, preparing for a battle. He gave commands, sharp and incisive, discussed the preparations with his officers, and seemed quite happy over the prospect of victory. He died on August 30, a few weeks short of his sixty-eighth birthday. Anne survived him by fifteen years.

In June 1900 the citizens of Mobile dedicated a statue in his memory. The admiral stands on the quarterdeck of the *Alabama*, binoculars in one hand, scanning the horizon. He looks, as always, less impressive than he should. The plaque at the front of the base reads, "Sailor, Patriot, Statesman, Scholar, and Christian Gentleman." The plaque behind the statue adds: "Still after these many years, his patriotism and heroic deeds inspire us to cherish our American liberties!"

The *Alabama* Found

In the late 1970s, as a training exercise for sonar operators, French Navy minesweepers began to search the area off Cherbourg where the *Alabama* sank. About six miles offshore, the location is extraordinarily difficult to investigate. The water is cold, as the survivors from the *Alabama* discovered, less than sixty degrees Fahrenheit even in summertime. Brisk tidal currents agitate the channel except for brief periods, twice a day, when the tides are turning. The water averages some two hundred feet deep, so visibility at the bottom is quite murky, only a couple of feet, even under direct sunlight. At that depth, scuba divers near their sensible limit for safe operations. They risk the cognitive derangements of diving narcosis if they spend more than about fifteen minutes on the ocean floor.

In October 1984, personnel on the minesweeper *Circe*, under Commander Bruno Duclos, picked their way through nearby wrecks from World War II and located a wooden ship of the *Alabama*'s dimensions. They caught a glimpse of a cannon that might have been one of the Blakely pivot guns on the Confederate cruiser. Divers brought up some dishes and an iron ventilator, and then two bronze gun tracks from one of the pivot cannon. With them, Max Guérout, a marine archaeologist and retired French Navy captain, tentatively identified the wreck as the *Alabama*. Almost three years passed, apparently for reasons of military security and scholarly caution, before Guérout announced the discovery in September 1987 at an international conference on maritime history at Charleston, South Carolina. The most significant ship of the Civil War was officially found, 123 years after being sunk, and she awaited exploration.

An underwater survey the following spring, under Guérout's direction, produced the first detailed description of the remains. The *Alabama* lies on her starboard side at a thirty-degree angle. (The starboard list so evident during the battle was retained in her burial.) Less than one-third of the wooden hull has survived the tides and marine organisms. A sandbank has accumulated on the starboard side, offering some protection for that part of the hull. The port side is essentially gone. Boilers have protected the midsection. The bow and stern have worn away down to a level below the lower deck. As the *Alabama* foundered, her bow rose into a nearly vertical position and many objects tumbled toward the stern. Thousands of metal, glass, and porcelain artifacts remain on the ship and scattered around the nearby seabed, clustered at the aft portion of the wreck.

Exploration and retrieval have been complicated by disagreements among France, Britain, and the United States over which nation has jurisdiction over the site and ship. In 1864, the battle took place in international waters as defined at that time: three miles off shore. But with the improvement of long-range naval gunnery, that boundary was later extended to twelve miles. By a contemporary definition, the wreck lies within French authority. Eventually French and American investigators worked out a joint project that has performed annual dives on the site. A French miniature submarine with robot arms and a three-dimensional video camera has improved the searching.

Many assorted artifacts have been retrieved: a gimballed oil lamp, a cream pitcher, a water glass, nails, brass screws, a thimble, tarnished Brazilian coins from the cruiser's stops at Bahia or Fernando de Noronha; a copper kitchen chimney, a pewter kettle, a green glass jar and lid, a lead sounding weight, a brass oarlock, a brass pulley, cups and saucers, an iron pulley, and various mysterious fragments of iron machinery. The particular prizes to date have been three of the four porcelain flush toilets, with a lovely English boating scene still bright in the bottoms of the bowls; the ship's iron wheel with the Confederate motto *"Aide-toi et Dieu t'aidera"* still clearly inscribed; the ship's bell; and the aft Blakely pivot cannon, the fearsome weapon that consistently brought Yankee merchantmen to heel but then failed in the final battle with the *Kearsarge*.

A current exhibit at the Museum of Mobile includes many of these items, along with photographs and the elaborate sword and scabbard that Louisa Tremlett so lovingly cared for. None of the recovered *Alabama* artifacts has significantly expanded historical understanding of the ship, her men, or what they did. The objects are interesting to ponder, in the cool, dim light of the museum, but they don't really have much to say. Still, they do provide a direct, visceral, almost tangible connection to the distant cruiser. Eventually the channel tides will sweep away the wooden hull entirely, and only these bits and pieces will remain.

Acknowledgments

I did most of the research for this book at my favorite joint, the Boston Public Library in Copley Square, and at the S. E. Wimberly Library of Florida Atlantic University in Boca Raton. Special thanks to Henry Scannell of the BPL's microtext department, John Dorsey, and Roberta Zonghi of Rare Books and Manuscripts. Vivian Spiro, my longtime colleague in the Associates of the Boston Public Library, invited me to an event at the library's Sargent Gallery in the fall of 2004 that raised my intellectual sights. Much of the new material presented in this book was drawn from files of various Union and Confederate newspapers among the vast hoard of microfilmed newspapers at the Widener Library of Harvard University. I again exploited the dependable holdings of the Massachusetts Historical Society and the Boston Athenaeum. Edwin C. Bridges, director of the Alabama Department of Archives and History in Montgomery, kindly expedited my research there in the Semmes Family Papers, the major collection of manuscript materials by and about Raphael Semmes.

Among current descendants and relatives of the admiral, I owe particular thanks to Anderson Humphreys, who conceived, co-wrote, and published the indispensable family history *Semmes America* (1989), and sent me a package of Semmes items; Luke Finlay and Anne Finlay Schenck, who loaned and showed me Semmes materials collected by their father, Brigadier General Luke William Finlay; and Thomas Middleton Semmes, who sent me carefully scanned copies of some significant pages from the Semmes family Bible in his possession.

Elizabeth T. Spencer and Buddy Spencer generously let me see materials from the papers of Warren F. Spencer in their custody. Professor Spencer's careful biography of Semmes (1997) has become the standard source on the admiral's life before the Civil War. William Marvel, author of an important book on the *Alabama* and *Kearsarge*, published in 1996, gave me useful advice during the early stages of my research. When I told him I was contemplating a book on Semmes and the *Alabama*, he helpfully asked, "Another one?" I have tried to keep this skeptical question in mind.

Thanks for assistance with my research to Michael Hammerson, who I hope will eventually write his biography of Francis W. Tremlett; John Buescher, for help with the history of American spiritualism; Marina Klaric of the W. S. Hoole Special Collections Library of the University of Alabama, Tuscaloosa; Mary Johnson of the Mobile Genealogical Society; Jim Johnson and Patricia M. LaPointe of the Memphis Public Library; Andrew Davis of the National Maritime Museum, Greenwich, England; John Rhodehamel of the Huntington Library; John M. Coski of the Eleanor S. Brockenbrough Library, Museum of the Confederacy, Richmond; Dave W. Morgan of the Museum of Mobile; and the staffs of the Tisch Library of Tufts University, the Manuscript Division of the Library of Congress, the National Archives, the Virginia Historical Society in Richmond, the Rare Book, Manuscript, and Special Collections Library of Duke University, and the Southern Historical Collection at the Wilson Library, University of North Carolina, Chapel Hill.

Of friends and family members, Dr. Heather E. Fleming and David Evans rescued me from various computer mysteries. Bruce Tulgan and Debby Applegate raised my spirits at a crucial moment. Judith Harper, my fellow historian of the Civil War, helped with bibliographical lunches and general encouragement. Jan Swafford, both a writer and a composer, loaned me his Civil War books and performed an expert sight-reading for me of "The Alabama," a rousing old Confederate song in honor of Semmes and his ship. My wife of twenty years, Alexandra Dundas Todd, a writer and sociology professor, again understood and even tolerated the absences, recurring absent-mindedness, and sharply variable moods of a writing husband—and all of this during a difficult time in her own life.

At Alfred A. Knopf, Andrew Miller acquired this project and then line-edited the manuscript with meticulous care and the most extraordinary handwriting. Andrew also showed me how the illustrations could well be distributed through the text of this book, and he commiserated with me, as a fellow sufferer by marriage, over the usual late-season fortunes of the Boston Red Sox. His assistant, Dixon Gaines, helped out at various stages of the publication process. Walter Havighurst expertly copyedited the final manuscript.

During the last two decades, personal computers and the Internet have revolutionized historical research just as they have affected almost every aspect of modern life. It may be that any historical work written before these technological boons will eventually have to be done again. For example, the American Periodical Series of microfilmed nineteenth-century magazines has been available for half a century—but the material formerly could only be accessed by laboriously reading through the actual volumes. Now the entire collection may be digitally searched, and I thereby turned up fourteen significant references to Semmes that were previously unknown to historians. Today, when any U.S. federal census from 1790 through 1930 can be name-searched at ancestry.com, and all 158 volumes of the *Official Records* of the Civil War armies and navies are searchable at Cornell University's "Making of America" website, and ancient files of such important newspapers as the *New York Times, Brooklyn Eagle, Philadelphia Inquirer,* and *Richmond Dispatch* may be digitally searched from any home computer, certain traditional notions of historical research must be revised.

Yet most newspapers of interest still cannot be plumbed so easily. A historian must, as ever, spend long, eye-glazing hours hunched over a microfilm reader or picking through thick files of manuscripts, all in the hope that the familiar regimen will be redeemed by an occasional discovery. This process has its hardships, but—one must remember—it's still a lot easier than actually writing the book.

We historians, so deeply rooted in the past, tend to favor stability and continuity, and some things fortunately don't change. This book's dedication reflects a personal and intellectual debt of long standing. Robin Straus has been my literary agent for twenty-seven years. Through five books, three publishers, and many changes for both of us, she has been a smart, steady, encouraging presence in my life. So now I want to say what I surely have not said often enough along the way: Thanks, Robin, for your counsel and persistence.

Stephen Fox
Somerville, Massachusetts
Deerfield Beach, Florida
DECEMBER 15, 2006

Notes

MANUSCRIPT MATERIALS

Charles Francis Adams Papers, Massachusetts Historical Society
Alabama contract and specifications, copy in Southern Historical Collection, Wilson Library, University of North Carolina, Chapel Hill
Garnett Andrews Papers, Southern Historical Collection, Wilson Library, University of North Carolina, Chapel Hill
Letters of Ezra Bartlett, Rare Books and Manuscripts, Boston Public Library
Joshua Bates Diary, Baring Archive, London
Baylor Family Papers, Virginia Historical Society, Richmond
Clement Claiborne Clay Papers, Rare Book, Manuscript, and Special Collections Library, Duke University
William H. Cushman Papers, Manuscript Division, Library of Congress
Frederick M. Dearborn Collection, Houghton Library, Harvard University
Doubleday and Company Collection (Bruce Catton Research Notes by E. B. Long), Manuscript Division, Library of Congress
Thomas H. Dudley Papers, Huntington Library, San Marino, California
Finlay Family Papers, in custody of Anne Finlay Schenck, New Haven, Connecticut
Hamilton Fish Papers, Manuscript Division, Library of Congress
Robert Bennet Forbes Papers, Massachusetts Historical Society
Foreign Office Papers, Public Record Office, Kew, England
Gustavus Vasa Fox Papers, Naval History Society Collection, New-York Historical Society
Henry Hotze Papers, Manuscript Division, Library of Congress
John McIntosh Kell Papers, Rare Book, Manuscript, and Special Collections Library, Duke University
William S. Lindsay Papers, Caird Library, National Maritime Museum, Greenwich, England
Log Book of the *Alabama*, W. S. Hoole Special Collections Library, University of Alabama, Tuscaloosa
John N. Maffitt Papers, Southern Historical Collection, Wilson Library, University of North Carolina, Chapel Hill

James M. Mason Papers, Manuscript Division, Library of Congress

Materials in Record Group 45, National Archives

    Letters Sent by the Secretary of the Navy to the President and Executive Agencies 1821–86, Microcopy No. 472

    Miscellaneous Letters Received by the Secretary of the Navy, 1801–84, Microcopy No. 124

    Records Relating to Confederate Naval and Marine Personnel, Microcopy No. 260

    Subject File of the Confederate States Navy, 1861–65, Microcopy No. M1091

Matthew F. Maury Papers, Manuscript Division, Library of Congress

Navy Collection, Eleanor S. Brockenbrough Library, Museum of the Confederacy, Richmond

Letters of William Nevius, "Misc, Nevius" file, New-York Historical Society

Elizabeth B. Nicholas Papers, Virginia Historical Society, Richmond

James H. North Diary, Southern Historical Collection, Wilson Library, University of North Carolina, Chapel Hill

Journal of Charles A. Poole, G. H. Blunt Library, Mystic Seaport, Mystic, Connecticut

Benedict J. Semmes Papers, Southern Historical Collection, Wilson Library, University of North Carolina, Chapel Hill

Semmes Family Bible, with notations by Raphael Semmes and others, in custody of Thomas Middleton Semmes, Gladstone, Oregon

Semmes Family Papers, Alabama Department of Archives and History, Montgomery

Raphael Semmes, *Electra* Journal, 1848–52, photocopy, Museum of Mobile

Raphael Semmes Letterbook, 1848–58, Manuscript Division, Library of Congress

Raphael Semmes Papers, Rare Book, Manuscript, and Special Collections Library, Duke University

Raphael Semmes Papers, Virginia Historical Society, Richmond

Raphael Semmes ZB file, Naval Historical Foundation, Washington Navy Yard

Harvey M. Smith Jr. Collection, Kenan Research Center, Atlanta History Center

Warren F. Spencer Papers, in custody of Elizabeth T. Spencer, Charlottesville, Virginia

Charles G. Summersell Papers, W. S. Hoole Special Collections Library, University of Alabama, Tuscaloosa

Charles Sumner Papers, Houghton Library, Harvard University

Francis W. Tremlett Papers, Eleanor S. Brockenbrough Library, Museum of the Confederacy, Richmond

Journal of William Wainwright, G. H. Blunt Library, Mystic Seaport, Mystic, Connecticut

Charles Wilkes Papers, Manuscript Division, Library of Congress

John A. Winslow Papers, Manuscript Division, Library of Congress

NOTE ON JOURNALS

The principal source for this book is the journals that Raphael Semmes kept during the cruises of the *Alabama* and *Sumter.* They were published, with a few deletions, in the *Official Records of the Union and Confederate Navies in the War of the Rebellion* (1894), Series 1, as follows:

Sumter journal, May 24, 1861–April 11, 1862, in volume 1, pp. 691–744.

Alabama journal, August 20, 1862–January 4, 1863, in volume 1, pp. 783–817; January 5, 1863–March 31, 1864, in volume 2, pp. 720–807; and April 1–June 16, 1864, in volume 3, pp. 669–77.

Citations to these journals are by date (volume and page number); thus: Journal, May 24, 1861 (1:691).

ABBREVIATIONS OF MAJOR SOURCES

BUS James D. Bulloch, *The Secret Service of the Confederate States in Europe; or, How the Confederate Cruisers Were Equipped* (2 vols., 1884)

CFA Charles Francis Adams Papers, Massachusetts Historical Society

CGB *Correspondence Concerning Claims Against Great Britain Transmitted to the Senate of the United States* (7 vols., 1869–71)

CGT *The Case of Great Britain as Laid Before the Tribunal of Arbitration, Convened at Geneva* (3 vols., 1872)

CWH *Civil War History* (quarterly journal, 1955–)

ELJ Raphael Semmes, *Electra* Journal, 1848–52, photocopy, Museum of Mobile

FOP Foreign Office Papers, Public Record Office, Kew, England

FUJ *The Journal of George Townley Fullam: Boarding Officer of the Confederate Sea Raider* Alabama, ed. Charles G. Summersell (1973)

HUS Anderson Humphreys and Curt Guenther, *Semmes America* (1989)

ILN *Illustrated London News*

JMK John McIntosh Kell Papers, Rare Book, Manuscript, and Special Collections Library, Duke University

Journal Raphael Semmes, Journals of the *Alabama* and *Sumter*, in ORN (see below)

KER John McIntosh Kell, *Recollections of a Naval Life* (1900)

LBA Log Book of the *Alabama*, W. S. Hoole Special Collections Library, University of Alabama

MEM Raphael Semmes, *Memoirs of Service Afloat, During the War Between the States* (1868)

MEX Raphael Semmes, *Service Afloat and Ashore During the Mexican War* (1851)

MOC Eleanor S. Brockenbrough Library, Museum of the Confederacy, Richmond

MOJ *The Journal of Benjamin Moran, 1857–1865*, ed. Sarah Agnes Wallace and Frances Elma Gillespie (1949)

NYH *New York Herald*

NYT *New York Times*

ORA *The War of the Rebellion: A Compilation of the Official Records of the Union and Confederate Armies* (128 vols., 1880–1901; cited by series, volume, and page number)

ORN *Official Records of the Union and Confederate Navies in the War of the Rebellion* (30 vols., 1894–1922; cited by series, volume, and page number)

PFA   *Papers Relating to Foreign Affairs, Accompanying the Annual Message of the President* (1862 and later years)

SEC   *The Cruise of the Alabama and the Sumter: From the Private Journals and Other Papers of Commander R. Semmes, C.S.N.* (2 vols., 1864)

SFP   Semmes Family Papers, Alabama Department of Archives and History, Montgomery

SHC   Southern Historical Collection, Wilson Library, University of North Carolina, Chapel Hill

SIT   Arthur Sinclair, *Two Years on the Alabama* (2d ed., 1896)

SLB   Raphael Semmes Letterbook, 1848–58, Manuscript Division, Library of Congress

SPR   Warren F. Spencer, *Raphael Semmes: The Philosophical Mariner* (1997)

SPV   Raphael Semmes Papers, Virginia Historical Society, Richmond

TAC   John M. Taylor, *Confederate Raider: Raphael Semmes of the* Alabama (1994)

PROLOGUE   Escape and Debut

3   "You cannot conceive, my dear wife": Raphael Semmes to Anne E. Semmes, July 7, 1862, SFP.

4   "It now requires no very far-reaching prophet": Allan Nevins, *The War for the Union: War Becomes Revolution, 1862–1863* (1960), p. 91.

4   "My paramount object": *The Collected Works of Abraham Lincoln*, ed. Roy P. Basler (1953), 5:388.

4   "But whatever may betide them": Raphael Semmes to Anne E. Semmes, July 7, 1862, SFP.

5   "I am sorry, my darling daughter": Raphael Semmes to Electra Semmes, August 11, 1862, SFP.

5   "My personal interests": BUS, 1:32; on Bulloch see *Confederate Veteran*, February 1901 and December 1909.

5   "the nearest approach to Col. Newcome": *Confederate Veteran*, January 1903.

5   "that most beautiful": ibid., November 1905.

5   Thomas H. Dudley: Brainerd Dyer in *CWH*, December 1955.

6   "not as a general thing": David Hepburn Milton, *Lincoln's Spymaster: Thomas Haines Dudley and the Liverpool Network* (2003), pp. 32–33.

7   "They did not know for what purpose": BUS, 1:62, 68.

7   building of such a ship: ibid., 1:226.

7   "The foreman who": Milton, *Lincoln's Spymaster*, p. 40.

7   Dudley's spies reported: ibid., pp. 42–43.

8   mostly political reasons: see discussion in Chapter 5, pp. 116–17.

8   "I think we shall stop her": CGB, 3:14.

8   the *Agrippina: Nautical Magazine* (London), March 1863; BUS, 1:237; Peter Barton in *Mariner's Mirror*, November 1999.

8   "they were going to have some fun": George King deposition, September 27, 1862, CGB 3:50.

8   bizarre, inexplicable twists: Diary of Charles Francis Adams, July 21–23, 31, 1862, and Adams to Thomas Dudley, July 27, 1862, CFA; Frank J. Merli, *The Alabama, British Neutrality, and the American Civil War,* ed. David M. Fahey (2004), p. 70; Merli, *Great Britain and the Confederate Navy, 1861–1865* (1970), pp. 92–93.

8   "a private but most reliable": BUS, 1:238.

8   Sir John Harding went insane: Milton, *Lincoln's Spymaster,* p. 46.

8   "you are strictly": James D. Bulloch to Clarence R. Yonge, July 28, 1862, Thomas H. Dudley Papers.

9   Departure of *Alabama:* LBA, July 28–31, 1862; Milton, *Lincoln's Spymaster,* pp. 46–48; Richard I. Lester, *Confederate Finance and Purchasing in Great Britain* (1975), pp. 75–76.

9   strong gales with hard squalls: LBA, August 4, 1862.

10   "proved herself": Merli, *British Neutrality,* p. 133.

10   "She was, indeed, a beautiful thing": MEM, p. 404.

10   "Her model was": ibid., p. 402.

10   "she became sweet": ibid., p. 408.

11   Semmes's appearance: *London Star,* April 19, [1862], in *Alabama* folder, miscellaneous box 3, Navy Collection, MOC.

12   "Now, my lads": John Latham deposition, January 8, 1864, PFA (1864), 1:91.

12   "The others hung back": Journal, August 20, 1862 (1:784).

12   Scene on *Alabama:* SIT, pp. 14–15.

12   "said he was deranged": Henry Redden deposition, September 3, 1862, CGB 3:46.

13   "but any of you": Latham deposition, 1:91.

13   £20,000: Clarence Yonge deposition, April 2, 1863, PFA (1863), p. 193.

13   "The modern sailor": Journal, August 24, 1862 (1:785).

13   "Banishing every sentiment": ORN, 1:1:777.

14   First night at sea: Journal, August 24, 1862 (1:786).

14   "It was the most obvious thing": MEM, p. 424.

14   "We are still": Journal, August 28, 1862 (1:786).

15   Capture of *Ocmulgee:* LBA, September 5–6, 1862; William Stanley Hoole, *Four Years in the Confederate Navy: The Career of Captain John Low* (1964), pp. 59–60.

15   sorry to inform: CGB, 3:75.

15   estimated the value: ORN, 1:3:677.

15   "We seem to be": Journal, September 24, 1862 (1:791).

16   rough estimates: ORN, 1:3:677–78.

16   "A splendid vessel": Theodore Julius statement, October 15, 1862, FO 5/1318, file 196, FOP.

16   "I fear that neither": PFA (1862), p. 237.

17 Report by skipper of *Baron de Castine: Baltimore Sun*, November 3, 1862.

17 "Can one vessel": *NYH*, November 3, 1862.

1 The Captain and the Ship

18 "While in the United States Navy": David D. Porter, *The Naval History of the Civil War* (1886), pp. 602–4.

19 "The inertness": ibid., p. 604.

19 split in Maryland: Barbara Jeanne Fields, *Slavery and Freedom on the Middle Ground: Maryland During the Nineteenth Century* (1985), pp. 6–9.

19 Semmes's family background: Harry Wright Newman, *The Maryland Semmes and Kindred Families* (1956), pp. 1–3, 43–44, 47–49, 55, 286–87; HUS, pp. 274–75, 286.

19 Semmes's parents: Newman, *Semmes*, pp. 65, 76, 80; HUS, p. 295.

19 sleeping in each other's arms: Raphael Semmes to Samuel Semmes, August 12, 1865, in *Confederate Veteran*, July 1927.

20 "reared on the banks": MEM, p. 75.

20 Joseph Semmes: William W. Warner, *At Peace with All Their Neighbors: Catholics and Catholicism in the National Capital, 1787–1860* (1994), pp. 70–71, 250.

20 Uncle Benedict: HUS, pp. 298–99.

20 "The habit of study": Raphael Semmes to Electra Semmes, August 11, 1862, SFP.

20 Semmes at military academy: TAC, p. 14.

20 "the shreds and patches": MEX, p. 261.

20 Uncle Alexander: Newman, *Semmes*, pp. 64–65, 76.

20 Uncle Raphael: HUS, pp. 295–98.

20 appointed a midshipman: S. Spencer Semmes in *Southern Historical Society Papers*, vol. 38 (1910), pp. 28–29.

21 typical Navy sailing ship: George Jones, *Sketches of Naval Life* (1829), 1:40–45, 98–101; Daniel Ammen, *The Old Navy and the New* (1891), pp. 34–35, 64–65; Charles Nordhoff, *Man-of-War Life* (1895), pp. 46–51.

22 midshipmen's mess: Charles Wilkes, *Autobiography of Charles Wilkes, U.S. Navy, 1798–1877* (1978), pp. 126–27.

22 Semmes's betting habit: MEX, p. 291.

23 "As a controversialist": J. N. Maffitt in *South-Atlantic* (Wilmington, North Carolina), November 1877. For an example of Semmes as sea lawyer, see the thirteen-page letter from him to David Conner, September 11, 1846, Autograph file, Simes Collection, Houghton Library, Harvard University.

23 Semmes sent a sharp rebuttal: *Military and Naval Magazine of the United States*, November 1833.

23 "The public will see": Raphael Semmes to editor, *Pensacola Gazette*, November 4, 1836, reprinted in *Army and Navy Chronicle*, November 24, 1836.

23 Semmes's clash with Dallas: James E. Valle, *Rocks and Shoals: Order and Discipline in the Old Navy, 1800–1861* (1980), p. 269.

24 Cincinnati in 1834: Charles Theodore Greve, *Centennial History of Cincinnati and Representative Citizens* (1904), 1:547.

24 "a stately, handsome": W. Adolphe Roberts, *Semmes of the Alabama* (1938), p. 18.

24 early photograph: HUS, p. 312.

24 Oliver Spencer: Oliver M. Spencer, *Indian Captivity: A True Narrative* (1835), pp. 5–6.

24 annual friendly visit: ibid., p. 154.

24 Miami Exporting Company: Greve, *Cincinnati*, 1:109–11, 140–42, 575.

24 Spencer home address: Cincinnati City Directory (1819, 1825).

25 in 1812 he pledged: Henry A. Ford and Kate B. Ford, *History of Cincinnati, Ohio* (1881), p. 150.

25 opened his home to the newly arrived Quakers: Greve, *Cincinnati*, 1:496.

25 Spencer as minister: ibid., 1:533; Cincinnati City Directory (1825, 1829).

25 Marriage of Semmes: marriage certificate, May 2, 1837, Finlay Family Papers.

25 Birth of Samuel Spencer: notations in Raphael Semmes's handwriting in Semmes family Bible, currently owned by Thomas Middleton Semmes.

25 Anne as Catholic: Roberts, *Semmes*, p. 261.

25 Two children's conversion: ibid.

26 "Money has no charms": Raphael Semmes to Anne Semmes, January 4, 1863, SFP.

26 bought farmland: Roberts, *Semmes*, p. 18; TAC, pp. 19–20.

26 "a very pleasant colony": Maffitt in *South-Atlantic*, November 1877.

26 "my fellow citizens": ELJ, April 15, 1848.

26 "served during the whole": Raphael Semmes to J. P. Kennedy, November 27, 1852, SLB.

26 *Somers* sinking: MEX, pp. 93–99; report by John H. Wright, *New Orleans Picayune*, reprinted in *New York Anglo American*, January 9, 1847; MEM, pp. 276–78, 346–47.

27 "Our hitherto quiet": MEX, p. 125.

27 troops were landed: ibid., pp. 125–41.

27 Semmes joined the Army: SPR, pp. 42–43; Raphael Semmes to Winfield Scott, May 8, 1847, and Scott to Semmes, May 9, 1847, SLB.

27 he and Lieutenant Ulysses S. Grant: SPR, pp. 74–75.

28 "distinguished gallantry": Philip F. Thomas to Raphael Semmes, July 11, 1848, SLB.

28 *Porpoise* manuscript: "Cruise of the <u>Porpoise</u> in the Caribbean," file 3:3, SFP; on the cruise, see Richard S. West Jr., *The Second Admiral: A Life of David Dixon Porter, 1813–1891* (1937), pp. 41–43.

28 brother Henry: Charles Frederic Goss, *Cincinnati: The Queen City, 1788–1912* (1912), 1:178.

28 brother Oliver: ibid., 1:769–70.

28 "as a tribute": MEX, dedication.

28 "There never yet was": ibid., p. vi.

29 women screaming: ibid., p. 138.

29 "Politicians, with a few": ibid., p. 41.

29 "the petty theater": ibid., p. 67.

29 "an inferior people": ibid.

29 "Time, with his scythe": ibid., p. 126.

29 "One of the most interesting": *De Bow's Review*, September 1851.

29 "The most unprejudiced": *Godey's Lady's Book*, October 1851.

29 "A work of standard merit": *Harper's Magazine*, October 1851.

30 Semmes as tightly wound: Roberts, *Semmes*, p. 26.

30 smiled, but he hardly ever laughed: John M. Kell to J. N. Maffitt, January 6, 1878, John N. Maffitt Papers.

30 Birth date of Anna: SPR, p. 76.

30 Naming of Anna Spencer Semmes: Anna, later married to Charles B. Bryan of Memphis, and active in the DAR, listed her name as Anna Spencer Semmes Bryan in its directory; see *Directory of the National Society of the Daughters of the American Revolution* (1901), p. 570. Some sources give the name as Anna Elizabeth Semmes.

30 Eden Hall school: *Metropolitan Catholic Almanac* (1861), pp. 66, 303; *Philadelphia Press*, July 8, 1864.

30 Anna claimed a birth date: see her obituaries in *Memphis Press-Scimitar*, October 7, 1936, and *Memphis Commercial-Appeal*, October 8, 1936.

31 a brief visit in early July 1846: Raphael Semmes to David Conner, September 11, 1846, Autograph file, Simes Collection.

31 "to be near": ELJ, January 15, 1848.

31 "I feel sad": ibid., March 4, 1848.

31 "Every day I am becoming": ibid., April 1, 1848.

31 "No letters yet": ibid., April 8, 1848.

31 "At Home!": ibid., May 17, 1848.

31 found the welcome news: ibid., July 7, 1848.

32 wrote a fond letter: Raphael Semmes to Anne Semmes, July 7, 1862, SFP.

32 "for the convenience": Raphael Semmes to W. Ballard Preston, October 4, 1849, SLB.

33 "I read, and read": ELJ, March 28, 1848.

33 Quotations from Byron: MEX, pp. 190, 205, 408; MEM, pp. viii, 30, 107, 119, 165, 176, 177, 216, 265, 295, 439.

34 Semmes's description of Maffitt: MEM, p. 354.

34 "a voice like a woman's": *The Times* (London), February 4, 1863.

34 "He had no particular taste": David D. Porter, *The Naval History of the Civil War* (1886), p. 602.

34 "Although his courage": ibid., p. 656.

34 "He had the rare": R.C.R. in *United Service*, July 1890.

34 "Nothing particularly striking": E. T. Eggleston in ORN, 1:12:190.

34 "For he was a man": note by William S. Lindsay, ca. 1867, in file LND/7, pp. 469–71, William S. Lindsay Papers.

35 Navy promotion system: [Matthew F. Maury] in *Southern Literary Messenger,* April 1840; Charles Wilkes, *Autobiography of Charles Wilkes, U.S. Navy, 1798–1877* (1978), p. 45; A. T. Mahan, *From Sail to Steam: Recollections of a Naval Life* (1907), pp. 13, 15; James E. Valle, *Rocks and Shoals: Order and Discipline in the Old Navy, 1800–1861* (1980), pp. 12–14, 28.

35 "We of the naval": MEX, p. 51.

35 "Ambitious as I am": Raphael Semmes to David L. Yulee, n.d., in Miscellaneous "S" file, Naval Historical Society Collection, New-York Historical Society.

35 tried lumbering: ELJ, March 4–May 22, [1852].

35 Commander's pay scale: *American Almanac and Repository of Useful Knowledge* (1857), p. 119.

36 "I have not been afloat": Raphael Semmes to J. C. Dobbin, October 21, 1855, SLB.

36 "the first vacant command": Raphael Semmes to J. C. Dobbin, February 23, 1856, SLB.

36 Command of the *Illinois: Captains of the Old Steam Navy: Makers of the American Naval Tradition, 1840–1880,* ed. James C. Bradford (1986), p. 199.

36 "I respectfully request": Raphael Semmes to J. C. Dobbin, December 15, 1856, SLB.

36 "a perfectly independent one": Raphael Semmes to Samuel Spencer Semmes, May 30, 1859, Garnett Andrews Papers.

36 "I love my country": ELJ, April 1, 1848.

37 South and Cavaliers: Robert E. Bonner in *CWH,* March 2002.

37 "the great extent": Raphael Semmes to Anne Semmes, August 21, 1860, SFP.

37 "The great government": Raphael Semmes to Alexander Stephens, December 11, 1860, SFP.

37 "I think States enough": Raphael Semmes to Howell Cobb, January 26, 1861, in *The Correspondence of Robert Toombs, Alexander H. Stephens, and Howell Cobb,* ed. Ulrich Bonnell Phillips (1913), p. 533.

38 "I do not think": Raphael Semmes to J.L.M. Curry, February 6, 1861, SFP.

38 Samuel as Unionist: Harry Wright Newman, *Maryland and the Confederacy* (1976), pp. 247–48; Samuel M. Semmes to Charles Sumner, September 16, 1863, Charles Sumner Papers.

38 Oliver resigned commission: "Biographical Memoranda" by Oliver J. Semmes, February 28, 1907, in folder 27, box 5510, Charles G. Summersell Papers.

38 "Kiss your dear": Raphael Semmes to Electra Semmes, March 26, 1861, SFP.

38 "If you can get safely": Raphael Semmes to Anne Semmes, May 28, 1861, SFP.

39 "The fierce and savage": Raphael Semmes to Electra Semmes, May 3, 1861, SFP.

39 "a small organized system": Raphael Semmes to J.L.M. Curry, February 6, 1861, SFP.

39 "There is a growing disposition": MEX, p. 82.

41 "was like a chieftain": BUS, 1:20.

41 *Sumter* background: *NYH*, August 20, 1861.

41 flush deck was added: *The Times* (London), January 29, 1862.

41 "I could have kicked": John M. Kell, newspaper interview, quoted in Blanche Kell, "Life and Letters of J. M. Kell," p. 26, in box 12, JMK.

41 Her first trial run: Raphael Semmes to Stephen Mallory, June 14, 1861, SFP.

41 buoyant and dry: MEM, p. 342.

41 *Sumter*'s running of the blockade: "Journal of a *Sumter* Officer," *Harper's Weekly*, August 16, 1862; MEM, pp. 114–19.

41 "Night beautiful": Journal, June 30, 1861 (1:694).

42 *Golden Rocket* burning: MEM, pp. 128–29.

42 Early captures by *Sumter*: *NYH*, July 15, 21, August 2, 1861.

42 The limitations of the *Sumter*: Raphael Semmes to Stephen Mallory, November 9, 1861, ORN 1:1:628–31.

42 Rumors flew around: *NYH*, August 2, 1861.

42 actual total for the first ten ships: Semmes to Mallory, November 9, 1861, ORN 1:1:635.

42 Porter's pursuit: ORN, 1:1:65, 69, 91–92, 108.

43 "use every endeavor": ibid., 1:1:120.

43 "Great excitement": Journal, November 14, 1861 (1:721).

44 "I have at last got hold": *NYT*, December 16, 1861.

44 Escape from Martinique: KER, p. 164; ORN, 1:1:213–14; MEM, pp. 261–65.

44 "This was truly": Journal, November 23, 1861 (1:724).

44 wrecked off Trinidad: *NYH*, September 13, 1861.

44 captured near Barbados: *NYT*, November 9, 1861.

44 Impostor on *Edinburgh*: *NYT*, November 8, 1861.

45 "It is of no use": Journal, November 25, 1861 (1:725).

45 "As ugly looking": Journal, December 11, 1861 (1:729).

46 "Alas!": Journal, December 25, 1861 (1:732).

46 "I could scarcely believe": *The Times* (London), January 29, 1862.

46 Survey of ship: John M. Kell et al. to Raphael Semmes, January 28, 1862, SFP.

47 "The crippled condition": Raphael Semmes to J. M. Mason, January 24, 1862, ORN, 1:1:660.

47 "There is not a shipbuilding firm": Kenneth Warren, *Steel, Ships and Men: Cammell Laird, 1824–1993* (1998), p. 35; on John Laird, see *ILN*, July 27, 1861.

47 Henry Laird: *Engineering*, June 2, 1893; *Engineer*, June 2, 1893; *Transactions of the Institution of Naval Architects* (1893), pp. 239–40.

47 The Lairds had pioneered: Stephen Fox, *Transatlantic: Samuel Cunard, Isambard Brunel, and the Great Atlantic Steamships* (2003), pp. 143–44.

48 wooden hull resisted thick fouling: ibid., p. 144.

48 wooden hull cost more: BUS, 1:60–61.

48 *Alabama* specifications: copy of building contract, 1861, in SHC.

48 "oscillating" arrangement: *The Advent of Steam: The Merchant Steamship Before 1900*, ed. Robert Gardiner and Basil Greenhill (1993), pp. 32, 167.

49 *Alabama*'s sailing qualities: John M. Kell in *Century*, April 1886; Porter, *Naval History*, p. 631.

49 Layout of upper deck: Andrew Bowcock, *CSS* Alabama: *Anatomy of a Confederate Raider* (2002), p. 79.

49 *"Aide-toi"* as general motto: interview with John M. Coski, MOC, October 17, 2005.

49 *Alabama*'s guns: James Tertius deKay, *The Rebel Raiders: The Astonishing History of the Confederacy's Secret Navy* (2002), p. 89; SIT, p. 8; Richard I. Lester, *Confederate Finance and Purchasing in Great Britain* (1975), pp. 141–42.

50 Captain's stateroom: *Cape Town Mail*, August 19, 1863, reprinted in *NYT*, October 8, 1863; *NYH*, August 2, 1863; William Stanley Hoole, *Four Years in the Confederate Navy: The Career of Captain John Low* (1964), p. 66.

50 Layout of lower deck: Hoole, *Four Years*, p. 45; Charles Grayson Summersell, *CSS Alabama: Builder, Captain, and Plans* (1985), "Profile of Inboard Works" in sleeve at back of book.

51 "It is rarely that a ship": SIT, p. 149.

51 "I think": Norman C. Delaney, *John McIntosh Kell of the Raider* Alabama (1973), p. 129.

2   "A Pirate on the High Seas"

52 Semmes as Stonewall: *Macon Daily Telegraph*, October 21, 1863; *Confederate Veteran*, August 1918.

52 *Alabama* as Flying Dutchman: *NYH*, December 20, 1862; *New York Albion*, January 3, 1863.

53 dangerous fun: a phrase borrowed from Jesse Winchester's song of that name, on his album *Third Down, 110 to Go* (1972).

54 Effect of long chase on captain's mood: SIT, p. 131.

54 men waiting on the upper deck knew: ibid., p. 93.

56 *Benjamin Tucker:* MEM, pp. 439–40; Journal, September 14, 1862 (1:790); CGT, 3:446.

57 *Elisha Dunbar:* MEM, pp. 442–44; Journal, September 18, 1862 (1:790–91); CGT, 3:447–48.

57 "My gallant little ship": MEM, p. 443.

58 Gifford might actually have saved: SIT, p. 33.

59 "like a child": letter of Edward M. Anderson in *Georgia Historical Quarterly* (winter 1975), ed. W. Stanley Hoole; and see Hagar's later protest, CGB, 3:192–93.

59 Semmes felt moved: MEM, p. 459.

59 *Herald*'s claimed circulation: *NYH*, February 21, 1862.

59 "A Pirate on the High Seas": *NYH*, October 17, 19, 1862.

60 the *Herald* leveled an even more serious charge: *NYH*, October 17, 1862; for later denials of this accusation, see MEM, p. 459, and SIT, p. 113.

60 "The deck is more or less wet": Journal, September 19, 1862 (1:791).

61 Semmes angry over mistreatment of purser: KER, p. 191.

61 clerk maintained an ongoing file: *New Bedford Standard*, November 3, 1862.

61 Copies of the latest papers would pass: SIT, pp. 56–57.

61 vows of revenge: SEC, 1:372.

61 "little better than": MEX, p. 82.

62 "Do not believe": Raphael Semmes to Anne Semmes, January 4, 1863, SFP.

62 Kell: see KER; and Norman C. Delaney, *John McIntosh Kell of the Raider Alabama* (1973).

63 Kell's beard: James Morris Morgan, *Recollections of a Rebel Reefer* (1917), p. 189.

63 "I think," he later wrote: KER, p. 9.

63 "So far from being a mutineer": MEM, p. 123; and see W. Ballard Preston to Raphael Semmes, July 3, 1849, with note by Semmes, SLB.

63 "priest-ridden superstitions": KER, p. 239.

66 the five lieutenants: SIT, pp. 20, 202, 302–5, 314; MEM, pp. 416–17; obituary of Armstrong, *Confederate Veteran*, July 1904; Charles Grayson Summersell, *CSS Alabama: Builder, Captain, and Plans* (1985), pp. 29–30.

66 Freeman: SIT, pp. 317–18; Summersell, *Alabama*, pp. 30–31.

66 Howell: *The Papers of Jefferson Davis*, ed. Haskell M. Monroe et al. (1971), 5:42.

67 Evans: SIT, pp. 139, 323–24.

67 Fullam: FUJ, pp. xvi–xvii.

67 Smith: *New Orleans Picayune*, September 29, 1912; FUJ, p. 149.

67 "Smith had a peculiar man": SIT, p. 326.

67 Only Kell and Freeman were over thirty: ibid., p. 226.

67 Generation of the 1850s: Gary W. Gallagher, *The Confederate War* (1997), pp. 72, 96.

68 "As though she was": Anderson in *Georgia Historical Quarterly* (winter 1975).

68 "We are nothing": NYH, October 19, 1862.

68 Reports of poor discipline: CGT, 3:425, 428; CGB, 3:76, 78; *NYH*, October 19, December 12, 1862.

68 "from the groggeries": Journal, December 29, 1862 (1:816).

69 "Many of my fellows": ibid.

69 "I have never seen": Journal, November 16, 1862 (1:805).

69 often lifted rum: SEC, 2:103–4.

69 Semmes paced the deck: SIT, p. 225.

69 he could guess about the general direction: ibid., pp. 117–18.

70 "The men feel": ibid., p. 84.

3   For Money and Fighting

71 Plan for attacking New York: Norman C. Delaney, *John McIntosh Kell of the Raider* Alabama (1973), p. 135; *New Bedford Standard*, November 3, 1862.

71 Capture of *Tonawanda: NYH*, November 13, 1862.

72 "I found that our women": Theodore Julius deposition, CGB, 3:77.

72 "I hope," Semmes shot back: *NYT*, November 3, 1862.

73 Hurricane: SIT, pp. 44–46; FUJ, pp. 37–38.

73 Kell . . . had witnessed: Blanche Kell, "Life and Letters of J. M. Kell," p. 28, box 12, JMK.

74 Damage to ship: LBA, October 16, 1862.

74 Semmes . . . thought it was: MEM, p. 475.

74 "I must capture": Journal, October 16, 1862 (1:796).

74 "While they are running": Journal, October 26, 1862 (1:799).

75 had to drop his plan: KER, p. 195.

75 "As coal was both fuel": Raphael Semmes to James D. Bulloch, November 19, 1862, Navy Collection, miscellaneous box 2, MOC.

75 "We were considerably": FUJ, p. 46.

75 "We were placed": *NYH*, December 12, 1862.

75 "a prize more valuable": Journal, November 8, 1862 (1:804).

76 "We are to be embarrassed": Journal, November 8, 1862 (1:803–4).

76 "awkward position": SIT, p. 49.

76 dreamed about his children: MEM, p. 497.

76 Crew's uprising at Martinique: ibid., pp. 511–13; TAC, p. 131.

77 "We gave our crew": letter from Edward M. Anderson in *Georgia Historical Quarterly* (winter 1975), ed. W. Stanley Hoole.

77 "We were afraid": ORN, 1:1:592.

77 up to five million: *Bankers' Magazine*, May 1863.

78 "The capture of one or two": Stephen Mallory to John N. Maffitt, October 25, 1862, John N. Maffitt Papers.

78 A million dollars in gold: MEM, p. 520.

78 "I am looking": Journal, November 28, 1862 (1:807).

79 "This night will answer": Journal, December 2, 1862 (1:809).

79 "Several sail in sight": Journal, December 5, 1862 (1:810).

79 "S-a-i-l h-o!": MEM, p. 530.

79 Appearance of *Ariel*: SEC, 2:2–3.

79 "Everybody in the best": FUJ, p. 61.

80 Pursuit of *Ariel*: SIT, pp. 58–59.

80 rapt passenger saw: *A Pioneer of 1850: George Willis Read, 1819–1880*, ed. Georgia Willis Read (1927), p. 132.

80 ducked down behind the pine bulkheads: A. T. Mahan, *From Sail to Steam: Recollections of a Naval Life* (1907), p. 181.

80 Capture of *Ariel*: ORN, 1:1:578–80; *NYH*, December 28, 29, 1862; KER, pp. 203–6.

80 took away $8,000 in Treasury notes: Raphael Semmes to Stephen Mallory, January 4, 1863, ORN 1:1:779.

80 "Passengers, you're safe": *Baltimore Sun*, December 30, 1862, reported that

Semmes gave this reassuring speech, but he was never on board the *Ariel;* Semmes's later account does not identify the speaker except as "my handsomest young lieutenant," who was evidently Armstrong; see MEM, pp. 533–34.

82 crewmen of the *Ariel* cheered: SIT, p. 63.

82 "I was sorry": letter from Edward M. Anderson in *Georgia Historical Quarterly* (winter 1975).

82 "Having procured one": Plantation Bitters ad, *NYH*, December 31, 1862. Given the anarchic ethics of patent-medicine advertising, the Semmes letter might have been forged, but it has been accepted as genuine by W. Adolphe Roberts, *Semmes of the Alabama* (1938), pp. 127–28, and later biographers. On Plantation Bitters, see Stephen Fox, *The Mirror Makers: A History of American Advertising and Its Creators* (1984), pp. 16–17.

83 "It is important": Journal, December 13, 1862 (1:812).

83 "I hope to strike": Journal, December 15, 1862 (1:812).

83 "The clouds look hard and wintry": Journal, December 17, 1862 (1:812).

83 "They will live in history": Journal, December 25, 1862 (1:814).

84 "Constant cruising": Journal, December 28, 1862 (1:815).

84 Banks expedition: Raphael Semmes to Stephen Mallory, May 12, 1863, ORN, 1:2:683–84.

84 could do everything but talk: MEM, p. 540.

84 "Land ho!": ibid., p. 541.

85 "Everyone delighted": FUJ, p. 70.

85 "What ship is that?": Journal, January 11, 1863 (2:721); KER, p. 208.

86 "This is the Confederate States": SIT, p. 71.

86 "The conduct of our men": FUJ, p. 76.

86 "Give it to the rascals": ibid., p. 77.

86 six holes near the waterline: CGT, 1:139; and see drawing of damage, noting thirteen holes (six at waterline), in roll 7 (AD), "Subject File of the Confederate States Navy, 1861–1865," microcopy M 1091, RG 45, National Archives.

86 "I thought the wheel": *Nautical Magazine*, March 1863.

86 no more than one hundred yards apart: FUJ, p. 71; Clarence Yonge to "Esteemed Friend," January 20, 1863, Thomas H. Dudley Papers. In his official report, Semmes gave the distance as 150 to 400 yards, but most of the battle evidently took place at closer quarters; Semmes to Mallory, May 12, 1863, ORN, 1:2:684.

86 casualties were remarkably light: ORN, 1:2:20.

86 "The main brace": FUJ, p. 173.

87 "He does everything": *Philadelphia Evening Bulletin*, January 27, 1863.

4 Impacts: North and South

88 "With the South": *The Journals and Miscellaneous Notebooks of Ralph Waldo Emerson*, ed. Ralph H. Orth et al. (1982), 15:208.

89 "I'm going to destroy": *Baltimore Sun*, November 8, 1862.

05 "produced a profound sensation": *Charleston Daily Courier*, January 6, 1863.

05 "another victory": ibid., January 26, 1863.

05 Confederate government as democracy: Gallagher, *Confederate War*, p. 127.

06 two most persistent newspaper critics: Rable, *Confederate Republic*, p. 86.

06 demanded that Davis switch: ibid., p. 196.

06 "We and all the world": *Charleston Mercury*, October 25, 1862.

06 "The Alabama at intervals": *Richmond Examiner*, January 23, 1863; and see *Examiner*, January 9, May 27, 1863.

06 Benjamin conceded to Moore: George Moore to Lord Lyons, November 28, 1862, file FO 5/840, 25, FOP.

07 illiteracy rate among whites: James M. McPherson, *Drawn With the Sword: Reflections on the American Civil War* (1996), p. 19.

07 "Like all people much given": Drew Gilpin Faust, *The Creation of Confederate Nationalism: Ideology and Identity in the Civil War South* (1988), p. 16.

07 "But a ruggeder field": Edward C. Bruce, "The Sea-Kings of the South," *War Poetry of the South*, ed. William Gilmore Simms (1866), pp. 190–94.

08 "Verse is stronger": *Richmond Examiner*, October 17, 1863.

08 "southern orality": Faust, *Confederate Nationalism*, p. 18.

08 song to Semmes: E. King and Fitz William Rosier, "The Alabama," in Paul Glass and Louis C. Singer, *Singing Soldiers: A History of the Civil War in Song* (1968), pp. 186–88.

09 Kate Stone diary: *Brokenburn: The Journal of Kate Stone, 1861–1868*, ed. John Q. Anderson (1972), p. 169.

09 "Push these ships": ORN, 2:2:333, 367.

5   Impacts: Anglo-America

11 Britain choosing sides: R.J.M. Blackett, *Divided Hearts: Britain and the American Civil War* (2001), pp. 100–107.

11 quite limited democracy: Dean B. Mahin, *One War at a Time: The International Dimensions of the American Civil War* (1999), p. 26.

11 "men in general": ibid., p. 40.

11 "Slavery has in reality": *The Letters of Charles Dickens*, ed. Graham Storey et al. (1965–2002), 10:53–54, and 10:157–58, 190, 254, 268.

12 "one side for empire": Mahin, *One War*, p. 27.

12 Role of *The Times* (London): Allan Nevins, *The War for the Union: War Becomes Revolution, 1862–1863* (1960), pp. 245–46; and see Charles Mackay, *Through the Long Day* (1887), 2:215–18.

12 "There is, throughout England": PFA (1862), p. 53.

12 he regarded Lincoln: MOJ, p. 1092.

12 "He has never raised himself": Diary, December 16, September 14, October 19, 1862, CFA.

89 "The defence of New York Harbor": Gustavus Fox to George W. Blunt, September 11, 1862, *Confidential Correspondence of Gustavus Vasa Fox*, ed. Robert Means Thompson and Richard Wainwright (1918–19), 2:374.

89 "From the accounts": Charles Wilkes to Gideon Welles, September 29, 1862, reel 17, Charles Wilkes Papers.

89 "Any of our three-masted": *Boston Traveller*, November 4, 1862.

90 "Disabuse your mind": Henry A. Wise to Hamilton Fish, November 15, 1862, letterbook 49, Hamilton Fish Papers.

90 John Murray Forbes: *Dictionary of American Biography*, 3:508.

90 "Here on the coast": John Murray Forbes to Gustavus Fox, November 19, 1862, Gustavus Vasa Fox Papers.

90 "What vexes me": Samuel F. Du Pont to wife, November 10–11, 1862, Samuel Francis Du Pont, *A Selection from His Civil War Letters*, ed. John D. Hayes (1969), 2:283n.

91 The men on the *Alabama* were always puzzled: SIT, p. 48; and see David D. Porter, *The Naval History of the Civil War* (1886), pp. 634–35, 642.

91 Welles's pursuit of *Alabama*: ORN, 1:1:416–17, 431, 470–72, 476–77, 483, 493.

91 Interplay of military news and homefront: Gary W. Gallagher in *Ken Burns's The Civil War: Historians Respond*, ed. Robert Brent Toplin (1996), pp. 42, 57–58; Gary W. Gallagher, *The Confederate War* (1997), pp. 8, 12.

92 belonged to residents of Boston and New York: Robert Greenhalgh Albion and Jennie Barnes Pope, *Sea Lanes in Wartime: The American Experience, 1775–1945* (2d ed., 1968), pp. 153–54.

92 "What if some fine morning": *Boston Post*, October 11, 1862.

92 "Whether the authorities": ibid., October 17, 1862.

92 "This is galling": ibid., November 3, 1862.

92 "The terror of the ocean": *NYH*, October 17, 1862.

92 "too swift": *NYT*, October 16, 1862.

92 "The intelligence of our captures": Journal, October 28, 1862 (1:801).

92 New York Chamber of Commerce meeting: *NYH*, October 22, 1862.

93 Gideon Welles dispatched: ORN, 1:1:517, 522–25.

93 a dozen Union warships: ibid., 1:19:338.

93 Welles dutifully tried to cover: ibid., 1:1:510–11.

93 Navy Department rewards: *Philadelphia Evening Bulletin*, October 22, 1862.

93 "Here is your opportunity": Porter R. Chandler in *American Neptune*, January 1973.

94 twice his gunpower: MEM, p. 515.

94 Escape from the *San Jacinto*: ORN, 1:1:549–55; FUJ, pp. 52–53; Journal, November 18–19, 1862 (1:805–06); *The Times* (London), December 25, 1862; *NYH*, December 14, 15, 1862; CGT, 1:509–11.

94 A New York magazine paid tribute: *Vanity Fair*, January 1863.

94 Rumors of *Alabama*: *Baltimore Sun*, November 10, 1862.

94 about to invade the small: *NYH*, November 27, 1862.

95 "The undisturbed sway": *NYH*, November 8, 1862.

95 steamship *Vanderbilt*: *Harper's Weekly*, November 22, 1862; Cedric Ridgely-Nevitt, *American Steamships on the Atlantic* (1981), pp. 230–33.

95 Other U.S. warships: *New Bedford Standard*, November 1, 1862.

95 "Your main object": ORN, 1:1:533.

95 stayed out for three weeks: ibid., 1:1:563–64.

95 "I do hope": Charles Baldwin to Gustavus Fox, December 9, 1862, Fox Papers.

96 "I cannot but think": Baldwin to Fox, December 30, 1862, Fox Papers.

96 Welles . . . ordered Baldwin: ORN, 1:2:60.

96 "The only ship": *NYH*, December 28, 1862.

96 "The first great and imperative duty": Gideon Welles to Charles Wilkes, December 15, 1862, Wilkes Papers.

96 "I am aware": ORN, 1:2:54.

97 "This is the vessel for me": William W. Jeffries in *Journal of Southern History*, August 1945.

97 "filling his pockets": ibid.

97 Eighteen vessels in pursuit: *NYT*, January 1, 1863.

97 "It is a sickening record": ibid., November 3, 1862.

97 "no one suspecting": ORN, 1:19:582.

97 "Look out for the *Alabama*": ibid., 1:19:584.

97 "There is not in the United States": *New York Tribune* quoted in *Vicksburg Daily Whig*, January 22, 1863.

98 "The English must certainly": Percival Drayton to Samuel Du Pont, February 7, 1863, *Civil War Letters*, ed. Hayes, 2:425.

98 "It is annoying": *Diary of Gideon Welles* (1911), 1:214.

98 Off the Cape Fear River: ORN, 1:8:518–19.

98 "We are all feeling": *Civil War Letters*, ed. Hayes, 2:329.

98 "We are out": ibid., 2:458.

98 Union Navy's success rate: I computed these percentages from the statistics cited in Stephen R. Wise, *Lifeline of the Confederacy: Blockade Running During the Civil War* (1988), pp. 72, 110.

98 "that all our small blockaders": ORN, 1:19:537.

98 felt obliged to divert: ibid., 1:13:487.

98 Welles sent another ship: ibid., 1:1:605.

98 "to keep a whole fleet": *Boston Post*, April 7, 1863.

99 over $63,000: *New Bedford Standard*, October 14, 17, 1862.

99 Increased war risk insurance: ibid., October 17, 1862; *NYH*, December 30, 1862.

99 "We are the more emboldened": CGT, 3:450.

99 as high as 10 percent: ORN, 1:2:356.

99 Reduction in gold shipments: Albion and Pope, *Sea Lanes*, p. 163.

99 "The commerce between Liverpool": London newspaper quoted in *Charleston Mercury*, December 25, 1862.

99 Shift in Philadelphia exports: J. Matthew Gallman, *Mastering Wartime: A Social History of Philadelphia During the Civil War* (1990), p. 281.

100 "Our commerce will soon": Robert Bennet Forbes to Gideo[n] 1863, ORN, 1:2:382.

100 New York Chamber of Commerce again "resolved": *NYH*, Fe[b]

100 "which hurts Semmes": *Boston Post*, February 24, 1863.

100 *New York World* . . . acidly suggested: quoted in *Liberator*, Janua[ry]

100 "There was an old fogy": *New York World*, April 15, 1863, quote[d] *erary Messenger*, June 1863.

100 imaginary biography: *Vanity Fair*, December 20, 1862.

101 Winslow Homer drawing: *Harper's Weekly*, April 25, 1863.

101 odd story from Washington: *Boston Saturday Evening Gazette*, [

101 "will of course set all New York": *With Lincoln in the White Ho[use:* Letters, Memo]randa, and Other Writings of John G. Nicolay, 1860–1865*, ed. M[ ] (2000), p. 98.

103 Mary Todd Lincoln and spiritualism: Jean H. Baker, *Mary Tod[d Lincoln: A Biogra]phy* (1987), pp. 217–22.

103 *Gazette*'s story was reprinted: Carl Sandburg, *Abraham Linc[oln: The War Years]* (1939), 3:343.

103 a spiritualist newspaper in Boston: *Boston Banner of Light*, Jun[e] retraction in *Boston Saturday Evening Gazette*, June 6, 1863. Th[e name] Shockle" does not appear anywhere else in the voluminous s[ ] and publications of this period.

104 half of them had expired: George C. Rable, *The Confederate R[epublic: A Revolution] Against Politics* (1994), p. 133.

104 no naval correspondents: J. Cutler Andrews, *The South Re[ports the Civil War]* (1970), p. 508.

104 first wisp of Confederate news: *Richmond Examiner*, Septemb[er]

104 printed a list: *Charleston Mercury*, September 29, 1862.

104 had acquired her former name: *Augusta Daily Constitutionalis[t,*]

104 correctly noted instead: *Savannah Republican*, quoted in *Aug[usta Daily Constitu]tionalist*, October 15, 1862.

104 first news of the *Alabama*'s whaling bonfires: *Augusta Da[ily*] October 17, 1862, and *Charleston Daily Courier*, October 17, [1862.]

104 "the great naval hero": *Charleston Mercury*, October 20, 186[2.]

104 A day later, the rival: *Charleston Daily Courier*, October 21, 1[862.]

104 "Retaliation at Sea": *Mobile Register and Advertiser*, October [ ]

104 "What a mighty difference": ibid., November 15, 1862.

105 no loyal Southern: *Mobile Register and Advertiser*, November [ ]

105 "The sensitive nerve": *Richmond Dispatch*, October 31, 186[2,] November 4, 1862.

105 "Semmes coolly slid": *New Orleans Picayune*, December 27, [1862.]

105 a chasing enemy ship: *Richmond Examiner*, January 16, 1863[.]

105 listed the eighteen Union warships: *Vicksburg Daily Whig*, J[ ]

105 "If Semmes survives": *Charleston Mercury*, January 26, 1863[.]

113 "chill and repellent": Charles Francis Adams [Jr.], *Charles Francis Adams* (1900), p. 325.

113 "I cannot well suit myself": Diary, November 25, 1862, CFA.

113 Wilkes and the *Trent:* Charles Wilkes, *Autobiography of Charles Wilkes, U.S. Navy, 1798–1877* (1978), pp. 769–75.

113 "I fear the North": *Letters of Charles Dickens,* ed. Storey et al., 9:531, 549.

113 "I consider that we are dished": Henry Adams, *The Letters of Henry Adams,* ed. J. C. Levenson et al. (1982–88), 1:263–64.

113 "The whole British nation": ORN, 2:2:148–49.

114 Liverpool as Confederate center: Brainerd Dyer in *CWH,* December 1955.

114 Fraser, Trenholm: Stephen R. Wise, *Lifeline of the Confederacy: Blockade Running During the Civil War* (1988), pp. 46–47, 63.

114 *The American Union:* Blackett, *Divided Hearts,* pp. 62–63, 138.

114 argued that tariffs, not slavery: James Spence, *The American Union: Its Effect on National Character and Policy* (1861), pp. 119–65.

114 "It has been very generally read": ORN, 2:3:425.

114 good business for him as well: Blackett, *Divided Hearts,* p. 92.

115 Henry Hotze: ibid., pp. 144–45; Charles P. Cullop, *Confederate Propaganda in Europe, 1861–1865* (1969), pp. 18–21; Robert E. Bonner in *CWH,* September 2005.

115 "A great success": *Mobile Register and Advertiser,* quoted in *Southern Literary Messenger,* November–December 1862.

115 Hotze . . . celebrated . . . Semmes: *London Index,* May 1, 1862.

115 "I have come to take the Captain": MEM, p. 349; and see Raphael Semmes to F. W. Tremlett, May 5, 1862, SPV.

115 The Tremletts: Charles Priestley in *Crossfire* (American Civil War Round Table—United Kingdom), December 2003; Edwin W. Besch, Michael Hammerson, and Dave W. Morgan in *Military Collector & Historian* (winter 2001–2); interview with Michael Hammerson, London, November 2005; *The Times* (London), June 13, 1913; KER, p. 179; Blackett, *Divided Hearts,* p. 104.

115 Lindsay visiting the United States: file 753a, p. 111, William S. Lindsay Papers.

115 "How can a nation": note by Lindsay, September 1867, file LND/7, p. 483, Lindsay Papers.

115 Lindsay's motives: Charles M. Hubbard, *The Burden of Confederate Diplomacy* (1998), p. 142.

116 "My interests were entirely with the North": note by Lindsay, n.p., file LND/7, Lindsay Papers.

116 "a brave and down-trodden nation": *NYT,* July 24, 1863.

116 Lindsay always denied: ibid., July 16, 1863, August 30, 1864.

116 "A man of highest": ORN, 2:3:398.

116 Mason and Lindsay: W. S. Lindsay to James M. Mason, October 17, 22, November 20, 1862, James M. Mason Papers.

116 Seward ordered Adams: Mahin, *One War,* p. 126.

116 Debate in House of Commons: MOJ, pp. 1040–44.

116 balancing act: this is my own conjecture—that the *Alabama* was allowed to escape because, a week earlier, Palmerston had argued against mediation.

117 American visitors to England: MOJ, p. 1024.

117 "England, in particular": Raphael Semmes to Electra Semmes, August 11, 1862, SFP.

117 Gladstone met with Hotze: Howard Jones, *Union in Peril: The Crisis Over British Intervention in the Civil War* (1992), p. 149.

117 "We may have our own opinions": *The Times* (London), October 9, 1862; and see Robert L. Reid in *CWH*, December 1969.

119 "It is very manifest": PFA (1862), p. 219.

119 Russell . . . denied any past mistakes: ibid., p. 200.

119 "But for the material support": *Philadelphia Evening Bulletin*, November 3, 1862.

119 "If this craft be": *Harper's Weekly*, December 27, 1862.

119 Welles's annual report: *Hunt's Merchants' Magazine*, January 1863.

119 "It is our weak point": Gustavus Fox to Duncan McLean, November 15, 1862, Gustavus Vasa Fox Papers.

119 "The subject which presses": Diary, December 23, 1862, CFA.

119 "Her Majesty's government": PFA (1863), p. 145.

119 "I wonder what Great Britain would say": Charles Francis Adams to Edward Everett, February 13, 1863, CFA.

120 "It suits well": *United Service Magazine*, December 1862, quoted in *Living Age*, January 17, 1863.

120 "with so large a Navy": Lord Russell to Lord Lyons, December 26, 1862, file FO 5/1318, 419, FOP.

120 "the Laird rams": *Engineer*, March 13, 1863; George Warren to George B. Upton, November 3, 1862, Fox Papers; O. R. Mumford to Gideon Welles, January 16, 1863, roll 431, Miscellaneous Letters Received by the Navy, 1801–84; BUS, 1:380–88, 394.

121 "We cannot leave the home market": Gustavus Fox to George B. Upton, October 30, 1862, Fox Papers.

121 Forbes-Aspinwall mission: Douglas H. Maynard in *Mississippi Valley Historical Review*, June 1958.

121 "You must stop them": Gustavus Fox to John Murray Forbes, April 1, 1863, *Letters and Recollections of John Murray Forbes*, ed. Sarah Forbes Hughes (1900), 2:23.

122 Victory for the North: Allan Nevins, *The War for the Union: The Organized War, 1863–1864* (1971), p. 1.

122 "Our men must prevail": John B. Jones, *A Rebel War Clerk's Diary*, ed. Earl Schenck Miers (1958), p. 181.

122 "The subjugation of the South": George Moore to Lord Russell, January 15, 1863, file FO 5/909, 88, FOP.

122 "The Confederates are resolved": Lord Lyons to Lord Russell, March 10, 1863, file FO 5/879, 161, FOP.

123 Many people in Richmond: *Richmond Examiner*, February 2, 1863.

123 Wilkes was . . . arrogantly bumbling: William W. Jeffries in *Journal of Southern History*, August 1945; Lord Lyons to Lord Russell, December 16, 1862, file FO 5/840, 18, FOP; *Nautical Magazine*, November 1862.

123 "We are indeed drifting": John Bigelow, *Retrospections of an Active Life* (1909–13), 1:632.

6 The Turncoats

124 "We are very much": Journal, January 12, 1863 (2:722).

124 "dull, hard-looking sky": Journal, January 16, 1863 (2:723).

125 "Her arrival at this port": *Liverpool Commercial Advertiser*, reprinted in *NYH*, March 6, 1863.

125 "The necessity of the repairs": Hugh Dunlop to Alexander Milne, January 23, 1863, FO 5/1319, 21, FOP.

125 "If I remain": ibid.

125 Semmes in Jamaica: MEM, pp. 554–57.

126 Semmes's speech at the Merchants' Exchange: *Cincinnati Daily Commercial*, February 12, 1863; *New Orleans Picayune*, February 22, 1863.

126 "It is impossible to describe": FUJ, p. 80

126 Desertions in Kingston: ibid., p. 81.

127 Clarence Yonge: ORN, 2:2:448–49; *NYH*, March 11, 1863.

127 "a name that causes Yankee hearts": Clarence Yonge to "Esteemed Friend," January 20, 1863, Thomas H. Dudley Papers.

128 Semmes and the rubber dolls: *New Orleans Picayune*, March 17, 1863.

128 "a mere skeleton": ibid.

128 "Sick list largely increased": Journal, January 27, 1863 (2:725).

128 "Several of my rascals": Journal, March 27, 1863 (2:735).

129 *Alabama* was reported: *NYH*, January 16, 20, February 7, 1863; *Charleston Mercury*, February 14, 1863; *Saturday Evening Post*, March 14, 1863.

129 "It is high time": *Boston Post*, February 20, 1863.

129 "A gloomy Sabbath": Journal, February 8, 1863 (2:727).

129 "I have more and more reason": Journal, February 15, 1863 (2:728).

130 "We have thus doubled": Journal, March 2, 1863 (2:731).

130 *Florida*: Royce Shingleton, *High Seas Confederate: The Life and Times of John Newland Maffitt* (1994), pp. 58–67; John N. Maffitt to Stephen Mallory, February 1863, and Maffitt to his children, March 13, 1863, John N. Maffitt Papers.

130 "England is so much": *Saturday Evening Post*, April 11, 1863.

130 officers and men alike played: Journal, March 22, 1863 (2:734).

131 "Must say that I was treated well": *NYH*, June 16, 1863.

131 Encounter with *Chili*: FUJ, p. 102.

131 "He said that he would": Charles Francis Adams to William H. Seward, April 3, 1863, CFA; and see Diary, April 1, 1863, CFA.

132 Moran on Yonge: MOJ, pp. 1140–41.

132 Henry Redden's deposition: CGB, 3:45–47; and see the later statement by Redden in New York, November 2, 1862, ORN 1:1:527.

133 "She is now at her hellish work": MOJ, p. 1064.

133 George King's deposition: CGB, 3:50.

134 John Latham's deposition: PFA (1864), 1:90–92.

135 Yonge's account book: now in the Dudley Papers.

136 Clarence Yonge's deposition: PFA (1863), pp. 190–96.

137 Adams at once sent copies: ibid., p. 190.

138 "I am finally domiciled": Clarence Yonge to Thomas Dudley, April 11, 1863, Dudley Papers.

138 *Alabama*'s condenser: SIT, p. 96.

138 Capture of the *Louisa Hatch:* MEM, p. 594.

139 "a godsend": KER, p. 216.

139 "It was the very quality": SIT, p. 101.

139 Fernando de Noronha: MEM, pp. 596–98.

140 "a sprightly, bright mulatto": Journal, April 12, 1863 (2:739).

140 "The roses were very sweet": Journal, April 19, 1863 (2:741).

140 "The island, after the rain": Journal, April 21, 1863 (2:741).

141 "We have had a glorious outing": SIT, p. 109.

141 "mutually polite": PFA (1863), p. 1166.

141 "countenance and support": ibid., p. 1168.

141 Frostier reception of the *Florida:* John N. Maffitt to Stephen Mallory, May 11, 1863, Maffitt Papers.

141 Capture of the *Sea Lark:* FUJ, pp. 110–11; CGB, 4:425–26.

141 "They put my officers": *NYH*, June 15, 1863.

142 "Visitors innumerable": FUJ, p. 112.

142 "We are having capital success": BUS, 1:267.

142 ordered Semmes to leave: Journal, May 17, 1863 (2:745).

142 The tardy tender at last: Peter Barton in *Mariner's Mirror*, November 1999.

142 "The *Alabama* . . . was therefore": BUS, 1:269.

143 "wormy biscuit": *Philadelphia Evening Bulletin*, June 30, 1863.

144 "Sir, . . . your vessel": *NYH*, July 3, 1863.

144 "of the worst description": ibid.

144 "with great scorn": ibid., September 2, 1863.

145 *Alexandra* case: Kevin J. Foster in *Prologue* (fall 2001); Frank J. Merli, *Great Britain and the Confederate Navy, 1861–1865* (1970), pp. 160–77.

145 Yonge testimony: CGB, 5:64–78. (I have condensed the testimony and paraphrased the defense attorney's questions, but have not changed the sequence of questions and answers.)

147 "The ministry are feeble": Diary, June 11, 1863, CFA.

147 "The enemy of course are jubilant": John Murray Forbes to Gideon Welles, June 25, 1863, Henry Hotze Papers. How this letter wound up in Hotze's possession is a mystery; perhaps it was intercepted at sea.

148   "which has served not only": Clarence Yonge to Thomas Dudley, July 21, 1863, Dudley Papers.

148   "I can then make arrangements": Yonge to Dudley, [July 1863], Dudley Papers.

7   Cape Town Zenith

149   "I think well of your suggestion": MEM, p. 353.

150   had to keep his fires banked: BUS, 1:274.

150   "Our ship has certainly": Journal, June 15, 1863 (2:749–50).

150   "a mere skeleton": *New Orleans Picayune*, March 17, 1863.

150   "a little weazen": *Philadelphia Evening Bulletin*, June 30, 1863.

150   red nose covered with pimples: *NYH*, July 3, 1863.

150   "not improved by exposure": *The Times* (London), June 23, 1863.

150   "The fact is": Journal, June 29, 1863 (2:753).

151   "All these things": Journal, June 30, 1863 (2:753).

151   "The bread supply": Journal, June 27, 1863 (2:752).

151   they caught the *Anna F. Schmidt:* Robert R. Newell in *American Neptune*, January 1965.

151   "Such Boston bread": KER, p. 221.

151   "Dark blue days": *The Diary of George Templeton Strong: The Civil War, 1860–1865*, ed. Allan Nevins and Milton Halsey Thomas (1952), 3:295.

152   "The country is wonderfully demoralized": David Farragut to Gustavus Fox, March 7, 1863, *Confidential Correspondence of Gustavus Vasa Fox*, ed. Robert Means Thompson and Richard Wainwright (1918–19), 1:328.

152   the Yankee invasions . . . had not broken: Gary W. Gallagher, *The Confederate War* (1997), p. 58.

152   "The temper of our people": Diary, March 20, 1863, CFA.

152   "predominating feeling": Dean B. Mahin, *One War at a Time: The International Dimensions of the American Civil War* (1999), p. 175.

152   the *Georgia:* Frances Leigh Williams, *Matthew Fontaine Maury: Scientist of the Sea* (1963), pp. 405–7.

152   "A day of reckoning": *NYH*, April 16, 1863.

152   "No man can delude himself": Charles Francis Adams to Edward Everett, April 29, 1863, CFA.

152   Secret mission of Forbes and Aspinwall: Douglas H. Maynard in *Mississippi Valley Historical Review*, June 1958.

152   "It was indeed socially": Sarah Forbes Hughes, *Letters and Recollections of John Murray Forbes* (1900), 2:17.

153   "a daughter of the pirate": *NYH*, November 7, 1862.

153   Spencer Semmes in war: HUS, pp. 423–24.

153   Oliver Semmes in war: ibid., pp. 425–27; Richard Taylor, *Destruction and Reconstruction: Personal Experiences of the Late War* (1879), pp. 131–34.

153 "I am glad": Raphael Semmes to Electra Semmes, August 11, 1862, SFP.

154 "Secession Impudence": *Cincinnati Daily Commercial,* reprinted in *Dallas Herald,* July 26, 1862.

154 More worrisome items: *Cincinnati Daily Commercial,* October 23, 1862, January 3, February 13, 1863.

154 "severely riddled": ibid., February 16, 1863.

154 "All about the capture": W. Adolphe Roberts, *Semmes of the Alabama* (1938), p. 117.

154 searched her house and baggage: ORA, 2:2:261.

154 sent her an occasional allotment: Stephen Mallory to Paymaster, July 9, December 11, 1863, and to Bolling Baker, December 12, 1863, in Semmes's ZB file, Naval Historical Foundation, Washington Navy Yard.

154 "You must be of good cheer": Raphael Semmes to Anne Semmes, January 4, 1863, SFP.

155 "traitors" and "terrible dangers": *Cincinnati Daily Commercial,* March 5, February 24, 1863.

155 Burnside's order: William Marvel, *Burnside* (1991), pp. 231–32.

155 lieutenant . . . escorted them: SPR, p. 168; *The Times* (London), May 20, 1863; Roberts, *Semmes,* pp. 222–23.

155 Thomas J. Semmes: *New Orleans Picayune,* January 23, 1898.

156 Spencer granted leave: Benedict J. Semmes to Eo Semmes, June 26, 1863, Benedict J. Semmes Papers.

156 "a very estimable lady": Fred J. Cridlund to William S. Lindsay, October 4, 1863, file LND/7, p. 357, William S. Lindsay Papers.

156 Background of "Buxton": Edwin C. Fishel, *The Secret War for the Union: The Untold Story of Military Intelligence in the Civil War* (1996), pp. 86–88.

156 spy for the Union: ORA, 1:5:339–41, 613–14.

156 Buxton in Richmond: Cridlund to Lindsay, October 4, 1863.

157 "A gloomy, desert-looking place": Journal, July 30, 1863 (2:757).

157 "Three of them have run off": Journal, August 1, 1863 (2:758).

157 "plump, ruddy Dutch girls": Journal, August 3, 1863 (2:758).

158 examined the mustaches: MEM, p. 639.

158 "The *Alabama* in sight": Cape Town newspaper, reprinted in *Charleston Mercury,* December 30, 1863.

158 Capture of the *Sea Bride:* MEM, pp. 648–52; FUJ, p. 134.

159 "As we approached": Blanche Kell, "Life and Letters of J. M. Kell," p. 29, box 12, JMK.

159 "Hundreds crowded on board": ibid.

159 "What can't be cured": *Charleston Mercury,* December 30, 1863.

159 Semmes proudly reeled off: *Cape Argus,* August 20, 1863, quoted in *ILN,* October 10, 1863.

161 "There is but one subject": *Charleston Mercury,* December 30, 1863.

161 "You are a native African": ibid.

161 "Take a seat": *Advertiser and Mail*, August 19, 1863, quoted in *NYT*, October 8, 1863.

162 "My own countrymen": Edna and Frank Bradlow, *Here Comes the Alabama: The Career of a Confederate Raider* (1958), p. 70.

162 "I am sure . . . President Davis": Raphael Semmes to Anne Semmes, August 8, 1863, in *Mobile Advertiser*, reprinted in *Charleston Mercury*, December 30, 1863.

163 recent Union consul: Alan R. Booth, *The United States Experience in South Africa, 1784–1870* (1976), p. 145.

163 "There is hardly a man": Bradlow and Bradlow, *Here Comes the Alabama*, p. 67.

163 "The ship is nothing more": ibid., p. 119.

164 Fullam journal published: *Charleston Mercury*, November 25, 1863; CGB, 4:181–201.

164 Townshend poem: Bradlow and Bradlow, *Here Comes the Alabama*, p. 49.

164 "Here comes the Alabama": ibid., following title page, and p. 115.

164 photographer came aboard: Journal, August 12, 1863 (2:760).

165 "We have had a reasonable degree": Raphael Semmes to F. W. Tremlett, August 12, 1863, SPV.

165 mail steamer from England: Journal, August 14, 1863 (2:760).

166 "Everything he does": Maynard in *Mississippi Valley Historical Review*, June 1958.

166 "Every Englishman": W. H. Aspinwall to Gustavus Fox, April 25, 1863, Gustavus Vasa Fox Papers.

166 Welles at last bestirred himself: ORN, 1:2:251–53.

166 "Detaining you in the West Indies": Gustavus Fox to Charles Baldwin, June 3, 1863, Fox Papers.

166 "You may believe, sir": ORN, 1:2:408.

167 "I can only hope": ibid., 1:2:409.

167 the crucial decision was made: ibid., 1:2:426–27.

167 The two reports: ibid., 1:2:427.

168 another near miss: ibid., 1:2:445–47.

168 Sale of the *Sea Bride*: Bradlow and Bradlow, *Here Comes the Alabama*, p. 72.

168 "We are on the Yankee track": Journal, September 4, 1863 (2:763).

168 "We had a rough": Journal, September 7, 1863 (2:764).

169 "a very large steamer": SIT, p. 162.

169 "He thinks the Vanderbilt": *Cape Argus* quoted in PFA (1863), p. 379.

169 twenty-one sailors who had deserted: *Alabama* muster roll, reel 17, "Subject File of the Confederate States Navy, 1861–1865," microcopy M 1091, RG 45, National Archives; SIT, p. 174; MEM, pp. 670–71.

169 urgent telegrams: Journal, September 24, 1863 (2:766).

170 The scene in Simon's Bay: MEM, pp. 672–73; Journal, September 24, 1863 (2:766–67).

170 "In my present crippled condition": ORN, 1:2:468.

8 The Track of Fire to Singapore

171 a dime novel: [Leon Lewis], *The Track of Fire; or, A Cruise with the Pirate Semmes* (1863), copy in Rare Books and Manuscripts, Boston Public Library.

171 Wheeler a pseudonym: Albert Johannsen, *The House of Beadle and Adams and Its Dime and Nickel Novels* (1950–62), 3:39.

171 Beadle dime books: ibid., 1:30–126; *North American Review*, July 1864.

172 "The history of Capt. Semmes": Lewis, *Track of Fire*, p. 3; next eight quotations from ibid., pp. 4–5, 6, 13, 20, 110. The *NYH*, November 19, 1863, reported the *Alabama* was cruising in the Bay of Bengal; perhaps this was the author's source for that conjecture.

174 "I am supremely disgusted": Journal, September 8, 1863 (2:764).

174 "No sail in sight!": Journal, September 12, 1863 (2:765).

174 "Greatly discouraged": Journal, September 16, 1863 (2:765).

174 "We shall fight it out": ibid.

175 "A weary, monotonous": SIT, p. 181.

175 von Meulnier and Schroeder: ibid., pp. 172–73, 321–23.

175 raspy sounds of holystones: Herman Melville, *White Jacket; or, The World in a Man-of-War* (1850; Grove Press ed., 1956), p. 92.

175 Bartelli as steward: SIT, pp. 106, 234.

176 "I was the Commander": Joseph T. Durkin, *Stephen R. Mallory: Confederate Navy Chief* (1954), p. 410n.

176 "How I used to hate him": Norman C. Delaney, *John McIntosh Kell of the Raider Alabama* (1973), p. 147.

176 "You were kind": ibid.

176 "the only man we fellows": ibid.

176 Boatswain's role: Melville, *White Jacket*, p. 107.

176 "Make it so, sir": SIT, p. 24.

177 Midday dinner: ibid., pp. 24–25.

177 familiar commands: ibid., pp. 120–21.

177 "one of our greatest losses": Journal, September 25, 1863 (2:767).

177 Evans, Fullam, and O'Brien: SIT, pp. 20, 320–21, 324.

177 Glee club and dances: ibid., p. 237.

178 Sinclair with book aloft: ibid., p. 67.

178 "Off Galveston": Frank Townshend, "The Fight of the 'Hatteras' and 'Alabama,'" in Frank Moore, *Anecdotes, Poetry, and Incidents of the War* (1866), p. 91.

179 "I presume this run": Journal, October 21, 1863 (2:776).

179 water leaked through the tortured seams: Journal, October 14, 1863 (2:773).

180 "As usual, when not well": Journal, October 25, 1863 (2:777).

180 "This is the first time": Journal, October 26, 1863 (2:777).

180 "It was one of the finest sights": *The Times* (London), January 26, 1864.

180 Larrabee, later reported: Affidavit by Isaiah Larrabee, November 14, 1863, file FO 5/1322, FOP.

181   the American clipper *Winged Racer:* CGB, 4:427.

181   "We thought the *Winged Racer*": KER, p. 234.

181   "a most disorderly set": *New Bedford Mercury,* January 30, 1864, reprinted in *NYH,* February 1, 1864.

181   Capture of the *Contest:* Journal, November 11, 1863 (2:780–81); MEM, pp. 693–95.

181   "She had all sail set": William Nevius to Peter Nevius, December 11, 1863, in "Misc, Nevius" file, New-York Historical Society.

182   "We had never captured": SIT, p. 189.

182   "that it seemed a shame to burn": KER, p. 235.

182   "a most rascally": William Nevius to Peter Nevius, December 11, 1863.

182   "Crew much dissatisfied": statement by James D. Babcock, ORN, 1:2:562.

184   "mutinous and seditious conduct": FUJ, pp. 159–60.

184   "bring the disorderly to their senses": Journal, November 17, 1863 (2:782).

184   "We must have constant bustle": SIT, p. 193.

184   Semmes bending over maps: ibid., p. 191.

184   "Our captain begins to show the wear": ibid., p. 193.

185   "My ship required overhauling": ORN, 1:2:707.

185   French officials had heard: Journal, December 5, 1863 (2:786).

185   "these caricatures of humanity": Journal, December 5, 1863 (2:785).

185   "We see nothing": Journal, December 8, 1863 (2:786–87).

186   "A lengthened cruise": Journal, December 15, 1863 (2:789).

186   "Our young officers": ibid.

187   Culprits released: Journal, December 16, 1863 (2:789).

187   Reception in Singapore: John Cameron, *Our Tropical Possessions in Malayan India* (1865), p. 271. (Cameron was editor of the *Straits Times* of Singapore.)

187   Coal from P&O: SIT, pp. 208–9.

187   "The *Alabama* once seen": *Straits Times,* January 8, 1864, reprinted in *The Times of India* (Bombay), January 25, 1864.

187   *kappal hantu:* Cameron, *Our Tropical Possessions,* p. 273.

188   "no sign of impatience": ibid., p. 275.

188   "The business is almost exclusively": Journal, December 23, 1863 (2:791).

188   "It pays an enormous license": ibid. (2:792).

188   twenty-two Yankee ships: SIT, p. 210.

188   "The enemy's East India": ORN, 1:2:707–8.

189   Drinking and fight at hotel: SIT, pp. 210–11.

9   Running Down

190   Capture of *Martaban:* ILN, April 2, 1864; SIT, pp. 217–18; *Nautical Magazine,* March 1864.

190   "I *shall* sit down!": letter of Samuel B. Pike to *Straits Times,* reprinted in *The Times of India* (Bombay), January 25, 1864.

190 Semmes's version: Journal, December 24, 1863 (2:792); MEM, pp. 718–19.

191 "Good Lord!": Isaac Colby in *Records and History of the Marine Society of Newburyport* (1906), reprinted in *Civil War Times*, October 1971, ed. Norman C. Delaney.

191 "Can't you read?": ibid.

191 "They entered the cabin": Lawrence R. Brown, "Burnt Out by the Alabama," typed MS in Mariners Museum Library, Norfolk, Virginia; copy in file 31, box 5510, Charles G. Summersell Papers.

191 They told Brown they would like to quit: *The Times of India* (Bombay), January 21, 1864.

191 "there seemed to be little order": Brown, "Burnt Out."

192 "I never touch a port": Journal, December 31, 1863 (2:794).

192 "Alas! another year of war": Journal, January 1, 1864 (2:794).

192 "It won't do": Journal, January 8, 1864 (2:795).

193 "Captain, I am going to burn your ship": *The Times of India* (Bombay), February 4, 1864.

193 "While she was burning": ibid.

193 "a careworn and anxious man": *Cochin Chronicle*, January 23, 1864, reprinted in *The Times of India* (Bombay), cumulative issue, January 29–February 14, 1864.

194 "The sky was of the deepest blue": Journal, January 22, 1864 (2:797).

194 "My vagabonds on shore": Journal, February 11, 1864 (2:800).

195 "It is three years": William Marvel, *The Alabama and the Kearsarge: The Sailor's Civil War* (1996), p. 225. This significant entry was deleted from the Journal as published in the ORN, apparently because of the reference to Lincoln. William Marvel discovered it by comparing the published version with the manuscript Journal in the Semmes Family Papers.

195 "The Yankee Government and people": Journal, March 29, 1864 (2:807).

196 Lincoln's initial blunders: these included strategic errors such as forcing a premature assault at Manassas, diverting McDowell's troops to chase Jackson when they were needed for the campaign against Richmond, and sending his friend John A. McClernand to Vicksburg, duplicating Grant's forces. Lincoln also sometimes signed papers from Seward without reading them, and in general did not display basic skills of leadership. "He has no will, no power to command," Attorney General Edward Bates noted in the fall of 1861. "He makes no body afraid of him." See Doris Kearns Goodwin, *Team of Rivals: The Political Genius of Abraham Lincoln* (2005), pp. 343, 374, 394, 442, 478.

196 Effect of proclamation in Britain: Howard Jones, *Abraham Lincoln and a New Birth of Freedom: The Union and Slavery in the Diplomacy of the Civil War* (1999), pp. 151–52.

196 Spence shunned by agents: ORN, 2:3:567, 661.

196 "The Emancipation Proclamation": Henry Adams, *The Letters of Henry Adams*, ed. J. C. Levenson et al. (1982–88), 1:327.

197 "The emancipation movement": Douglas H. Maynard in *Mississippi Valley Historical Review*, June 1958.

197 "Nothing will move England": Diary, June 11, 1863, CFA.

197 "I did not believe the enemy": James M. McPherson, *Battle Cry of Freedom: The Civil War Era* (1988), p. 663.

197 state elections that fall: Allan Nevins, *The War for the Union: The Organized War, 1863–1864* (1971), pp. 155, 159, 177–78.

197 "I think our Govt.": William S. Lindsay to John Slidell, November 6, 1863, William S. Lindsay Papers.

197 "England is too rich": Journal, March 29, 1864 (2:807).

197 "Yesterday we rode": *The Journals of Josiah Gorgas, 1857–1878*, ed. Sarah Woolfolk Wiggins (1995), p. 75.

198 "I have never actually despaired": Robert G. H. Kean, *Inside the Confederate Government: The Diary of Robert Garlick Hill Kean*, ed. Edward Younger (1957), pp. 119, 122.

198 "If we had only twenty Alabamas": *Richmond Dispatch*, October 28, 1863, in D. P. Crook, *The North, the South, and the Powers, 1861–1865* (1974), p. 322n.

198 the *Florida* . . . was laid up: Chester G. Hearn, *Gray Raiders of the Sea: How Eight Confederate Warships Destroyed the Union's High Seas Commerce* (1992), pp. 99–120.

198 The *Georgia* had proven ineffective: ibid., pp. 242–43.

198 Bulloch's attempts to build: ORN, 2:2:423–24, 536.

198 "We are alone in this war": *Richmond Dispatch*, November 12, 1863.

199 Isaac Oakford: MOJ, pp. 17, 25, 208, 568–69, 625, 1011, 1296, 1352.

199 "I told him the Department": Gustavus Fox to R. B. Forbes, July 28, 1864, Gustavus Vasa Fox Papers.

199 George B. Upton: *Dictionary of American Biography*, 10:130–31; CGB, 3:160–62.

199 handed Oakford $5,000: Fox to Forbes, July 28, 1864.

199 Oakford sailed to Liverpool: Isaac Oakford to Gustavus Fox, August 12, 1863, Fox Papers.

199 "I will stop the ships": Oakford to Fox, August 29, 1863, Fox Papers.

199 "I have had no easy job": Oakford to Fox, September 9, 1863, Fox Papers.

200 called Oakford a scoundrel: Fox to Forbes, July 28, 1864.

201 The war in fact was always about slavery: on the centrality of slavery in Confederate nationalism, see Anne Sarah Rubin, *A Shattered Nation: The Rise and Fall of the Confederacy, 1861–1868* (2005), pp. 100–102, 106–8.

201 Semmes owned three slaves: copy of will of Raphael Semmes, February 5, 1852, Warren F. Spencer Papers, lists Matilda and her sons, Edward and Henry, all slaves.

201 relations "more or less of mutual regard": MEX, p. 17.

201 "free niggerdom": Journal, July 30, 1861 (1:699).

201 "niggerdom will not work": Journal, August 28, 1861 (1:706).

201 "I then stated to him": Journal, September 10, 1861 (1:709).

201 "to whom I explained": Journal, November 10, 1861 (1:719).

201 Slave Ned on *Sumter*: MEM, pp. 201–2; ORN 1:1:627; Raphael Semmes to [Stephen Mallory], ca. November 10, 1861, SFP.

202 David Henry White: MEM, pp. 465–66; SIT, pp. 37–38.

202 "The Pirate Steals": *NYH*, November 13, 1862.

202 "This lover of slavery": *Jamaica Watchman*, January 29, 1863, reprinted in *Cincinnati Daily Commercial*, February 18, 1863, and (in part) in *Charleston Daily Courier*, February 25, 1863.

202 "the rant of white-chokered negrophilists": *Cape Town Mail*, August 19, 1863, reprinted in *NYT*, October 8, 1863.

202 "Yes . . . we belong to the country": Journal, February 9, 1864 (2:799).

203 Grant later remarked: Ulysses S. Grant, *Personal Memoirs* (Library of America edition, 1990), p. 735.

10 Cherbourg

204 "now abroad for the benefit": newspaper clipping, unidentified, pasted into entry for April 28, 1864, manuscript Journal, SFP.

204 Wedding of Electra: *Mobile Daily Advertiser and Register*, February 20, 1864.

205 "Much doubt exists": Fred J. Cridlund to William S. Lindsay, October 4, 1863, file LND/7, p. 357, William S. Lindsay Papers; and see ORN, 2:3:992, 1005.

205 Lindsay wrote Anne: note by Lindsay, ca. 1867, file LND/7, p. 355, Lindsay Papers.

205 Pendleton Colston: *NYT*, September 25, 1866.

205 "a very clever and promising man": B. J. Semmes to Eo Semmes, February 2, 1864 [misdated 1863], Benedict J. Semmes Papers. This letter is filed with the 1863 correspondence, but the content shows that Semmes wrote it in 1864 and mistakenly dated it 1863; in addition, the letter was written on the blue stationery that Semmes used in 1864 but not in 1863, and was dispatched from Dalton, Georgia, like other letters that B. J. Semmes wrote in February 1864. In February 1863 he was in Fayetteville, Tennessee.

206 "one of the safest places": Fred J. Cridlund to Lord Russell, March 28, 1864, FO 5/970, 174, FOP.

206 "lying, blasphemy, drunkness": Cridlund to Russell, November 16, 1863, FO 5/908, 119, FOP.

206 fashionable attitude: on life in Mobile during the war, see Kate Cumming, *Kate: The Journal of a Confederate Nurse*, ed. Richard Barksdale Harwell (1959), pp. 189–91, 245–58, especially p. 257; on social excesses in wartime, see Anne Sarah Rubin, *A Shattered Nation: The Rise and Fall of the Confederacy, 1861–1868* (2005), pp. 60–64, 67–68.

206 "Electra was certainly": B. J. Semmes to Eo Semmes, February 2, 1864 [misdated 1863], B. J. Semmes Papers.

206 Electra's birthday party: ibid.

206 Smallpox in Mobile: *Mobile Daily Advertiser and Register*, March 25, 1864.

206 Electra's miracle: B. J. Semmes to Eo Semmes, March 4, 1864, B. J. Semmes Papers.

206 "She has been recd": B. J. Semmes to Eo Semmes, March 3, 4, 1864, B. J. Semmes Papers.

207 "Gaily along the rebel came": George H. Boker, "Captain Semmes, C.S.A.N.," in Frank Moore, *Rebellion Record* (1865), vol. 9, "Poetry and Incidents" section, p. 1.

207 "Our bottom is in such a state": Journal, May 21, 1864 (3:674).

207 "The lame hunter": Journal, May 23, 1864 (3:674).

208 "And thus, thanks to an all-wise Providence": Journal, June 10, 1864 (3:676).

208 "probably to refit": PFA (1864), 1:641.

208 vice consul at the port cabled the news: ORN, 1:3:51–52.

208 "The character of this vessel": PFA (1864), 3:101.

209 *Kearsarge* pursuing Semmes: ORN, 1:1:320–21; *Philadelphia Evening Bulletin,* October 27, 1862; PFA (1862), pp. 591–92.

209 "Shall we never have the pleasure": Journal of William Wainwright, January 15, 1863.

209 "We was unable": ibid., April 13, 1863.

209 "The great trouble with us being": ibid., June 30, 1863.

209 "We are always behind": ibid., July 5, 1863.

209 "I do not think we have": *Army and Navy Journal,* December 26, 1863.

210 "Much dissatisfaction with Capt. Winslow": MOJ, p. 1280.

210 "I wish that we could be doing": Journal of Charles A. Poole, June 6, 1864.

210 "Nothing to mar": ibid., June 10, 1864.

210 "I must say": ibid., June 11, 1864.

210 Winslow received Dayton's telegram: ORN, 1:3:50.

210 Scene on the *Kearsarge:* William H. Badlam, *Kearsarge and Alabama* (1894), p. 25. (Badlam was an engineer on the *Kearsarge.*)

210 "I for one": Journal of Charles A. Poole, June 12, 1864.

211 many bets were placed: Journal of William Wainwright, June 13, 1864.

211 Strawberries, milk, beef: Journal, June 12, 1864 (3:676).

211 "She will require to be recoppered": ORN, 1:3:651.

211 "She is a fine looking steamer": Ezra Bartlett to George Bartlett, June 14, 1864, Rare Books and Manuscripts, Boston Public Library.

212 "Kell . . . I am going out to fight": KER, p. 245.

213 "I saw his mind": ibid.

213 "I am tired": interview with John Kell by Wood Holt in *Atlanta Constitution,* ca. 1885, in scrapbook F-2103, JMK. In another interview, in 1883, Kell more decorously quoted Semmes as saying, "I am tired of running from that flaunting rag!"; see Norman C. Delaney, *John McIntosh Kell of the Raider* Alabama (1973), p. 159. The "dirty rag" version seems more likely to me.

213 "I desire to say": ORN, 1:3:648.

213 he sent to shore the paymaster's: ORN, 1:3:651.

213 "What glory for us": Ezra Bartlett to George Bartlett, June 14, 1864.

213 "Fearlessly the seas we roam": Alex H. Cummins, "Song of the Privateer," in *Songs and Ballads of the Southern People,* ed. Frank Moore (1886), pp. 248–49.

214 "My crew seem to be": Journal, June 15, 1864 (3:677).

214 Winslow returned from an errand ashore: John M. Browne in *Overland Monthly*, February 1875.

214 Winslow told his crew: Journal of William Wainwright, June 15, 16, 1864.

214 "I want to catch Semmes": John A. Winslow to his wife, June 13, 1864, in file 221, Doubleday and Company Collection.

214 "Well there is no signs": Journal of William Wainwright, June 16, 1864.

214 Sudden alarm and harbor pilot: Journal of Charles A. Poole, June 16, 1864.

214 "Every man is confident": ibid.

215 "Banter is the order": SIT, p. 263.

215 Wilson mordantly put it: ibid., p. 261.

215 Semmes and Adams: *The Times* (London), June 20, July 6, 1864; *The Collected Letters of George Meredith*, ed. Clarence Lee Cline (1970), 1:274–75.

215 "Coaling ship": Journal, June 16, 1864 (3:677).

215 "if she met his approval": Diary, June 17, 1864, box 58, Matthew F. Maury Papers.

216 local Confederates felt so sure: James Morris Morgan, *Recollections of a Rebel Reefer* (1917), p. 187.

216 *Deerhound: The Times* (London), July 15, 1858; *Transactions of the Institution of Naval Architects* (1880), p. 226.

216 John Lancaster: *The Times* (London), December 5, 1868, April 24, June 28, 1884; *Proceedings of Institution of Mechanical Engineers* (1884), pp. 402–3.

216 a Confederate sympathizer: John Lancaster to James M. Mason, June 24, 1864, James M. Mason Papers.

216 later testimony of three members: CGB, 3:281–90.

216 Brent Johnston . . . later recalled: ibid., 3:301–3.

216 "He was a very quiet, silent man": [Alicia Maria Falls], *Foreign Courts and Foreign Homes* (1898), p. 282.

217 "Well we are ready": Journal of William Wainwright, June 18, 1864.

217 Chronometers transferred: SIT, p. 87; James Bryant Jr. to Fraser, Trenholm, November 19, 1864 (copy), SFP.

217 "Have you heard": Falls, *Foreign Courts*, p. 284.

217 Lancaster and his family arrived: PFA (1964), 2:230–32.

217 "Oh, pa": CGB, 3:288.

218 "In Cherbourg Roads the pirate lay": Thomas Buchanan Read, "The Eagle and Vulture," in Read, *Poetical Works* (1874), 3:287.

218 weekend excursion train: E. Parmalee Prentice in *Harper's Magazine*, November 1910.

218 two German officers: SIT, p. 260.

218 "The officers, including Semmes": *Richmond Enquirer*, August 19, 1864.

218 Preparations on *Alabama:* SIT, p. 266.

219 Semmes addressed men: MEM, p. 756.

219 Semmes's strategy: SIT, pp. 264, 287–88.

219 To some observers it appeared: CGB, 3:293.

219 "Here she comes!": *Boston Evening Transcript*, June 21, 1922.

219 The battle: MEM, pp. 756–63; KER, pp. 247–49; SIT, pp. 266–83; John M. Kell in *Century*, April 1886; *The Times* (London), June 21–23, 28, July 5, August 13, 1864; *Colburn's United Service Magazine*, July 1864; ORN, 1:3:59–65, 69–71, 77–81; Browne in *Overland Monthly*, February 1875, and in *Century*, April 1886; *Washington Post*, September 22, 1892; Frederick Milnes Edge, *An Englishman's View of the Battle Between the Alabama and the Kearsarge* (1864); *New Orleans Picayune*, September 29, 1912.

220 Semmes tried to come closer: SEC, 2:290.

220 seemed to a sailor on the *Kearsarge: Boston Evening Transcript*, June 21, 1922.

221 The sound of the gunfire echoed: *Manchester Guardian*, June 23, 1864.

221 "We all laughed and talked": William H. Cushman to his mother, June 19, 1864, William H. Cushman Papers.

221 "Confound them": Edge, *Englishman's View*, p. 29.

224 "We had hardly got warmed up": Cushman to his mother, June 19, 1864.

224 "I took my last look": Journal of William Wainwright, June 19, 1864.

224 "But for God's sake": John Lancaster to Lord Russell, July 16, 1864, FO 5/1323, FOP.

225 "She has gone to the bottom!": Maurice Bell, "The Alabama," in *Bugle-Echoes*, ed. Francis F. Browne (1886), pp. 224–25.

225 Kell swam a few yards away: Kell interview by Wood Holt in *Atlanta Constitution*, ca. 1885.

226 "A little": Blanche Kell, "Life and Letters of J. M. Kell," part 30, box 12, JMK.

226 "He is drowned": SIT, p. 289.

226 Semmes implored Lancaster: KER, p. 251.

226 officers . . . urged Winslow: Badlam, *Kearsarge and Alabama*, p. 29; *Boston Evening Transcript*, June 21, 1922.

226 "Had I deemed him mean enough": John Winslow to his wife, June 20, 1864, file 221, Doubleday Collection.

226 landed forty-one men: CGT, 3:550.

227 Casualties on *Alabama*: list by Francis L. Galt in series II, box 1, Harvey M. Smith Jr. Collection; ORN, 1:3:665.

227 "It is the proudest moment": Ezra Bartlett to George Bartlett, June 19, 1864.

227 "The Yankees were very tardy": Edward M. Anderson to a friend, June 28, 1864, in *Georgia Historical Quarterly* (winter 1975), ed. W. Stanley Hoole.

227 Semmes and Kell on Monday: Kell interview by Wood Holt in *Atlanta Constitution*, ca. 1885.

228 Semmes was criticized: ORN, 2:3:1155.

228 he contrived a specious explanation: Raphael Semmes to James Mason, June 21, in *The Times* (London), June 23, 1864.

228 chains shielded only one-quarter: Eugene B. Canfield in *Naval History*, August 2004.

228 three of the *Alabama*'s officers: TAC, p. 213; Arthur Sinclair to John Kell, April 7, 1896, JMK; *New Orleans Picayune*, September 29, 1912.

228 "Semmes knew all about it": SIT, p. 274.

228 "He was very much worn": KER, p. 261.

228 only one prior injury: Francis Galt to Anne Semmes, September 3, 1877, SFP.

229 "He paralysed the commerce": *Manchester Guardian*, June 21, 1864.

229 *World* printed a list: George W. Dalzell, *The Flight from the Flag: The Continuing Effect of the Civil War Upon the American Carrying Trade* (1940), p. 246.

229 "The *Alabama*'s sunk": *Letters of Meredith*, ed. Cline, 1:295.

229 Quotations from Meredith's chapters: SEC, 1:1, 8; 2:276, 298.

230 the book came out in New York: *NYT*, September 2, 1864.

230 Cost of sword: Brava Maury to brother, June 28, 1864, Maury Papers.

230 Description of sword: *Army and Navy Journal*, September 3, 1864.

230 Lady de Houghton's flag: Raphael Semmes to Louisa Tremlett, January 15, 1868, SPV; MEM, p. 785.

230 Semmes dined at Laird's home: Semmes's lecture, 1874, to Catholic Young Men's Society, file 2:18, SFP.

230 Louisa Tremlett: photograph in file 3:19, SFP.

232 Quotations from Semmes's letters: Raphael Semmes to Louisa Tremlett, November 11, 1864, MOC; and Semmes to Tremlett, March 6, 1865, SPV.

232 "stolen fruits": Louisa Tremlett to Raphael Semmes, May 14, [1866], SFP.

232 "a formal purpose": Diary, June 24, 1864, CFA.

232 official protest to Lord Russell: PFA (1864), 2:295–97.

232 "By all the rules": *Army and Navy Journal*, August 27, 1864.

232 Semmes's false name and passport: MS draft of memoir, chapter 1:1, file 3:1, SFP.

232 "when we made the swift journey": Raphael Semmes to Louisa Tremlett, October 11, 1869, SPV.

232 "delightful day at Waterloo" and next two quotations: Louisa's ivory diary, SPV.

233 "I never saw him looking better": ORN, 2:2:818.

233 "My movements will be so uncertain": *New Orleans Picayune*, September 29, 1912.

11 Afterward

235 "I felt a strange thrill": Raphael Semmes to Louisa Tremlett, November 11, 1864, MOC.

236 a bland note that everybody was in good health: Raphael Semmes to F. W. Tremlett, March 6, 1865, SPV.

236 "When ready to come on": Stephen Mallory to Raphael Semmes, telegram, December 24, 1864, SFP.

236 expecting that . . . he could return home soon: Semmes to F. W. Tremlett, March 6, 1865, SPV.

237 overland journey: MEM, pp. 799–801.

237 "material resources greater": *Columbia Southern Guardian*, January 13, 1865.

237 "totally uncalled for": *Charlotte Bulletin*, January 14, 1865, reprinted in *Richmond Whig*, January 20, 1865.

238 "looking as hard and determined": *An Irishman in Dixie: Thomas Conolly's Diary of the Fall of the Confederacy*, ed. Nelson D. Lankford (1988), pp. 63, 65.

238 "Dreary, weary, lonely": Semmes's journal, February 27, 1865, in *Alabama Review* (April 1975), ed. W. Stanley Hoole.

238 "The Vandals seem": ibid.

238 "We have plenty of men": Semmes to F. W. Tremlett, March 6, 1865, SPV.

239 "looked mad and ragged": *NYT*, June 12, 1865.

239 the story later passed down: SPR, p. 187.

239 Semmes wrote to his English friend Lindsay: W. S. Lindsay to Raphael Semmes, July 8, 1865, replying to Semmes's letter of May 31, SFP.

240 five thousand former Confederates: Daniel E. Sutherland in *CWH*, September 1985.

240 "I came out of the war": Raphael Semmes to W. S. Lindsay, August 8, 1865, file LND/7, p. 477, William S. Lindsay Papers.

240 chronometers were sold in England: Fraser, Trenholm to Raphael Semmes, August 16, 1865, SFP; Anne Semmes to Electra Semmes Colston, October 1, 1865, SFP.

240 "disappointed and mortified": Raphael Semmes to Anne Semmes, May 28, 1861, SFP.

241 "You have been frequently in my thoughts": Raphael Semmes to Samuel Semmes, August 12, 1865, *NYT*, January 4, 1866.

241 "My own course has been a neutral one": Samuel Semmes to Raphael Semmes, August 29, 1865, SFP.

241 "But I am afraid": Anne Semmes to Electra Semmes Colston, October 1, 1865, SFP.

242 license to practice law: October 31, 1865, in file 3:5, SFP.

242 "Attorneys at Law": advertisement in *Mobile Register and Advertiser*, November 1, 1865.

242 "I think . . . we shall": Raphael Semmes to Pendleton Colston, December 5, 1865, SFP.

242 Semmes's arrest: Elizabeth Bethel in *Journal of Southern History*, November 1956.

242 "No name connected": John A. Bolles in *Atlantic Monthly*, July 1872.

243 "I told him I thought": *Diary of Gideon Welles* (1911), 2:436, 472.

243 on a steamship bound . . . to New York: Dabney Herndon Maury, *Recollections of a Virginian in the Mexican, Indian, and Civil Wars* (1894), pp. 221–22.

243 "His health is good": Pendleton Colston to Anne Semmes, January 5, 1866, SFP.

243 "I have ever found": TAC, p. 241.

244 "The President said": *Diary of Welles*, 2:474.

244 he was elected a judge: Raphael Semmes to Pendleton Colston, May 9, 1866, SFP.

244 "Are we to be handed over": Caldwell Delaney, *Confederate Mobile: A Pictorial History* (1971), p. 255.

244 Semmes and *Gazette: NYT*, September 25, November 24, 1866.

244   Semmes and Louisiana college: Walter L. Fleming in *New Orleans Picayune*, May 14, 1911; Elizabeth Joan Doyle in *Alabama Review*, July 1952.

244   Semmes and *Bulletin:* Raphael Semmes to W. S. Lindsay, August 19, 1867, file LND/7, p. 479, Lindsay Papers.

244   "the drudgery of a daily press": Doyle in *Alabama Review*, July 1952.

244   "to restore . . . the Star Spangled Banner": *NYT*, June 16, 1867.

245   "We scanned the countenances": *Memphis Bulletin*, quoted in *Knoxville Whig*, August 7, 1867.

245   The owners of the *Bulletin* disagreed: Doyle in *Alabama Review*, July 1952.

245   "His whole appearance": *Cincinnati Daily Gazette*, January 15, 1868.

245   "The expression of his countenance": *Cincinnati Commercial*, January 14, 1868.

246   "With a little more animation": *Cincinnati Daily Gazette*, January 15, 1868. For other accounts of Semmes's lectures, see *Macon Weekly Telegraph*, December 17, 1866; Diary of Trueman G. Avery, March 12, 1868, Rare Book, Manuscript, and Special Collections Library, Duke University; and David Macrae, *The Americans at Home: Pen-and-Ink Sketches of American Men Manners and Institutions* (1870), 2:121–26.

247   "book of the sea": Raphael Semmes to *The Times* (London), October 28, 1868, SPV.

247   "the wonders and beauties of nature": MEM, p. 674.

247   "that patient little stone-mason": ibid., p. 171.

247   "gloomy asceticism of character": ibid., p. 39.

247   "Whilst the civilization": ibid., p. 56.

248   Cavalier myth: Robert E. Bonner in *CWH*, March 2002.

248   "a beautiful woman": MEM, p. 116.

248   Union force at Galveston: ibid., pp. 519–20.

248   "we never had any trouble": ibid., p. 427.

248   "if such license": ibid., p. 451.

249   "The canting, hypocritical Yankee": ibid., p. 187.

249   journal entries later in the fall: Journal, September 10, November 10, 1861 (1:709, 719).

249   reaching ten thousand copies: Raphael Semmes to *The Times* (London), October 11, 1869, SPV.

249   "The shameless record": *Putnam's Magazine*, June 1869; and see a similar review in *Atlantic Monthly*, April 1869.

250   "My <u>dearest</u> Miss Louisa": Raphael Semmes to Louisa Tremlett, November 11, 1864, MOC.

250   "My dearest Miss Louisa": Raphael Semmes to Louisa Tremlett, March 6, 1865, SPV.

251   "You see what trouble": Louisa Tremlett to Raphael Semmes, October 18, [1865], SFP.

251   "I spent the whole of last summer": Raphael Semmes to Louisa Tremlett, November 17, 1865, SPV.

252 "You are much oftener in our thoughts": Louisa Tremlett to Raphael Semmes, October 29, 1867, SFP.

252 "My dear Miss Louisa": Raphael Semmes to Louisa Tremlett, January 15, 1868, MOC.

253 "I am making a comfortable living": Raphael Semmes to Louisa Tremlett, October 11, 1869, SPV.

253 "He has quite cut me": Louisa Tremlett to Blanche Kell, February 15, [1871], box 5, JMK.

253 In Alabama, outbreaks of white violence: Eric Foner, *Reconstruction: America's Unfinished Revolution, 1863–1877* (1988), p. 442.

253 "The people of the South": Raphael Semmes to Louisa Tremlett, October 28, 1868, SPV.

253 wished to annex Canada: J. Bartlet Brebner, *Canada: A Modern History* (rev. ed., 1970), pp. 279, 288–94.

254 "the *Alabama* claims": Jay Sexton in *Diplomatic History*, September 2003; Adrian Cook, *The Alabama Claims: American Politics and Anglo-American Relations, 1865–1872* (1975).

254 the case proved that he was: Raphael Semmes to F. W. Tremlett, July 22, 1871, and March 31, 1872, SPV.

254 "He was, probably, . . . the man to carry out": Bolles in *Atlantic Monthly*, July 1872.

254 "Very few of these letters": John A. Bolles in *Atlantic Monthly*, August 1872.

255 "Mobile, and Boston are situated": Raphael Semmes to editor, *Atlantic Monthly*, August 10, 1872, Rare Book, Manuscript, and Special Collections Library, Duke University.

255 "For the last few years": Raphael Semmes to F. W. Tremlett, January 5, 1872, MOC.

255 Friends bought the Semmeses a house: TAC, p. 262.

255 "the Great Admiral": Joel Hunter in *Confederate Veteran*, July 1924.

256 "It comes from the victor": *Mobile Daily Register*, April 28, 1874.

256 "I think I am improving": Raphael Semmes to Anne Semmes, February 5, 1877, SFP.

256 Final illness: W. Adolphe Roberts, *Semmes of the Alabama* (1938), p. 263.

256 he imagined that he was back: *Saturday Evening Post*, October 13, 1877.

EPILOGUE The *Alabama* Found

257 Discovery of *Alabama* wreck: Max Guérout in *Mariner's Mirror*, November 1988.

258 Exploration and recovery of wreck: C. S. Lambert in *American History Illustrated*, October 1988; Max Guérout in *National Geographic*, December 1994.

259 exhibit at the Museum of Mobile: at the time of my visit in July 2005.

Index

Page numbers in *italic* refer to illustrations.

A NOTE ABOUT THE AUTHOR

Stephen Fox is a freelance historian based in Boston. He studied American history at Williams College and at Brown University, where he received his doctorate in 1971. After two years of college teaching, he decided to pursue an independent scholarly career outside the academic world. *Wolf of the Deep* is his seventh book. Of his previous works, perhaps the best known are *The Mirror Makers*, on the history of American advertising, and *John Muir and His Legacy*, a history of American environmentalism organized around the life of the founding president of the Sierra Club. Mr. Fox's articles have appeared in *Sierra, Wilderness, Smithsonian, Orion, American Heritage of Invention and Technology*, the *Journal of American History, The Boston Globe, The New York Times*, and elsewhere. He has served on the boards of PEN New England and of the Associates of the Boston Public Library. His wife, Alexandra Dundas Todd, is a writer and professor emerita of sociology at Suffolk University.

A NOTE ON THE TYPE

This book was set in Janson, a typeface long thought to have been made by the Dutch-man Anton Janson, who was a practicing typefounder in Leipzig during the years 1668–1687. However, it has been conclusively demonstrated that these types are actually the work of Nicholas Kis (1650–1702), a Hungarian, who most probably learned his trade from the master Dutch typefounder Dirk Voskens. The type is an excellent example of the influential and sturdy Dutch types that prevailed in England up to the time William Caslon (1692–1766) developed his own incomparable designs from them.

Composed by North Market Street Graphics,
Lancaster, Pennsylvania

Printed and bound by Berryville Graphics,
Berryville, Virginia

Designed by Soonyoung Kwon